Before They Were

Cardinals

Sports and American Culture Series

Bruce Clayton, Editor

Before They Were Cardinals

Major League Baseball in Nineteenth-Century St. Louis

Jon David Cash

University of Missouri Press
Columbia and London

University of Missouri Press, Columbia, Missouri 65201
Printed and bound in the United States of America

First paperback printing, 2011
5 4 3 2 1 15 14 13 12 11

Library of Congress Cataloging-in-Publication Data
Cash, Jon David.
Before they were cardinals : major league baseball in nineteenth-century St. Louis.
p. cm.—(Sports and American culture series)
Includes bibliographical references and index.
ISBN 9780-8262-1935-0 (pbk.: alk. paper)
1. Baseball—Missouri—Saint Louis—History-19th century. I. Title: Major league baseball in nineteenth-century St. Louis. II. Title. III. Series.
GV863.M82 5253 2002
796.357'09778'669034—dc21 2002024568

™ This paper meets the requirements of the American National Standard for Permanence of Paper for Printed Library Materials, 239.48, 1984.

Designer: Jennifer Cropp
Typesetter. Bookcomp, Inc.
Printer and binder: Thomson-Shore, Inc.
Typeface: Adobe Caslon

This book is dedicated to my family and friends who helped to make it a reality

Contents

Acknowledgments

It would require another book to credit properly all of the gracious people who have provided encouragement. First and foremost, I want to thank everybody in my family. My parents, David and Hazel Cash, deserve special credit for their contributions toward helping me finish Graduate School at the University of Oregon. This study of nineteenth-century St. Louis baseball, originally my doctoral dissertation, could never have been completed without the patience and support given by my major adviser, Daniel Pope, and the executive assistant to the Dean of the Graduate School, Toby Deemer. I also want to thank the other individuals who served on my dissertation committee: Jack Maddex, Richard Maxwell Brown, Larry Singell, and Kelly Eakin. Many of the graduate students of that era offered words of reassurance and acts of generosity. My appreciation goes out to all of them and especially to Lori Gates, Delores McBroome, Ernest Boyd, Larry Bagby, Steve Smith, Hope Benedict, Leah Kirker, Sally Morita, Roxanne Easley, and Beth Wilson. Away from the pressures of graduate school, I could always depend on the friendship of Tom Lutz and two sisters, Janice and Joyce Findley.

I owe a large debt of gratitude to the University of Missouri Press for turning my dissertation into a book. This project would never have been possible without the steadfast commitment of Clair Willcox. Jane Lago also shared insightful suggestions. Karen Caplinger and Beth Chandler kindly waited for me to complete their marketing questionnaire and then provided enthusiastic promotional efforts. John Brenner contributed skillful copyediting comments.

Along the way, innumerable people helped me. I want to thank the entire staff of the State Historical Society of Missouri in Columbia, and, in particular, Christine Montgomery for cheerfully answering all of my abundant inquiries about obtaining photographic prints. I also benefited greatly from the advice of the staff of the Missouri Historical Society in St. Louis and the assistance of Ellen Thomasson in supplying photographic prints from there. At the University of Arkansas–Monticello Library, Randall Watts guided me through the process of rounding up and corralling the final stray publishing citations for the Bibliography. Besides the libraries of the University of Oregon and the University of Arkansas–Monticello, I also enjoyed the comforts and collections of libraries on the campuses of Oregon State University, the University of Missouri, the University of Arkansas–Fayetteville, Hendrix University, and the University of Louisiana–Monroe. I gained additional information and valuable support from the public libraries in Crossett, Arkansas; Monroe, Louisiana; and Eugene and Corvallis, Oregon.

Over the years, a variety of individuals have motivated me. On one fateful 1984 night, Jon Gibson, David Edwards, and Bryan Holland were with me in Fayetteville, Arkansas, when the Cardinals' Joaquin Andujar shut out the Atlanta Braves and inspired the launching of my scholarly study of St. Louis baseball. At the University of Oregon, my intramural softball teammates helped me to understand not only the profound satisfaction of sharing championship seasons but also the solace of striving for success in less productive years. Last, but far from least, thanks to all of the numerous college students in both Oregon and Arkansas who have voiced their support. I want to express my gratitude particularly to four students who have worked in the office of the School of Social and Behavioral Sciences at the University of Arkansas–Monticello, where I have taught since 1996. All four of these student workers—Leah Dennington, Wendi McSwain, Carrie Carter, and Jarett Lamb—have been aware of my efforts to write this book and managed to bolster my will to finish it. Carrie Carter merits further praise for preparing computer disks from my original manuscript.

To everybody mentioned in these acknowledgments and anybody else who I may have inadvertently forgot to mention, please read the dedication on page v. This book is for you!

Prologue *Fall Festival*

What do you imagine the American people would think of me if I wasted my time going to the ballgame?

—President Grover Cleveland, declining an invitation to a major-league baseball game in 1886

On October 7, 1885, Thomas A. Hendricks, the vice president of the United States, looked out from the balcony of the Southern Hotel on a parade making its way through the crowded street below. More than a quarter-million people were milling around, many carrying torches that sent flames leaping fifteen feet into the air. Some torchbearers were periodically setting off Roman candles, and other parade participants fired double-barreled shotguns skyward.[1] Hendricks, an Indianan who was serving President Grover Cleveland in the first Democratic administration since the outbreak of the Civil War, assumed that the pandemonium below was a well-intentioned effort to welcome him to St. Louis. Sure that he was the focal point of the crowd's attention, he began to deliver a political speech to his audience: "This, gentlemen, is an honor that I did not expect. It is a genuine surprise to me. It must only be in the West that the greatness of the vice presidency is recognized. I know that Missouri is a good old Democratic state, but I did not suspect for a moment that my arrival would provoke the enthusiasm which I see displayed before me—"

The vice president was quickly cut off by a young torchbearer, who loudly interrupted the political oration by gesturing eagerly at a stocky, mustached man on the street and exclaiming, "There's Gleason! There's Gleason!"

Hendricks was suddenly perplexed. Regaining his voice, he queried the youth: "Gleason? Gleason? And who, may I ask, is Gleason?"

"Just the greatest shortstop the Browns ever had," the torchbearer said, quickly filling in what must have seemed a major gap in the vice president's education. "And that is one of the reasons why we are going to beat Chicago for the championship."[2]

Vice President Thomas A. Hendricks. State Historical Society of Missouri, Columbia.

Southern Hotel, St. Louis. State Historical Society of Missouri, Columbia.

Bill Gleason. State Historical Society of Missouri, Columbia.

Before They Were

Cardinals

Introduction

Take Me Out to the Nineteenth-Century Ball Game

> Baseball in 1870 resembled fast-pitch softball more than . . . modern baseball.
>
> —Bill James, *Historical Baseball Abstract* (1988)

If present-day baseball fans could travel by time machine back to May 6, 1875, to witness the St. Louis Brown Stockings play their first game against the Chicago White Stockings, they would see a sport that, while recognizable as baseball, differed substantially from the modern game in its rules and prevailing style of play.

Some differences would be obvious even before the game began. The contest would start not with the home team taking the field, but with a coin flip. After summoning the team captains, the lone umpire—the game would not adopt umpiring crews until the twentieth century—would award the winner of the coin toss the choice of either batting first or last. The winning captain would not necessarily choose the psychological advantage of batting last. In nineteenth-century ball games, the ball used for the first pitch was expected to remain in use throughout the game; fouls and errant throws were retrieved, even from out of the stands if necessary, usually without regard to wear or damage to the ball. Therefore, given a choice, a captain sometimes opted to get the first cracks at a shiny, undamaged baseball.[1]

Modern fans might also be surprised to realize that none of the 1875 fielders wore baseball gloves. Fielding gloves did not become prevalent until the 1880s, and some players chose not to use them for a decade after that, perhaps because the primitive gloves of the nineteenth century resembled a pair of work gloves more than a modern baseball mitt.[2]

While watching the 1875 pitcher take his warm-up tosses, fans from the present would make a series of observations. First, they would note that he did not toe a horizontal rubber slab atop an elevated mound. Instead, he stood within the flat confines of a six-foot-square pitcher's box, within which he could move freely. The pitcher frequently started his delivery from a back corner of the box, making a running start across it at a diagonal angle. Although the pitcher's box would undergo several changes in dimensions, it would survive in some form until the start of the 1893 season. In 1893 the pitching rubber arrived, and shortly thereafter the pitching mound made its first appearance, although it received no official recognition until 1903, when the major leagues decreed that the mound should not exceed fifteen inches in height.[3]

Next, present-day fans would see that an 1875 pitcher threw every pitch either underhanded or sidearm. Overhand deliveries were not yet permitted, although restrictions would soon ease. By 1883, pitchers were permitted to use a three-quarters "from the shoulder" delivery; the overhand delivery gained universal acceptance in June 1885. Astute modern fans might also notice that in 1875 home plate was located considerably closer to the pitcher than it is now. The distance later would be increased twice, from 45 feet to 50 feet in 1881 and then to the present distance of 60 feet, 6 inches in 1893. These rule changes would transform the role of the pitcher. In 1875, one pitcher could still handle the pitching chores for virtually all of his team's games. The new overhand delivery, however, placed increased stress upon throwing arms. This problem was further complicated by the longer pitching distances and expanded playing schedules. As a result, ball clubs would be forced to divide the workload among several pitchers. Latter-day pitchers would have no opportunity to compile as many wins as the game's earliest ace pitchers.[4]

In addition to the legal running start and the short distance to home plate, several other rules favored the pitcher in 1875. For one thing, he could afford to throw more pitches out of the strike zone. Under the ball-strike count in effect, a batter only earned a walk after the pitcher had thrown nine balls. Throughout the 1880s, the major leagues would steadily lower the number of balls needed to draw a walk. Also, batters would not receive first base as compensation for being hit by a pitch until the 1880s. Instead, the umpire simply called a ball, and the at-bat continued. Furthermore, until the 1880s, a pitcher could retire a batter whenever one of his fielders caught a foul ball on the first bounce.[5]

Like pitchers, hitters operated by different rules in 1875, some of which greatly improved their chances of reaching base safely. One rule allowed the fair-foul hit, a batted ball that "landed in fair territory and immediately caromed foul." A successful fair-foul sliced away from infielders into foul territory, making it almost impossible for the batter to be thrown out at first base. One player who built a career around the fair-foul rule was Ross Barnes, a three-time batting champion with the Boston Red Stockings and Chicago White Stockings. During the first six years of major-league baseball, from 1871 to 1876, Barnes hit better than .400 four times and averaged .397 for the six-year span. Then, following the 1876 season, the National League eliminated the fair-foul hit. The new rule insisted that a fair grounder "must stay within the foul lines until it passes a base or until it is fielded." Deprived of the most important weapon in his hitting arsenal, Barnes averaged only .269 in the remaining three years of his career.[6]

The new fair-foul rule did not hurt the hitting style of Lipman Pike, a four-time home run champion in the 1870s. Pike's totals, however, were ludicrous by today's standards—he won his four slugging titles by hitting a combined total of eighteen home runs. This had everything to do with the composition of nineteenth-century baseballs: game balls consisted of a cover wrapped loosely around a rubber-centered ball of yarn. In 1910 a cork center would add some new life to the baseball. But the so-called dead-ball era would not really end until 1920 when the American League introduced a livelier ball that owed its increased resiliency primarily to tighter wrapping. The National League soon adopted the livelier ball as well. Additionally, by the 1920s the major leagues were no longer trying to get through entire games with a single baseball, and hitters benefited from hitting clean and undamaged balls. In February 1920 it became illegal for pitchers to deface the baseball or apply a foreign substance to it, thus putting an end to the spitball, emery ball, shine ball, mud ball, cut ball, and licorice ball. Only a select group of seventeen prominent spitballers were allowed to continue employing the pitch for the duration of their careers. Influenced by the fatal beaning of Ray Chapman in August 1920, umpires started regularly replacing any damaged baseballs; ball clubs also initiated the practice of permitting fans to keep all balls hit into the stands. With fresher and livelier baseballs always in play, home runs proliferated at an astonishing pace. In both the National and American Leagues, more home runs were hit in the 1920s than in the preceding two decades combined.[7]

As the home run became more commonplace, the game's leading sluggers actually hit a smaller percentage of the overall total of home runs. In Pike's best season, 1872, his league-leading six home runs accounted for 17.1 percent of the thirty-five home runs hit in the National Association that year. Thus, the 1872 season marked one of only twenty-one occasions in baseball history when a league's leading home run hitter accounted for more than 10 percent of all the league's home runs. Nineteenth-century players achieved this feat eleven times; in the twentieth century, Babe Ruth alone accomplished it eight times. The achievement has never been duplicated since Ruth last performed it in 1928. A nineteenth-century home run was a rare commodity, somewhat akin to an unexpected bolt of lightning. Sluggers capable of supplying home runs, such as Pike, were regarded as entertaining novelties.[8]

While watching Pike and other 1875 hitters as they took their turns at bat, present-day fans would detect a number of advantages that batters no longer enjoy. First, each hitter could still request that the pitcher throw either a high or low pitch to him. Second, pitchers faced a much smaller strike zone: home plate was a twelve-inch square, and would not become the modern five-sided, seventeen-inch-wide target until 1900. Third, a foul ball did not count as a strike. Finally, a hitter could accumulate two strikes and still afford to take another called strike. The umpire would merely warn the hitter to swing at good pitches. Until 1881, when this rule changed, hitters frequently received a fourth strike.[9]

In the remaining years of the nineteenth century, the major leagues would continually adjust the rules of the game, seeking the right balance in the contest between pitchers and hitters. Some of these rule changes favored the pitchers, and others were advantageous to hitters. The joint National League–American Association rules conference in 1887 would eliminate the right of the batter to request that the pitcher throw either a high or low pitch; in compensation to hitters, the leagues granted an additional strike, so that for the 1887 season pitchers were required to register four strikes for a strikeout. The four-strike rule, plus the decision to grant hitters credit for a base hit whenever they drew a walk, resulted in chaos: after five seasons in which the National League and American Association had jointly produced a cumulative .247 batting average, the two leagues averaged .325 for the 1887 season. Until 1887, no League or Association player had compiled a .400 batting average during the decade of the 1880s; in 1887, the American Association alone produced eleven players who were credited with a batting average that reached or exceeded the .400 mark.[10]

Consequently, after the 1887 season, the leagues rescinded the concessions given to hitters at the joint 1887 rules conference. Major-league baseball returned to a three-strike requirement for strikeouts for the 1888 season, and ceased to regard walks as either a base hit or an official at-bat. Batting averages plummeted. The two leagues averaged only .239, the lowest mark to that point in major-league history. So the rules were changed again, to tilt the balance back toward the hitters. For 1889 the major leagues dropped the number of balls required to draw a walk from five to four; batting averages rose to .263, the highest level attained since 1877 (with the single exception of the fluky 1887 season). But after batting averages consistently declined for three years from 1890–1892, the rules makers took action again, expanding the distance between the pitcher and the batter to 60 feet, 6 inches. For the remainder of the 1890s, major-league hitters reaped the rewards of this rule change. They averaged .288 from 1893–1899, a sustained offensive barrage previously unprecedented in the game's history.[11]

Accordingly, at the dawn of the twentieth century, baseball rules were revised yet again. In 1900 the beleaguered pitcher received relief in the form of the enlarged and reconfigured home plate, and foul balls soon began to be counted as strikes until the last strike. This modern foul-ball rule gained universal acceptance prior to the 1903 season. By then, most modern rules were in effect. During the 1890s major-league baseball had even adopted the game's limited form of a free substitution rule and the often-confusing infield fly rule. Nineteenth-century baseball underwent constant and dramatic rule changes, but after 1903, rules makers played a less significant role in the development of the game. The twentieth-century playing style would be changed most profoundly by the advent of the lively baseball—a change occurring outside of the realm of official playing rules. Of course, rules tinkering has continued even into recent baseball history, most notably in such changes as lowering the mound to offset the advantage pitchers seemed to demonstrate during 1968, the "Year of the Pitcher," when batting averages plunged to an all-time low mark of .237, and in the American League's adoption of the controversial designated hitter rule in 1973 to boost offensive production.[12]

In 1875, major-league baseball had only just begun the long evolutionary process that would shape the modern game, most particularly the modern pitcher-versus-hitter duel. Modern fans on their time-traveling expedition to the 1875 St. Louis–Chicago contest would experience bewilderment over the game being played on the field before them. But they also would be reassured by many similarities between the nineteenth- and twentieth-century ball game. There were the four bases, arranged in the expected locations at the familiar ninety-foot distances. One team took the field, and the other took its turn at bat. The team on defense controlled the ball. The team on offense continued batting until the defensive team recorded three outs. Then, the two teams switched roles. A regulation game repeated this ritual nine times, although darkness frequently shortened nineteenth-century contests—there were no lights at the playing fields. If the game was tied after nine innings and sufficient daylight remained, the teams would play as many extra innings as needed to determine a victor.

Most reassuring of all, the modern fan would feel at home with the crowds of St. Louis and Chicago partisans in the grandstands. The fans would be instantly recognizable, displaying their intense, timeless civic spirit, secure in believing that their city fielded the finest baseball team in the land.[13]

Part I

The Rise and Fall of Major League Baseball in St. Louis, 1875–1877

1

St. Louis versus Chicago

St. Louis, for the first time, appreciates the fever attending the support of a professional team.

—*St. Louis Dispatch,* on the eve of the first professional baseball game between the St. Louis Brown Stockings and the Chicago White Stockings, May 6, 1875

Long before the Brown Stockings took the field against the White Stockings on May 6, 1875, a heated rivalry had developed between the cities of St. Louis and Chicago. In 1870, as the federal census neared completion, the civic rivalry between St. Louis and Chicago reached a new peak. Due to the strength of its river commerce, St. Louis had long been the dominant center of trade for the Middle West. But through its ties to a growing national railroad network, Chicago was destined to overtake its regional rival. The Civil War, by totally disrupting St. Louis's Mississippi River trade, had accelerated this process.[1] By 1870, Chicago was poised to eclipse St. Louis in not only economic output but also overall population. Thus St. Louis civic boosters looked to the 1870 census as a chance to show that their city could still outshine Chicago.

These civic leaders included William McKee, the primary owner of the *Missouri Democrat,* to whom President Ulysses S. Grant had bestowed control of federal patronage in St. Louis. McKee exercised this power to manipulate the results of the 1870 census. He persuaded the federal census-takers, whose jobs were beholden to him, to withhold the St. Louis census figures until after the totals from Chicago were returned. Then the St. Louis census-takers simply filed fraudulent returns. This subterfuge succeeded in conveying the entirely false impression that the population of St. Louis had remained larger than that of Chicago.[2]

The outcome of the 1870 census only delayed the inevitable conclusion of the St. Louis–Chicago trade rivalry. Symbolically, the trade rivalry would not end until the 1880 census revealed that Chicago had officially surpassed St. Louis in population. But even before the 1870 census, an economic stake had been driven through the heart of St. Louis's trade aspirations. On May 10, 1869, in the faraway Utah Territory, Leland Stanford, the founder of the Central Pacific

Railroad, drove the golden spike that completed the nation's first transcontinental rail line. In the post–Civil War economy, the transcontinental railroad sealed Chicago's economic ascendancy over St. Louis.[3] Nevertheless, despite Chicago's growing affluence, St. Louis remained an important economic force. Furthermore, local entrepreneurs frequently gave notice that St. Louis had not yet conceded defeat as they constantly sought to enhance trade and discover new fields of competition.

The baseball diamond served as one of the new arenas in the old urban rivalry. Competition between the two cities became the most pressing motive for civic leaders to organize a professional baseball team in St. Louis. The Chicago White Stockings had been the first team to copy the model of success employed by baseball's original self-proclaimed professional club, the undefeated 1869 Cincinnati Red Stockings. In 1870, civic boosters and baseball enthusiasts from Chicago raised twenty thousand dollars to recruit players for a professional team that could challenge the Cincinnati club. The 1870 White Stockings defeated the Cincinnati Red Stockings to lodge their claim as the premier baseball club in the West. They trained for this task by traveling to St. Louis in late April to inflict lopsided defeats upon the two finest local amateur clubs of the era, the Empires and the Unions, outscoring them 36–8 and 47–1 respectively. The Empires lost badly to the White Stockings again in October, this time by a score of 46–10. On the same October trip the White Stockings also overwhelmed another local amateur organization, the Atlantics, 46–8. In 1871 the Chicago White Stockings became one of ten charter members in the first all-professional baseball league, the National Association of Professional Baseball Players. To prepare for the season, the White Stockings took another late April jaunt to St. Louis, where they easily triumphed over the Atlantics, 22–2, and crushed the Empires, 34–8.[4]

St. Louis amateurs tried to compete against other National Association teams, but the games resulted in humiliatingly one-sided losses to the Philadelphia Athletics, Brooklyn Atlantics, and Boston Red Stockings. Yet in August 1873 the league-champion Red Stockings drew a crowd of three thousand in St. Louis, a large audience for that era, to see a defeat of the Empires, 24–4. The turnout prompted the *St. Louis Democrat* to observe that a local professional club "certainly would pay, as St. Louis takes as much interest in outdoor sports as any other city in the Union." In April 1874 the Chicago White Stockings returned to St. Louis in preparation for their upcoming National Association season. Competing against various St. Louis clubs, the White Stockings won eight consecutive games and outscored the local amateurs by a combined score of 179–53. At the end of this series of embarrassing defeats, the *St. Louis Daily Globe* despaired that local promoters would discover it "impossible to gather baseball laurels against Chicago" until they created a professional team. Adding insult to injury, the White Stockings signed two of the top local amateurs, Empire pitcher

Dan Collins and Red Stocking infielder Johnny Peters, before going back to Chicago. Later in 1874 the White Stockings defeated the Empires and Red Stockings with ease on six separate occasions, by an emphatic combined score of 93–14. Chicago's professional club extended its winning streak over St. Louis amateurs to twenty games.[5]

The scene was set. In the fall of 1874 St. Louis civic boosters raised twenty thousand dollars to organize a professional baseball team, to be called the Brown Stockings, that would begin play the following season in the National Association. Four hundred shares at fifty dollars apiece were sold to finance a club capable of competing with the professional outfits from the East. C. Orrick Bishop, a member of the Brown Stockings' board of directors, later recalled that the primary motive for him and other shareholders to invest in the team was "civic pride," as they "didn't expect to make any money." The *St. Louis Dispatch* described the impetus for forming the Brown Stockings as a desire to compete with the city's foremost trade rival. "Chicago could ill brook Cincinnati's success in the diamond field," it explained, "and St. Louis in turn desires to lower the standard of a rival."[6]

The team's shareholders represented the upper echelons of St. Louis society. The president of the Brown Stockings, J. B. C. Lucas II, was reputedly the wealthiest man in the city, an heir to the fortune of a socially prominent French family that had helped pioneer the development of St. Louis. His grandfather, appointed territorial judge and a commissioner of land claims by President Thomas Jefferson in 1805, had invested in local real estate that produced a fortune after the land boom following the War of 1812. James H. Lucas, father of the original Brown Stockings' president, expanded the family's real estate empire during the 1850s by developing Lucas Place, the city's most exclusive residential district for most of the remaining nineteenth century. Upon his death on November 9, 1873, he left a will bequeathing one million dollars to each of his seven children. Two of his sons, J. B. C. Lucas II and Henry V. Lucas, used part of their inheritance to promote baseball in St. Louis.[7]

By his presence at the head of the Brown Stockings' board of directors, J. B. C. Lucas established an aristocratic tone for other major investors. His cousin, Charles H. Turner, a wealthy realtor from another socially prominent family, served as secretary of the organization. The team's board of directors included such influential citizens as Joseph P. Carr and C. Orrick Bishop. The Carr family also traced its St. Louis roots back to the early Louisiana Territory. C. Orrick Bishop, on the other hand, belonged to a family of comparative newcomers to the city of St. Louis, although he had grown up in the city in an affluent area dubbed "Aristocratic Row," on Eighth Street between Olive and Locust Streets, approximately a half-dozen blocks east of Lucas Place. Bishop had played amateur baseball while attending Westminster College in Fulton, Missouri, and pursuing legal studies in Louisville. His playing career ended when he opened a law

J. B. C. Lucas II. State Historical Society of Missouri, Columbia.

practice in St. Louis during 1867, but Bishop remained active in promoting local amateur baseball.[8] This long-time love for the sport persuaded Bishop to accept a major role in the development of the Brown Stockings. Team officials, impressed by his intimate knowledge of the game, appointed him as managing director and entrusted him with recruiting players for the team. Approaching this mission very seriously, Bishop spent a month away from his thriving legal practice to travel the East Coast in search of ballplayers. He focused his efforts in Brooklyn and Philadelphia, cities whose teams had previously traveled to St. Louis.

Bishop signed three players—shortstop Dickey Pearce, right fielder Jack Chapman, and first baseman Herman "Dutch" Dehlman—from the roster of the 1874 Brooklyn Atlantics. While in Brooklyn, Bishop also secured the services of Lipman Pike, who had played the previous season with the Hartford Dark Blues. Pike and Pearce rated among the best players in the game. Near the end of the amateur era, Pike had been one of a few select players who were publicly recognized as professionals. In 1866 the Philadelphia Athletics had reportedly paid

C. Orrick Bishop. State Historical Society of Missouri, Columbia.

Pike a total of twenty dollars a week. Following the formation of the National Association, Pike had led the first professional league in home runs in each of its first three seasons (1871–1873). Pearce played a significant role in pioneering the position of shortstop. Prior to 1856, the standard defensive alignment of baseball teams had featured a fourth outfielder, akin to a softball rover, but no infielder in the huge gap between second base and third. Pearce, a smart player assigned to be a fourth outfielder, moved instead into the modern-day shortstop position. It quickly became apparent that a shortstop could cut off a multitude of base hits into left field, and other teams soon copied Pearce's innovation. Even though Pearce was thirty-eight and nearing the end of his career when he agreed to play in St. Louis, baseball insiders still considered him the finest-fielding shortstop in the National Association. In 1870 Pike and Pearce had been teammates, along with Chapman, on the Atlantics. They had participated in the most famous game yet played in baseball's brief history: Brooklyn's eleven-inning 8–7 win over the previously undefeated Cincinnati Red Stockings.[9]

Bishop discovered the rest of his starting nine in and around Philadelphia: third baseman Bill Hague, catcher Tom "Reddy" Miller, second baseman Joe Battin, left fielder Edgar "Ned" Cuthbert, and pitcher George Washington Bradley. While the Brown Stockings' "Brooklyn Connection" provided a quartet of battle-tested performers, only one member of the "Philadelphia Connection" had extensive playing experience. Hague, a native Philadelphian who had never seen action in a single National Association game, had played the preceding season for the Easton, Pennsylvania, amateur team. Miller and Battin had used exceptional performances with the Easton team as their springboard to the Philadelphia Athletics of the National Association. Miller joined the Athletics late in the 1874 season. Known as an excellent defensive catcher, he showed a surprisingly lively bat in four Association games, amassing eight base hits in sixteen at bats. Battin had made a similarly dazzling debut with the Athletics in 1873. He collected three hits in five at bats, scored four times, and assured himself of a starting position on their 1874 Philadelphia team.[10]

Unlike these three relative newcomers, Cuthbert traced his playing days back to the era before professionalism. In 1865 the Philadelphia native joined a local amateur team, the Keystones. Credited as the first ballplayer either to steal a base or to slide into a base, Cuthbert served, like Dickey Pearce, as one of the game's foremost innovators. After playing for five years on various Philadelphia ball clubs, Cuthbert allowed promoters of the 1870 Chicago White Stockings to lure him west of the Alleghenies for the first time in his career. He returned to Philadelphia the following season, however, and made a vital contribution to the National Association's first pennant-winner, the 1871 Athletics. Cuthbert led the 1871 team in runs scored and stolen bases, then hit a career-high .338 for the Athletics in 1872 before jumping to their newly formed local rivals, the Philadelphia Whites. With the 1873 Whites, Cuthbert tied for the stolen base championship of the National Association. In 1874 the Chicago White Stockings again enticed Cuthbert away from Philadelphia, and for the fourth consecutive season Cuthbert topped his team in both runs scored and stolen bases. During the off-season, Cuthbert wintered in Philadelphia. While there, he met with Bishop and accepted an offer to play in St. Louis, soon to become Cuthbert's permanently adopted home.[11]

The last member of Bishop's Philadelphia quintet, George Washington Bradley, was an amateur pitcher who had made an improbably rapid climb to fame within Pennsylvania baseball circles. Bradley began the 1874 season in Philadelphia as a third baseman on the Modocs, a team described as "a third rate amateur club."[12] Jack Smith, manager of the Easton, Pennsylvania, ball club, discovered

Bradley's playing prowess and persuaded him to play for Easton. Bradley happened to be assigned the task of pitching batting practice one fateful day. The Easton hitters experienced such difficulty connecting with Bradley's pitches that Smith decided to give the young player a chance to start against a New York amateur club. Bradley was so impressive in this initial outing that Smith, who previously had been the team's starting pitcher, relegated himself to the bench and turned the position over to Bradley. Bradley then drew the attention of professional clubs by pitching Easton to successive victories over three National Association teams—the Brooklyn Atlantics, Philadelphia Whites, and Philadelphia Athletics. The Athletics offered contracts to both Bradley and his catcher, Reddy Miller, after Easton held them to a single run and completed a sweep of the two Philadelphia teams. Miller accepted, but Bradley declined because he was reluctant to share the pitching duties with Dick McBride, the team's player-manager and an entrenched star.[13] St. Louis, however, desperately needed a pitcher. Therefore, Bishop easily persuaded Bradley to reunite with his old battery mate, Miller, as teammates on the brand-new Brown Stockings.

Bishop had put together a fine team, and the Brown Stockings' shareholders commended him for performing his duty "in a manner highly satisfactory to his confreres in the new venture."[14] But by hiring a starting lineup of ballplayers born in either New York or Pennsylvania, Bishop had risked alienating some sectors of St. Louis society that yearned to see the city represented by homegrown talent. The *St. Louis Democrat,* for example, observed, "It will be noticed, and with regret, we think, that there is not one single player from the city on the nine."[15] A local amateur club, the Red Stockings, appealed to that local sentiment by turning professional themselves, entering the National Association alongside the Brown Stockings in 1875.

Yet the Brown Stockings quickly and decisively triumphed in the battle for popularity within St. Louis, for several reasons. By February, when the Red Stockings decided to turn professional, the Brown Stockings had already trained for an entire month inside the Missouri Gymnasium. Trailing the Brown Stockings in conditioning, the Red Stockings encountered "an exceedingly rainy" spring that hindered efforts to overcome the early start of their local rivals. Thomas McNeary, the president of the Red Stockings, faced a similar problem in attracting shareholders. Nearly every St. Louisan with any inclination to buy stock in a baseball team had already invested in the Brown Stockings. Once the season started, two other factors emerged in favor of the Brown Stockings. First, the team adhered to advice from the *Democrat* to "put in just one St. Louis boy, even if he had to play as an 'assistant to a substitute.'" Two native-born players, utility man George Seward and eighteen-year-old backup pitcher James Galvin, eventually played for the Brown Stockings in their inaugural National Association season. Galvin went 4–2 in the first season of a professional career that eventually led to more than 360 wins and his 1965 induction into the Baseball Hall of Fame. Second, the Brown Stockings were simply a much better ball club than the Red Stockings. By June 26 the Brown Stockings had surged to a record of 12–5, while the Red Stockings had lost thirteen of fourteen contests. Fan support, as always, followed the winners, and dwindling attendance forced the Red Stockings to abandon their National Association experiment in July after posting a 4–15 record.[16]

The success of the Brown Stockings had been powerfully foreshadowed in their three initial National Association games. On opening day—May 4, 1875—the Brown Stockings defeated the upstart Red Stockings, 15–9. The Brown Stockings raced to a 14–1 lead after seven innings and coasted to victory despite the Red Stockings' furious eight-run rally in the eighth. More than twenty years later one of the Brown Stockings' shareholders, E. H. Tobias, still recalled how the game showcased the vast disparity between the teams: "Every one of the Brown Stockings was of massive mold and great experience, while the Reds were mere striplings with limited experience." The *St. Louis Dispatch* acknowledged the existence of "a slight prejudice" against the Brown Stockings because of their reliance upon "imported players." It predicted, however, that this resentment would soon vanish: "In time this feeling will rapidly give way. Not a professional club in the country with the solitary exception of the [St. Louis Red Stockings] is composed entirely of local players, but several localities grow to take the same interest in their men, and give them their full sympathies."[17]

The win over the Red Stockings set the stage for the first showdown between competing professional teams representing St. Louis and Chicago. To win the hearts of local baseball supporters, the Brown Stockings needed to defeat the team that St. Louisans hated most—the White Stockings. On May 6 they would get their chance.[18]

Anticipation for the matchup had been building for months, among "those who know the merits of the game of ball, and those, also who had not the remotest conception as to how it was played." The *St. Louis Dispatch* depicted the contest as a new aspect of the all-encompassing competition between the two cities: "The habitual rivalry between the 'Garden City' [Chicago] and the 'Mound City' [St. Louis] which has entered the pulpit, the political, mercantile and social worlds . . . has naturally insinuated itself as a feature of the present trial, and the fight will be bitter indeed." "Never in the history of baseballdom," agreed the St. Louis correspondent of the *Chicago Tribune,* "has there been a greater fever in this city than over the game to be played tomorrow. The rivalry which has so long existed between the two cities has no doubt added to the enthusiasm."[19]

The day of the big game dawned bright and sunny, contributing immensely to the cheerfulness that the *Dispatch* perceived: "Everyone interested in the day's sport—we might have said the entire city—were early from 'roost,' and gave a mental thanksgiving for obtaining what they had . . . anxiously hoped for—a fine May 6. All accordingly put on a holiday grin and thought less of the everyday vexations of life." The *Democrat* observed "a seemingly endless string" of horse-drawn carriages making their way along Grand Avenue en route to the ballpark. Grand Avenue Park dated back to 1866, when its baseball diamond had been laid out by Augustus Solari, an amateur ballplayer and member of the Empires who had secured a five-year lease on John Dunn's corn field. Solari and the Empires had selected the site because it was located near the Fair Grounds, where several streetcar lines converged. Grand Avenue Park had previously served as the home for both the Empires and the Unions, but the St. Louis–Chicago contest of May 6, 1875, marked its first time to host a game between two professional teams.[20]

A crowd of about eight thousand squeezed into the ballpark, while another two thousand scrambled for "seeing distance upon the outside, in every imaginable quarter, on house-top and in trees." The *Dispatch* mentioned that the "densely packed" grandstand contained a substantial number of women, whom the newspaper praised for their "good effect on many who might otherwise have been boisterous and demonstrative." The event was, in short, a festival on a scale seen before in St. Louis only on special occasions. The *Democrat* compared the atmosphere to "Thursday of Fair Week, when all St. Louis is out to see and be seen."[21]

Most eyes in the crowd focused on the warm-up tosses of St. Louis's ace pitcher, George Washington Bradley, after the Brown Stockings took the field. The first Chicago batter to match skills against the St. Louis battery of Bradley and Miller was Richard "Dick" Higham, the White Stockings' catcher. The *Dispatch,* in its position-by-position comparison of the two teams, had opined, "Miller has the advantage of Higham in every respect behind the bat; better in temper and disposition; he is possessed of keen judgement, a quality lacking in Higham, who loses [his] head badly." Whatever personal flaws he might have had, however, Higham could hit, averaging better than .300 for his career. He started the game by lining Bradley's opening pitch into right field for a base hit. St. Louis's shaky beginning continued as Higham advanced to second on Miller's passed ball and went to third when the St. Louis catcher compounded his mistake by making an errant throw toward second. But just as suddenly as the scoring threat had developed, St. Louis extricated itself from the inning without allowing any runs to be tallied. Scott Hastings smashed a sharply hit grounder that was scooped by St. Louis third baseman Bill Hague, who then threw to Miller in time to put out Higham at home. Finally, after Hague had assisted on a force-out of Hastings at second, Miller ended the inning stylishly by throwing

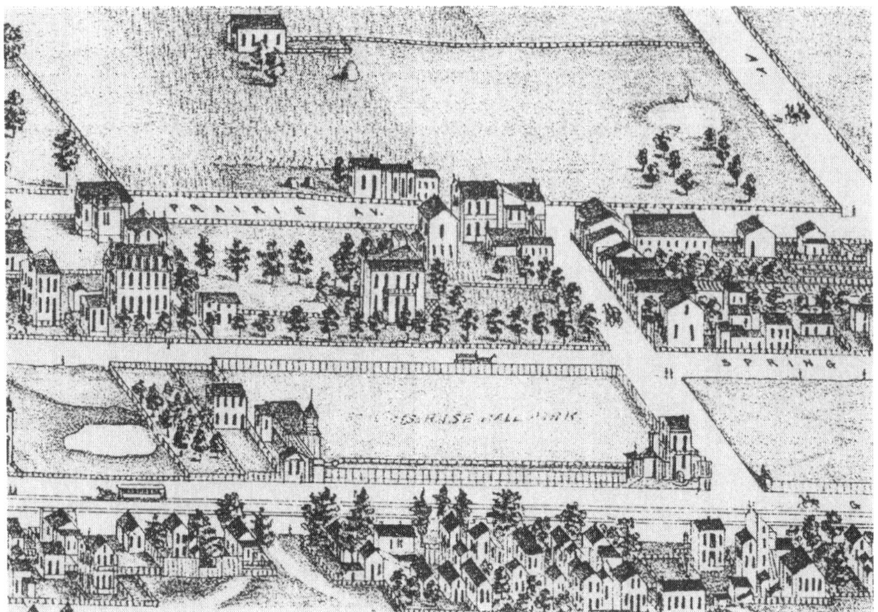

Grand Avenue Park in 1875. State Historical Society of Missouri, Columbia.

out White Stockings' base runner William Warren White when he attempted to steal second.[22]

In their half of the first, the St. Louis lead-off hitter was, appropriately enough, Ned Cuthbert, who would play in winning home debuts on St. Louis ball clubs in three different professional leagues—the National Association, the National League, and the American Association. Cuthbert hit a grounder back to Chicago pitcher George "The Charmer" Zettlein. Zettlein bobbled the ball, losing the opportunity to retire the hustling Cuthbert, who sped safely to first just ahead of the belated throw. This error proved costly to "The Charmer" when Cuthbert scored the game's first run on a two-out triple to the left-field fence by Jack Chapman. Bill Hague followed with a single up the middle of the diamond, driving home Chapman to give the Brown Stockings a two-run lead at the close of the first inning.[23]

As the innings unfolded, the Brown Stockings continued to provide plenty of scoring for the local faithful. They added another run in the second when Dutch Dehlman drove a "red hot rip-snorter" down the left-field foul line for a single, moved to third on a muffed fly ball, and then scored on Cuthbert's groundout. In the fourth inning the Brown Stockings started to turn the game into a rout with four more runs. Dehlman began the rally again with another single to left. Next, Reddy Miller doubled into the gap between outfielders in left-center, advancing Dehlman to third. Cuthbert drove home Dehlman once again and reached base himself on an infield single. Miller and Cuthbert both scored when the Brown Stockings' captain, "Bad Dickey" Pearce, doubled to right field. Cuthbert, renowned for his fast base running and aggressive slides, was portrayed as "striding some six feet" at a time between the bases. The *Dispatch* felt that only this "terrific baserunning" allowed Cuthbert to enjoy "a narrow escape at home base," and the *Democrat* reported that Cuthbert slid across the plate "amid thunders of applause." Pearce scored the last run of the fourth inning, completing his trip around the bases on a ground-out and a Chicago error. Jack Chapman—nicknamed "Death to Flying Things" in the East due to his outfielding abilities and dubbed "the beauty" or "the handsome rightfielder" in St. Louis because of his status as the favorite of female fans—furnished the pivotal hit for the two runs St. Louis scored during the sixth inning. Following a single from Cuthbert, Chapman lined a pitch into the gap in left-center for his second triple of the game. He then scored on a Chicago error to give the Brown Stockings a lead of 9 to 0. In the seventh inning, St. Louis produced its tenth and final run. Joe Battin tripled into the gap in right-center and scored on Dehlman's infield single.[24]

Meanwhile, Bradley retired the White Stockings' hitters with relative ease. Going into the ninth inning, he had shut out Chicago on only three hits. The superb defensive play of the St. Louis nine assisted Bradley in posting the long string of zeroes beside Chicago's name on the scoreboard. In Chicago's half of the fourth inning, Higham hit a sinking liner toward short center, where Brown Stockings' center fielder Lipman Pike made "a magnificent forward running catch . . . taken near the ground, the effect throwing him over." The *Democrat* described Pike's diving catch against Higham as "the prettiest catch of the day." However, local sportswriters also praised second baseman Battin for making a long run to snare a fly ball down the line in right field, third baseman Bill Hague for a catch in foul territory, and Pike again for grabbing another fly ball that threatened to drop in short center field.[25]

The White Stockings sent the top of their order to bat against Bradley in the ninth inning for a last-ditch effort to salvage at least a bit of pride by preventing a St. Louis shutout. Bradley, though, induced Higham to send an easy grounder to shortstop Pearce, who relayed the ball to Dehlman at first base in time for the out. Hague handled another grounder, this one off the bat of Scott Hastings, and threw the ball over to Dehlman for the second out. William Warren White singled to provide the White Stockings' fourth hit of the game, adding some extra suspense for spectators intent upon shutting out, or "Chicagoing," Chicago.[26] James Devlin, a promising pitching prospect and Chicago's starting center fielder,

Baseball is still played on the site of the old Grand Avenue/Sportsman's Park, now the Herbert Hoover Boys and Girls Club. In this 1993 photograph, a young baserunner rounds third and heads for home. Photo by the author.

stood intently at the plate, hoping to drive White home and finally put the White Stockings on the scoreboard. Instead, Bradley elicited the third ground-out of the inning as Devlin sent the ball bounding toward Pearce, who flipped it over to second baseman Battin to force out White.[27]

Pandemonium instantly broke out in the crowded grandstand. "The entire assemblage," the *Dispatch* reported, "rose to their feet and shouted until they were hoarse, danced, sang and threw their hats into the air as though they were taking leave of their senses. They kissed, wept and laughed over each other, embraced, shook hands, slapped each others' back, ran to and fro like madmen." And, the paper noted, the afterglow of triumph lingered long into the evening: "About town last night, everywhere, the excitement regarding the great victory was most intense. In hotel, shop, restaurant, bar room, in the home circle and on the street, but little was talked of save the terrific 'poulticing' the Browns had administered to the Chicago Whites."[28]

Table 1.
Box Score of Game on May 6, 1875
Brown Stockings 10, White Stockings 0

CHICAGO	AB	R	H	RBI	TB	PO	A	E
Highamn C-RF	4	0	1	0	1	7	1	0
Hastings RF-C	4	0	0	0	0	1	0	0
White 3B	4	0	1	0	1	0	0	1
Devlin CF-P	4	0	1	0	1	1	2	0
Hines LF	3	0	0	0	0	2	1	0
Keerl 2B	3	0	0	0	0	1	5	1
Peters SS	3	0	0	0	0	0	5	1
Glenn 1B-CF	3	0	0	0	0	9	0	1
Zettlein P-1B	3	0	1	0	1	6	1	2
	31	0	4	0	4	27	15	6

ST. LOUIS	AB	R	H	RBI	TB	PO	A	E
Cuthbert LF	5	3	2	2	2	0	0	0
Pearce SS	5	1	1	2	2	0	2	1
Pike CF	5	0	0	0	0	2	0	0
Chapman RF	5	2	2	2	6	1	0	0
Hague 3B	5	0	1	1	1	3	4	0
Bradley P	5	0	0	0	0	2	3	0
Battin 2B	5	1	3	0	5	5	2	0
Dehlman 1b	5	2	3	1	3	12	0	1
Miller C	4	1	1	0	2	2	4	2
	44	10	13	8	21	27	15	4

Chicago	0 0 0	0 0 0	0 0 0- 0
St. Louis	2 1 0	4 0 2	1 0 0- 10

2B-Miller, Pearce 3B-Chapman 2, Battin

	IP	H	R	ER	BB	SO
ST. LOUIS						
Bradley (W, 2–0)	9	4	0	0	0	1
CHICAGO						
Zettlein (L, 1–1)	7	13	10	5	0	1
Devlin	2	0	0	0	0	1

Time: 2 hours *Umpire:* Adam Wirth of the St. Louis Empires
Sources: *St. Louis Republican,* May 7, 1875; *St. Louis Democrat,* May 7, 1875.

St. Louisans awoke the next morning, opened their local newspapers, and read reports about the preceding day's ball game. The accounts were filled with passages bursting with civic pride. The *Democrat* exclaimed in a boldface headline, "We Have Met the Enemy and They are Ours."[29] In the same vein, the *St. Louis Republican* rejoiced, "Time was when Chicago had an excellent baseball club, the best in the West, but that was before St. Louis decided to make an appearance on the diamond field and there, as everywhere else, attest the supremacy of the Western city with the greatest population, the most flourishing trade, the biggest bridge, and the prettiest women."[30]

Both newspapers also exulted at the discomfort felt by Chicago boosters. The *Democrat* snickered, "Baseball is not Chicago's stronghold; but there is a little game called brag in which that city excels."[31] Similarly, the *Republican* proclaimed, "St. Louis is happy. Chicago has not only been beaten in baseball, but outrageously beaten. With all the bragging of that boastful city . . . the result only illustrates once more the old truth that bluster does not always win. In this, as other things, St. Louis proves stronger."[32]

The *Dispatch* informed St. Louisans that Chicago's loss was the worst suffered since the formation of the White Stockings and blamed the Chicagoans' "ill-advised braggadocio." The *Democrat* expressed hope "that the unpleasant experience of the visitors from the Lake City will not be without its good results in the future; perhaps they will be less venturesome with opinion as to personal prowess, thereby rendering the companionship of defeat less disagreeable." In fact, neither the *Dispatch* nor the *Democrat* provided any evidence that suggested the White Stockings had been confidently predicting victory prior to the game. Rather, these local newspapers were projecting onto the White Stockings' ballplayers character traits which St. Louisans disliked in Chicago civic boosters. Defensive citizens of St. Louis had tired of comments such as the one by the *Chicago Tribune* that "the difference between Chicago and St. Louis business men" was that St. Louisans wore "their pantaloons out sitting and waiting for trade to come to them" while Chicagoans wore "their shoes out running after it." Baseball, as one perceptive scholar has noted, offered a "salient" alternative to the economic competition between the cities, a contest in which there was no necessity "to peruse the complex data of the financial pages or to hypothesize on the comparative resources of each community." One had only to look at the scoreboard. The *Dispatch* felt the 10–0 victory was so important that the date would be considered a milestone in the city's history: "May 6, 1875, will be remembered for long years to come by St. Louisans."[33]

Only two days later, on May 8, the Brown Stockings and White Stockings met again in St. Louis for the finale of their two-game opening series. Again, Grand Avenue became "one great jam of vehicles of all sorts" as citizens hurried to the ballpark in search of the best available seats. The game would not begin until 4 P.M., but people began to line up outside Grand Avenue Park even before the gates opened. By 2:30, the *Democrat* noted, "Every available seat, except such as offered by mother earth, had been taken within the enclosure. It is estimated that there were fully nine thousand people present . . . and among the spectators were a large number of ladies." Spectators shared a good-natured camaraderie. One seated man jokingly advised an unseated friend of his named John, "You should have come out earlier." John replied, "How early must a man come? I started just after breakfast, but the crowd was so thick that I couldn't make time." The seated spectator responded, "I came out last night and brought my bed, and didn't get a very good seat either. You see, we must start in several days ahead after this." The problem of locating a good seat, however, proved surmountable for the famous General William Tecumseh Sherman, who commandeered a spot in the press box.[34]

George Washington Bradley returned as the starting pitcher for St. Louis, but the White Stockings this time chose to give Jim Devlin the pitching assignment. Devlin fared much better than George Zettlein had. However, St. Louis nicked away at Devlin for single runs in both the third and fourth innings, and scored twice more in the fifth to take a 4–0 lead. The running game played a crucial role in the Brown Stockings' offense. In the third inning, Dickey Pearce and Lipman Pike both singled with one out. The duo then executed a double steal of second and third. Pearce scored when an unnerved Devlin uncorked a wild pitch. The Brown Stockings' final two-run rally began when Ned Cuthbert led off the fifth inning with a single and subsequently stole second. Cuthbert came around to score on a passed ball and a ground-out.[35]

This lead seemed more than sufficient as Bradley continued to baffle White Stockings' batters, extending his streak of consecutive scoreless innings against Chicago to seventeen. But in the ninth inning, just when it appeared that Bradley would pitch another shutout, Chicago launched a frenzied comeback that aptly illustrated "the glorious uncertainty of baseball." The White Stockings parlayed a lead-off walk and three successive base hits into two runs. Furthermore, Chicago had the potential tying runs perched on first and second with no outs. Although the Brown Stockings retired the next two batters on ground-outs, another run scored. John Glenn, the last hope for Chicago, approached the plate with the Brown Stockings clinging to a 4–3 lead and the tying run only ninety feet away at third base. At that stage of the game, "excitement" among spectators reached "a high pitch." Most of the people in the stands felt their tension turn to relief when Glenn knocked a grounder toward St. Louis third baseman Bill Hague, who fielded the ball and threw it to first baseman Dehlman in time to record the final out.[36]

The *Democrat* described another exuberant victorious response from the crowd: "Hats were thrown into the air regardless of expense, and everybody tried to yell themselves hoarse." In Chicago, local newspapers mocked the importance that St. Louis placed on the outcome of the two games. The *Chicago Tribune* complained, "The city of St. Louis has risen to its feet in a spirit of exultation and is rending the air with ecstatic exclamations, and making itself ridiculous generally." Meanwhile, the *Chicago Times* resorted to sarcasm: "In mere matters of business, we have had our way. St. Louis did not care particularly to interfere. . . . But all that is nothing beside this defeat in baseball. . . . Her citizens should feel proud of an achievement that places her at once in the front rank of brains and culture."[37]

The Chicago newspapers, however, had missed the point of the celebration in St. Louis. In only a matter of months, prominent St. Louisans had devised and successfully carried out a scheme to end a series of baseball setbacks to Chicago. If these civic leaders could win the St. Louis–Chicago baseball rivalry so easily, it seemed clear to them that the trade competition between the cities was also theirs for the taking. The *Democrat* explored this theme in an eight-stanza poem entitled "A Tale of Two Cities—A.D. 2000." The poet, Jack Frost, predicted the effect of the two baseball games upon the future of the St. Louis–Chicago rivalry:

> A village, once, of low degree,
> A city's rival tried to be.
> The city now in triumph stands.
> The village—leveled to the sands.
>
> This mournful tale's designed to tell
> How, like the frog who tried to swell
> Until he'd be an ox in size,
> Soon burst this town of many lies.
>
> From out her miasmatic smells
> One morn came nine athletic swells,
> Who would their humbler rivals meet,
> And crush them with a sore defeat.
>
> They met these rivals on the green;
> They ne'er were more surprised, I ween,
> For though they hard and harder fought,
> Their puny efforts counted naught.
>
> Again they met—but, while you know,
> Brains fed on lake fish larger grow,
> And while to man great use they've been
> A game of ball they cannot win.

As lions, came this buffer crew
Intending mighty things to do;
Like badly beaten fowls they went,
With feathers drooping, crushed and bent.

This little village seemed accursed;
Soon all her gaudy bubbles burst.
She proved what me thought her before,
A wind-bag burgh—and nothing more.

Where this wretched village stood
Now stands a sign of painted wood.
On it these words: "Upon this spot
Chicago stood, but now stands not;
Her time soon came, she had to go;
A victim, she, of too much blow."[38]

Of course, Chicago did not become a ghost town simply because its team lost two baseball games in St. Louis. Despite the optimism of St. Louis civic leaders, Chicago exploited links to the new transcontinental railroad system to defeat its river rival in the hard-fought contest for economic supremacy. Baseball, however, provided a new arena in which St. Louis would more than hold its own. The St. Louis–Chicago baseball rivalry quickly became institutionalized. Today, the St. Louis Cardinals and the Chicago Cubs continue the same classic baseball rivalry begun by the Brown Stockings and White Stockings in May of 1875.

2

"Champions of the West"

> Because [the National Association of Professional Baseball Players] was in name an association of players rather than clubs, historians have tended to assume that during its five-year life span, professional players themselves controlled the organization of the game. The brief interlude of "worker's control" came to an end, in this view, when the National League of Professional Baseball *Clubs* was established in 1876 and placed control firmly in the hands of baseball's businessmen. . . . In point of fact, the two organizations were more alike than has been supposed. Players did not run the first professional association.
>
> —Warren Goldstein, *Playing for Keeps: A History of Early Baseball,* 1989

The *Chicago Tribune* reacted angrily to the White Stockings' opening defeats in St. Louis. The newspaper admonished the team, telling it that "the way they have commenced in St. Louis is not the way Chicago people do business." The *Tribune* threatened these "white-legged young gentlemen purporting to hail from Chicago" that "If they propose to continue the use of the name Chicago, they must . . . wipe out St. Louis." The 1875 Chicago White Stockings failed to heed this directive. The St. Louis Brown Stockings' final record of 39–29 placed them a respectable fourth in the thirteen-team National Association, easily outdistancing the sixth-place White Stockings, who endured a record of 30–37.[1]

Boosted by the Brown Stockings' success, St. Louis replaced Chicago as the National Association's top attraction at the box office. Nevertheless, like the owners of other major-league teams of the era, the Brown Stockings' upper-class investors missed a golden opportunity to reach out to the working classes. They failed to schedule games on Sunday afternoons when most workers enjoyed their only day off. Despite the lack of Sunday games, the 1875 Brown Stockings drew to Grand Avenue Park a record total of 78,500 spectators, an average of more than 2,300 per game. Chicago, previously the National Association's leader in home attendance, lagged 23 percent behind.[2]

Consequently, the White Stockings' team president, William Hulbert, spent much of the 1875 season seeking to strengthen his ball club. In June 1875 Hulbert reached contractual agreements for the following year with the so-called "Big Four" from the league's perennial powerhouse, the Boston Red Stockings—pitcher A. G. Spalding, second baseman Ross Barnes, first baseman Cal McVey, and catcher "Deacon" Jim White. He made the same type of agreement with slugging first baseman–third baseman Adrian "Cap" Anson of the Philadelphia Athletics. Hulbert undertook these actions fully conscious that he was violating a National Association rule. The league barred clubs from signing, during the course of a season, players already under contract to another team.

Facing possible disciplinary action from the National Association, Hulbert covered his bets by forming a new league: the National League. He first succeeded in negotiations with three western river cities—St. Louis, Cincinnati, and Louisville. In January 1876 baseball representatives from these three cities met at a Louisville hotel, the Galt House, with a Chicago delegation of Hulbert, A. G. Spalding, and *Tribune* sports editor Louis Meacham. The four cities tentatively agreed to create a new league, the Western League, but Hulbert emphasized that their real objective was to persuade an equal number of eastern teams to join them. Prior to the Louisville meeting, Hulbert had confidently predicted to Charles A. Fowle, secretary of the St. Louis Brown Stockings' board of directors, "You and I can carry the day for everything that we want. Then, firmly established with four powerful clubs welded together, we can easily influence such of the remainder that we desire to join us."[3]

The St. Louis and Chicago baseball executives shared a mutual distaste for certain National Association policies. Their major sources of discontent centered around player-owner relations, instability caused by the presence of too many small-market franchises and the oversaturation of some of the biggest markets, a disproportionate balance between eastern and western teams, and concerns about the effect of gambling upon the game's image.

The St. Louis and Chicago baseball franchises initially formed an alliance in opposition to the turmoil that surrounded the legality of player contracts. In March 1875 at the annual National Association convention, both teams appeared before the Judiciary Committee to settle cases involving the disputed rights to players who had signed duplicate contracts. The Judiciary Committee ruled against St. Louis, awarding Hartford the rights to catcher Tom Miller, and against Chicago as well, siding with the Philadelphia Athletics in a struggle over the services of shortstop Davy Force. Tom Miller had signed three times before the 1875 season, first making a commitment to St. Louis, then pledging his labor to Hartford, and finally agreeing once again to play for St. Louis. The Judiciary Committee voided Miller's original St. Louis contract on the grounds that the signing of the document had not been properly witnessed. This represented a major embarrassment to the Brown Stockings' managing director, C. Orrick Bishop, who, in spite of his status as a noted attorney, had failed to secure a legally binding contract. Hartford, however, brought the Miller case to an amicable resolution. Since they had already signed another catcher, Doug Allison, Hartford permitted St. Louis to purchase the rights to the services of Miller, who did actually want to play for the Brown Stockings.[4]

No such compromise emerged in the rancorous fight over Davy Force. During the 1874 season Force had starred for the White Stockings, compiling a .313 batting average. On November 2 he signed a contract promising a return engagement in Chicago for the following season. Shortly thereafter, however, Force received a more enticing offer from the Philadelphia Athletics and, on December 5, signed another contract with them. The case went before the same Judiciary Committee that had decided the Miller case. On the grounds that the original contract was the one with the White Stockings, the committee awarded Chicago the rights to Force's labor.

But Charles Spering, a team official of the Athletics and the newly elected president of the National Association, managed to reverse this decision. First, Spering convinced the general session of convention delegates to wait until the next day to hear the Judiciary Committee's report on the Force case. This one-day delay allowed Force's fate to be determined by the incoming Judiciary Committee rather than the outgoing committee that had already voted in favor of Chicago. The composition of the new five-man committee included three representatives from Philadelphia teams. Each of these men possessed a vested interest in having Force, one of the National Association's top players, serve as a gate attraction in Philadelphia ballparks. The new committee voided Force's contract with Chicago on the grounds that the White Stockings' management, for reasons never divulged, had antedated its November 2 signing date to September 18. In 1875, after being awarded to the Athletics, Force posted a .311 batting average for his new team.[5]

C. Orrick Bishop would label the Force case as "the primary cause" behind the organization of the National League. He later recalled, "Although Hulbert had to acquiesce in the award, it stung him deeply and he never forgave the Association for it." Having both lost cases about disputed player contracts, Bishop and Hulbert quickly developed a friendship, born out of their mutual defeats and Bishop's belief that Force "rightfully belonged to Chicago." Bishop subsequently explained that Hulbert "appeared to have taken a fancy to me . . . and soon wrote me a letter advocating the formation of a new association."[6]

This spark ignited when Bishop and Hulbert exchanged "several letters" on the subject.[7] The pair discovered that their St. Louis and Chicago ball clubs harbored a number of other shared grievances. The Brown Stockings and White Stockings were the best-drawing clubs in the National Association, yet as western organizations they were still a distinct minority within a league dominated by eastern interests. Both the Brown Stockings and the White Stockings had been infuriated by the refusal of two eastern teams, the Brooklyn Atlantics and the New Haven Elm Citys, to make any western appearances during the 1875 season. (Eastern clubs nourished the same resentments against the Keokuk Westerns and St. Louis Red Stockings for not making an eastern road trip.)[8]

These scheduling complaints were symptomatic of deeper problems. The National Association suffered from the presence of unstable franchises such as the small-market operations in New Haven and Keokuk, while even some big-market ball clubs such as the Brooklyn Atlantics or St. Louis Red Stockings fell apart because they could not compete with more popular local competitors. Six of the thirteen National Association teams failed to complete a full schedule during the 1875 season; nevertheless, another fifteen organizations were seeking admission for 1876.[9]

Unstable franchises existed in both the East and the West, but further scheduling problems were created by the uneven balance between teams hailing from those two regions. The National Association lacked a fixed schedule, leaving each team with the responsibility of arranging its own games. The results were chaotic. Eastern clubs usually played against other eastern clubs. Western teams played most of their games against other western teams. East-West contests were rare, and since most teams hailed from the East, eastern clubs played far more games than their western counterparts. For instance, throughout the opening month of the 1875 season, nine eastern teams played exclusively among themselves while four western teams competed solely against each other. This haphazard scheduling ensured that in the early stages of the season eastern teams played more than twice as many games as western teams. In early June the unbeaten Boston Red Stockings finally traveled to St. Louis; on June 5 the Brown Stockings dealt the three-time defending league champions their first defeat, 5–4. Moving within two games of Boston in the loss column, the Brown Stockings should have been in a position to dream of overtaking them at the top of the National Association standings. The Association's disorderly scheduling process, however, prevented any cogent comparison between the Red Stockings, winners in twenty-six of twenty-seven contests, and the Brown Stockings, victors in nine of twelve games. Under these circumstances, western teams regarded themselves as a sort of unofficial division within the National Association. The two strongest western ball clubs, the Brown Stockings and the White Stockings, felt as though they were competing for the "Championship of the West" whenever they faced each other.[10]

The final concern of the St. Louis and Chicago franchises revolved around widespread rumors that gamblers controlled the outcome of certain National Association games. Gambling scandals extended back into baseball's amateur era, and the National Association utterly failed to establish public confidence in the honesty of the sport. A. G. Spalding, the pitching star who would become the president and major stockholder of the White Stockings six years after joining them as player-manager in 1876, later recalled the National Association era as a time when "a few players . . . had become so corrupt that nobody could be certain as to whether the issue of any game in which the players participated would be determined on its merits."[11]

The founders of the National League, led by the Chicago–St. Louis alliance, sought to provide remedies to the problems that the National Association had encountered. Working from a rough draft prepared by Hulbert, Bishop drew up a constitution for the new organization. In the January meeting in Louisville this document was approved by the organizers of the Cincinnati and Louisville teams. The four western partners then authorized Hulbert and Fowle to act as a special committee in future negotiations with eastern clubs.[12]

On February 2, 1876, Hulbert and Fowle met with delegates from the Boston Red Stockings, Philadelphia Athletics, Hartford Dark Blues, and New York Mutuals at the Grand Central Hotel in New York City. Skillfully using the projected Western League to achieve their ends, Hulbert and Fowle offered the eastern representatives a choice between either joining them or competing against them. The two westerners then presented the constitution that Bishop had drawn up for a proposed National League. Late that night, following a full day of discussion, the eastern teams decided their interests would be best served by rejecting the increasingly unstable National Association in favor of an equal partnership with the West.[13]

The Red Stockings and the Athletics, as the twin victims of Hulbert's raid on eastern playing stars, posed the greatest threat to this agreement. In overcoming their objections, Bishop believed the new constitution's major selling point had been the provisions calling for "some distinct understanding in regard to players so that there would be no more clashes between clubs about them." The National League required all player contracts to be filed with the league secretary. Upon receiving a copy of any player contract from one ball club, the secretary would immediately notify all other league clubs. This procedure prevented players from signing duplicate contracts.[14]

By forbidding "open betting" at any of their games, the National League attempted to discourage gamblers from attending. Also, to allay fears about dishonest players, the National League's leaders inserted a "blacklist" clause into the constitution providing that when releasing any ballplayer, a team should send to the secretary written documentation attesting "the release shall have been granted for a cause that does not in any manner reflect upon the character of the player." If a club did not extend an "honorable discharge" to a released player, the constitution stated, "It shall be inferred . . . that such player has been in fact dismissed, discharged, or expelled." Under these circumstances, a player could not sign with another league club, unless an appeal persuaded the board of directors to reinstate him.[15]

Besides striving to regulate player contracts, National League founders sought to establish an exclusive organization composed of a few select teams. League membership, generally limited to the nation's largest urban markets, would be evenly divided between eastern and western teams. Since the National League prohibited the presence of more than one team in any city, each franchise would obtain a territorial monopoly. In return, each franchise agreed to play a standardized schedule of ten games, five at home and five away, against every other team in the league. Finally, the National League took three steps to restrict its membership to the most financially stable ball clubs. First, the constitution raised the annual membership fee for each team from ten dollars to a hundred. Second, only teams owned by joint-stock corporations were admitted as charter members. This second step effectively froze out a group of cooperative teams that had participated in the National Association. These cooperative teams, which had been organized by the players themselves, paid their own expenses out of gate receipts and shared any remaining profits. Finally, the league's constitution required that any new members must represent a city possessing a population of at least seventy-five thousand.[16]

When play began in the spring of 1876, the National League stood alone as the sole major league in the country. Having lost six of its seven surviving teams from the 1875 season, the National Association simply dissolved. The first National League game in St. Louis took place on May 4, 1876, between the Brown Stockings and the White Stockings. A crowd of four thousand attended at Grand Avenue Park, and hometown partisans were delighting in a 2–1 lead in the third inning when "the rain came down with such force and persistency as to drive the men off the field."[17] Since the game had not gone the five innings necessary to become an official contest, it was rescheduled for the following afternoon.

The previous day's lead emboldened many St. Louisans inclined to wager on the Brown Stockings. National League moralists had banned gambling from the ballpark, but they were unable to change prevailing social attitudes on the subject. St. Louisans of the era were eager to lay down their money and frequently bet on contests such as baseball games, horse races, or even in one case a steamboat race from New Orleans to St. Louis between the fastest vessels traveling the Mississippi River. However, the games leading up to the 1876 home opener had discouraged anyone from staking much on the Brown Stockings' chances against Chicago. The White Stockings, vastly improved after adding Boston's Big Four and Anson, had won their first four contests, while the Brown Stockings had recorded only one win against three losses in games played at Cincinnati and Louisville. The *St. Louis Globe-Democrat* reported that betting had been "exceedingly slow" at the Southern Hotel on the night of May 3. But after St. Louis outplayed the White Stockings for three innings on May 4, gambling increased for the next day's game. By the next morning, the *Chicago Tribune* maintained, "Betting here is rather brisk, though the backers of the home club demand long odds—generally two or three to one."[18]

Meanwhile, a lively controversy erupted over the St. Louis team management's refusal to reimburse spectators their price of admission for the canceled contest. The *Globe-Democrat* issued a stinging editorial proclaiming, "Thousands of people, who took the chances of the weather yesterday to encourage the game of baseball, were entitled either to see a game, after having paid their money, or to have the money refunded." The newspaper then suggested that management should allow spectators to use tickets issued for the rain-curtailed game to gain entry the following day. Otherwise, the loss in public relations would far outweigh the fleeting financial gain derived from keeping the money. "If the people who pay full price to see a game can be turned out of the grounds at the end of two or three innings, whenever it rains," the paper pointed out, "they will take very good care not to subject themselves to the risk of rain . . . and they will largely avail themselves of the American privilege of staying away." The Brown Stockings' management defended itself merely by declaring "the custom that no money nor tickets shall be refunded . . . is so universal that no other rule has ever existed since the game was known."[19]

Fulfilling the prophecy of the *Globe-Democrat,* a smaller gathering turned out on May 5 than had attended the rained-out game the preceding afternoon. Two thousand spectators, only half of the previous day's crowd, saw George Washington Bradley outduel Chicago's A. G. Spalding, 1–0. In the first inning, Spalding's own throwing error enabled a St. Louis runner to reach second base. Lipman Pike then singled into right field and drove home the game's lone run.[20]

Prior to the game, the *Chicago Tribune* had boasted that the Brown Stockings' "playing is vastly inferior to the Chicagos at the bat and in the field." After the game, the *Tribune* despaired, "St. Louis . . . seems fated to tip over some pet theory of the Garden City in the baseball way."[21] In his first St. Louis appearance as a White Stocking, Spalding suffered a frustrating defeat that foreshadowed the problems he would usually encounter when his Chicago club faced the Brown Stockings. Spalding's poor record against the Brown Stockings, as a pitcher and later as an owner, would mark the greatest athletic disappointments in the success story of his life. The initial National League season of 1876 established that pattern.

After losing their first game in St. Louis, the White Stockings recovered to win the National League pennant, but the Brown Stockings were the only team to defeat them in a season series. St. Louis not only defeated Chicago, six games to four, but also emerged victorious in its own season series with every other National League club. By that unofficial criterion, St. Louis claimed to be the best team in the League. The *Globe-Democrat* proclaimed that the Brown Stockings "stand confessedly the actual champions in the race for the pennant, by having won the series of the ten games from the Chicago club."[22] At the close of the preceding season, the *Tribune* had reveled in declaring the White Stockings "champions of the West" because they had won their series with St. Louis, even though the Brown Stockings had posted a better overall record. With the roles reversed in 1876, however, the *Tribune* feigned incredulity at the *Globe-Democrat*'s assertion. "The most extraordinary claim of the season," it protested, "is that made to the championship of the West by the St. Louis club's friends." Because of the disagreement, the two teams arranged an unofficial postseason showdown. The *Tribune* advertised this five-game series as the "Northwestern Championship" or the "Championship of the West."[23]

The postseason series started with a pair of games in St. Louis on October 5 and 7. As a side attraction to the city's bigger fall festival, the Mississippi Valley Fair, the games drew fifty-five hundred spectators. Both contests bore out the records of Spalding and Bradley as the National League's best pitchers in 1876. Spalding had led the league in wins (47) and winning percentage (.797). Bradley had finished second in wins with 45, but posted the circuit's lowest earned run average (1.23) and topped all other hurlers in shutouts (16). In the opener, Spalding pitched a five-hit shutout for a 2–0 victory. Bradley countered with a six-hit shutout of his own in the second game, which the Brown Stockings won, 4–0.[24]

Bradley and Spalding engaged in another tight pitching duel as the "Championship of the West" resumed in Chicago on October 9. Bradley narrowly triumphed, 3–2, although the *Tribune* attributed his margin of victory to the defensive errors of the White Stockings. "The Browns won a very creditable victory, all things considered," it admitted. "To be sure, the Whites made more clean hits off Bradley than the Browns could get off Spalding, but the errors made by White and Anson turned the tide and gave the victory." By contrast, the *Globe-Democrat* described the St. Louis defensive performance as "one of the . . . sharpest fielding games ever seen in this city." Center fielder Lipman Pike served as the hitting star for the Brown Stockings with two hits (including a triple), a run scored, and two runs batted in.[25]

The *Tribune* blamed the sparse hitting in Game Three of the "Championship of the West" upon the stormy conditions under which the contest took place: "The wind was of a character to render batting a mere matter of chance. A strong gust, almost amounting at times to a gale, blew from the southwest." Adding to the *Tribune*'s vivid description of the weather's impact, the *Globe-Democrat* noted, "The hitting, in the teeth of a fierce southwest wind, was necessarily weak. . . . Most of the fielding work was done around the bases."[26]

For more than a century now, the fans and players of St. Louis baseball teams have been accustomed to checking the weather conditions in the Windy City prior to the start of a game against their arch-rivals. A wind blowing in toward the batters pretty much assures a low-scoring game. If the wind is blowing out from home plate, however, a high-scoring battle promises to unfold. Thus, the dramatic increase in the number of runs scored during Game Four the following day may have indicated that the wind switched directions and began blowing out. Validating this hypothesis, the official weather report reveals that the "brisk" southwesterly winds of October 9 shifted into "fresh" northwesterly winds for October 10.[27]

The tired arms of Bradley and Spalding could also have explained the deluge of runs that finally burst forth in Game Four. During the 1876 regular season, the two hurlers had been called upon to pitch an average of no more than three games per week. However, on October 10, both Bradley and Spalding appeared for the fourth time in only six days. Yet each team was determined to stick with its best pitcher, since a St. Louis victory would clinch the "Championship of the West" for the Brown Stockings. A Chicago win would make the fifth and final game of the series, scheduled for neutral Milwaukee, a decisive contest.

The *Tribune* depicted the fourth game as "a most remarkable circus," and the *Globe-Democrat* reported, "The ball was lively, and, as the fielding was poor, a large score was made on both sides." St. Louis and Chicago combined to produce an amazing total of 39 runs, 43 hits, and 32 errors, before the Brown Stockings emerged victorious by a score of 21–18. The heroes for St. Louis were once again Pike, whose five hits paced the Brown Stockings' 22-hit attack, and Bradley, who, though hit heavily at times, gamely kept St. Louis ahead at the end of every inning and also clouted his first major-league home run.[28]

Even though St. Louis had already won the "Championship of the West," the two teams still traveled to Milwaukee to play the fifth and final game. In another action-packed affair on October 11 they combined for 31 runs, 28 hits, and 32 errors. The Brown Stockings again prevailed, 16–15.[29]

At the start of the 1876 season the *St. Louis Republican* had predicted that baseball competition would be enhanced "not only [by] the natural rivalry which exists between St. Louis and Chicago, but [from] the fact that Chicago has this year

The 1876 St. Louis Brown Stockings, "Champions of the West." Front row, left to right: Joe Battin, John Clapp, Tim McGinley, Lipman Pike, Ned Cuthbert (sprawled on the ground), Mike McGeary, Dennis Mack. Back row, left to right: Joe Blong, George Bradley (holding baseball), Herman Dehlman, Dickey Pearce. State Historical Society of Missouri, Columbia.

made the most strenuous efforts ever made by a city to secure the championship to herself." The newspaper then called upon the Brown Stockings to thwart the ambitions of "the tall-priced Chicagoites" and their "phenomenal nine." By winning the "Championship of the West," the Brown Stockings allowed the *Globe-Democrat* to gloat that the White Stockings were "our meat" and the *St. Louis Dispatch* to boast, "St. Louis has beaten Chicago for the Western championship. In fact the only thing the 'Garden City' can beat us in is mortgages."[30]

The St. Louis–Chicago rivalry constituted one of the few bright spots in the National League's debut season. The year had been filled with problems. Only the pennant-winning White Stockings turned a profit. Their closest competitors, St. Louis and the Hartford Dark Blues, attracted only half as many fans as they had the year before. Overall, attendance at National League games dropped more than 31 percent from that of the National Association the preceding season. Baseball fans apparently resented the fact that the National League had doubled admission prices to fifty cents. Late in the 1876 season, citing financial hardships, the New York Mutuals and the Philadelphia Athletics both refused to make their last western road trip. On December 7, 1876, using punitive powers granted un-

Table 2.
Box Score of Game Four in the "Championship of the West," October 10, 1876

Brown Stockings (21)

	AB	R	H	PO	A	E
Pike CF	7	2	5	2	1	0
Clapp C	6	3	3	4	0	9
McGeary 2B	6	2	2	0	5	2
Battin 3B	6	2	1	0	2	2
Cuthbert LF	6	3	4	1	0	0
Blong RF	7	2	2	3	0	1
Bradley P	6	3	1	1	4	1
Mack SS	6	3	3	1	2	0
Dehlman 1B	6	1	1	15	1	3
	56	21	22	27	15	18

White Stockings (18)

	AB	R	H	PO	A	E
Barnes 2B	6	3	3	3	6	2
Anson 3B	6	2	1	5	0	3
McVey 1B	6	4	5	8	0	0
Peters SS	6	3	3	0	3	1
White C	6	1	4	7	1	1
Hines CF	6	2	2	1	0	1
Spalding P	6	1	2	0	2	1
Glenn LF	6	1	1	3	1	2
Addy RF	5	1	0	0	0	3
	53	18	21	27	13	14

	1 2 3	4 5 6	7 8 9	Final
Chicago	1 1 3	0 1 3	5 1 3	18
St. Louis	2 2 4	4 7 0	0 2 0	21

2B-Barnes, Anson, Peters 2, Pike, McGeary, Cuthbert, Blong
3B-Barnes, White
HR-McVey, Bradley
Source: *Chicago Tribune,* October 11, 1876.

der its constitution, the National League expelled the two teams. This action upheld the requirement that each league team must complete a full schedule against every other member of the organization. However, since William Hulbert stubbornly declined to accept any other New York or Philadelphia clubs as replacements, the National League denied itself access to the nation's two largest cities.[31] Faced with the unraveling of their plan to establish an elite group of large-market teams, the National League also found itself confronted by another specter: gambling.

3

The Collapse of the Original Brown Stockings

> The announcement that Hall, Devlin, Nichols, and Craver had been expelled from the Louisville club for crooked conduct was the all-absorbing topic in baseball circles yesterday, and the general impression prevailed that it would result in killing the national game "deader than a mackerel." The news, of course, created greater excitement in St. Louis than elsewhere, as two of the expelled players were relied on to help bring the championship here next season.
>
> —William MacDonald Spink, sports editor of the *St. Louis Globe-Democrat,* November 1, 1877

In 1876 the St. Louis Brown Stockings had gloriously concluded their initial National League season by defeating the Chicago White Stockings for the "Championship of the West." In 1877, however, their season would end in such turmoil that they would leave the league entirely.

From the start, the 1877 season constituted St. Louis's first true disappointment in professional baseball. The Brown Stockings' woes began less than two weeks after their final game against Chicago, as soon as the arch-rival White Stockings lured George Washington Bradley away to pitch for Chicago during 1877. St. Louis baseball fortunes further declined when Lipman Pike signed to play with Cincinnati. Pike, with averages of .346 in 1875 and .323 in 1876, had been the Brown Stockings' top hitter. Allegedly the fastest man in the sport, Pike also excelled defensively as a swift center fielder. The defections of their two best players gutted the team's offensive, defensive, and pitching capabilities, pushing the Brown Stockings down into the National League's second division. In 1877 they suffered through their first losing record, 28–32, to finish fourth out of six clubs. The Brown Stockings could only find solace in the fact that the two teams who trailed them in the standings—Chicago and Cincinnati—were the same clubs that had raided their stars. A. G. Spalding had decided to finish his active playing career in 1877 with one last season at first base. Bradley, however, failed to adequately replace him as a pitcher, going just 18–23 with the White Stockings.

Pike won the National League home run championship, but his heroics were not enough to keep Cincinnati from finishing last in the league for the second consecutive year.[1]

While the Brown Stockings were playing their last games of the season, team executives worked to improve the roster so that the team could win again. They chose to emulate the tactics that the Chicago White Stockings had successfully used in 1875, when William Hulbert had signed four players from the Boston Red Stockings and another player, Philadelphia's Cap Anson, to contracts for the following season. St. Louis's strategy two years later was virtually identical. The Brown Stockings' secretary, Charles Fowle, and treasurer, Charles Turner, signed three players from the Louisville Grays, who appeared to be on their way to the National League pennant, and Chicago shortstop Johnny Peters to contracts for 1878.

This approach backfired when two of the Louisville players recruited by St. Louis, pitcher James Devlin and outfielder George Hall, soon became implicated in a gambling scandal. Late in the season the Grays lost seven straight road games and blew the pennant to Boston. Louisville officials privately started an investigation in mid-September, shortly after the Grays returned home from their disastrous road trip. *Louisville Courier-Journal* sportswriter John Haldemann, the nephew of the club's president, had observed Hall, utility infielder Al Nichols, shortstop Bill Craver, and others suddenly sporting diamond rings and stickpins in a conspicuous display of wealth. Haldemann threatened to investigate on his own if the Grays' board of directors did not launch a full-scale examination of the suspected players. Walter Haldemann's status as owner of both the Louisville Grays and the *Courier-Journal* ensured that the ball club would follow up on the accusations made by the newspaper.

On October 23 and 24, St. Louis hosted the 1877 league-champion Boston Red Caps in a pair of exhibition games staged to showcase the prospective 1878 Brown Stockings. St. Louis won both contests, 9–1 and 2–0. Devlin pitched brilliantly, limiting Boston to only one hit in the first game and shutting them out on six hits the following day.[2] Ironically, Devlin's renewed pitching effectiveness against the Red Caps helped convince the *Courier-Journal* that the hurler had not been bearing down for the Grays in the regular season.

Devlin and Hall both returned to Louisville after the exhibition games in St. Louis. On October 26, Louisville team officials duped them into giving the confessions that led to their suspensions four days later. By leading each ballplayer to believe that the other had given a full confession, they elicited more information than either Devlin or Hall had originally intended to provide. Both players denied involvement in throwing the seven questionable road games against Hartford and Boston, but they did acknowledge making arrangements with a

New York gambler, James McCloud, to fix two non-league games and a contest with the Cincinnati Red Stockings. They also identified another teammate, the rarely used Al Nichols, as the man who had introduced them to McCloud. The *Courier-Journal* was contemptuous of the willingness of Devlin and Hall to admit their transgressions freely. The newspaper conceded that the two players "could have had a jolly good time skipping around on the St. Louis grounds next season" if they had "locked their jaws, had they refused to answer a single question put to them, or had they worked the thing on a lying ticket all the way through." Therefore, it described the players as "the most ignorant of rascals" and "two true-blooded numskulls."[3]

The talkative ballplayers then led the Louisville directors to the next crucial piece of evidence, revealing that McCloud had communicated with them by telegraph. Louisville officials, highly suspicious of the third player signed by St. Louis in the midst of the season (catcher Charles Snyder) as well as of former Brown Stockings' third baseman Bill Hague, required all the Grays to authorize the club to examine their Western Union records. Their telegrams implicated Devlin, Hall, and Nichols, but not Snyder or Hague. On October 30 the Louisville board of directors suspended Devlin, Hall, and Nichols for "selling games, conspiring to sell games, and tampering with players." They also suspended Bill Craver, the one Gray who had refused to allow access to his telegraph records, for "disobedience of positive orders, general misconduct, and suspicious play in violation of his contract and the rules of this league." In a description of National League shortstops, the *Courier-Journal* had previously expressed doubts concerning Craver, comparing him and St. Louis's Davy Force as "slippery roosters, artful dodgers, eels of a superlative degree of lubrication, little jokers whom now we see and now we don't, algebraic problems with two unknown quantities; a bad crowd."[4]

When the focus of the National League gambling scandal shifted to St. Louis, Force and three other Brown Stockings suddenly became subjects of intense scrutiny themselves. In response to the Louisville suspensions, William MacDonald "Billy" Spink, the sports editor of the *St. Louis Globe-Democrat,* wrote a series of articles about corruption in baseball. Spink had pioneered sports journalism in St. Louis. At the age of fifteen he had emigrated to St. Louis from Canada to take a job as a telegraph operator for Western Union. Five years later, in 1860, he wrote the first accounts of St. Louis baseball to be published in local newspapers. When Western Union officials employed hard-line tactics to defeat a strike by the Telegrapher's Union, Spink quit his job and became a full-time newspaperman. He covered sports in St. Louis for twenty years with the *Democrat, Dispatch,* and *Globe-Democrat.* After his 1884 death, two brothers, Al and Charles, carried on the Spink legacy in St. Louis sports journalism.[5]

William MacDonald Spink. State Historical Society of Missouri, Columbia.

William Spink predicted the effect that the banishment of Devlin and Hall might have upon baseball in St. Louis: "If the charges against them can be sustained, it is almost a foregone conclusion that the St. Louis club will 'throw up the sponge' and never again place a nine in the field." Since Spink now strongly suspected that "the days of professional baseball are numbered," the *Globe-Democrat*'s sports column temporarily ceased to promote the game and instead pursued an investigation into the negative effect of gambling. Spink alleged that two Brown Stockings had conspired with Chicago gambler Mike McDonald to fix the St. Louis–Chicago game of August 24, which the White Stockings had won, 4–3.[6]

The movements of a profiteering middleman, identified by Spink only as "a certain St. Louis sharp," had tipped off Brown Stocking officials to the plot.

Shortly after Spink revealed the scandal, the *Chicago Tribune* maintained that the middleman had been L. W. Burtis, a National League umpire. Spink did not deny that assertion, and following the close of the 1877 season, Burtis never umpired another major-league game. During the days directly preceding the game in question, the middleman had been seen socializing with Mike McDonald in Chicago. After this individual returned to St. Louis, McDonald had mailed "a considerable sum of money" to him. On the day of the game, the middleman had placed a sizeable wager upon the White Stockings and dispatched a telegram that advised McDonald, "Buy wheat. Smith is all right. Jones will assist."[7]

Spink subsequently charged that the Brown Stockings had lost the game when a pair of their players made pivotal errors "at precisely the right moment." In the immediate aftermath of the loss, the Brown Stockings' board of directors had hired a detective to ascertain whether these two ballplayers were "Smith" and "Jones." The detective discovered that, prior to the game, one of the suspected players had telegraphed a cryptic message to a Philadelphia acquaintance: "We'll go to Chicago, but don't know when." Spink observed, "As St. Louis had . . . paid its last visit to Chicago for the season, and the sender had no business to transact in that city, the idea naturally suggested itself that the word 'Chicago' in the dispatch meant a good deal more to the recipient than it would have done to an outsider." In other words, since gambling pools were available to bet on the results of each inning or an entire game, Spink reasoned that the player had been surreptitiously advising a friend to wager on the White Stockings to win the game, but not on the outcome of individual innings. Later that night, the detective had followed McDonald's assistant to "the back room" of a St. Louis saloon. There, this middleman met the two corrupt members of the Brown Stockings and paid them off. Then, before departing, the middleman had warned the ballplayers, "For God's sake, don't lose your nerve tomorrow."[8]

The directors of the St. Louis club had cautioned Brown Stockings' captain Mike McGeary about the conspiracy. In the next day's game, McGeary "made a judicious change" when it appeared that one of the players "attempted to duplicate his errors." By transferring the suspected player "to a position where, as luck happened, he had little to do," McGeary also alerted the other conspirator about the suspicions of the team's management. St. Louis—with one of its crooked players removed from an influential to a remote position and the other scared into giving an honest effort—defeated Chicago. Despite all of their shady dealings, McDonald and his assistant ended the week empty-handed.[9]

Comparing Spink's postseason allegations with his late August accounts of the two ball games, it seems clear that he intended to target pitcher Joe Blong and third baseman Joe Battin as the dishonest Brown Stockings. Blong, relieved of his pitching duties and sent to the outfield in the second inning of the August

25 game, had been the suspected player who changed positions. In his report of the August 24 game, Spink noted that the White Stockings tied the score during the seventh inning on "a miserable error by Battin." Chicago claimed the victory the next inning when "Battin gave the visitors the winning run by failing to hold an easy throw." Evaluating the player performances of August 24, Spink complained, "The game was lost, after it had been won, by Battin, who has been the weakest spot in the St. Louis ninc all scason. In the early part of the contest, Blong pitched well, but towards the end went to pieces, his wild pitching and lack of headwork . . . proving very costly." A day later, Spink emphasized the glaring improvement in Battin's performance: "Battin braced up at the bat and in the field yesterday, which was a source of gratification to his many friends. . . . Joe can play ball as well as any one, but he is apt to be a trifle careless at times."[10]

Spink went on to claim that the scandals in Louisville and St. Louis represented only particular examples of a larger gambling problem that extended to every National League team. William Hulbert, the president of both the White Stockings and the National League, promised that the annual league meeting in December would provide "an excellent time and place to strike an effective blow" at "the thieves and scoundrels."[11] It soon became apparent, however, that Hulbert intended to limit the gambling investigations to Louisville and St. Louis.

The *Chicago Tribune,* expressing the views of the White Stockings' management, reacted to Spink's accusation of widespread corruption throughout the entire National League with much less enthusiasm than his exposé of the St. Louis scandal. The *Tribune* challenged Spink to prove that there had been any crooked play by Chicago players. It directly accused the *Globe-Democrat* of responding to "stealing in members of its present and prospective teams" by throwing "mud at random in the chance of making someone as dirty as the thrower."[12]

Meanwhile, the *Tribune* continually pressured the Brown Stockings' board of directors to discipline Blong and Battin. It also urged them to investigate two Brown Stockings whom the *Tribune* considered equally guilty—Davy Force and Mike McGeary. In analyzing both the August and November coverage that the *Globe-Democrat* provided of the "fixed" St. Louis–Chicago game, the *Tribune* conceded, "Battin and Blong are the men it is gunning after." Yet the *Tribune* suggested there was also "a flavor of Force in the pot," since the St. Louis shortstop had committed a run-costing error in the lost game.[13]

In its description of the August 24 game, the *Globe-Democrat* had left slightly open the possibility that Force, rather than Battin, might have been Blong's accomplice. Battin, though, clearly seemed the more obvious suspect. Furthermore, in his original comments about the scandal, Spink had promised that the Brown Stockings' directors would drop the suspected players from the team. Significantly, neither Blong nor Battin figured in St. Louis's plans for the following season, while Force did. The Brown Stockings intended to shift Force to Battin's former position of third base and clear the shortstop role for one of their new additions, Johnny Peters.[14]

Certainly, no ambiguity ever existed over the St. Louis perception of McGeary. Spink portrayed him as a hero for turning the tables on Blong in the August 25 game. The Brown Stockings' directors included McGeary as a prospective member of their 1878 team. But despite his popularity in St. Louis, McGeary could not escape from his bad reputation elsewhere. He had been a target of gambling rumors since 1875.[15]

Henry Chadwick, the most prominent eastern baseball writer, joined the *Tribune* in insisting that the Brown Stockings discipline Blong, Battin, Force, and McGeary. Chadwick initially claimed in one newspaper, the *Brooklyn Eagle,* that the National League had blacklisted all four suspected Brown Stockings along with the Louisville Four. In reality, the National League planned to withhold all disciplinary proceedings until its December meeting. Next, in another newspaper, the *New York Clipper,* Chadwick demanded, "What action had been taken by the St. Louis Club in regard to the reported expulsion of Force, Battin, Blong, and McGeary?"[16] Chadwick had been the only person to suggest that these four ballplayers were expelled. Thus, Chadwick's method of persuasion depended upon planting a false rumor and then piously pleading for a response to his own unsubstantiated accusation. William Spink, in the *Globe-Democrat,* vehemently protested Chadwick's irresponsible journalism:

> The *New York Clipper* this week contains its customary "shot" at McGeary, asking what action has been taken by the St. Louis Club in regard to his expulsion. Will the *Clipper* have the manliness to publish the statement authorized by the St. Louis Club Directors that they never had a more faithful man in their employ, or one in whom they have ever placed or at present place more implicit confidence than in M. H. McGeary? Should this paragraph catch Frank Queen's eye, the proprietor of the *Clipper* will do an honest player the justice which Chadwick denies him.[17]

The Brown Stockings' board of directors not only issued an emphatic defense of McGeary but also chose not to take any action against the team's other suspected players. "The reason why the two St. Louis players supposed to be crooked are not expelled," the *Missouri Republican* explained, "is because the actual proof of their guilt is wanting. The club directors are well satisfied who the guilty ones are, but they could not prove it in a court of law, and hence they do not care to publish their names." Initially, in looking ahead to the National League's annual meeting, William Spink implored the directors of each team to set aside their legal concerns, "ignore all technicalities," and eliminate a "dozen dishonest men" from the playing ranks. Angered by the continual attacks upon McGeary's character, Spink eventually decided that C. Orrick Bishop—the Brown Stockings' director who was an expert in criminal law—had been correct in clinging to the principles of the American judicial system. After the *Tribune* deduced that Blong and Battin had been the two unnamed Brown Stockings accused by the *Globe-Democrat* of throwing the August 24 game against Chicago, Spink even offered a half-hearted defense of Battin: "There is no proof to show that Battin has been guilty of any crooked work." Shortly afterward, when Force received a "good conduct" discharge to join the Buffalo club in the International Association, the *Tribune* exaggerated the extent of Spink's defense of Battin in order to criticize his investigation into the St. Louis gambling scandal: "The *Globe-Democrat* took great pains within a short time to say that Battin was pure as the driven snow, and that sized it down to two, Blong and Force. And now Force turns up with a clean, slick and clear release and certificate. . . . Can it be that Joe Blong was in himself the two men who sold the game?"[18]

In defense of nineteenth-century ballplayers suspected of dishonesty, one may point out that reports of crooked players, which ran rampant during the final years of the National Association and the first years of the National League, often proved to be utterly inaccurate. For example, in July 1876 the *Tribune* printed a purported telegram from St. Louis alleging that Bradley had signed to play the following year with the Philadelphia Athletics. The wire added that Bradley's new eastern allegiance made "it common talk here . . . [that] the Browns will not try to win a game from the Hartfords." Bradley responded to the report by pitching three consecutive shutouts in five days against Hartford, the last one a no-hitter. Louis Meacham, the sports editor of the *Tribune,* sheepishly issued a retraction. However, Chadwick, while admitting that the Hartford series represented "what the St. Louis nine can do when they one and all put their shoulders to the wheel," still insisted, "What they can do when they go in to win is one thing; what they have done and will do again is quite another." It must be remembered that Chadwick, in his writings about the influence of gambling upon baseball, characteristically combined irrationality with assurances of absolute moral certainty. Few St. Louisans believed the charges of Chadwick and the *Tribune* in 1876. William Spink had dismissed the original charge made by the *Tribune* as evidence "that all fools are not yet dead."[19]

The scandals of 1877, though, caused a profound loss of faith in professional baseball, even among its previous boosters. The gambling scandals could not have occurred at a worse time for the Brown Stockings' board of directors. The *Tribune* reported that all six National League teams lost money during the 1877 season. It also identified St. Louis, with a deficit of eight thousand dollars, as the city suffering the greatest loss. In 1876 and 1877 combined, the Brown Stockings had drawn fewer fans to National League games than they had attracted in their only National Association season of 1875. These bleak financial realities had driven the Brown Stockings' directors to sign the three Louisville players to contracts for 1878 before the 1877 season ended. They had hoped thereby to persuade civic-minded St. Louisans to invest in the Brown Stockings' bid to build a team capable of winning the National League pennant. They tried the same approach they had used two years earlier to build a squad that could beat Chicago. Once again, a group of the city's wealthiest businessmen offered some of the game's top stars higher salaries to transfer from their current teams to the Brown Stockings. Until the gambling revelations, this plan had been working to the apparent satisfaction of the Brown Stockings' directors. In the week following the two exhibition victories of the prospective 1878 Brown Stockings over the Boston Red Caps, a total of twenty-five hundred dollars was raised in support of the 1878 team. More contributions were expected to roll in at a shareholders' meeting scheduled for the night of October 31.[20]

But by October 31 chaos reigned within St. Louis baseball circles. The Louisville team had already suspended Devlin and Hall, and were still investigating Snyder. Earlier that day, William Spink had made his suggestion in the *St. Louis Globe-Democrat* that two Brown Stockings had been guilty of throwing games. J. B. C. Lucas II called the shareholders' meeting to order. He informed the thirty or forty shareholders present that the purpose for calling them together had been to raise money to pay the 1877 Brown Stockings their overdue final paychecks. The board of directors, which felt it had borne a disproportionate share of the team's operational costs, contributed $2,000 toward reducing their debt to the players and called on the shareholders to make up the difference—a reported $2,791. Acting upon a suggestion from Secretary Charles Fowle, Lucas appointed a six-man committee to solicit donations. During a recess, the committee carried on solicitations actively, but it managed to collect less than a fifth of the outstanding debt.[21]

When the meeting resumed, one questioner asked Lucas whether, by paying off the 1877 debt, the shareholders could assure that St. Louis would field a National League team in 1878. Lucas provided an evasive, but shocking, answer. First, he announced that, unless the 1877 debt was erased, St. Louis would not remain in the league. But he quickly added that even if the debt was erased, he could not personally guarantee the continuation of National League baseball in St. Louis, since he was severing his connection to the sport.[22] The meeting soon adjourned with the Brown Stockings now led by a lame-duck president and the team's supporters still more than $2,000 short of meeting expenses for 1877.

A little more than a month elapsed between the shareholders' conference and the beginning of the National League's annual winter meeting. During that time, rumors flew regarding the future of the Brown Stockings' organization and the fate awaiting the four team members accused of foul play. The *Chicago Tribune* depicted the state of baseball in St. Louis as "extraordinary." "First," it chortled, "they charge certain of their players with crookedness, and assert that the loss of games through that crookedness was the cause of the deficit in their treasury. In the same breath they call for subscriptions to the amount of $2791 to pay the players who lost the games and thus caused the deficits." The *Tribune* assessed the prospects of National League baseball continuing in St. Louis as "doubtful."[23]

Back in St. Louis, the sports editor of the *Missouri Republican* searched for a silver lining within his own gloomy prognosis for the 1878 Brown Stockings. Al Spink, the younger brother of William MacDonald Spink, admitted that the team's demise was "quite probable." However, after expressing the hope that "a year of quiet will revive public interest," Spink reckoned the gambling scandals ultimately would have a curative effect upon the sport: "In the long run, it will be beneficial. . . . The wound will be painful, but it will heal in time, if there is anything good left in the original. And baseball is the same noble game today that it ever was, and it is not going to die; it cannot die, because of its very nobility."[24]

Meanwhile, William Spink, writing for the *Globe-Democrat,* explored a number of alternatives for the future development of St. Louis baseball. He originally predicted the St. Louis, Chicago, Louisville, and Hartford clubs would all drop out of the National League, leaving only Boston and Cincinnati as surviving representatives. Under this scenario, Spink thought the league would simply cease to exist, thereby terminating the era of professional baseball. In its place he envisioned a return to a purer form of intercity competition of the kind that had flourished during the heyday of amateur baseball: "St. Louis . . . can afford to do away with professional baseball, having amateurs by the score who are almost as skillful as men who are paid to play, and the enthusiasm which was aroused in the days of the Unions and Empires, and later of the Empires and Red Stockings, will be again witnessed." Two weeks later, when the Chicago White Stockings completed plans to field a National League team in 1878, Spink changed his mind. Influenced heavily by the rivalry between the cities, Spink could not bear to see St. Louis deprived of major-league baseball status at the same time that Chicago maintained its National League membership. Therefore, he now urged the Brown Stockings' shareholders to make good "the trivial amount" that they were legally obligated to pay the 1877 players. In return, Spink offered both a promise and a threat: "If the stockholders evince an intention to pay off the debt of the present season, the directors will secure a first-class nine, one capable of winning the championship in '78—otherwise the chances are that this city has seen the last of professional ball-playing for some years to come."[25]

Despite the renewal of the *Globe-Democrat*'s promotional efforts, the Brown Stockings' shareholders remained reluctant to come forth with the requested donations. William Spink blamed their reluctance mostly on the gambling scandals: "The Collection Committee report that [they] . . . are met by the argument that the crooked developments of the past season have robbed the national game of its interest, and that there is no guarantee that players will not repeat it next year." However, he also believed the directors' complaint that the shareholders lacked a genuine commitment: "The stockholders evidently invested in the organization for the sport to be derived from it, but without any intention of making good any deficiencies which might arise." Besides these factors, uncertainty hindered the attempts at fund-raising. Although William Spink claimed that St. Louis would field a championship-caliber team if the shareholders erased the debt from the 1877 season, the directors had not signed anybody to replace either Devlin or Hall. Therefore, in the *Missouri Republican,* Al Spink noted that the directors seemed more interested in "trying to raise the money to pay off for 1877, than planning for a nine in 1878." He alleged instead that if the shareholders indeed made the contributions requested from them, the directors would merely use the money to "quit professional baseball honorably."[26] The *Republican,* likely more accurate than William Spink, hardly encouraged shareholders to invest in the future of the Brown Stockings.

National League president William Hulbert visited St. Louis only a week before the beginning of the annual league meeting. Following Hulbert's visit, William Spink again acknowledged the distinct possibility that the Brown Stockings would resign its membership: "If St. Louis has a club next season, there will be some startling developments at Cleveland next week. Should she decide not to place a team in the field, it is doubtful whether charges will be preferred against her crooked players." The Brown Stockings did not even send representatives to Cleveland. On December 5 the National League accepted a letter of resignation from the team's board of directors. Henry Chadwick speculated that the Brown Stockings pursued this option to avoid an embarrassing investigation. "The action of such gentlemen as Messrs. Bishop and Fowle, of the St. Louis Club . . . is not what was looked for at their hands," he wrote. "We understand that direct charges would have been made at the League convention against several of the St. Louis players had the club not resigned."[27]

The National League, which upheld the suspension of the four Louisville players accused of dishonesty, never addressed the guilt or innocence of the St. Louis players. Blong played professional baseball in 1878 with a team representing Springfield, Massachusetts, but he never participated in another major-league game. Battin also never played again in the National League, although he did return to major-league baseball in the 1880s with the American Association and

Union Association. Both Force and McGeary returned to the National League in 1879 after one-year absences. Force rejoined the National League after his new team, the Buffalo Bisons, transferred from the International Association. Perhaps mindful of how the National League had tainted his reputation, Force wrote a letter unsuccessfully imploring the Buffalo club to stay out and avoid the more expensive traveling costs. When Mike McGeary signed with the Providence Grays, the *Tribune* smirked that he would "undoubtedly prove to be the largest kind of thorn" in the manager's side. Instead, McGeary teamed in the infield with Bill Hague, one of the suspected Louisville players and another former Brown Stocking, to spark Providence to the 1879 National League pennant.[28]

Providence had been one of three cities the National League admitted in 1878 to compensate for defections following the scandals of 1877. The league also had added teams from Indianapolis and Milwaukee. They replaced St. Louis, Hartford, and Louisville. All three departing cities had left the league as a reaction to the gambling scandals and their club's financial deficits. The deficits and scandals fed off each other. For example, after an 1876 season in which only the Chicago White Stockings avoided a deficit, the National League adopted new cost-cutting policies. Each player would be charged thirty dollars for his uniform, and on road trips would have fifty cents a day in meal money deducted from his salary. Joe Battin had protested these financial measures by initially refusing to sign another contract with the Brown Stockings. In 1877, despite the National League reducing team expenses, every team still lost money, with both the Brown Stockings and the Louisville Grays unable to fulfill payroll obligations to their players. The disgruntled Battin had relented and returned to the Brown Stockings, but his batting average fell from .300 in 1876 to only .199 in 1877. In the field, Battin's play also had dramatically declined, dropping from first to last among the National League's third basemen. William Spink had indicated that these deteriorating performances were linked to Battin accepting payments from gamblers to throw games. Fixing games could not be justified by either the National League's new financial policies or the failure of the St. Louis and Louisville clubs to meet their payroll obligations on time. Nevertheless, these factors had certainly served as powerful motives to lure discontented players astray. Then, once the gambling scandals were publicized, potential investors had grown disillusioned and increasingly reluctant to spend money on a baseball club.[29]

The National League's new franchises in Indianapolis and Milwaukee lasted merely one season. In 1879 the league regained its original eight-team format by adding clubs in Cleveland, Buffalo, Syracuse, and Troy, New York. The Syracuse franchise also lasted only one season and was replaced the next year with a team from Worcester, Massachusetts.[30] Reeling from all of these defections, the National League somehow managed to survive. But in its first five years of existence it utterly failed to achieve its goal to become an exclusive organization of elite big-market teams evenly divided between the East and the West. By 1880 the National League had stooped to using three cities—Syracuse, Troy, and Worcester—that did not reach the requirement of seventy-five thousand inhabitants demanded in the league's constitution.[31] Also abandoned was the concept of maintaining geographical balance between the East and the West. The National League had been transformed into an organization that was top-heavy with northeastern clubs: Troy, Worcester, Providence, Buffalo, and Boston.

The smaller northeastern clubs were dominated by the league's two big-market teams, Boston and Chicago. In 1879, Boston and Chicago secured passage of the "reserve clause" rule. The reserve clause sought to bind the game's top players to a single team, preventing them from "revolving" among the league's different teams in bidding wars. Chicago and Boston had won three of the first four National League pennants, and both clubs wished to preserve a core of players from those successful teams without risking raids from other teams. Initially, the reserve clause applied to only five players per team. It enabled teams to reserve the services of their best players for the following season and prevent them from bargaining in a free market.[32]

Cincinnati, the last of Chicago's original western partners still in the league, clashed with its former ally in 1880 over the reserve clause. The Cincinnati Red Stockings wanted to improve a weak team by enticing established stars away from other teams. In 1879 William Hulbert had gained support for the reserve clause by stressing its effectiveness as a cost-cutting device. A year later, faced with Cincinnati's complaint that the reserve clause perpetuated a competitive imbalance tilted toward Chicago and Boston, Hulbert suddenly switched gears. He now consolidated approval among smaller-market teams by defending the reserve clause as "a vital necessity" in their attempts to compete against the big-market teams.[33]

Despite finishing last in three of the National League's first five seasons, the Red Stockings had supplemented their gate receipts by adding an average of three thousand dollars a year in income from beer and refreshment concessions. Worcester had spent much of 1880 attacking Cincinnati's "questionable custom" of selling beer in its ballpark and leasing its grounds on Sundays to non-league teams. O. P. Caylor, the sports editor of the *Cincinnati Enquirer*, delivered a ringing denunciation of Worcester. "Puritanical Worcester is not liberal Cincinnati by a jugful," he wrote sarcastically, "and what is sauce for Worcester is wind for the Queen City. Beer and Sunday amusements have become a popular necessity in Cincinnati . . . We drink beer as freely as you used to drink milk." Chicago sided with Worcester in this dispute. The *Chicago Tribune*, a reliable gauge of William Hulbert's prejudices, denounced "beer-peddling" as "an unnatural and incompatible adjunct, a disgrace and a curse to baseball." In a similar tirade published two weeks later, the *Tribune* complained that "this association of beer and baseball" was "degrading, offensive [and] ruinous" to the game and to public morals.[34]

On October 4, 1880, the National League convened a special meeting in Rochester, New York. Every club, with the exception of Cincinnati, pledged to support amendments prohibiting the sale of liquor on league grounds and the leasing of league ballparks for Sunday games. Two days later, prodded by Hulbert, the National League expelled Cincinnati for refusing to promise to abide by these agreements once they were officially adopted. Caylor criticized Chicago's moral principles as hypocritical: "We respectfully suggest, that while the League is in the missionary field, they turn their attention to Chicago and prohibit the admission to the Lake Street grounds of the great number of prostitutes who patronize the game up there."[35]

Angered by Chicago's control of National League affairs, Caylor had previously threatened to establish a rival league. However, by 1880, the National League had already brushed aside challenges from such transitory organizations as the International Association and the original Northwestern League. Thus the *Tribune* had expressed disdain at Caylor's threat: "By all means form an anti-League association, with Cincinnati, St. Louis, and a few other villages as members. The League would be glad to get rid of some dead wood." Once the National League had evicted Cincinnati, the *Tribune* again dismissed all concerns that Caylor might organize a rival league: "There isn't the least danger that any player of prominence will join these paper clubs, and, if any of them are formed, they will be composed of what the League had no use for."[36]

The *Tribune* drew confidence from the skeptical views of professional baseball expressed in newspapers of cities exiled from the National League such as St. Louis, Philadelphia, and New York.[37] It was smugly believed that those cities would never again support a major-league team. Perhaps the *Tribune,* when it celebrated Cincinnati's eviction, would have been less confident if it had known about the unheralded entrance into St. Louis baseball circles that same October by a German immigrant saloon owner named Chris Von der Ahe. Brewery interests in the German-influenced western river cities of St. Louis and Cincinnati were about to dramatically alter the world of major-league baseball.

Part II

The Resurrection of Major League Baseball in St. Louis, 1878–1886

4

Beer and Baseball

> [Chris Von der Ahe] did as much for baseball in St. Louis and the country at large as any man ever associated with the game.
>
> —Al Spink, founder of the *Sporting News,* in *The National Game,* 1910

If not for the support extended in the early 1880s by Chris Von der Ahe, major-league baseball probably would have died in St. Louis and might indeed have come to an end throughout the nation. Christian Frederick Wilhelm Von der Ahe had been born on October 7, 1851, in Hille, a German farming community in the province of Westfalia. His father has been described as "a large dealer in grain . . . and one of the most successful merchants" in Westfalia. In 1867 Chris Von der Ahe immigrated as a teenager to the United States. Since he belonged to a prosperous family, it seems likely that he left home to avoid conscription into Prussian military service.[1]

Von der Ahe spent six weeks in New York City and then moved to St. Louis. Beginning in St. Louis as a grocery clerk, he had saved enough by 1870 to acquire a small combination grocery and saloon. On March 3, 1870, Von der Ahe married Emma Hoffman, a native-born Missourian of German lineage. Four years later he opened a spacious establishment at Grand and St. Louis Avenues that functioned as a joint grocery, delicatessen, saloon, and beer garden.[2] He would emerge as the savior of St. Louis baseball in the autumn of 1880.

Between 1878 and 1880, baseball struggled to survive in St. Louis. In 1878, after the original Brown Stockings resigned from the National League, five former players (left fielder Ned Cuthbert, shortstop Dickey Pearce, third baseman Joe Battin, pitcher Joe Blong, and second baseman–manager Mike McGeary) had joined forces on an independent semi-professional St. Louis club. This restructured team, also known as the Brown Stockings, competed against another St. Louis club, the Red Stockings. Thomas McNeary, the original owner of the Red Stockings, had reorganized his team that year and stocked it with local amateurs. In the opening week of the 1878 season the Brown Stockings defeated the Red Stockings in three out of four games. But the team disbanded when some of the players drifted away to accept better offers elsewhere.[3]

Chris Von der Ahe. State Historical Society of Missouri, Columbia.

The aborted 1878 season compounded the sense of disillusionment with baseball that had followed the gambling scandals of 1877. The gambling scandals had severely tested the loyalty of St. Louis baseball enthusiasts. Still, a surprisingly large crowd of two thousand attended the first Brown Stockings–Red Stockings game of 1878. Attendance declined at the next two contests, partly due to confusion over the site of the second game and the handicap of cold weather for the third meeting. However, on May 5, a large number of spectators, totaling one thousand, gathered for what turned out to be the fourth and final tilt between the ball clubs.[4]

One of the original Brown Stockings, Ned Cuthbert, was sufficiently encouraged to revive the Brown Stockings yet again the following year. The 1879 team tried several strategies to overcome lingering local antipathy. First, Cuthbert sought to improve the image of team members. In 1878 the Brown Stockings had used two men, Joe Blong and Joe Battin, who had been accused of throwing games to Chicago. Rather than relying on former major leaguers, Cuthbert recruited most of his 1879 team from the ranks of St. Louis amateurs. He included only three members of the old National League Brown Stockings—himself, Dickey Pearce, and first baseman–outfielder Arthur Croft—all of whom had been above reproach in the 1877 gambling scandals. Consequently, the opening-day crowd welcomed the 1879 Brown Stockings "with all the old-time enthusiasm, the veterans especially."[5]

Yet fewer fans attended the early season games in 1879, although those who did remained as fervent as ever. In 1875 the Brown Stockings had attracted an average of more than 2,300 people per game. The independent Brown Stockings of 1878 had twice drawn an audience of a thousand or more. But in 1879 no more than seven hundred people viewed any of the Brown Stockings' opening thirteen victories. To combat this problem, the team halved the price of admission in the hope that "the working classes, who have always been staunch supporters of the national game, may not be taxed beyond their means."[6]

The reduced admission fee—twenty-five cents—had no initial impact upon attendance figures. In the opinion of the *St. Louis Globe-Democrat,* attendance suffered because of the Brown Stockings' utter dominance of the best St. Louis amateur clubs.[7] Therefore, in addition to cutting admission prices and improving the team's image, the Brown Stockings found it necessary to schedule more competitive opponents.

As a result, the Brown Stockings embarked on their only road trip of the 1879 season. They traveled to Cincinnati and Louisville to challenge a pair of semiprofessional clubs, the Stars and the Eclipse, who claimed to be the state champions of Ohio and Kentucky, respectively. In exchange, both the Stars and the Eclipse promised to play return engagements at St. Louis.[8] In Cincinnati the Brown Stockings posted consecutive victories over the Stars. They followed a relatively easy 10–4 win on Saturday, August 2, with a narrow eleven-inning 16–15 triumph in front of a large Sunday afternoon crowd of three thousand. Traveling on to Louisville, the Brown Stockings played their third game in three days. Prior to the road trip, the team had played only once a week, winning thirteen straight Sunday afternoon games at Grand Avenue Park. Such a schedule had enabled George "Jumbo" McGinnis to pitch every game. The daily demands of the road trip, though, placed a great strain upon McGinnis's pitching arm. When his aching arm forced McGinnis to abandon the pitching duties, the Brown Stockings sustained their first defeat of the season—losing to the Louisville Reds, 14–8. After a day of rest, McGinnis returned to pitch the Brown Stockings to a 6–1 victory over the Eclipse, a team that had previously beaten the Reds in four of the five games played between them.[9]

Although both the Stars and the Eclipse reneged on promises to appear in St. Louis, the Brown Stockings still benefited from the successful road trip. Their victories in Cincinnati and Louisville convinced many area residents of the accuracy of the *Globe-Democrat*'s claim that "the Brown Stockings . . . now have a nine well able to cope with any professional team in the country." Shortly after the team returned to St. Louis, heightened local interest manifested itself. On Sunday, August 17, the Brown Stockings defeated the defending Missouri amateur champions, the Athletics, for the sixth time that season, but this time the attendance doubled the biggest crowd that the two teams had previously drawn. Among the twelve hundred people present, William MacDonald Spink recognized "many solid admirers of the game, who have not been seen at ball matches since the good old days when St. Louis used to knock the stuffing out of the Chicagos, when both were represented in the League."[10]

On their road trip the 1879 Brown Stockings had generated favorable publicity, which then stimulated attendance at home. Thomas McNeary, the former owner of the St. Louis Red Stockings, had been impressed with the large gathering drawn to Grand Avenue Park for the Brown Stockings–Athletics game of August 17. After that contest, McNeary persuaded Cuthbert to play the remainder of the season at Compton Avenue Park. This move, which might have created confusion or anger among certain segments of the public, quite possibly contributed to a decline in attendance. Whatever the cause, the Brown Stockings did not attract more than six hundred fans in any of their first six games on the Compton Avenue site. Despite these disappointing turnouts, the team continued its mastery of local amateurs and defeated the Memphis Riversides and a couple of clubs hailing from Belleville, Illinois, as well.[11]

The superb record of the 1879 Brown Stockings, by now the winners of twenty-four out of twenty-five games, sparked the season's last resurgence of interest in St. Louis baseball. In mid-October a number of local ballplayers who played professionally or semi-professionally elsewhere were returning to St. Louis for the winter. These players formed a "Picked Nine," and on the final two Sundays of the 1879 baseball season, October 19 and 26, they attempted to spoil the undefeated home record of the Brown Stockings. Each game drew a thousand spectators to see the Brown Stockings claim their twenty-second and twenty-third home wins of the year, 9–3 and 16–13.[12]

Cuthbert's Brown Stockings had restored pride to St. Louis baseball. As they won game after game, more and more St. Louisans returned to the ballpark. After drawing less than a thousand people to each of their first fourteen home games, the 1879 Brown Stockings attracted at least a thousand for three of their last nine contests, including the final two. Therefore, local sportswriter Al Spink later recalled the season as a pivotal one in the history of St. Louis baseball: "During the close of the season of 1879 the game showed signs of returning to life."[13]

But if Al Spink stopped short of describing the next baseball season as a setback, he certainly believed that the game had missed an opportunity to take a major stride forward. Spink complained that in 1880 the Brown Stockings still frequently played in front of "what Shakespeare would have termed a beggardly array of empty benches." He especially regretted a game in St. Louis against Indianapolis. On that particular afternoon the Brown Stockings failed to accumulate enough in gate receipts to reimburse the Indianapolis players for streetcar fares from the ballpark back to their hotel. Yet when attendance peaked in 1880, the crowds equaled those drawn on the best days of 1879. For example, on Sunday, September 5, 1880, the *Globe-Democrat* estimated that "over one thousand people" turned out for the second game in a five-game season-ending series between the Brown Stockings and the again resuscitated Red Stockings. The *Missouri Republican* noted, "Seldom this season has the Grand Avenue Park been better filled."[14]

The plans of August Solari, however, were not affected by another late-season surge of support. With his latest five-year lease on Grand Avenue Park set to expire, Solari decided not to spend sixty-five hundred dollars to renew the lease, planning instead to dismantle the ballpark. In early October, without explanation, Solari suddenly announced, "Next week I am going to get out of here. I am going to take down the stands, the benches and everything else." Bemoaning this development, the *Missouri Republican* asked, "Who is there that loves the national game that will not be pained to hear that the old park is to be defaced?"[15]

On the heels of Solari's statement, Chris Von der Ahe arrived to save St. Louis baseball. Ned Cuthbert had already spent months urging Von der Ahe to promote baseball. Cuthbert tended bar at Von der Ahe's drinking establishment, the Golden Lion Saloon, located only a block away from Grand Avenue Park. The two men had first discussed the sport's effect upon beer sales on a fateful Sunday afternoon after the Brown Stockings and Red Stockings had competed at Grand Avenue Park. Cuthbert served as a player-manager for the Red Stockings, and after the game he walked down to the Golden Lion. There, Cuthbert met some of his teammates to quench their thirst with a few postgame beers. After a while, Von der Ahe visited the ballplayers' table. Puzzled, the saloon owner asked Cuthbert to explain why some customers hurriedly guzzled a few beers before 2 P.M., then disappeared for a couple of hours, and finally returned after 4 P.M. in a mood to while away several hours with leisurely drinking. Cuthbert provided the answer: "They're all at the ballgame."[16]

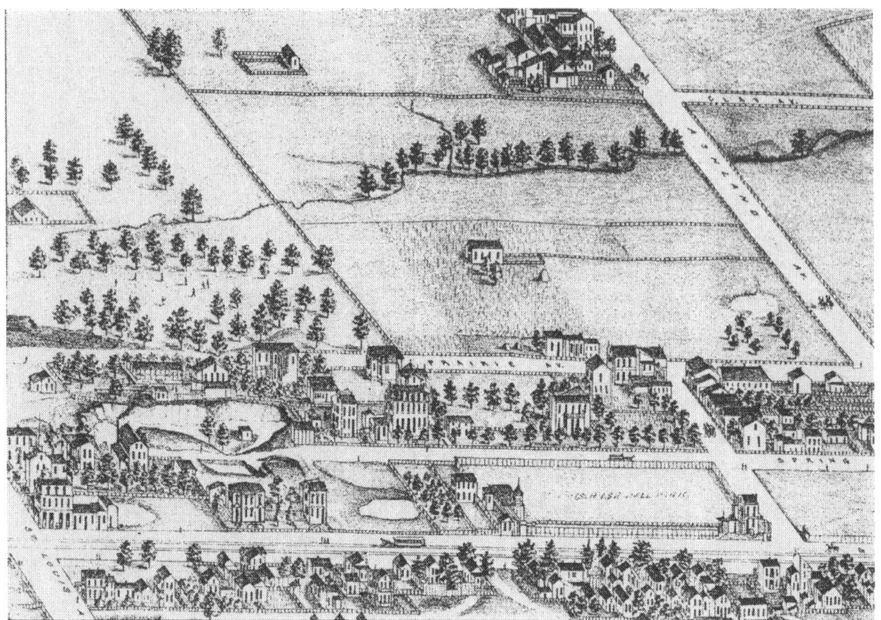

The area around Grand Avenue/Sportsman's Park. Near the lower left corner is Chris Von der Ahe's saloon, at Grand and St. Louis Avenues, a block away from Grand Avenue Park. State Historical Society of Missouri, Columbia.

Over the ensuing months, while at work, Cuthbert regaled his boss with anecdotes about the days when he had roamed the outfield for the "Champions of the West." He also captivated Von der Ahe with tales of the riches awaiting the man who bought the concession rights to baseball. The German immigrant did not understand very much about the game, but he quickly grasped the potential for profit. Many years later, he recalled, "It was 'Eddie' who talked me into baseball. . . . He picked me out, and, for months, he talked league baseball, until he convinced me that there was something in it."[17]

Initially, Von der Ahe offered to provide Solari with financial assistance in exchange for the concession rights at Grand Avenue Park. Solari rejected the proposal. However, when Solari ceased promoting baseball, Von der Ahe took over the lease of the ballpark. At the time, Grand Avenue Park languished in shambles. According to Al Spink, it consisted of merely a baseball diamond with "a weather beaten grandstand and a lot of rotten benches." Yet Spink believed that Von der Ahe could revitalize St. Louis baseball by refurbishing the grounds "as they were in the olden times when they were looked upon as the best in the country." Thus the Sportsman's Park and Club Association was formed. It sold five thousand dollars' worth of stock to finance renovation of the newly renamed Sportsman's Park. As the largest investor, Von der Ahe operated as president. John W. Peckington, another local saloon owner who shared Von der Ahe's hopes for a profitable marriage between beer and baseball, functioned as vice-president. Al Spink, secretary of the group, handled most of the day-to-day business arrangements.[18]

Their renovation project restored some lost grandeur to the ballpark. Following the Brown Stockings' resignation from the National League in 1877, Solari had torn down the nine-thousand-seat grandstand and erected a fence that divided the playing field in half. From 1878 through 1880, baseball at Grand Avenue Park had been played on this half-field in front of minuscule crowds seated precariously on dilapidated benches. The Sportsman's Park and Club Association immediately uprooted Solari's fence and returned the playing field to its proper dimensions.[19] Then, after leveling the old bleachers, the organization started to build anew.

By the beginning of the 1881 baseball season, Sportsman's Park featured a new double-decked, covered grandstand and safely secured wooden benches. Construction continued during the course of the season, and the overall seating capacity increased from 2,500 to 6,000 when rows of uncovered bleacher seats were added down the first-base line. Later, in 1886, the bleachers were extended around the outfield fences and down the right-field and left-field foul lines, and the park's capacity reached 12,000.[20]

Asymmetrical outfield distances constituted the most unusual feature of the ballpark. While the left-field fence was 350 feet from home plate, right field stood only 285 feet away. The right-field wall, if it could be called that, was a two-story house where Augustus Solari had been living. Solari vacated the residence when he relinquished the lease to the ballpark. After the Sportsman's Park and Club Association took over the lease, Chris Von der Ahe transformed the house into a beer garden with handball courts and lawn bowling. The area was regarded as part of the playing field until October 1888, and spectators frequently beheld the bizarre sight of right fielders racing through the beer garden to chase down long drives.[21]

Al Spink, besides supervising the renovation of the ballpark, also shouldered the task of bringing in visiting teams. He first contacted O. P. Caylor of the *Cincinnati Enquirer.* Acting on Spink's advice, Caylor formed a makeshift team and gave it the traditional "Red Stockings" moniker. Then Spink and Caylor arranged for the Brown Stockings and Red Stockings to meet in the "grand opening" of Sportsman's Park. On Saturday, May 28, 1881, six hundred spectators sat scattered across the freshly painted grandstand or with raised steins in the right-field beer garden to toast the occasion. Since leaving the National League, St. Louis clubs had usually played only one Sunday game per week. Consequently,

Al Spink. State Historical Society of Missouri, Columbia.

the *Missouri Republican* considered the May 28 contest to be a significant experiment: "This is the first game of importance played in St. Louis upon a week day in years. Those lovers of the national game who are opposed to Sunday playing will now have a chance to give the week-day fun a 'boost.' If it is the right kind of a 'boost,' there will be more of it." Although the Saturday turnout proved somewhat disappointing, the Brown Stockings still thrilled those who witnessed the game. St. Louis outscored Cincinnati 15–9, while "the ball several times was knocked nearly out of sight, and the crowd went wild."[22]

The contest received considerable local coverage in the Sunday morning newspapers. Many area residents who had not attended a game in years were now tempted to go see the redesigned ballpark. On Sunday afternoon four thousand people swarmed into Sportsman's Park. This overflow crowd, twice the size of any assembled at a Brown Stockings' game between 1878 and 1880, watched St. Louis thrash Cincinnati, 16–2. St. Louisans had clearly demonstrated their

Sportsman's Park. State Historical Society of Missouri, Columbia.

preference for Sunday baseball; in an era in which a six-day, ten-hours-per-day work week was the norm, Sunday was the only day that most workers had free for relaxation.[23] Sunday ball games entertained weary workers with a sporting event, sunshine, fresh air, and cold beer. But while Sunday remained the big payday for Von der Ahe and the Brown Stockings, the 1881 season proved that weekday games could serve a promotional purpose.

Nearly three decades later, recognizing the significance of these opening games at Sportsman's Park, Al Spink described the Cincinnati series as a monumental breakthrough: "We began to see daylight and to again hope for better things."[24] His allocation of the gate receipts at the time, however, better revealed the modest expectations of this semi-professional era of St. Louis baseball. Spink set aside 60 percent of the receipts to be distributed among the Brown Stockings' players. In 1879 the players had received 75 percent of the gate receipts from Augustus Solari. But by reducing their share of the gate to help finance the renovations to Sportsman's Park, the players prospered. In 1879 peak attendance had been twelve hundred; at a quarter per admission, this turnout had produced gate receipts of $300, and the players thus divided $225 as their share. On May 29, 1881, the four thousand spectators generated $1,000 in gate receipts, providing the players with $600 to divide among themselves as a product of their 60 percent share.[25]

The Brown Stockings' management retained the other 40 percent of the proceeds for the upkeep of Sportsman's Park, to cover advertising expenses, and to reimburse the travel expenses of visiting teams. The visitors received no share of the gate receipts. They were only compensated for their railroad fares, hotel accommodations, and streetcar rides to and from the ballpark.[26] Under this system of distribution, Von der Ahe received his financial reward from concession rights, primarily beer sales.

Out of these humble economic origins, a new professional baseball league arose. Following the successful Cincinnati series, Spink convinced some of the nation's best semi-professional ball clubs to visit St. Louis. Ned Cuthbert, returning as the Brown Stockings' player-manager, guided the 1881 team to a superb record of 35–15, with one tie. Attendance increased as the season progressed, peaking whenever the Brown Stockings were matched against top-flight competitors such as the Brooklyn Atlantics, the Akrons, the Philadelphia Athletics, or the Louisville Eclipse. Sunday crowds as large as six thousand crammed into Sportsman's Park for games against the Athletics and the Eclipse. Von der Ahe, now an avid convert to the sport, purchased a controlling interest in the Brown Stockings near the end of the 1881 season.[27]

Labeling these events "an old-time baseball revival," the *Globe-Democrat* praised Von der Ahe for resurrecting "a regular corpse" and transforming it "into the liveliest being imaginable." The St. Louis baseball renaissance coincided with renewed enthusiasm in other large cities excluded from the National League. Consequently, Von der Ahe and his Brown Stockings banded together with five other clubs to create a new professional baseball league, the American Association. On November 2, 1881, at the Hotel Gibson in Cincinnati, the American Association announced its formation. The charter members represented the six major cities—Philadelphia, Baltimore, Pittsburgh, Cincinnati, Louisville, and St. Louis—from the old river traffic network that had flourished in preindustrial days when St. Louisans boasted commerce always followed natural avenues of trade. Now, the former business partners united again. Besides seeking profits, the American Association embarked on a crusade to promote Sunday baseball and beer in the ballparks. Brewery interests had bought into all six Association clubs and were the primary investors in St. Louis, Cincinnati, Louisville, and Baltimore.[28]

The presence of the brewmasters brought conspicuously different business practices to the new American Association. In the National League, Chicago White Stockings' owner William Hulbert had persuaded the other team owners to ban beer sales and Sunday games from any of their parks. The founders of the American Association condemned these restrictions as the "tyrannical articles" of the National League constitution. The rowdier Association had no such emphasis on this form of morality. American Association teams were encouraged to schedule Sunday games wherever local law permitted the custom (originally St. Louis, Cincinnati, and Louisville). To further stimulate attendance, the new league catered to the working class by offering twenty-five cent tickets, half the price of admission that the National League demanded.[29]

The American Association–National League debates over liquor sales, Sunday games, and ticket prices mirrored deeper divisions within the United States. A recent landmark political study described "the prohibition question" as "the paramount state or local issue, year in and year out, throughout most of the Midwest (and much of the rest of the country) in the 1880s." Democrats such as Von der Ahe were usually staunch opponents of prohibition; Republicans such as Hulbert generally advocated for it. Prohibition received widespread support from large sectors of native-born Americans, such as Hulbert; opposition to prohibition proved popular among European immigrants, such as Von der Ahe. Similarly, native-born Protestants tended to prefer an "American Sabbath," believing Sunday should be set aside solely as a day of worship. On the other hand, European immigrants, whether they were Catholic, Jewish, or German Lutherans, normally championed the "Continental Sabbath," in which Sunday was viewed as a day of rest and recreation. The two leagues' competing ticket policies reflected separate demographic appeals as well. The National League's fifty-cent ticket price, equivalent to about six dollars today, had been adopted with the goal of drawing increased patronage from the upper and middle classes. This high price of admission, combined with opposition to liquor sales and Sunday games, diminished support for the National League among the ethnic working classes. The American Association, however, actively courted working-class spectators with liquor sales, Sunday games, and quarter tickets. In fact, American Association leaders reveled in their working-class appeal while proudly proclaiming allegiance to the Association's slogan: "We Have Brought Baseball to the People."[30]

The proponents of National League moralism treated the American Association with contempt, mocking their new rival as a "Beerball League" or a "Beer and Whiskey Circuit." The *Chicago Tribune* predicted that the Association would "degrade and disgrace baseball, to be sure, but only in cities like Cincinnati and St. Louis, where, through immoral practices and disreputable associations, the game has long ceased to be regarded as fit for the patronage of respectable ladies and gentlemen." Hulbert, the National League's president, chided the American Association for seeking "the patronage of the degraded" rather than emulating his league's policy of striving for the "support and respect of the best class of people."[31] Obviously, National Leaguers continued to believe in the need to attract the upper and middle classes with a strong emphasis upon morality. But by attacking their rivals with epithets such as "Beerball League," they succeeded only in further establishing an identity for the American Association along the very battle lines that the newcomers had chosen.

The two baseball leagues, spurred by their divergent business and social beliefs, developed a heated rivalry. Their intense competition stimulated public interest in both leagues. In 1882 National League attendance rose 26 percent from the preceding season, and for the first time in its seven-year history it exceeded the total attendance that the National Association had drawn in 1875. However, even these achievements paled in comparison to the dramatic success of the American Association. The average attendance at American Association games surpassed that of National League games by 30 percent. While National League clubs had rarely enjoyed a profitable season, all six American Association teams turned profits in 1882.[32] The confident new league proceeded boldly with plans to add a pair of new ball clubs for the 1883 season, the New York Metropolitans and the Columbus Buckeyes.

The National League reacted warily to the American Association's prosperity. Eventually, it adopted a strategy that combined conservatism, confrontation, and accommodation. In all likelihood, William Hulbert would have followed a more belligerent course, but the White Stockings' owner passed away on the eve of the 1882 season. Despite Hulbert's death, the National League maintained his conservative policies regarding liquor-selling and Sunday baseball.

Nevertheless, the National League took aggressive steps to confront the American Association's advantage in some of the nation's most attractive markets. In 1882 the six Association cities touched a population base of slightly more than 2 million, significantly larger than the eight-team National League's market of slightly more than 1.5 million.[33] In 1883 the Association expected to reap the rewards of bringing major-league baseball back to New York City, the nation's largest market. The National League responded by scrapping its two smallest markets—Troy, New York, and Worcester, Massachusetts—and replacing them with New York City and Philadelphia. Thus after a six-year absence the National League finally regained access to the nation's two largest markets and began direct competition with the American Association's franchises there. But the older league also offered its new rival an olive branch. Under the terms of the 1883 National Agreement, the National League officially acknowledged the major-league status of the American Association and the integrity of its contracts with ballplayers. In return, the Association agreed to accept the National League's reserve clause. Also, for the first time, the reserve clause was expanded to include virtually the entire roster of each club.[34]

Both of the major leagues benefited from the National Agreement. Due to their conflicting business philosophies, they still waged a fierce rivalry. However, they both now accepted the reserve clause, protecting every team from the prospect of costly player raids. Of course, this increased stability had been gained at the expense of the players' marketplace freedom. Ironically, while each club received protection for the rights to their players, the leagues did not receive protection for the rights to their franchises. Later, the security of the National Agreement would be threatened by both the restrictions on the players' marketplace freedom and the lack of restrictions on franchise freedom. All in all, though, the National Agreement helped to pave the path for professional baseball's first profitable decade—the Golden Age of the 1880s.[35]

In 1883 the American Association became the first major league ever to reach the one million mark in total attendance for a season. The crowds at Association games outpaced those of the National League by 40 percent. Nevertheless, the National League's attendance also continued to rise, climbing 34 percent above its own all-time high of a year before. Available records reveal that Association teams earned bigger profits than the League clubs. The two most profitable Association ball clubs, the Philadelphia Athletics ($75,000 in profits) and the St. Louis Browns ($50,000), each earned more than the League's biggest moneymaker, the Boston Red Caps ($48,000). Furthermore, the earnings of a third Association team, the Cincinnati Reds ($25,000), exceeded the amount accumulated by the League's second-most profitable club, the Chicago White Stockings ($20,000). Altogether, American Association teams cleared somewhere in the neighborhood of $150,000. At the most, the profits of the National League clubs reached $125,000, and they may even have fallen short of $100,000.[36]

During the 1883 season Von der Ahe's team adopted a shortened nickname and emerged as pennant contenders. In the Association's debut season the St. Louis Brown Stockings had been a competitive disappointment, but a financial success. They had led the major leagues in home attendance, playing in front of a record total of 135,000 customers (an average of 3,068 per game). Von der Ahe deserved much of the credit. First, he satisfied a public demand in St. Louis for the combination of major-league baseball, quarter tickets, Sunday games, and beer in the ballpark. Second, he made skillful use of local advertising in both English- and German-language newspapers. Finally, he excelled as a promoter and showman, hiring bands to entertain before home games and, at the end of the day, hauling away the cash proceeds in a wheelbarrow.[37]

But Von der Ahe realized a winning team could generate even larger profits. In St. Louis, the Brown Stockings' lackluster record had been the only negative aspect to the 1882 season. After sweeping Louisville in the home-opening series, they had remained atop the American Association standings as late as June 8 and were still in close contention for the pennant until July. Then on a disastrous month-long road trip the Brown Stockings had lost fourteen of eighteen games.

They had ended the 1882 season with a record of 37–43, fifth among the league's six teams.[38]

Consequently, prior to the 1883 season Von der Ahe dismissed Ned Cuthbert as the team's manager and hired Ted Sullivan to replace him. Under Cuthbert, the Brown Stockings' roster had been typical of the average experience level of American Association players. Most Association teams had not resorted to widespread raids on National League rosters. Of the 113 players who participated in the American Association's inaugural campaign of 1882, 63 possessed no previous major-league experience. Another eleven players had participated in fewer than ten major-league games, meaning that almost two-thirds of the 1882 Association players had either little or no previous major-league playing experience. A mere 19 of the original players had been members of National League clubs in either 1881 or 1882. Similarly, out of 22 players who saw action with the 1882 Brown Stockings, 13 had never played in the major leagues before, while three others had previously participated in fewer than ten major-league games. Therefore, almost 73 percent of the 1882 Brown Stockings either had no previous major-league experience or only a very limited major-league background. The 1882 team included just one player who had belonged to an 1881 National League roster: Tom "Sleeper" Sullivan, a St. Louis–born catcher who had jumped from the National League's Buffalo Bisons to play baseball in his hometown. Thus even the case of Sullivan illustrated Cuthbert's emphasis upon signing local players. Six of the Brown Stockings' nine regular starters in 1882 were either native or transplanted St. Louisans; all of these local products, except for Sleeper Sullivan, had played for the semi-professional Brown Stockings of the preceding season.[39]

Ted Sullivan transformed the Browns after he took over as manager. He used seven members of Cuthbert's 1882 team for at least part of the following season, but only three of these players spent the entire 1883 season on the Browns' roster. The holdovers were pitcher Jumbo McGinnis, shortstop Bill Gleason, and first baseman Charles Comiskey. McGinnis and Gleason had both advanced from within the ranks of the semi-professional Brown Stockings. George Washington "Jumbo" McGinnis, a St. Louis glassblower, had been the Brown Stockings' star pitcher since the 1879 season. In 1882 he had compiled a record of 25–18. McGinnis would anchor the St. Louis pitching staff for its initial three American Association seasons, winning more than twenty games each year. Bill Gleason had played shortstop, alongside his older brother Jack at third base, on the 1878 St. Louis Red Stockings, the 1879 Dubuque (Iowa) Rabbits, the 1880 St. Louis Red Stockings, and the 1881–1882 Brown Stockings. In 1883 the Browns sold the services of brother Jack to the Louisville Eclipse. However, Bill Gleason remained entrenched as the Browns' shortstop from 1882 to 1887. He had notched the highest batting average on the 1882 St. Louis ball club (.288) and also topped all Association shortstops in putouts, assists, double plays, and total chances. During his six major-league seasons with St. Louis, Gleason would score an average of 92 runs per year and post a .275 batting mark.[40]

Charles "Commy" Comiskey, meanwhile, would eventually exert more of an influence upon St. Louis baseball than any other nineteenth-century player. Comiskey, a native of Chicago, had pursued a professional baseball career in defiance of his father's objections. His father, an Irish immigrant who arrived in the United States in 1848, won election as an alderman on the Chicago City Council in 1859, the same year that Charles was born, and also was the superintendent of shipments in Chicago's cattle yards and a deputy U.S. revenue collector for President Andrew Johnson. John Comiskey, described as a "serious minded" man, had been greatly disturbed by his son Charles's attachment to baseball, considering the game to be "frivolous." He had even tried to force Charles to pursue the plumbing trade instead.[41]

Charles Comiskey avoided that fate through the assistance of a long-time friend: Ted Sullivan. The two had met as schoolboys on the baseball diamond at St. Mary's College in Dodge City, Kansas.[42] In the summer of 1876 Sullivan was managing a team known as the Milwaukee Alerts. Sullivan finagled fifty dollars from Thomas Shaughnessy, president of the Canadian Pacific Railroad and the sponsor of the amateur Alerts, to fix a hole in the fence around the ballpark, then used the money to pay Comiskey for pitching a single month. The arrangement helped Comiskey evade his father's demands to give up baseball and take up a more serious occupation. At the end of the season, though, Comiskey reluctantly returned to Chicago and started learning the trade of plumbing from a "master plumber" named Hogan. In 1878 Sullivan again rescued Comiskey. By that point Sullivan had moved to Dubuque, Iowa, where he operated the Western News Agency and was in the process of forming a baseball team. Comiskey had pitched in the 1877 season for the Elgin Watch Team of Elgin, Illinois, but had resumed his off-season training as a plumber under the watchful eyes of Mr. Hogan. Sullivan hired Comiskey to perform a dual job. For the next four years, Comiskey received fifty dollars a month for playing baseball during the season and a 20 percent commission year-round from selling newspapers or snacks to passengers on the Illinois Central Railroad.[43]

In 1879 Sullivan managed the Dubuque Rabbits, including Comiskey and the Gleason brothers, to the championship of the Northwestern League. Sullivan had organized the entire league, but it quickly folded because the overwhelming superiority of the Dubuque club suffocated interest elsewhere. The Rabbits then reverted to their former independent status. In 1881 they visited Sportsman's Park to play the Brown Stockings, losing 9–1, but Comiskey handled twelve fielding chances flawlessly at first base and also doubled for one of only two hits that the Rabbits collected against "Jumbo" McGinnis. Al Spink had been extremely impressed by Comiskey's performance, and during the off-season he mailed the young first baseman a contract offer of ninety dollars a month for the 1882 season.[44]

In his first major-league at-bat, Comiskey had tripled to drive home St. Louis's first run in the American Association. The triple marked the prelude to a solid rookie year. Comiskey hit .243, the third-highest average among the Brown Stockings' regulars. His most impressive achievements, though, took place in the field, where he not only led Association first basemen in putouts and total chances but also pioneered a new style of first-base play. In 1882 the prevailing defensive strategy was for first basemen to station themselves close to the bag and serve primarily as a target for the throws of the other three infielders. Comiskey, however, roamed far from the bag and became a fourth infielder. He may not have introduced the practice of first basemen playing off the bag, but it seems certain that he played farther away from first base and demonstrated more mobility in covering the diamond than any of his predecessors at the position. In writing about first-base play, Comiskey made no claim that he had originated the art of playing off the base, but he did claim, "I always played my position ten or fifteen feet deeper than the other first basemen."[45]

Comiskey quickly established himself as one of Chris Von der Ahe's favorite players. He had convinced Von der Ahe to hire Ted Sullivan as the Browns' manager. Al Spink credited Sullivan's "great skill" in recruiting ballplayers as the key to turning the Browns from a "crude organization" to a baseball power. Sullivan brought in veteran players from all over the country. No longer would the Browns depend upon inexperienced local products. To the nucleus of McGinnis, Gleason, and Comiskey, Sullivan added eight newcomers in either regular or semi-regular playing spots—catcher Pat Deasley, second baseman George Strief, third baseman Arlie Latham, catcher–left fielder Tom Dolan, left fielder Tom Mansell, center fielder Fred Lewis, right fielder Hugh Nicol, and pitcher Tony Mullane. All eight possessed National League playing experience,[46] and none of them were from St. Louis. In 1883 Sullivan frequently fielded a Browns' lineup with more foreign-born players (Nicol from Scotland and Mullane and Deasley from Ireland) than players with St. Louis origins.

Out of all the newcomers, Arlie Latham lasted the longest in St. Louis baseball. Walter Arlington Latham grew up in Lynn, Massachusetts, working as a teenager in the local shoe industry and playing on various semi-professional baseball teams around the state. Latham spent two months of the 1880 season in the National League, but the Buffalo Bisons released him when his batting average slipped to .127. After observing Latham's performance on a Philadelphia semi-pro team, Ted Sullivan brought him to St. Louis in 1883 as the Browns' starting third baseman. Latham held the position for the next seven years. During this stint he hit .267, scored an average of 118 runs a year, and became the most prolific base stealer in the game. Turning somersaults or cartwheels while running the bases and indulging in nonstop chatter throughout games, Latham also acquired a reputation as an eccentric. This image later earned him a title as "the first of the Clown Princes of Baseball."[47]

Latham, however, did not make as large an immediate impact as pitcher Tony Mullane. Born in Cork, Ireland, Mullane emigrated to the United States as a child. In 1880 he attracted the attention of the National League's Detroit Wolverines with his pitching exploits for a top-flight semi-professional ball club from Akron. After winning only one of five pitching decisions for Detroit in 1881, he jumped to the American Association for its debut season, joining the Louisville Eclipse. In 1882 he pitched the Association's first no-hitter, struck out more batters than any other pitcher in the league, and logged a 30–24 record—the first of what would become five consecutive thirty-win seasons. Thanks to the absence of a reserve clause in the American Association at the time, he had no trouble in joining the Browns in 1883. Flaunting a handlebar mustache and occasionally wielding an unusual ambidextrous pitching style, Mullane played the game with a flair that marked him as one of the most popular nineteenth-century players.[48]

With the Browns in 1883, Mullane recorded thirty-five wins, his single-season career-high. He paired with Jumbo McGinnis, a twenty-eight-game winner, to keep St. Louis in pennant contention. On July 27 the Browns departed St. Louis for an extensive road trip, precariously clutching a one-game lead over the Philadelphia Athletics. When they returned on September 8, they had lost both the Association lead and their manager.[49]

The preceding homestand had ended on a sour note. Following a 5–4 loss to Louisville, Von der Ahe fined Latham five dollars for getting thrown out at home on an attempted double steal. Von der Ahe often indulged in this type of behavior, sometimes fining players for illogical offenses such as not positioning themselves in the spot where an opposing batter happened to hit the ball. These incidents demonstrated the negative effect that Von der Ahe sometimes exerted. Although he contributed promotional genius and eagerly spent money to build a stronger ball club, he lacked an adequate knowledge of the game's strategy and thus harmed the Browns whenever he directly intervened in baseball operations. Faced with this particular fine, Latham rebelled. "You have no right to fine me," the third baseman argued. "I used my best judgment. I thought I could get there. I won't stand it." Von der Ahe quickly silenced Latham by threatening to increase the fine to fifty dollars if he did not stop squawking. But Ted Sullivan jumped to Latham's defense, creating a conflict between the Browns' owner and manager.[50]

With the relationship between Von der Ahe and Sullivan already beginning to deteriorate, the events of the long road trip sealed Sullivan's rapid fall. In Columbus, Ohio, two Browns' players, Pat Deasley and Fred Lewis, got drunk and assaulted their manager; they spent the night in jail. By the time the Browns reached Baltimore, the story had already been reported in both the *St. Louis Post-Dispatch* and the *St. Louis Globe-Democrat.*[51] On August 19 the *Post-Dispatch* received a telegram from Baltimore, ostensibly sent by Deasley and Lewis, which maintained, "The article in your paper stating that we assaulted Manager Sullivan is a contemptible and malicious statement." The *Post-Dispatch,* however, presented convincing arguments in its defense, questioning the accuracy and authenticity of the players' telegram, and citing as an unlikely coincidence its receipt of a similar telegram from Ted Sullivan. Revealing that it had been urged by an unidentified member of the Browns' board of directors to suppress their original article on the arrests of Deasley and Lewis, the *Post-Dispatch* concluded, "Manager Sullivan knows he will be blamed for the want of discipline and this telegram is an attempt to square himself."

But the *Post-Dispatch* did not simply stop at refuting the ballplayers' telegram: the newspaper also published details of other distressing lapses in team discipline on the road trip. The allegations included two other fights, one between Mullane and Bill Gleason and another in which Tom Dolan was sufficiently provoked to "hammer" Deasley. Finally, claiming that both Deasley and Lewis had been jailed previously in St. Louis, the *Post-Dispatch* suggested that the two men posed a chronic threat to team morale. All of these damaging accusations were printed beneath the headline "Why the Browns Lose," on the same page with another article that summarized how the last-place Baltimore Orioles had scored three times in the ninth inning to defeat Mullane.[52]

Nevertheless, when the Browns rolled into New York City in late August they were still clinging to first place. On August 27 Mullane pitched the Browns to an 8–3 triumph over the New York Metropolitans, maintaining the team's one-game edge over the Philadelphia Athletics. When the Athletics lost to Louisville the next afternoon, the Browns' lead grew to a game and a half.[53]

However, the date of August 29, 1883, would be a very bleak day for the St. Louis Browns. That afternoon McGinnis pitched against the Metropolitans while Mullane, a versatile athlete, started in left field. The Metropolitans bashed McGinnis's ineffectual pitches all around the Polo Grounds. In the midst of a 7–1 setback, Von der Ahe ordered Sullivan to make a pitching change. The Browns' owner wanted Mullane and McGinnis to switch positions. Realizing that Mullane desperately needed to take a day off from the physical rigors of pitching, Sullivan refused to comply with Von der Ahe's demand. Mullane had pitched the Browns' last three games over the course of only four days. McGinnis, on the other hand, had not pitched in a week, and Sullivan hoped that he would regain

Ted Sullivan. In 1883, after taking over as manager, Sullivan built the St. Louis Browns into a pennant contender. This achievement, though, did not ensure Sullivan a harmonious relationship with the team's owner, Chris Von der Ahe. State Historical Society of Missouri, Columbia.

his sharpness if given more innings to pitch. Von der Ahe had voiced another fundamentally unsound idea about baseball strategy and again placed a strain upon his relationship with Ted Sullivan.[54]

Making matters even worse for the Browns, the Athletics gained victories both on and off the baseball diamond. On the field, Philadelphia overpowered Louisville, 11–3. Off the field, they won the right to reschedule a game against the Metropolitans that they had previously forfeited. Jimmy Williams, the secretary-treasurer of the American Association, ruled in favor of the Athletics' appeal of the forfeited game, which they had conceded because injuries had prevented them from fielding a full nine. Now a healthy Athletics' squad would be allowed to make up the game. Compounding this injustice, Williams permitted the Metropolitans to shift their home game to Philadelphia, where the New Yorkers could profit from the record-breaking crowds that the Athletics were drawing, even though the game originally was to have taken place in New York.[55]

In a single day, the Browns' game-and-a-half lead had vanished. The Athletics were now tied with the Browns, and they had an opportunity to go into first place in the makeup game against the Metropolitans. Late that night, Von der Ahe personally conducted a surprise curfew check. Discovering most of his players absent from their hotel rooms, he furiously berated Sullivan for allowing them to be out on the town.[56] On the following day, the *Post-Dispatch* filed this notice:

> It is announced from New York that Sullivan has withdrawn from the management of the St. Louis club. The reasons for the withdrawal are alleged to be dissensions in the club, some accounts of which have already been given in the *Post-Dispatch*, and the truth of which are pretty well proven by the final result. It is also stated that President Von der Ahe took Sullivan to task for not enforcing stricter discipline, and that a stormy scene occurred between the two men. Sullivan, at any rate, has withdrawn, and his place is filled for the present by Charley Comiskey.[57]

Under the twenty-four-year-old Comiskey, the Browns salvaged their last two games in New York. But on the first day of September the Athletics defeated the Metropolitans in their makeup game. They now led the Browns by half a game. On September 3, in Philadelphia, the two pennant contenders squared off for the opener of a four-game showdown. The pitching matchup pitted Mullane against George Washington Bradley, the revered hero of the original Brown Stockings. Mullane prevailed, 7–5. His thirty-first win of the season pushed the Browns back into first place by half a game.[58]

On the very next day, however, the Browns forced Mullane to shoulder the pitching duties again. This decision defied logic. McGinnis, already a twenty-three-game winner, could have pitched with four days of rest. It seems certain that Von der Ahe insisted upon giving the starting assignment to Mullane. The owner's intrusion damaged the Browns' pitching rotation. Meanwhile, the Athletics pulled off a shrewd acquisition. They added a fresh pitching arm by purchasing a rookie, Jumping Jack Jones, from the National League's Detroit Wolverines. Jones, in his Philadelphia debut, opposed Mullane. Appearing for a second straight day and pitching his forty-fifth game of the year, the St. Louis pitcher faltered under the strain, while Jones, pitching for only the thirteenth time in the 1883 season, turned in a much stronger performance. The Athletics crushed the Browns, 11–1, and moved into first place to stay. They solidified their hold on first with one-run victories over the Browns, 5–4 and 4–3, in the final two games of the series.[59]

Jones would prove instrumental in preserving Philadelphia's advantage. After joining the Athletics, he pitched three games in just four days and won each outing, including a pair of victories against the Browns. For the month, Jones would win five games against only two losses, and his heroics allowed the Athletics to survive the extended absence of their ace pitcher, Bobby Mathews. The thirty-one-year-old Mathews, a veteran of eleven major-league seasons, had pitched in forty-one games and was even more worn down than Mullane. He missed more than two weeks of the September stretch drive, seeing no action for sixteen days from September 2–17. In his absence, the pitching of Jones and Bradley guided the Athletics to seven consecutive triumphs.[60]

The Browns returned home to St. Louis, resumed the practice of alternating pitching assignments between Mullane and McGinnis, and took five of their next seven contests. But they could not gain any ground on Philadelphia. On September 21 the Athletics, leading the Browns by two and a half games, arrived in St. Louis for a pivotal three-game series. In the first contest, a weary Mathews staggered to a 13–11 decision over Mullane. McGinnis then evened the series with a 9–6 victory against Jones. A record crowd of 16,800 turned out to see the third game on Sunday, September 23. Bradley threw a masterful three-hitter to defeat Mullane and the Browns, 9–2.[61]

All hope seemed gone for the Browns. The Athletics, now holding a three-and-a-half-game lead with just one week left in the season, had already clinched at least a tie for first place. To guarantee the American Association championship, they needed to win only one of their last four games at Louisville or for the Browns to lose any of three encounters with Pittsburgh. Amazingly, the race nearly ended in a tie. On both Wednesday and Thursday, the Louisville Eclipse knocked off the Athletics while the Browns beat the Pittsburgh Alleghenys. Suddenly, the Browns trailed by a mere game and a half. But the next day Jones rescued the Athletics once more, pitching Philadelphia to a ten-inning 7–6 victory that clinched the pennant. The Athletics claimed the league title over the Browns by one game.[62]

In 1883 Chris Von der Ahe fell just short of providing St. Louis with its first pennant-winner. Greater successes awaited just over the horizon. Still, through the popularity that the American Association had attained in its initial two seasons, Von der Ahe had already blazed the trail to baseball profits. The Browns attracted 243,000 people to their forty-nine home dates in 1883, an average of almost five thousand spectators per game. Although the *Globe-Democrat* estimated the team's profit at $50,000, Von der Ahe boasted that he had made $70,000 on the 1883 Browns.[63]

The profitable American Association soon spawned an imitator. On September 12, 1883, the Union Association organized in Pittsburgh. A twenty-six-year-old St. Louisan, Henry V. Lucas, served as the new league's president and contributed financially to each of its teams, including his own St. Louis Maroons.

The youngest son of James Lucas, Henry Lucas had been dubbed "the Prince Fortunatus of St. Louis" by his friends. As a teenager he had witnessed many of the games of the original St. Louis Brown Stockings, whose board of directors had been headed by his oldest brother, J. B. C. Lucas II. Al Spink later recalled that in 1882 and 1883 Henry Lucas had become "an everyday attendant at the games played by the St. Louis Browns." A ballplayer himself on the amateur level, Henry Lucas had even converted part of his country estate into a baseball diamond.[64]

Given his enthusiasm for the game and the million dollars he had inherited from his father, Henry Lucas hungered to own a major-league baseball team. The 1883 National Agreement, though, thwarted his ambition. According to one section of the National Agreement, which protected the territorial rights of each existing National League and American Association franchise, Von der Ahe's Browns possessed the exclusive rights to play major-league baseball in St. Louis. If Lucas wanted to operate a team in his native city, he would have to supply an entirely new league. The Union Association arose as his grandiose plan to overcome the obstacle imposed by the National Agreement.[65]

Lucas spurred other investors into helping him support teams in eight cities—Baltimore, Boston, Philadelphia, Washington, Altoona, Chicago, Cincinnati, and St. Louis. In St. Louis, Lucas received economic assistance for his own club, the Maroons, from two of the city's most prosperous brewers, Ellis Wainwright and Adolphus Busch. Eager to emulate the achievements of the American Association, brewery interests provided funding to four of the original eight Union Association franchises. A Baltimore mattress manufacturer, A. H. Henderson, controlled the Baltimore and Chicago ball clubs. George Wright, owner of a sporting goods store and a former star player, agreed to run the Boston organization. In exchange, the Union Association promised to use the lively Wright and Ditson baseball that he manufactured. Pennsylvania Railroad executives backed the team in Altoona.[66]

These Union Association entrepreneurs hoped to eclipse the two established major leagues by attacking their reserve clause. In its constitution, the Union Association specifically condemned the reserve clause for making "the player almost the slave of the club." Lucas excoriated it as "the most arbitrary and unjust rule ever suggested." Advising that the reserve clause "ought to be broken," he predicted ballplayers would "no more submit to [it] than to have rings put in their noses and be led by them."[67] The Union Association believed opposition to the reserve clause would allow it to recruit the best ballplayers away from the other two major leagues. Then, with the finest playing talent cornered, the Union Association could become the most popular major league and claim the same type of profits that the American Association had earned in 1882 and 1883.

Lucas soon served notice to Von der Ahe of the magnitude of the impending struggle. Von der Ahe had offered Tony Mullane a $1,900 contract for the 1884 season, and Mullane had been offended. This offer would have given Mullane a $500 raise over his 1883 salary, but it still fell short of the $2,100 contract that teammate Jumbo McGinnis had allegedly signed for the upcoming season. Lucas then stepped in, offering Mullane a $2,500 contract, with $500 payable in a cash advance, and successfully enticed the Browns' top pitcher to sign with the Maroons. For St. Louis baseball enthusiasts, the "Union Baseball War" had officially commenced.[68] During the next year, the Browns of Chris Von der Ahe, the German immigrant and self-made man, vied for St. Louis baseball supremacy against the Maroons of Henry V. Lucas, an heir to the fortune of one of the city's oldest and wealthiest French families.

5

Von der Ahe versus Lucas

> The truth is that St. Louis is at present in a sort of baseball craze or frenzy. If Mr. Lucas, after all of his lavish and tremendous expenditures does not make a success of his Union venture, he will have at least the mild satisfaction of knowing that his rivalry has provoked . . . the most widespread interest ever manifested in the national game in this city—and that is saying a great deal, for it has always ranked as one of the best of baseball centers.
>
> —*St. Louis Post-Dispatch,* commenting on the rivalry between Henry Lucas's St. Louis Maroons and Chris Von der Ahe's St. Louis Browns, May 10, 1884

Tony Mullane never played a game in the Union Association. Prior to the start of the 1884 season, the American Association and the National League had each adopted the Day Resolution. Named after its sponsor, John Day, the owner of the New York franchises in both the League and the American Association, the resolution provided that any players from their leagues who jumped to the Union Association would be blacklisted. When the Day Resolution passed, Mullane panicked. He feared that his major-league future would become tied to the survival of the fledgling Union Association. Unwilling to accept such a risk, Mullane decided to return to the American Association.[1]

Chris Von der Ahe had included Mullane on the St. Louis Browns' reserve list, and the Browns still held the American Association rights to the pitcher's services. However, Von der Ahe did not want to re-sign Mullane. To do so would have meant matching the lucrative $2,500 contract that Mullane had signed with Lucas. More significantly, Von der Ahe wanted to avoid a possible legal battle with Lucas over the issue of player rights. Therefore, he worked out an arrangement with the other owners of American Association and National League teams. He released Mullane from the Browns, and they allowed the pitcher to be claimed by the new American Association club in Toledo. The Toledo Blue Stockings then offered Mullane the same $2,500 contract that he had signed with Lucas's St. Louis Maroons, and he jumped back into the American Association.[2]

In subsequent legal proceedings held at St. Louis and Cincinnati, Lucas gained a pair of state court injunctions that prevented Mullane from playing for any team other than the Maroons. But Toledo appealed the case to Judge John Baxter of the U.S. Circuit Court in Cincinnati. Scornful of Lucas's case, Judge Baxter used very dubious legal principles to dissolve the injunction and allow Mullane to play for Toledo: "In announcing his decision, the Judge said he did not think the time of the court could be occupied by baseball matters. Ballplaying was nothing which benefited the public in any way. It was not a business, but it was merely a sport, which was beneath the dignity of the courts to notice." The state of Missouri disagreed with Judge Baxter's opinion. The St. Louis court order continued to prevent Mullane from legally playing in the city until 1887.[3]

The Mullane case illustrated the effectiveness of the Day Resolution as a deterrent to players who contemplated signing contracts with Union Association teams. However, the Day Resolution actually constituted only half of the overall strategy that American Association and National League club owners had devised. The other half of the plan called for higher salaries to players to induce them to stay put.[4] The St. Louis Browns' payroll reflected this trend. In the spring, Von der Ahe granted "a considerable increase in salaries." The projected yearly payroll showed that ten Browns would receive more than $1,575, the highest salary paid by the team the preceding season. In 1884, Von der Ahe budgeted an average salary of $1,798.08 per player.[5] By these tactics, the older leagues managed to retain most of their players.

Henry Lucas had badly miscalculated the resolve of major-league ballplayers. Throughout the 1883 season he had befriended players and listened sympathetically to their complaints. Players protested to Lucas that the National Agreement had imposed universal acceptance of the reserve clause and thereby once again eliminated their marketplace freedom. Lucas naively concluded his Union Association could simply denounce the reserve clause and then corner the finest playing talent.[6] He found instead that the vast majority of major-league players were not going to join the Union Association.

In 1884, most major-leaguers chose to remain in the two established leagues rather than risk allegiance to an upstart. Ballplayers were reaping the rewards of being highly skilled laborers who possessed talents in scarce supply. Even in the 1883 season, prior to the ensuing off-season pay raises, major-league baseball players received three to four times the average annual income a manufacturing worker earned. The salaries of the 1883 St. Louis Browns, for example, ranged from $1,200 to $1,575, at a time when the average annual income for a manufacturing worker was rising only from $345 in 1880 to $427 in 1890. Furthermore, the average manufacturing worker toiled ten hours a day, six days a week, twelve months a year.[7] Ballplayers, although they put in considerable practice time and tried to maintain off-season conditioning, were still essentially paid for playing a two-hour game on scheduled dates during a seven-month season. Their long off-season also presented them with a chance for an extended vacation, and many major-leaguers eagerly took advantage of that option. Thus, most established players decided that the older leagues offered them a comfortable livelihood and financial security, which would be endangered if they should cast their lot with the new, unproven Union Association.

As a result, out of the 273 ballplayers who played in the Union Association in 1884, only 71 had previously participated in more than ten major-league games. Most Union Association players—62 percent—possessed no previous major-league experience.[8] Hampered by the lack of well-known players, the Union Association found competition difficult in the glutted baseball marketplace.

During the course of the 1884 season, thirty-four teams claimed major-league status. In addition to the new league, the American Association expanded into four new markets (Toledo, Indianapolis, Washington, D.C., and Brooklyn). Of the four, only Brooklyn would eventually become a profitable franchise. The others did not last beyond the 1884 season, and the Washington club actually finished the year in Richmond. The American Association approved this ill-conceived expansion, despite skepticism about its prospects for success, out of a desire "to checkmate the Union Association."[9] *Sporting Life,* a Philadelphia-based weekly sports paper, had urged the American Association to restrict its expansion merely to Brooklyn and Indianapolis. Both the *Missouri Republican* and the *Philadelphia Times* had preferred to maintain the league's eight-team status quo. These two newspapers also protested the role that the National League had played in prodding the American Association to expand.[10]

The American Association had hoped to prevent potential markets from falling into the hands of the Union Association. Other than Brooklyn, though, these new markets were never a great advantage to any of the rival major leagues of the nineteenth century. The Union Association invaded Washington, D.C., anyway, and outdrew the American Association franchise there, but neither Washington club registered much of an impact at the box office. The fate of the Union Association ultimately hinged on the outcome of the struggle for large markets that had already shown a willingness to support major-league baseball. Union Association clubs challenged an established team from one of the older leagues in half a dozen cities—St. Louis, Cincinnati, Baltimore, Boston, Chicago, and Pittsburgh. Philadelphia earned the distinction of being the only city represented in all three organizations. In these pivotal markets, the two older leagues attracted crowds that ranged from 35 percent to 82 percent larger than the average attendance at Union Association games.[11]

The Union Association received the least fan support because it possessed the fewest heralded players, the most lopsided pennant race, and the least stable franchises. Henry Lucas had hired Ted Sullivan, the Browns' former manager, to build his St. Louis Maroons into a super-team. Sullivan succeeded, but at great cost to the overall welfare of the Union Association. Five years earlier, in 1879, the newly formed Northwestern League had disbanded after Sullivan's Dubuque team won their initial twenty-three games and "took all the heart out of the other Northwestern League cities." Five years later, Sullivan and the Maroons affected the Union Association in a similar fashion. The Maroons won their first twenty contests, and all speculation about the Union Association pennant race disappeared well before the traditional halfway point of the season—the Fourth of July.[12]

Undermined by this competitive imbalance, several Union Association clubs simply collapsed. Of the league's eight charter members, three failed to survive the 1884 season. The *St. Louis Globe-Democrat,* in covering the Maroons' fourth consecutive victory over the Altoona (Pennsylvania) Mountain Citys, graphically depicted the 14–5 mauling as "like seeing a giant jumping on an infant and throwing it in mid-air." With a record of 6–19, the last-place Altoona ball club folded on May 31. Altoona's withdrawal started a process in which Lucas, as the league's president and its primary financial supporter, scrambled constantly to keep eight teams afloat at the same time. Lucas replaced Altoona with Kansas City. Ted Sullivan left the Maroons to become the manager and part-owner of the Kansas City Unions, but the team quickly sank into the same last-place position occupied by its predecessors. At least more fans turned out to watch the ineptitude of the Kansas City club than had seen the mistakes of the Altoona team.[13]

In August, when the Union Association faced the dissolution of its Chicago and Philadelphia franchises, Lucas could not even locate a replacement team capable of lasting the remainder of the season. The financially struggling Chicago Browns transferred most of their players to Pittsburgh, but the Pittsburgh Stogies won just seven of eighteen games before folding in mid-September. Lucas filled in the vacant spot with the St. Paul Saints, who ignominiously completed the season by losing six of eight road games and never getting to play at home. The Wilmington (Delaware) Quicksteps entered the league in August as a substitute for the Philadelphia Keystones. The Quicksteps had been minor-league champions in the Eastern League, but they never adjusted to the Union Association. After losing sixteen of eighteen contests, Wilmington became another financial casualty in mid-September. Again, Lucas reached into the ranks of the minor leagues and persuaded the Milwaukee Cream Citys of the revived Northwestern League to finish the season in place of Wilmington. The Cream Citys, winning eight of their twelve Union Association outings, demonstrated that Lucas should have included them in his original plans.[14]

Wilmington and Milwaukee forged markedly different records in the Union Association. However, the mere presence of these minor-league teams underscored the utter failure of the Union Association to achieve its primary objective of cornering the finest talent. The St. Louis Maroons owed their superiority to the fact that they fielded the league's most experienced team. By generously breaking out his bankroll, Lucas lured such prominent major-league veterans as second baseman Fred "Sure Shot" Dunlap, third baseman Jack Gleason, right fielder George "Orator" Shaffer, center fielder Dave Rowe, and left fielder Lew "Buttercup" Dickerson. Another veteran, "Bollicky" Billy Taylor, headed the Maroons' pitching staff. In July, when Taylor jumped to the American Association's Philadelphia Athletics, Lucas replaced him with a hard-throwing and hard-drinking Californian, Charles Sweeney, who had been suspended by the Providence Grays of the National League. No other Union Association ball club could match the experience level of the Maroons until August. In that month, the Cincinnati Outlaw Reds raided three players (shortstop "Pebbly" Jack Glasscock, pitcher Jim McCormick, and catcher Charles Briody) from the Cleveland Blues of the National League. The Outlaw Reds soon became virtually invincible, winning thirty of their last thirty-two contests. Yet they could not possibly catch the St. Louis Maroons in the Union Association standings. The Maroons finished with a record of 94–19, twenty-one games ahead of second-place Cincinnati.[15]

Ironically, by running away with the Union Association pennant, the Maroons did not endear themselves to the baseball fans of St. Louis. When their season-opening win streak had reached fourteen, the *Globe-Democrat* observed that hometown crowds at the Maroons' games "appeared to desire the defeat of the St. Louis nine." Similarly, after the Boston Reds finally handed the Maroons their first defeat, the *Post-Dispatch* realized St. Louis spectators had "cheered the visitors" throughout the game. In St. Louis, the elements of surprise and unpredictability allowed the Browns to draw practically twice as many fans as the Maroons. Henry Lucas could faithfully duplicate the Sunday games and beer sales offered by Von der Ahe's St. Louis Browns, but he could not reproduce the American Association's frantic pennant race, in which the top five teams were separated by only three games on the Fourth of July.[16]

At the start of the season, the popularity contest between the Browns and the Maroons was bitterly waged. The Maroons initially benefited from favorable local coverage of Lucas and the Union Association. For example, the *Missouri Republican* insisted that the Union Association merited support for its attack upon the oppressive reserve clause: "Any St. Louis merchant or manufacturer who would try to dictate to his employees where and for what price they should work, and

A former Brown, Jack Gleason joined the St. Louis Maroons in 1884. State Historical Society of Missouri, Columbia.

would attempt to deprive them from working altogether unless they accepted his terms, would be hissed off the [Merchants Exchange] floor." The *Post-Dispatch* also condemned the "injustice" of the reserve clause and spoke of how Lucas's bold initiative reflected positively upon the entrepreneurial spirit of the entire city: "It has been said that St. Louisans are a slow-going lot, lacking the push, the energy and the get-up-and-get of their more Northern neighbors, but the work of Henry V. Lucas, the head and front of the Union Association, puts a damper on this statement." Such expressions of support stirred curiosity among St. Louisans. On April 20, a "bleak, desolate, and depressing" Sunday afternoon, the Maroons hosted Chicago in the opening game of the 1884 season. In spite of a steady drizzle and temperatures dipping near the freezing mark, an estimated ten thousand spectators saw St. Louis win, 7–2.[17]

Another experienced ballplayer, Dave Rowe, played center field for the 1884 St. Louis Maroons. State Historical Society of Missouri, Columbia.

Surprised by the size of the crowd, the *Globe-Democrat* boasted, "It is doubtful, if under similar circumstances, any other city in the country could produce such a gathering. Considering the conditions under which it was played, it was the most remarkable baseball event that ever occurred in the West, and, perhaps, the most remarkable in the annals of the game." When the St. Louis Browns opened their season on May 1, a comparably dreary Thursday afternoon, they drew only three thousand people to Sportsman's Park. Three days later, however, the Browns attracted an audience of ten thousand for their first Sunday game of the year. Through the first six home dates apiece, the Maroons narrowly outdrew the Browns. The Maroons pulled in a few more than 25,000 people at Union Park, while the Browns welcomed slightly more than 23,000 spectators into Sportsman's Park. On May 10 the *Post-Dispatch* credited the rivalry between the two St. Louis teams for creating "a sort of baseball craze or frenzy" in the city. But the *Post-Dispatch* believed a majority of St. Louisans would soon embrace one team or the other as their favorite: "The public . . . will attend where the best and most genuinely good article is provided for them. It may be at Mr. Lucas' park or

Charles Sweeney, a talented pitcher, jumped from the National League's Providence Grays to the St. Louis Maroons in July 1884. State Historical Society of Missouri, Columbia.

at Mr. Von der Ahe's, but they will lose no time in drawing their own deductions and judging for themselves."[18]

The following afternoon, for the first time, both teams played home games on the same Sunday. The Maroons faced the Washington Nationals, a team they had already defeated three times earlier in the week by the combined score of 42–10. Meanwhile, the Browns were playing the deciding game in a series against the Columbus Buckeyes. In the series opener on Friday, the Browns had edged the Buckeyes in ten innings, 3–2, for their sixth straight win. Columbus had rebounded the next day to give the Browns their first loss of the year. On Sunday, the Browns claimed a couple of victories. Between the lines of the playing field, the Browns defeated the Buckeyes, 6–3. More significantly, they drew a crowd of twelve thousand fans, while the Maroons lured only fifteen hundred spectators to see their 11–6 conquest of Washington.[19]

The games of May 11 represented a major turning point. The Browns firmly reestablished themselves as St. Louis's most beloved ball club and clearly relegated the Maroons to secondary status. Nevertheless, the Maroons continued to receive solid support. Their average home audience of 2,071 easily outdistanced any other Union Association team and ranked fifth among all major-league clubs. The Browns, for the second time in their three American Association seasons, topped the major leagues in attendance, with an average of 3,926 spectators for home games.[20]

The crowds at Sportsman's Park watched a Browns team in the thick of the tight American Association pennant race. Yet the 1884 Browns were still a team in transition. They were plagued by a pair of serious problems: a lack of pitching depth, and lapses in team discipline.

Chris Von der Ahe spent much of the 1884 season taking steps to replace Tony Mullane. His acquisitions ultimately resulted in the Browns fielding a much stronger ball club. James Edward "Tip" O'Neill, the first pitcher the Browns signed to offset the loss of Mullane, had played the previous season for the New York Gothams in the National League. As the dual owner of both the Gothams and the American Association's New York Metropolitans, John Day allowed his loyalty to the National League to outweigh his commitment to the Association. Therefore, he decided to transfer the contract of the Metropolitans' ace pitcher, Tim Keefe, to the Gothams. First, Day tested the viability of this tactic by moving O'Neill from the Gothams to the Metropolitans, where he could take over Keefe's pitching chores. However, in releasing O'Neill from the Gothams and signing him to a contract with the Metropolitans, Day violated a rule mandating that a player must wait ten days after his release from one club before signing with another. In fact, O'Neill's new Metropolitans' contract reached the American Association secretary a day ahead of notification that the Gothams had released him.[21]

Jimmy Williams had been hired by Von der Ahe in late October 1883 to manage the Browns. Nevertheless, he still remained the American Association secretary until December 12, pending the appointment of his replacement at the winter meeting. In his capacity of league secretary, Williams voided O'Neill's contract with the Metropolitans; then in his role as Browns' manager, Williams signed O'Neill to a St. Louis contract. The *Post-Dispatch* rejoiced that Williams's foiling of Day's scheme constituted "a great deal of retributive justice." National League president Abraham G. Mills, functioning as chairman of the Arbitration Committee, upheld the Browns' claim to O'Neill's services,[22] apparently basing his decision on a personal opinion that Day's flagrant violation of the ten-day

The 1884 St. Louis Browns. Standing, left to right: George Strief, George "Jumbo" McGinnis, Tip O'Neill, Joe Quest, Charles Comiskey, Bill Gleason, Hugh Nicol. Sitting, left to right: Harry Wheeler, Arlie Latham, John "Daisy" Davis, Tom Dolan, Pat Deasley, Fred Lewis. State Historical Society of Missouri, Columbia.

rule represented a more serious transgression than Williams's obvious conflict of interest.

To that point, though, O'Neill's background failed to suggest just how wise a purchase Williams had made. Believed to have been born in Canada—exactly where has baffled researchers from the United States for more than a century—O'Neill spent most of his youth in Woodstock, where his father was a hotelkeeper. "Tip" O'Neill originally attracted attention as a ballplayer in 1879 while pitching for his hometown team, the Woodstock Actives. His pitching propelled Woodstock, home in the 1860s to the original Canadian baseball champions, back into contention for the unofficial national amateur championship. In a season featuring a U.S. tour, the Actives claimed the mythical Canadian baseball title, although home and away losses against the Harriston Brown Stockings created a dispute that led to the temporary revival of an organized league—the Canadian Association of Ballplayers. Convinced that O'Neill had pitched excessively in 1879, Woodstock partisans believed he had suffered a career-ending arm injury. Viewed as a has-been, O'Neill left Canada virtually unnoticed to pursue his baseball ambitions in the United States. During the next three years he played semi-professional baseball for a variety of clubs including the Chicago Franklins, Detroit Metropolitans, and a barnstorming troupe sponsored by the Hiawatha Tobacco Company. In 1883, after joining the New York Gothams, O'Neill endured a frustrating major-league debut, winning five games while losing twelve. Even in the batter's box, O'Neill averaged only .197, giving few glimpses of the form that would win him fame as the first great Canadian-born hitter in the history of the game.[23]

Although arm problems continued to torment O'Neill, he served as the Browns' opening-day pitcher in 1884, leading the team to a 4–2 triumph over the Indianapolis Hoosiers. Behind the pitching of O'Neill and Jumbo McGinnis, the Browns started the season by winning ten of their first eleven games.[24]

After winning seven of eight games on their opening homestand, the Browns traveled to Indianapolis and swept three games from the Hoosiers. However, the problem of team discipline surfaced in Indianapolis. Prior to the first game there, the *Post-Dispatch* complained that "some of the boys began to 'pour liquor down their throats.'"[25] Shortly afterward, Browns' catcher Pat Deasley approached two women on the street. He apparently propositioned them, and, when his overtures were rejected, Deasley grabbed one of them by her arm. Both women escaped to the safety of a store that sold women's hats. Deasley steadfastly pursued them, and the Indianapolis police quickly arrived to arrest him "for drunkenness and insulting ladies." After being convicted on charges of drunkenness and assault, Deasley paid a ten-dollar fine and court costs for each offense.[26]

In the aftermath of Deasley's conviction, the Browns lost eight of their next eleven outings.[27] Rumors multiplied about the team's internal turmoil. In Toledo the Browns lost two of three games, and a trio of their players took part in a drunken brawl at the team's hotel. Second baseman Joe Quest and catcher Tom Dolan beat up Deasley. During their most recent loss, an embarrassing 16–2 shellacking at the hands of the first-year Brooklyn Trolley-Dodgers, the Browns had appeared to be the victims of poor physical conditioning. Two of their usual starters, Quest and center fielder Fred Lewis, had not played. Deasley had been injured in the course of the contest, and left fielder George Strief had barely managed to hobble through the game. Furthermore, neither McGinnis nor O'Neill were available to pitch. Williams had turned to the team's third pitcher, the stunningly inconsistent John "Daisy" Davis, whose performances were either brilliant or disastrous.[28] Davis had endured one of his poor days.

Once again, as with Ted Sullivan the preceding season, St. Louis newspapers blamed the manager for the decline in team morale. Back in St. Louis, a bewildered Von der Ahe read the reports about Williams's lack of control over the rowdy Browns. The Browns' president hastily departed on the Vandalia Railroad to join his team in Philadelphia. Upon arriving, Von der Ahe admitted "some of the men are disposed to impose upon [Williams'] good nature." He concluded, though, that rumors of team debauchery were "greatly exaggerated."[29]

Von der Ahe had deftly downplayed the disciplinary problem, but he did pursue an investigation into the physical health of his ball club. He believed that "one or two" of the players had fallen prey to "being indisposed whenever they have an excuse." Von der Ahe specifically ordered Lewis to play despite the center fielder's complaints about "a finger in fester," and he also suspected Quest of malingering. In contrast, Von der Ahe pointed to first baseman Charles Comiskey as a player who was "heart and soul in every game he goes into." The Browns would later seek intense competitors, like Comiskey, to man second base and center field. Although Lewis and Quest temporarily retained their positions, neither completed the season with the Browns.[30]

The Browns were more concerned, however, about the health of McGinnis and O'Neill. Obviously, they could not expect Davis to shoulder the pitching burden alone. McGinnis, after winning his initial six starts in just two weeks, experienced "lameness" in his arm. Over the next two weeks, he pitched four times and lost each outing. Fortunately, McGinnis recovered and quickly allayed Von der Ahe's fears about him. He twice defeated the defending American Association champion Athletics during a three-game series in Philadelphia. In the other game, O'Neill lost, 13–7, and his weary arm remained a source of worry.[31]

When the Browns reached Baltimore, Von der Ahe took O'Neill to visit a prominent local physician, who diagnosed the pitcher's condition as "inflammatory rheumatism." Von der Ahe derived some solace, though, from the physician's suggestion that "the best way to overcome the trouble was to exercise in warm weather." In spite of O'Neill's pained protestations, Von der Ahe ordered his pitcher to undergo an extensive throwing regimen. These strenuous workouts did, in fact, prove to be beneficial. O'Neill pushed past his pain to win the last two games he pitched on the road trip, 7–6 over the Baltimore Orioles and 3–2 against the Washington Statesmen. In the latter contest, O'Neill provided his own margin of victory, scoring the Browns' final run when he homered "on a beautiful drive to the center-field fence."[32]

This game-winning hit closed out the lengthy road trip on a triumphant note. It also foreshadowed O'Neill's major league future. As a pitcher, he had played in only a third of the Browns' thirty-three games, yet he led the club in hitting with a .353 batting average. No other member of the Browns was hitting .300. Consequently, when the Browns returned home, O'Neill received regular playing time in the outfield.[33] The experiment rapidly convinced the Browns' management that O'Neill could be far more valuable as an everyday outfielder than as an occasional sore-armed pitcher.

While on the road, the Browns had accumulated fourteen wins and eleven losses, giving them an overall win-loss record of 21–12. They had dropped from first to third place and now found themselves in an unprecedented pennant race, in which just four games separated the top seven American Association teams. For a while, the Browns revived their early season magic, thriving once again at Sportsman's Park. After losing their first game back, the Browns rebounded to capture the next eight contests.[34]

Then, with the team in a virtual deadlock for first place, team discipline broke down again.[35] In the early morning hours of July 2, St. Louis police arrested Lewis for creating a public disturbance. The Browns' center fielder, along with a member of the Baltimore Orioles, had been apprehended at what was likely a local bordello. That afternoon Deasley showed up drunk at Sportsman's Park. When Williams held him out of the game, Deasley bitterly condemned the team's manager to the crowd. Making matters even worse, the Browns in "a comedy of errors" lost to the Orioles, 15–12.[36]

Later that night, Von der Ahe met with the Browns' board of directors to implement appropriate disciplinary measures. The board initially decided to suspend Lewis for the remainder of the season and to assess Deasley a hefty fine. Three days later, it instead rescinded Lewis's suspension and substituted a large fine as his punishment. Also, both Lewis and Deasley were required to sign affidavits pledging they would abstain from alcohol for the rest of the baseball season.[37]

The board of directors was embarrassed by the antics of Lewis and Deasley. Throughout the ensuing three-game series against the New York Metropolitans, the Browns' inept pitching further shamed the organization. The Browns had planned to use their durable workhorse, Jumbo McGinnis, for both the morning and afternoon games of a Fourth of July doubleheader. In the morning game, though, the Metropolitans demolished McGinnis and the Browns, 17–0. This unforeseen outcome altered the pitching assignments. Davis started the afternoon game. He had demonstrated greater consistency of late, winning all five of his starts in the month of June, but two days earlier he had been driven from the pitcher's box in the 15–12 loss to the Orioles. In that dismal outing, he had allowed eleven runs in only three innings. This time, Davis promptly surrendered four runs to the Metropolitans. The Browns were forced for the second straight time to remove Davis and, out of desperation, bring O'Neill in from left field to take over the pitching duties. O'Neill fared slightly better than either McGinnis or Davis, but the hard-hitting Metropolitans still scored seven runs against him in eight innings. The Metropolitans beat the Browns, 11–8, to sweep the holiday doubleheader. A day later, they staged another offensive fireworks show against McGinnis and won again, 13–6. The Browns had lost four straight games, giving up an average of fourteen runs per game, and had fallen all the way to fifth place in the American Association.[38]

Von der Ahe immediately embarked upon a search for new pitching talent. In late July he acquired the rights to pitcher David Foutz from the Bay City, Michigan, club of the Northwestern League. Von der Ahe spared no expense in making the deal. First he paid Bay City a purchase price of $2,000. Then he extended a lucrative offer to Foutz, who quickly accepted the terms of a contract that allowed him to earn $1,600 for the duration of the season. Deasley, previously the highest-paid member of the Browns, received $2,500 for the entire 1884 season. Therefore, Foutz, joining the Browns slightly past the halfway point of the season, collected the largest monthly paycheck on the team as soon as he arrived. Von der Ahe insisted that the price would prove to be worthwhile since Foutz was "a bewilder and make no mistake."[39]

A Maryland native, Foutz started playing baseball in Baltimore. In 1882 he rose to prominence as a star pitcher and part-time center fielder for the champions of the Colorado State Baseball League, the Leadville Blues. The next year Foutz arrived at Bay City and publicized himself to the operators of the local professional team. He greatly embellished his actual achievements with the Leadville Blues, spinning a tall tale reminiscent of the exaggerations of gold prospectors in mining towns such as Leadville. The 1882 Leadville Blues had posted an overall record of 34–8 with one tie. Foutz had been the primary pitcher, but not the only pitcher, on the team. He nevertheless boasted in Bay City about winning forty of forty-one decisions in 1882. Despite this deception, the Bay City club obtained a versatile athlete in Foutz. By July 1884 he led the Northwestern League in batting average and also had compiled an outstanding pitching record of 17–4.[40]

Foutz proved to be an instantly effective acquisition for the Browns. In his major-league debut on July 29 in Cincinnati, Foutz defeated the Red Stockings, 6–5, striking out thirteen batters in a thirteen-inning, complete-game performance. Two days later he conquered Cincinnati again in ten innings, 3–2. These two triumphs moved the Browns past the Red Stockings into fourth place.[41]

Foutz pitched ten games in his initial twenty days with the Browns. He won eight of these contests and soon dominated local baseball discussions. When asked about the Browns' new pitcher, former Maroons' ace Billy Taylor snarled contemptuously: "Foutz is a tall man. . . . His delivery is a very puzzling down shoot. He has many superiors among the pitchers of the day, however." But the *Post-Dispatch* believed Taylor's perspective was tainted by the rivalry between the Browns and the Maroons. It argued instead that Foutz was indeed "one of the most skillful pitchers in the country," and, to support this premise, offered corroborating evidence from a teammate: "McGinnis, who is always modest and conservative in his opinions, says he judges him to be one of the best pitchers in America."[42]

By mid-August the sensational pitching of Foutz had boosted the Browns to third place, just four games behind the front-running Metropolitans. Then, suddenly, the Browns were deprived of both of their leading pitchers. Misfortune first struck the team in Cincinnati. McGinnis injured the tendons of his throwing arm, forcing him to abandon the road trip and return to St. Louis. McGinnis was out for more than a week and did not appear in another game until August 26. Von der Ahe lamented the "unfortunate" absence of McGinnis, yet he maintained faith that Foutz would be "capable of doing most of the pitching" and Davis could fill in enough to give Foutz sufficient rest. But on August 19, the same day that Von der Ahe's words appeared in the *Post-Dispatch,* Dave Foutz tried and failed to get out of his Louisville hotel bed. Stricken with malarial fever, he remained in Louisville until the first of September and did not pitch again until September 10.[43]

Without McGinnis or Foutz, the Browns were forced to depend upon Davis to supply the bulk of their pitching. Davis lost all six of his starts during Foutz's three-week illness and the Browns dropped back to fifth place. With the team's fortunes in decline, their old bugaboo of disciplinary problems resurfaced. Davis and Deasley fought each other in the dining room of the Louisville Hotel. Dolan, embittered about Deasley receiving a larger share of the catching duties, stormed across town to hook up with the rival Maroons. Lewis fell off the sobriety wagon with a resounding thud. He got drunk at the Marble Saloon, challenged every man on the premises to a fight, and was unceremoniously shown the door. In a rage, the Browns' center fielder grabbed "a beer keg and a box full of soda water bottles" and threw them through the saloon's window. St. Louis policemen arrested him "after considerable resistance"; the Browns then suspended him for the second time in the 1884 season.[44]

On September 4, 1884, Jimmy Williams resigned as manager, amid accusations that he had failed to provide "stern, strict discipline." More than two years later, Williams's tenure was still recalled in St. Louis as a time when the Browns had slipped down several rungs of the standings because of their manager's toleration of "Fred Lewis, who, with his little bottle ran everybody and everything." As he had a year earlier when Ted Sullivan resigned, Von der Ahe turned the managerial responsibilities over to first baseman Charles Comiskey.[45] Almost immediately, Comiskey benefited from Foutz's return and Von der Ahe's signing of another Northwestern League pitcher: Robert Lee "Bob" Caruthers.

The ailing Foutz had performed an invaluable scouting function when he recommended that the Browns purchase Caruthers from Minneapolis. Born in Memphis during the Civil War, Caruthers came from a distinguished family

Tom Dolan jumped from the Browns to the Maroons during the 1884 season. State Historical Society of Missouri, Columbia.

with roots in Kentucky and Tennessee. In 1876 the Caruthers clan moved to Chicago, where his mother's side of the family owned extensive real estate holdings. Over his mother's objections, Bob Caruthers took up the game of baseball. James Caruthers, a former chancery judge, encouraged his son to participate, hoping that strenuous exercise would toughen the slightly built youngster. Bob Caruthers soon displayed considerable skill within local amateur circles, and in 1883 he entered the professional ranks with the Grand Rapids, Michigan, club of the Northwestern League. A year later he joined the Minneapolis team in the same league. Although his win-loss record stood at a mediocre 15–16, he quickly proved Foutz to be a shrewd observer of pitchers. In his first game with the Browns on September 7, 1884, Caruthers went directly from the train station to

Sportsman's Park and defeated the Philadelphia Athletics, 6–2. In the last month of the 1884 season Caruthers won an impressive total of seven games and lost only twice.[46]

Meanwhile, Foutz returned to action, winning seven games as well during the season's final month. In a little less than two months of American Association play, Foutz notched a record of 15–6. Together, the pitching of Caruthers and Foutz reinvigorated the Browns, and the team again overtook Cincinnati for fourth place. The Browns, with a 67–40 record, finished the 1884 season only eight games behind the pennant-winning Metropolitans.[47]

The late-season emergence of Foutz and Caruthers enabled the Browns to release Davis in mid-September. With a 10–12 record, Davis had been the only pitcher on the 1884 staff to lose more games than he had won. The trio of Foutz, Caruthers, and O'Neill (who attained a win-loss record of 11–4) combined forces in 1884 to go 33–12, adequately compensating for the thirty-five games that Mullane had won the preceding year. But the 1884 season provided merely a small preview of the influence these three players would soon exert upon baseball in St. Louis. In terms of winning percentage, Foutz and Caruthers would soon lay claim to being the best one-two pitching combination in the entire history of baseball, nineteenth- or twentieth-century.[48]

A healthy Browns' pitching staff, headed by Foutz and Caruthers, completely freed O'Neill from the task of pitching. O'Neill settled in as the Browns' regular left fielder and conducted a reign of terror upon other Association pitchers. He averaged a .356 batting mark over the next five seasons. In his peak year of 1887, O'Neill became the only American Association player and one of just fifteen in major-league history to win the Triple Crown (leading the league in home runs, runs batted in, and batting average in the same season).[49]

At the close of the 1884 season, Von der Ahe stood on the brink of building a championship ball club. He decided the Browns could dispense with a pair of talented but troubled players: Lewis and Deasley. Von der Ahe promised the St. Louis baseball public that the absence of Lewis and Deasley meant the 1885 Browns would include "no boozers and lushers." Accordingly, the Browns released Lewis in late September, despite the fact that he had led the team with a .323 batting average. Lewis joined the St. Louis Maroons for the last weeks of the season, hitting an even .300 for Henry Lucas' ball club. Then, after the season ended, the Browns sold the services of Deasley to the New York Gothams for four hundred dollars. Deasley had led American Association catchers in fielding average in 1883. However, Von der Ahe acted in response to Comiskey's complaint that the Browns' catcher had been "a continual source of trouble to the team."[50]

The purge of Lewis and Deasley meant that Von der Ahe needed to locate a new center fielder and catcher. In addition, the Browns were looking for another second baseman. They had released Quest in mid-September and closed the season with an outfielder, Hugh Nicol, playing the position.[51] Von der Ahe and Comiskey started sifting through the wreckage of financially failed teams in search of gems to grace the diamond at Sportsman's Park. They salvaged four players from the remnants of the Toledo American Association club, the Baltimore Union Association team, and the Cleveland National League franchise, to complete the last links in a championship-caliber roster.

The Toledo Blue Stockings had lost ten thousand dollars in their only year of American Association play. On the evening of October 23 Von der Ahe received a telegram from W. J. Colburn, the president of the Blue Stockings' board of directors, requesting that Von der Ahe meet the next morning with Toledo's manager, Charlie Morton, at the Laclede Hotel in St. Louis. At their meeting, Morton proposed that Von der Ahe purchase some of Toledo's best players. The two gentlemen traveled to Ohio that evening to meet the directors of the Toledo ball club. Von der Ahe quickly struck a deal: the Blue Stockings' board of directors, still some four thousand dollars short of paying off their remaining 1884 debts, agreed to sell the services of five players to the Browns for twenty-five hundred dollars. "It has cost me more money than I ever expended in any similar venture, but I was determined not to let money stand between me and the players I needed," Von der Ahe explained. "I think I have got a winning nine, and I hope the public will appreciate my earnestness in trying to give them the best that money will procure."[52]

Indeed, the *Post-Dispatch* lavished praise upon Von der Ahe "for his enterprising stroke of policy." It depicted the Toledo deal, at different times, as "a four-base hit" or "one of the greatest hits on record." The newspaper likely exaggerated Von der Ahe's role in the transaction. Although the Browns' owner put up the money and handled the negotiations, Comiskey probably played a larger role in selecting the players that the team wanted. Most attention in St. Louis focused upon the projected return of Tony Mullane to the Browns and the arrival of second baseman Sam Barkley, whom the *Post-Dispatch* described as "a man who has been in more general demand than perhaps any other infielder in the country." However, it was one of the lesser known players in the transaction, center fielder Curt Welch, who turned out to be the best bargain the Browns acquired from Toledo. Comiskey had insisted on Welch's inclusion.[53]

Welch had averaged just .224 in his first year of major-league play. Yet Comiskey had perceived Welch's wondrous potential, and convinced Von der Ahe to take a chance on the young center fielder from East Liverpool, Ohio, despite the fact that Welch had already earned a reputation as an alcoholic. Von der Ahe promptly predicted Welch "will add to the field, to the batting, and he has no superior as a base-runner."[54]

Welch spent the next three seasons with the Browns. In that time he hit .277, led American Association outfielders in putouts each year and in fielding average twice, scored an average of 99 runs a year and drove in another 91 runs per year. Al Spink, in his 1910 memoir, recalled Welch as "a rough diamond, uncouth, uneducated, but a born athlete and player." Spink regarded Welch as "the greatest fielder of his day." A few years later, Charles Comiskey expressed the opinion that Welch still rated as "one of the greatest of all fly chasers and base runners."[55]

Sam Barkley, a native of Wheeling, West Virginia, also contributed significantly to the Browns' first pennant-winner in 1885. His .268 batting average and .921 fielding average at second base reflected a considerable improvement over the figures that Joe Quest had posted the preceding season. However, at the close of the 1885 season, Barkley requested a chance to play elsewhere, and Von der Ahe agreed to sell his services to another team.[56] A dispute soon ensued over the rights to Barkley; as we shall see, this conflict would gravely wound the American Association.

Tony Mullane, the most famous player purchased in the Toledo deal, managed to wiggle his way off the hook of a St. Louis baseball commitment for the second straight off-season. Von der Ahe could not legally sign any of the Toledo players until ten days after they had been officially released by their former club. In order to safeguard his investment against the ten-day rule, Von der Ahe persuaded each of the five players to sign a notarized statement that pledged their intention to play the next season for the Browns. The ten-day waiting period expired at midnight, November 4. Von der Ahe arranged a 1 A.M. meeting at a Toledo hotel to sign all five players. Mullane never appeared: at 12:15 he instead met with representatives of the Cincinnati Red Stockings and accepted their contract offer of five thousand dollars for the season, with two thousand paid in advance.[57]

Von der Ahe had already promised Mullane a five-hundred-dollar advance and agreed to make him the highest-paid Brown at thirty-five hundred dollars a year. Infuriated at Mullane's double-dealing, the Browns' president assured all concerned parties that there would be "trouble over the matter." Vowing that Mullane "would not now get a place on the team if he played for nothing," Von der Ahe grumbled: "I have Mullane's oath that he will play in St. Louis next season, made before a notary, and if he thinks as little of an oath as that, I don't think it would be much trouble for some party heavily interested in a game to put a few hundred dollars in a certain direction and have a game made to accommodate him." Therefore, rather than stake their own claim to Mullane, the Browns pursued a strategy to deny his services to the rival Red Stockings. The American Association ended up suspending Mullane for a year and forcing him to return one thousand dollars of Cincinnati's advance money as punishment for "conduct tending to bring discredit on the baseball profession, causing discontent and insubordination among all professional players, and setting an example of sharp practice almost equivalent to dishonesty."[58]

The *Post-Dispatch* complained that Mullane simply laughed all the way to the bank in 1885, a season for which he received his full salary from Cincinnati without playing a single game. The last laugh, though, was on Mullane. He would average more than 22 wins in seven full seasons with Cincinnati after joining them in 1886 and finish his career with 284 wins. He almost certainly would have won more than 300 games if he had been allowed to pitch during the 1885 season. All twenty pitchers in major-league history who have won 300 or more games have been selected to the Hall of Fame. Mullane never received a single vote in Hall of Fame balloting.[59]

Seeking further vengeance, Von der Ahe petulantly refused to pay the remaining money that he owed to the Toledo Blue Stockings' board of directors, pushing them into a lawsuit. Von der Ahe had paid $1,250 of the $2,500 promised to Toledo at the time the teams originally agreed upon the deal, with the other half payable after the five players signed a Browns' contract. The Toledo directors contended that they were entitled to a full payment of the second $1,250 for delivering four of the five players. Von der Ahe countered that the Toledo directors were not entitled to any of the second payment since they had failed to deliver Mullane. The court split the difference down the middle and awarded the Toledo club a grand total of $659.30, which included interest and court costs.[60]

The loss of Mullane took some of the luster off Von der Ahe's Toledo deal. However, Mullane's presence did not prove to be a necessary requirement for winning the pennant. In 1885, the durability of Caruthers and Foutz even limited McGinnis to only 112 innings of work.[61]

Instead of adding another pitcher, the Browns had greater need for someone to catch the tosses of the pitchers they already had. In December and January, Von der Ahe replaced his old catching tandem of Pat Deasley and Tom Dolan by reaching agreements with a pair of players from bankrupt teams. First, in December, he successfully concluded contract negotiations with William "Yank" Robinson. Then, a month later, Von der Ahe also signed Albert "Doc" Bushong.

Robinson, born in Philadelphia, had made his major-league debut in 1882, playing eleven games for the Detroit Wolverines of the National League. In 1884 he joined the Baltimore Monumentals of the Union Association. Robinson had displayed so many skills that the *Post-Dispatch* praised him as "the best all-around player in the Union Association." He participated in 102 games for the Monumentals—catching eleven games, pitching another eleven, and also seeing action seventy-one times at third base, on fourteen occasions as a shortstop, and in three appearances at second base. Robinson won three games and lost three as a pitcher, hit .267, and led Union Association third basemen in fielding average.[62]

The Baltimore Monumentals had lasted the entire 1884 season, posting a 58–47 record to finish third in their league. However, their owner, Robert Henderson, reportedly lost forty-two thousand dollars in his joint investments with the Monumentals and another Union Association team, the Chicago Browns. His Chicago franchise failed to survive the 1884 regular season, and the Monumentals dropped out of the Union Association in advance of the Unions' December winter meeting. Robinson had not played in either the National League or the American Association during 1883, and thus was not subject to the blacklisting provisions of the Day Resolution. In a lively bidding war for Robinson's services, Von der Ahe triumphed over the Baltimore Orioles and other Association teams as well as three National League clubs—the Chicago White Stockings, Providence Grays, and Philadelphia Quakers. Von der Ahe promised St. Louis baseball fans that his newest recruit was "one of the best players in the country."[63]

By signing Bushong, a refugee from the dissolved Cleveland Blues of the National League, Von der Ahe eliminated the need for the versatile Robinson to be the Browns' everyday catcher. "Doc" Bushong, another Philadelphian, derived his nickname from an off-season dentistry practice. He graduated in 1882 with a dental degree from the University of Pennsylvania and took post-graduate courses in Bourdeaux, France, during the off-seasons of 1883 and 1884.[64] Von der Ahe seemed just as impressed with Bushong the person as with "Doc" the baseball player, depicting his new catcher as "one of the most intelligent and gentlemanly men [I've] ever met—either as a ballplayer or outside of that profession."

In 1885, Bushong appeared in nearly all of the Browns' games, catching 85 of the team's 112 contests. While hitting a career-high .267, he led Association catchers defensively in putouts and assists. Charles Comiskey later recalled Bushong as "one of the gamest catchers I ever saw, one who never knew when he was beaten, or hurt either, for that matter." Bushong's presence enabled Robinson to roam over most of the playing field. Robinson hit .261 for the Browns in 1885 and played in 78 ball games—52 in left field when Tip O'Neill missed nearly three months of the season due to a leg injury, 19 at second base, twice at third base, once at first base, and five times taking the catching responsibilities. When Barkley departed following the 1885 season, Robinson took over as the Browns' regular second baseman for the rest of the decade. During his first four years with the Browns, Robinson compiled a batting average of .268 and scored an average of 91 runs per year.[65]

While Von der Ahe was rebuilding the Browns, Henry Lucas was struggling to keep the Maroons alive. On December 18, 1884, the Union Association staged its winter meeting in St. Louis. Although only five teams sent representatives, Lucas still publicly proclaimed that he intended to see the Unions take the field again in 1885. Behind the scenes, however, he surreptitiously negotiated with emissaries of the National League. These secret overtures soon blossomed into an open flirtation. Prior to forming the Union Association, Lucas had sought acceptance within the National League. But his desire had been detoured by the league's 1883 National Agreement with the American Association. In one section of the National Agreement, the two leagues consented to recognize the territorial rights of each existing National League and American Association franchise. The National League now wanted to add the Maroons in order to achieve two purposes: to terminate the threat that the Union Association posed, and to place a team in St. Louis to compete for control of the market against Von der Ahe's Browns. Lucas, tired of being the primary benefactor of a league that had lost somewhere between $50,000 and $250,000 in its first year of operation, viewed the more established National League as the best opportunity to recoup his financial losses.[66] Under the terms of the National Agreement, though, the National League could not accept the Maroons without first receiving permission from Von der Ahe.

Von der Ahe realized that Lucas posed less of a threat inside the National League than outside of it. The Union Association, with its assault upon the reserve clause, had struck a responsive chord in St. Louis. Von der Ahe, whose Browns were bound to the reserve clause through the National Agreement, had even resorted to spreading a rumor that he personally opposed the reserve system. Once the Maroons entered the National League, however, they would be forced to accept the reserve clause. If the Maroons submitted to the reserve clause, the Browns could derive two possible benefits: the Maroons would no longer use this issue as a means to appeal to public opinion, and the cost of player salaries might be reduced through the elimination of marketplace competition. To abandon the Union Association and join the National League, the Maroons would have to make other sacrifices. The National League would compel the Maroons to demand fifty cents as the cost of admission rather than the twenty-five-cent fee that was "the popular price of admission in St. Louis." Finally, the Maroons would be saddled with National League prohibitions against Sunday baseball and beer sales in the ballpark, restrictions that were adamantly opposed by most St. Louis baseball fans. Even National League president Nick Young, a firm opponent of beer sales and Sunday games, later conceded that his league's refusal to allow Sunday games had "undoubtedly cost [the St. Louis Maroons] their franchise."[67]

With the Maroons hindered by these unpopular National League policies, Von der Ahe understood that they would not be able to compete financially against the Browns. Also, if the Maroons joined the National League and became a partner in the National Agreement, Von der Ahe could look forward to the two teams settling the local championship in a series of profitable exhibition games. Initially, for all of these reasons, Von der Ahe had been inclined to grant Lucas permission to take the Maroons into the National League. But Lucas's behavior irked Von der Ahe. To begin with, Lucas tarried excessively before seeking Von der Ahe's support. Then, when Lucas finally did approach Von der Ahe about this vital favor, Von der Ahe felt that Lucas spoke to him in a very condescending tone.[68]

Two strong-willed men, from vastly divergent backgrounds, had clashed. Von der Ahe specifically criticized Lucas for being "so exact in his manner." This complaint likely referred to the Lucas family's propensity to present themselves as "proud and rich, and sticklers for rank and social distinction." Von der Ahe, as a self-made man, naturally resented Lucas's affluent heritage. However, he objected even more to Lucas's sense of superiority. Smug behavior caught Von der Ahe unprepared. After all, in Westfalia his father had been a prosperous merchant. So, with his pride wounded, Von der Ahe decided that Lucas should pay him ten thousand dollars for granting the Maroons a "valuable business privilege." He regarded this demand partially as compensation for damages that the Union Association had inflicted upon the Browns.[69]

In response, Lucas stated that he "positively declined" to make any financial settlement with Von der Ahe. When the Union Association convened again on January 15, 1885, Lucas did not attend, and the two teams present—the Milwaukee Brewers and the Kansas City Cowboys—officially dissolved the organization. Six days later, in New York, Lucas appeared at a special meeting of the National League. This meeting adjourned "without doing anything definite."[70] However, the league candidly discussed the possibility of admitting the Maroons without Von der Ahe's permission.

To American Association representatives sent to New York to monitor the meeting, the National League basically insinuated that it intended to admit the Maroons regardless of the consequences to the National Agreement. While the *Post-Dispatch* feared that the two major leagues might wage a chaotic "war to the knife," the National League and American Association appointed committees to attend a joint conference concerning the status of the Maroons, scheduled for Monday, January 26, at Pittsburgh.[71]

At this point, Democratic U.S. congressman John J. O'Neill resolved to forge a compromise between Von der Ahe and Lucas "without either having to abate a scintilla of self-respect." O'Neill and Chris Von der Ahe had a shared passion for baseball and politics. Von der Ahe in fact chaired the Democrats' district committee for the Eighth Congressional District, which O'Neill represented in Congress. Hence Von der Ahe's busy Golden Lion Saloon functioned as the "head office for the baseball club and political headquarters for the ward," a place where "baseball history was written, political careers were launched, and beer flowed in an endless stream." During the 1881 baseball season, when Von der Ahe started promoting the Brown Stockings, O'Neill quickly invested in the ball

BASE-BALL.

Will He Get Over Safely?

In this 1885 *St. Louis Post-Dispatch* cartoon, Henry Lucas walks a tightrope from the Union Grounds to the League Grounds. Chris Von der Ahe holds the key to the deal in one hand, while in the other he holds an ax that threatens to sabotage Lucas's plan. State Historical Society of Missouri, Columbia.

club. By 1883 Congressman O'Neill had replaced saloon owner John Peckington as the team's vice-president.[72]

As the Browns' vice-president, O'Neill had represented Von der Ahe at the National League meeting in New York. Heading back to St. Louis, O'Neill located Lucas aboard the same train and convinced him to meet with Von der Ahe again. Lucas, Von der Ahe, and O'Neill enjoyed dinner together on Saturday, January 24, at a fashionable St. Louis gathering place, Tony Faust's Restaurant. As the evening unfolded, O'Neill coaxed the two baseball team owners into reconciling their differences. In exchange for a rumored twenty-five-hundred-dollar payment from Lucas, Von der Ahe allowed the Maroons to enter the National League with his blessing.[73]

Henry Lucas later lamented his two years in the National League as a time when he "just didn't seem able to do anything right." In addition to facing local resentment over unpopular National League policies, the Maroons suffered from their failure to field a competitive team. They returned few of the players who had brought them the Union Association pennant. Two players, pitcher Billy Taylor and left fielder Lew "Buttercup" Dickerson, had already jumped to the American Association during the 1884 season. The American Association applied the Day Resolution to blacklist three other Maroons starters—third baseman Jack Gleason, center fielder Dave Rowe, and catcher Tom Dolan—for most of the 1885 season. Although some St. Louisans blamed the Maroons' misfortune upon these missing players, the stiffer National League competition probably had more to do with the team's poor record. The Maroons went from first place in the Union Association to last place in the National League in 1885, winning only 36 games while losing 72 and finishing 49 games behind the first-place Chicago White Stockings.[74] Handicapped by a poor team as well as National League prohibitions against beer sales, Sunday games, and quarter tickets, the Maroons attracted only about half as many spectators as they had drawn in the Union Association. Average attendance dropped from 2,071 in 1884 to 1,069 in 1885.

The 1885 baseball season confirmed Von der Ahe's assessment of the prospects for the two St. Louis ball clubs. His Browns, even with smaller crowds of their own, still more than doubled the attendance of the Maroons. The Browns' declining attendance, from an average of 3,926 fans per game in 1884 to 2,345 in 1885, ironically resulted from their own success on the diamond.[75]

Through hard work, the Browns had transformed themselves into a powerful juggernaut. They trained with greater zeal for the 1885 season than for any of their other years in the American Association. Three factors contributed to this new intensity. First, the Browns were now under the inspired leadership of Charles Comiskey—who, according to longtime friend Ted Sullivan, possessed "a volcano fire burning inside him to make himself famous." Second, Von der Ahe started taking a personal interest in the conditioning of his players. He not only insisted that, on fair-weather days, the Browns run several miles in local parks but also erected a gymnasium where they worked out for four hours a day whenever the weather was inclement. Third, Comiskey and Von der Ahe placed this priority upon getting in shape to prepare the Browns for a spring exhibition series, the first games ever played between Von der Ahe's Browns and Henry Lucas's Maroons. The *Post-Dispatch* described the public's interest in the Browns-Maroons matchup as "remarkable."[76]

The two teams originally were slated to compete four times, twice apiece at Sportsman's Park and the Union Grounds. However, rain canceled the final game, and frigid temperatures hampered attendance at the three contests that were played. Nevertheless, on Saturday, April 11, twenty-five hundred spectators turned out at Sportsman's Park for the first game and huddled together "blue of complexion and . . . under heavy overcoats from the effects of a raw northwest wind." These shivering spectators watched Dave Foutz limit the Maroons to only one hit in a 7–0 Browns' victory. Two days later, at the Union Grounds, the Maroons evened the spring series with a 6–4 win in front of two thousand chilled fans. Back at Sportsman's Park, Foutz pitched the Browns to the local championship, 8–0, allowing just four hits in another shutout performance.[77]

The blustery conditions reduced the crowd at this last game of the spring series to "a thin gathering." Poor weather continued to hinder attendance at the Browns' home opener of the American Association season. Only a "small crowd" showed up on April 18, a dreary Saturday, to see the Pittsburgh Alleghenys defeat the Browns, 7–0. The next day, though, was Sunday, the weather was warm and sunny, and a capacity crowd of ten thousand turned out to see Caruthers hurl a five-hit shutout to help the Browns gain revenge against the Alleghenys, 3–0. Over the next week, the Browns also split two-game series with both the Cincinnati Red Stockings and the Louisville Colonels. Then, in the concluding contest of their short opening homestand, the Browns attracted "an immense crowd" on Sunday, April 26. The game matched a pair of the Association's best pitchers, and Caruthers hurled a six-hit shutout to outduel Pittsburgh's Ed "Cannonball" Morris, 2–0.[78]

At the time, the victory simply gave the Browns a winning homestand and ensured a pleasant departure for the year's initial road trip. Nobody could have foreseen that the Browns' victory would mark the beginning of the longest home winning streak in major-league baseball history, which extended over the next eleven weeks of the season. After capturing three wins in five road outings, the Browns returned home in early May to compile the longest portion of their record home winning streak. They swept an entire fourteen-game homestand at Sportsman's Park—defeating the Philadelphia Athletics in four straight games, the Baltimore Orioles three times, the New York Metropolitans on four occasions, and the Brooklyn Trolley-Dodgers in the last three contests.[79]

Following the tenth of these triumphs, the *Post-Dispatch* confidently predicted, "It seems certain that the Browns are to win all the games played on the home grounds." The *Post-Dispatch,* of course, exaggerated. The Browns did not become indestructible simply by taking the field at Sportsman's Park. In the eleventh game of the homestand, for example, the Browns narrowly escaped with their winning streak intact. The New York Metropolitans scored seven runs in the first inning and forced the Browns to come from behind for an 11–9 victory. Yet the Browns had created an illusion of invincibility. Their dominance of the American Association affected local attendance just as adversely as had the Maroons' mastery of the Union Association. After the Browns' twelfth consecutive home victory, the *Post-Dispatch* observed with irony, "What seems to be the club's gain is Von der Ahe's loss. The attendance for the last two weeks has been very poor for the simple reason that . . . the Browns have been manifestly the superiors, out-batting and out-fielding all comers."[80]

By late May, when the Browns departed on an extensive five-week road trip, their home winning streak had reached fifteen games. They posted only a 14–12 record on the road, but actually added two games onto their Association lead over the second-place Pittsburgh Alleghenys. Sporting a five-and-a-half-game lead over Pittsburgh, the Browns returned to St. Louis for a Fourth of July weekend series. They defeated the Baltimore Orioles five times over the next five days, including a sweep of the traditional Fourth of July morning-afternoon doubleheader. The Brooklyn Trolley-Dodgers arrived in St. Louis as the next challengers to the home team's winning streak. Four days and four losses later, they left as the Browns' latest victims.[81]

The Browns had now prolonged their winning streak at Sportsman's Park to twenty-four games, just two victories short of the major-league record for consecutive home wins, held by the 1875 Boston Red Stockings. On July 14, one of their arch-rivals in the Association, the Philadelphia Athletics, opened a series at Sportsman's Park. Foutz tossed a three-hit shutout and the Browns bashed fifteen hits in a 7–0 triumph. Caruthers defeated the Athletics 8–4 the following day as the Browns tied the Red Stockings' record.[82]

A day later, on July 16, the Browns sought to break the record. In the second inning they produced nine runs to grab a 9–1 lead, but the Athletics stormed back and caught the Browns. Harry Stovey, perhaps the Association's finest player, slugged a two-run homer off McGinnis in the seventh inning, tying the game, 11–11.[83] In the eighth inning, the Browns adjusted their lineup to try to stem the Philadelphia onslaught. Foutz took over the pitching chores, coming in from left field and exchanging positions with McGinnis. After Foutz pitched a scoreless inning, the Browns tallied twice to reclaim the lead, 13–11. Foutz then retired the Athletics' initial three batters in the ninth inning, leaving the formidable Stovey (who had four hits in four official at-bats for the game with three doubles, a home run, and five runs scored) stranded in the on-deck circle as the game ended. Consequently, Foutz gained his twentieth win of the season and the Browns established a major-league record with their twenty-seventh straight victory at Sportsman's Park.[84]

When the teams met next on July 18, Philadelphia finally ended the Browns' home winning streak, administering an 8–3 drubbing. It was the Browns' first loss at Sportsman's Park since April 25. During the eleven weeks that the win streak had been intact, the Browns had moved into first place in the Ameri-

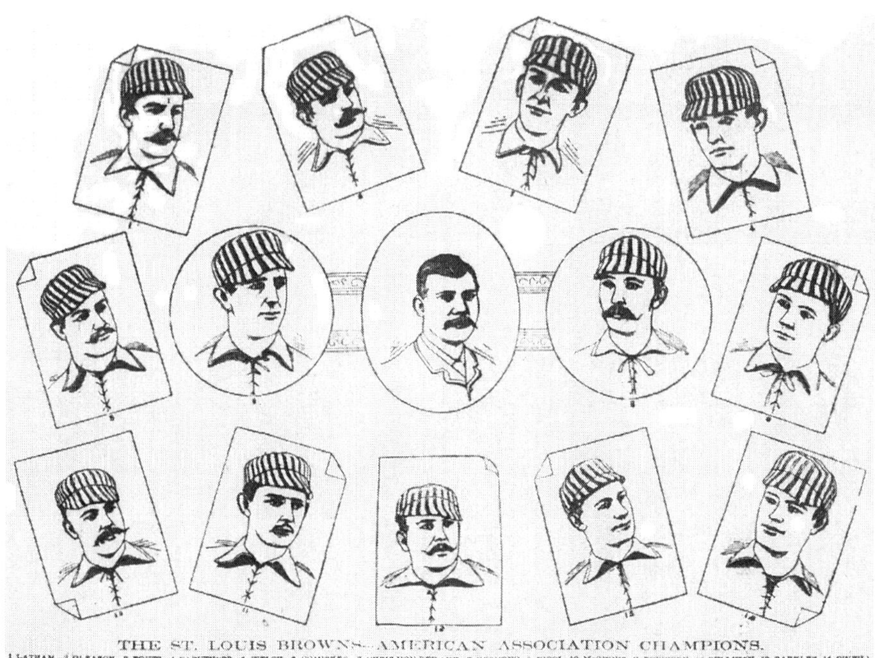
THE ST. LOUIS BROWNS—AMERICAN ASSOCIATION CHAMPIONS.

The 1885 St. Louis Browns. Top row, left to right: Arlie Latham, Bill Gleason, Dave Foutz, Bob Caruthers. Middle row, left to right: Curt Welch, Charles Comiskey, Chris Von der Ahe, Albert "Doc" Bushong, Hugh Nicol. Bottom row, left to right: George "Jumbo" McGinnis, William "Yank" Robinson, Dan Sullivan, Sam Barkley, James "Tip" O'Neill. State Historical Society of Missouri, Columbia.

can Association and built a nine-and-a-half-game lead over the second-place Cincinnati Red Stockings. Throughout the remaining months of the season, Cincinnati and Pittsburgh waged a close battle for second place. The Browns, however, continued to add to their lead. On September 10, in Baltimore, the team officially claimed its first American Association pennant. Foutz pitched the pennant-clincher in his hometown, defeating the Orioles 8–3 to give the Browns an insurmountable fourteen-game lead with only thirteen contests left to play.[85]

The champion Browns ended the 1885 season with a 79–33 record and outdistanced second-place Cincinnati by sixteen games. Early in October, returning from a long road trip, the Browns arrived back in St. Louis, where civic leaders welcomed and honored them at the twenty-fifth annual Mississippi Valley Agricultural and Mechanical Fair. In fact, the *Missouri Republican* described a parade honoring the Browns as "the great Wednesday night attraction of Fair

Sportsman's Park.
Vive la America.
Two Great Days!
Two Great Exhibitions,
Saturday & Sunday Afternoons,
OCTOBER 10 and 11.
Epitome of Western Life and History.

THE RENOWNED SIOUX CHIEF.
Sitting Bull,
And Staff, White Eagle, Fool Thunder, Crow Eagle and 65 braves.
All its thrilling features combined with America's National Game.
THE CHAMPION
ST. LOUIS BROWNS
VS.
THE CINCINNATIS
Both attractions for one admission. Doors open at 12—see the Camp. Game called at 2:30. Wild West immediately after the Ninth Inning.
Admission, 50c; Children, 25c.
Days to be Remembered.

Faced with local competition from Henry Lucas and the Maroons, Chris Von der Ahe outpromoted his rivals. Here, he advertises a doubleheader featuring the Browns and Buffalo Bill's Wild West Show, along with star attraction Sitting Bull. State Historical Society of Missouri, Columbia.

Week." An estimated quarter of a million people lined the streets of St. Louis, including Thomas A. Hendricks, the vice president of the United States, who as we already know had no idea what all the fuss was about. The parade culminated at Schnaider's Beer Garden where a reception had been prepared as a tribute to the Browns. Approximately one thousand guests and ticket-purchasers attended, and the *Republican* noted, "All were permitted to eat and drink to their heart's content. . . . Several kegs of beer were constantly on tap, and waiters were rushing about as fast as their feet would carry them." According to the *St. Louis Globe-Democrat,* the events of the evening marked a new epoch in baseball history: "In years past, it has been customary in other cities to give their returning victors similar receptions. The triumphal march of the St. Louis champions last night was on a grander scale. . . . It stands as the brightest page in the history of America's national game."[86]

The Browns were crowned as the undisputed masters of the St. Louis baseball world. Entering the 1885 season, Von der Ahe had faced the local challenge of Henry Lucas's Maroons, freshly transferred from the Union Association to the more prestigious National League. But the Maroons had finished last, while the Browns had raced to their first American Association pennant. Furthermore, Von der Ahe had profited from the American Association's popular promotional advantages over the National League (Sunday games, liquor sales, and quarter tickets). The Browns clearly remained St. Louis's favorite team, and in a postseason City Series they swept all four games against the Maroons. After the second of these losses, Henry Lucas had vowed: "You can count me out of the baseball business. This game has sickened me." Within a year, Lucas fulfilled his promise. In August 1886 he sold the team to local interests. The Maroons completed the 1886 season in St. Louis, but were subsequently sold to John Brush, who moved the team to Indianapolis and renamed it the Hoosiers.[87]

However, the Browns did not conclude the memorable 1885 season just with a series of triumphs over the Maroons. On October 14, 1885, exactly one week after their parade and reception, the Browns were in Chicago to play the opening game of the World Series versus the National League champion White Stockings. The matchup represented only the third postseason confrontation between champions of rival leagues and the first ever played under the moniker "World Series," a term created by St. Louis sportswriter Al Spink in anticipation of the Browns–White Stockings battle.[88] The Browns now aimed to be proclaimed the best team in the land.

6

"Champions of the World"

Messrs. Spalding and Von der Ahe placed in the hands of the editor of *The Mirror of American Sports* a written document to the effect that the sum of $1000 was to be paid to the club winning the series. As the record showed the contest to be a tie, by the written direction of Messrs. Spalding and Von der Ahe, the sums of $500 each were on the 28th day of last October paid to the Chicago and St. Louis clubs. Had the series stood three to two, St. Louis would have received $600 and Chicago $400 instead of $500 each. . . . All bets go with the main stake, and every person whose money has been paid away on the basis of St. Louis winning the majority of the series, is entitled to demanding the refunding of his money.

—*Spalding's Official Baseball Guide: 1886,* commenting on the disputed outcome of the 1885 World Series

When the two clubs met for the sixth game on the Cincinnati grounds on October 24, it was announced by Umpire John Kelly, in hearing of over one thousand spectators just preceding the beginning of the game that it had been agreed between the St. Louis and Chicago clubs that the game of that day would end their series, and, as each club had won two games, the result of the contest that afternoon would decide the series and the question of the championship. Captains Anson and Comiskey of the two clubs stood close by while this announcement was being proclaimed and neither, by word or gesture affirmed or denied it. The game proceeded and resulted in an overwhelming victory for the American Association Champions. . . . The press next day announced that the championship of America had been won by the St. Louis club. Later, however, the Chicagos laid claim to the unfinished game at St. Louis and declared the series had been a draw. There are, however, one thousand witnesses in Cincinnati who will readily

> testify that Umpire Kelly made the statement before the last game as above noted. Mr. Kelly, the oldest and best known umpire in the country, will also testify that he made the announcement at the request of both club captains. Thus, whatever of glory there may be in the title of Champions of America, the St. Louis Brown Stockings deserve to have it, and in the judgement of the baseball world have received the award.
>
> —*Reach's Official American Association Baseball Guide: 1886,* on the 1885 World Series

Chris Von der Ahe had traveled to Chicago in late September 1885 for a crucial series between the two top teams in the National League, the Chicago White Stockings and the New York Giants. He intended to challenge the National League winners to play a postseason series against his American Association champions, the St. Louis Browns. The White Stockings led the Giants by two games with only eight contests remaining in the season, but four of those games pitted them against the Giants. Once Chicago had defeated New York in the first two encounters, Von der Ahe had seen enough. He arranged a postseason schedule with A. G. Spalding, owner of the White Stockings, and returned to St. Louis with the news on the first day of October. That afternoon, the White Stockings beat the Giants again and clinched a tie for the National League pennant. New York, by salvaging the last game of the Chicago series, temporarily staved off elimination, but on October 6 they were defeated by the last-place Maroons in St. Louis, and the White Stockings clinched the title.[1]

Von der Ahe and Spalding agreed that their teams would play a dozen games scattered over eighteen days in seven different cities. After opening in Chicago, three games would be played in St. Louis. The next eight contests were scheduled for Pittsburgh, Cincinnati, Baltimore, Philadelphia, and Brooklyn. National League rules were to apply in Chicago; all other games were slated for American Association sites and would be governed by Association rules. However, Spalding, as a nativist, Republican, and National Leaguer, rigidly avoided scheduling any of the contests on a Sunday. Of course Von der Ahe, as a German immigrant, Democrat, and saloon owner, fell on the other side of this Gilded Age political divide.[2] Thus, even before the first pitch of the 1885 World Series, vital ingredients for a heated rivalry were already in place. The World Series not only would renew the civic rivalry between St. Louis and Chicago but also would bring together rival leagues that denounced each other on grounds of sharply differing philosophies.

If the two owners were studies in contrast, the teams and their managers also presented interesting differences. The managers, St. Louis's Charles Comiskey and Chicago's Adrian "Cap" Anson, shared certain characteristics. Yet, their contrasts were far more striking. Both played first base, for example, but their individual fielding styles differed dramatically. The smaller and quicker Comiskey roamed far from the bag and acted as another infielder. Anson stationed himself close to first base and served as a massive target for the throws of other infielders. Comiskey held an edge over Anson defensively and on the basepaths, but Anson maintained a large advantage as a hitter.[3]

Also, although both managers enjoyed phenomenal success in guiding their teams, they used vastly different tactics. Anson was a strict disciplinarian. He imposed a hundred-dollar fine on any White Stocking caught drinking beer and, while on the road, conducted thorough nightly room checks to search for curfew violators. Still, Anson gained respect from his players for fairly enforcing, without favoritism, the strict team rules. In contrast, Comiskey earned the friendship of the Browns, becoming the prototype of a "player's manager." He convinced Von der Ahe to institute a generous bonus system, which usually managed to offset or even exceed the amount that the eccentric Browns' owner took away in illogical fines. Unlike Anson, Comiskey preferred to look the other way whenever his players caroused and broke training rules. Comiskey tolerated Browns sneaking away behind his back to go off on drinking forays, but he cracked down when directly confronted.[4]

The Browns and White Stockings each had their share of heavy drinkers, but on the diamond itself they offered a stunning visual contrast. Chicago fielded a much more physically imposing team. Only one member of the 1885 White Stockings stood less than five feet, ten inches in height, while five members of the 1885 Browns fell short of that size. Mike "King" Kelly, one of Chicago's greatest players, believed that the sheer size of the White Stockings often intimidated opponents. Al Spink, the most influential St. Louis baseball writer of the era, later recalled that the Browns "were not stalwart looking but rather slight and slim waisted and when they met heavy nines like Chicago . . . they suffered in comparison." The bigger, stronger White Stockings boasted better hitting statistics, while the smaller, speedier Browns stole more bases and compiled higher fielding averages. Both ball clubs featured superb pitching and were noted for assailing umpires.[5]

The opening game of the 1885 World Series matched the best pitcher from each league against each other. John Clarkson had led all National League pitchers with 53 wins, while Bob Caruthers had won 40 games to top the American Association. Caruthers and St. Louis built a 5–1 lead going into the bottom of the eighth inning, but then the hometown White Stockings rallied for four runs, tying the game on second baseman Fred Pfeffer's three-run homer. With darkness descending on the field, umpire Dave Sullivan called the game before the ninth inning could begin.[6] The 5–5 tie clearly illustrated just how evenly matched the two teams were.

The teams next traveled to St. Louis, where the second game of the 1885 World Series would be the source of enduring controversy and a near riot at Sportsman's Park. On October 15 the first World Series game west of the Mississippi River got off to a rollicking start in front of a crowd of three thousand.[7] The White Stockings took a 1–0 lead in the top of the first inning, but the Browns immediately stormed back in the bottom half of the inning with three runs of their own. Homegrown hero Bill Gleason led off by doubling into right field. The Browns' center fielder, Curt Welch, then reached safely on an error by Chicago third baseman Ned Williamson, with Gleason staying at second base. Both runners advanced on a groundout. Then Comiskey knocked a sharply hit grounder toward second baseman Pfeffer, who tried to throw Gleason out at home plate, but Gleason was safe and the game was tied. Next, with Comiskey on first base and Welch at third, the Browns successfully executed a double steal. Comiskey reached second ahead of the throw from Chicago's catcher, King Kelly, while Welch galloped home. In a futile effort to catch Welch, Pfeffer threw wildly and allowed Comiskey to advance to third base. From there, Comiskey scored the last run of the inning on Kelly's passed ball. The fleet Browns had tallied three runs on just one hit, a pair of stolen bases, and three Chicago miscues.[8]

After five innings of play, the Browns still led, 4–2. However, frustrated St. Louis fans felt their lead could have been larger if not for several questionable calls by National League umpire Dave Sullivan. In the first inning, Sullivan had made an apparent mistake by calling Chicago's Kelly out on a steal attempt. Following that, every subsequent debatable decision went the way of the White Stockings. Sullivan initially drew the ire of St. Louis supporters in the third inning. He ruled foul a base hit down the right-field line by Browns' pitcher Dave Foutz that appeared to land "about a foot inside the foul line." The animosity of the crowd increased when Foutz, who had been called back from second base, then struck out. Later in the same inning, Sullivan called Browns' second baseman Sam Barkley out on a third strike "above his head." These two decisions greatly agitated the Sportsman's Park partisans, provoking a "storm of hissing and shouts of 'get the umpire.'"[9] They also set the stage for an angry outburst over another disputed call in the sixth inning.

Billy Sunday, later a famous preacher and fervent advocate of Prohibition, led off the fateful inning for the White Stockings by doubling to right field and then moving to third on a passed ball. Kelly hit a grounder to shortstop Gleason, who fumbled the ball before recovering in time to retire Kelly at first, while Sunday

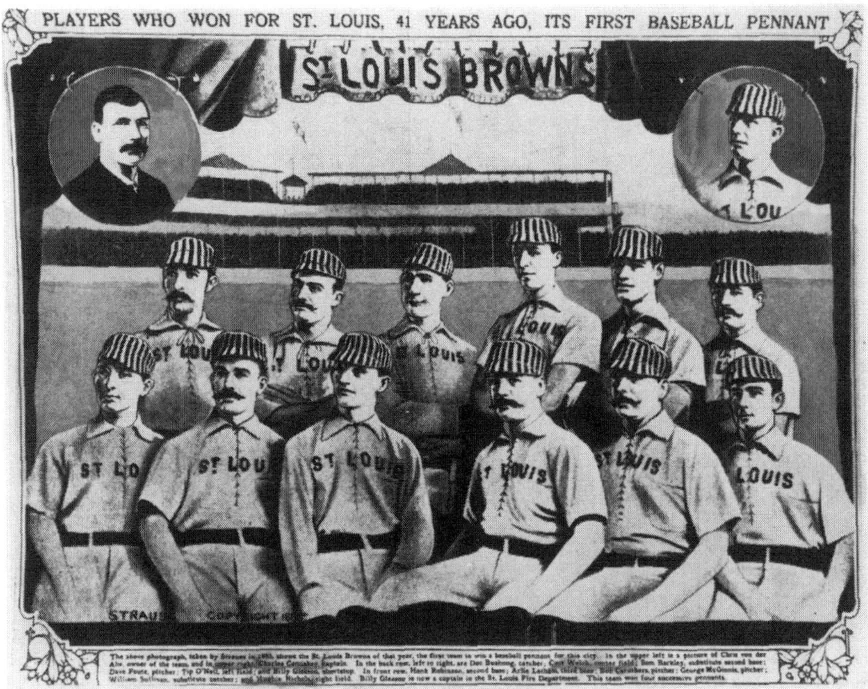

The 1885 St. Louis Browns pose in front of the grandstand at Sportsman's Park, where in October they hosted the first World Series game played west of the Mississippi River. Encircled upper left is Chris Von der Ahe, and upper right is Charles Comiskey. Front row, left to right: Yank Robinson, Arlie Latham, Bob Caruthers, George McGinnis, Dan Sullivan, Hugh Nicol. Back row, left to right: Doc Bushong, Curt Welch, Sam Barkley, Dave Foutz, Tip O'Neill, Bill Gleason. Missouri Historical Society, St. Louis. Photo by Strauss.

scored. Unfortunately, Sullivan, anticipating a play at the plate, watched Sunday crossing home rather than Kelly being thrown out at first. He then rendered a safe call on the play at first base. Even the *Chicago Tribune* later conceded that "the ball beat Kelly to the base [by] at least ten feet."[10]

Amidst cries of "robbery" from the crowd, Comiskey strode down the first-base line to confront Sullivan. He furiously demanded that Sullivan withdraw from umpiring duties for the duration of the contest. Sullivan decided to comply with Comiskey's wishes. He left the playing field, walked to the sidelines, and put on his overcoat. Anson, insisting that the White Stockings would not accept a change of umpires, then persuaded Sullivan to continue. While Sullivan returned to a chorus of "hisses and groans" from the crowd, Anson engaged in an on-field argument with Congressman John J. O'Neill, the Browns' vice-president.[11]

During the exchange between Anson and O'Neill, Comiskey resumed his quarrel with Sullivan. The Browns' manager still demanded that Sullivan relinquish the umpiring responsibilities; if Sullivan did not comply, he threatened to pull his team off the field. Sullivan responded with his own threat: if the Browns left the diamond, the besieged umpire vowed he would forfeit the game to Chicago. Wrangling ballplayers from both teams soon surrounded Sullivan and Comiskey. Sullivan made a half-dozen futile efforts to order the players to return to their proper positions before he finally resorted to giving Comiskey and Anson a two-minute deadline for getting their teams in place. Both clubs consented to Sullivan's command. After a ten-minute interruption, play proceeded again.[12]

Kelly, on first base thanks to Sullivan's umpiring blunder, stole second and scored the tying run on Anson's single into center field. Browns' right fielder Hugh Nicol dropped a fly ball off the bat of Pfeffer, but he recouped quickly and threw Anson out on a force play at second for the first "official" out of the inning. After Pfeffer stole second, Williamson sent a slow roller down the first-base line. The ball initially remained outside the foul line. But, spinning crazily, it curved inside the line at the last moment, hitting first base en route. Comiskey grabbed the ball and tossed it to Barkley, who covered first base, but Williamson beat the throw there. Pfeffer meanwhile scored all the way from second with the run that regained the lead for Chicago.[13]

Unleashing another howl of protest, Comiskey claimed that Sullivan had already called the ball foul and then reversed himself. Sullivan denied ever making a foul call on the play. Anson interjected himself into the argument, stating that his voice had been the one Comiskey heard. Comiskey suddenly switched tactics and contended the ball should have been declared foul under American Association rules. National League umpire Sullivan, thinking that this play was governed under an Association rule of which he was unaware, changed his mind and proclaimed the ball foul; in fact, the rule on determining fair or foul balls was the same in both leagues. Anson and Kelly called Comiskey's bluff. They indignantly insisted that the Browns' manager should at least be required to produce an American Association rulebook substantiating his position. When Comiskey proved unable to produce such a document, Sullivan again reversed his call and ruled the ball fair.[14]

At this point, while bickering ballplayers from each side swarmed the umpire to offer their own perspective on the play, the *Tribune* reported that "about two hundred men" left their seats and stormed the field with intentions to do bodily harm to Sullivan. Amidst the subsequent pandemonium, Sportsman's Park security personnel whisked Sullivan off the field to an awaiting carriage, the White

Stockings armed themselves with their baseball bats to fend off the uncontrolled mob, and the Browns left the ballpark.[15]

The question of precisely when the Browns departed the diamond later took on increased importance. Sullivan, from the safety of the Lindell Hotel, ruled the game forfeited to Chicago on the basis that Comiskey had pulled his men from the field of play. The Browns raised two objections: they had not left the field prematurely, but had exited with the White Stockings when both teams simultaneously were forced off by the rampaging spectators; and the declaration of a forfeit was invalid because Sullivan did not issue it on the playing site as required by the rules, but waited instead until he was ensconced at his hotel. Ironically, a Chicago newspaper offered a time sequence supportive of the Browns' version of events. The *Tribune* noted that "the spectators and players walked off the field in a bunch," thereby lending credence to the Browns' claim that they had been "forced off by the crowd." In another surprise, however, three St. Louis newspapers concurred with Sullivan's opinion that Comiskey pulled the Browns off the field before the fans rushed onto the diamond. These St. Louis newspapers differed only in how they assessed the propriety of Comiskey's action.[16]

Sullivan's experience illustrated the difficulties endured by umpires in the last two decades of the nineteenth century. Francis Richter, then the editor of *Sporting Life,* later recalled that "the '80s . . . developed a spirit of rivalry which led to much abuse of umpires by players."[17] Major-league umpires narrowly escaped harm at the hands of hostile crowds in Baltimore, Philadelphia, and Cincinnati, during the two baseball seasons before the St. Louis mob threatened the physical well-being of Sullivan. One umpire, Joseph Ellick, complained that the root of such tumult stemmed from the "kicking player . . . anxious to save face," who provided a "cue" for the hometown fans to vent their anger by seeking "to kill you and wish you an unpleasant time in the next world."[18] In the second game of the 1885 World Series, the last disputed call certainly matched Ellick's description. Comiskey, still fuming over Sullivan's earlier mistakes and angry at himself for not hastily fielding Williamson's grounder, had provoked hundreds of St. Louis fans into attempting an assault upon the suddenly endangered umpire.

The Browns and White Stockings renewed their rivalry on October 16, the day after their second game had disintegrated into complete chaos. Game Three again offered a competition between the leading pitchers in their respective leagues, Caruthers and Clarkson. It became the first contest of the 1885 World Series to be played to a true decision. Chicago scored once in the top of the first inning, but then the Browns jumped ahead with five runs in the bottom half of the inning, providing all the scoring they ultimately required. Still, even though their early lead eventually proved insurmountable, the advantage seemed vulnerable throughout most of the game. Caruthers avoided major damage, but he allowed the White Stockings a single run in each of the first three innings. Clarkson, rebounding from a difficult start, shut down the Browns through the fifth inning. The White Stockings' offense, which had led the National League in runs by a wide margin, thus received ample opportunities for a successful comeback.[19]

On three straight trips into the field, Caruthers assumed his pitching duties while clinging to a narrow 5–3 lead. Each time, from the fourth inning through the sixth, he preserved the Browns' edge. In the bottom of the sixth, the Browns rewarded their star pitcher by scoring a pair of insurance runs off Clarkson. With a more secure 7–3 advantage, Caruthers extended his scoreless streak to five and two-thirds innings before Chicago finally pushed another run across with two outs in the ninth. Caruthers, utterly undaunted, then recorded his seventh strikeout to complete the Browns' 7–4 victory. The St. Louis offense had been paced by Caruthers, left fielder Tip O'Neill, and third baseman Arlie Latham. Caruthers contributed a pair of runs batted in, while O'Neill scored twice and also drove home a pair of runs. Latham led the way with a game-high three hits, two runs scored, and two runs batted in.[20]

Cap Anson remained outwardly confident. The Chicago manager admitted, "The Browns are a good club. They are liable to beat us a game or two or more." But he also boasted, "Wait until they have played ten games with us and see where they will be." Despite his apparent cockiness, Anson seemed genuinely troubled. Prior to Game Four, he demanded a change of umpires and delayed the start of proceedings for half an hour. A St. Louis resident and former Browns' outfielder, Harry McCaffrey, had umpired the third game without excessive controversy. Even the *Tribune* had acknowledged that McCaffrey "gave very fair decisions."[21] Anson, though, suddenly insisted upon having a member of the St. Louis Maroons umpire Game Four. Comiskey refused to accept any member of his crosstown rivals. At one point of their ongoing debate, Anson suggested that the matter be decided by a coin flip. If he won, Comiskey could select any of the Maroons to umpire, and, if Comiskey prevailed, Anson would select a St. Louis resident off a list of willing candidates compiled by Comiskey. Comiskey rejected the notion of a coin flip. Finally, Anson relented, agreeing to allow McCaffrey to handle the umpiring duties. But McCaffrey, offended by Anson's implication that he had not been even-handed the day before, declined the umpiring assignment. In the end, Anson reluctantly settled for another St. Louis citizen, William Medart, who would prove almost as controversial from the Chicago perspective as Dave Sullivan had seemed to the Browns.

With the umpiring crisis temporarily resolved, Dave Foutz and Jim McCormick once more commenced their pitching rivalry, which had ended so abruptly in the second game. Foutz, with a 33–14 record, had trailed only his teammate Caruthers in winning percentage among American Association pitchers. McCormick, after joining the White Stockings, had posted a record of 20–4.[22]

Both Foutz and McCormick turned in excellent pitching performances in what would prove to be the lowest-scoring game of the 1885 World Series. After two-and-a-half innings of scoreless play, the Browns' speed generated a run. Latham singled into center to start the bottom of the third, stole second, and easily advanced to third when Foutz strategically hit the ball on the ground to the right side of the infield. Second baseman Pfeffer threw out Foutz at first base, but with only one out, Latham stood just ninety feet away from scoring. Caruthers, the Browns' right fielder for the day, followed by knocking a grounder to the White Stockings' third baseman. Wisely, Latham remained anchored on third base until Williamson fielded the ball and threw it to Anson at first. As soon as Williamson released the ball, Latham broke for home and scored with ease.[23]

Chicago took the lead in the top of the fifth. The White Stockings' shortstop, Tom Burns, began the inning with a single to left and moved to second on a passed ball. McCormick sent a grounder to the right side of the infield, and Burns went over to third. Browns' second baseman Barkley bobbled the ball, permitting McCormick to reach base safely. On a planned double steal, McCormick headed slowly toward second base, hoping to draw a throw that would enable Burns to break for home. The Browns' back-up catcher Yank Robinson, substituting for the injured Doc Bushong, responded with a deceptive ploy. He faked a throw to second, hoping to bait Burns into heading for home and then trap the confused White Stockings runner off base. Despite his ingenuity, Robinson's throw to third sailed wildly. Latham made an acrobatic catch at the same time that he was seeking to tag Burns, who had scrambled back to third base. Umpire Medart infuriated the White Stockings by ruling Burns out, although the *Missouri Republican* conceded that Latham caught the ball with one hand and then tagged the runner with his empty hand. Anson vociferously argued the call to no avail, and Medart's decision loomed even larger two batters later when the National League's home run champion, Abner Dalrymple, drove a Foutz pitch out of Sportsman's Park, scoring McCormick ahead of him and giving Chicago a 2–1 lead.[24]

The White Stockings, still justifiably angered that Medart's mistake had cost them a run, allowed their rage to reach a boiling point in the last two innings of the game. In the top of the eighth, they appeared to be on the verge of adding some precious insurance runs to their slender 2–1 lead. Kelly opened the inning by reaching base safely when Comiskey dropped Foutz's throw to first. Kelly proceeded to second on Anson's ground-out to Barkley. When Barkley threw Anson out at first, Kelly sprinted toward third base, seeking the strategic advantage of being there with only one out. Comiskey rushed a throw to third and the ball arrived just in time for Latham to put out Kelly. Kelly, a fast and daring baserunner, had gambled and lost. He then blamed his fate upon the umpire. Further frustrating the White Stockings, Pfeffer followed with a single to center, which would have scored Kelly if he had just remained at second on the preceding play. When Pfeffer tried to steal second and was thrown out, the White Stockings again greeted Medart's decision with wails of derision. The *Republican,* however, felt that the local umpire had been "unquestionably right" in calling both Kelly and Pfeffer out.[25]

The Browns promptly multiplied Chicago's anguish by regaining the lead in their half of the eighth inning. Latham again served as a catalyst, starting the rally with an infield hit that shortstop Burns could not grasp. Latham then scurried to second when McCormick's pitch escaped Kelly for a passed ball. Foutz, as he had done earlier, advanced Latham to third by grounding out to the right side of the infield, and Caruthers delivered Latham home again, this time with a single to left. Another passed ball allowed Caruthers to move up to second. Gleason tried to drive the ball up the middle, but McCormick seized it and trapped Caruthers in a rundown between second and third base. Pfeffer quickly tagged Caruthers out. In the meantime, Gleason had taken a wide turn around first, hoping to race into scoring position at second base if Caruthers could prolong the rundown long enough to permit such a maneuver. Pfeffer, after tagging Caruthers and noticing Gleason, decided to fire the ball to first and catch Gleason off base. This turned out to be a mistake. Pfeffer threw the ball so wildly that Gleason went all the way around to third base. The error proved pivotal when Welch smashed a grounder down the third base line and beat Williamson's throw to first for an infield hit, enabling Gleason to cross home with the go-ahead run.[26] Once again, the speed of the Browns had played a vital role. The Browns had hit only one pitch out of the infield in the eighth inning, but had put together a winning two-run rally with infield hits and aggressive baserunning to force fielding miscues.

In the ninth inning, before claiming victory, the Browns survived another White Stocking threat. Foutz retired the first Chicago batter, but a couple of defensive lapses jeopardized the Browns' lead. Barkley carelessly allowed a ground ball to roll right between his legs. Then, with Burns on first base, Comiskey dropped a pop-up that McCormick lofted into shallow right field. However, rather than brooding over his error, the Browns' manager alertly employed the same sort of ruse used successfully by Robinson back in the fifth inning. As Burns turned second base and headed for third, Comiskey faked a throw in that direction. The throwing motion implanted the thought in McCormick's mind that he could make a dash for second base while a play was being made on Burns at third. Having lured the Chicago pitcher off base, Comiskey sped toward McCormick, who had realized his misjudgment and was retreating back to first.

Umpire Medart ruled that Comiskey tagged McCormick out, precipitating the last and unquestionably angriest outburst of the White Stockings' many protests on the day. An account of the play contained in the *Tribune* reflected a distinct Chicago bias by adamantly claiming that McCormick "never moved" off first base at all. On the other extreme, the *St. Louis Globe-Democrat* perhaps displayed its own local prejudice by uncritically accepting the umpire's decision. In between these two widely divergent perspectives, the *Republican* reported: "Whether he had succeeded in getting back is a question on which the crowd was divided, some asserting that he was off the bag when touched, and others that he was on it."[27]

McCormick reacted to the call by sullenly refusing to leave first base. Sunday charged toward Medart, screaming: "That man was not out." Medart called Sunday "a liar," told him to shut up, and threatened, "If you don't do it, I'll make you." Sunday immediately assumed a boxing stance with fists clenched.[28]

At this point, Kelly interceded by grabbing Sunday and forcibly pulling his teammate to the sideline. McCormick rushed Medart next. Three separate newspaper accounts described the belligerent Chicago pitcher moving toward the umpire with "his face glowing like fire," "his face red with rage," or "with blood in his eye." As McCormick approached, Medart walked over to the sideline, appealing to Anson for help in restraining his men. After Anson apparently ignored the request, Kelly again avoided a violent confrontation by stepping between Medart and McCormick.[29]

Thanks to the peacekeeping efforts of Kelly and his considerable influence over the other White Stockings, the game finally resumed. With the potential tying run on third base and two outs, a local St. Louis amateur named James "Bug" Holliday represented the last chance for the White Stockings. Holliday had been pressed into service for a couple of reasons. First, the White Stockings had suspended their regular center fielder, George Gore, and second, Anson had wanted to give Clarkson, his ace pitcher, a day off.[30]

Holliday eventually put together a solid ten-year major-league career with Cincinnati, but on October 17, 1885, he was merely an eighteen-year-old youngster. Hitless in three previous at-bats, Holliday lifted a pop-up into foul territory behind third base. Spinning around, Latham turned his back to home plate, galloped after the ball, and made an impressive over-the-shoulder catch to give the Browns a hard-fought 3–2 win.[31]

The *Globe-Democrat* heralded Game Four as "one of the most exciting that has taken place at Sportsman's Park this season."[32] Actually, at that point, the hotly contested 1885 World Series had produced four close games in four days. It had been marred only by the constant carping about umpires. Ironically, Von der Ahe and Spalding solved the umpiring crisis at precisely the same time that their playing schedule caused a decline in fan interest.

The two owners resolved the controversy over selecting an umpire by hiring one of the nation's most esteemed officials, John O. Kelly, to serve in all the remaining games. The widely respected Kelly, nicknamed "Honest John," possessed four years of major-league umpiring experience and had presided over games in both leagues. However, the playing schedule presented two major problems. First, a four-day hiatus disrupted the continuity of the World Series. Second, making matters even worse, the World Series resumed not in either of the participating cities, but in Pittsburgh. The remainder of the original playing schedule called for eight games to be played over the course of the next ten days in Pittsburgh, Cincinnati, Philadelphia, and Brooklyn.[33]

Attendance at World Series games peaked in those cities where hometown clubs participated. A fairly typical Chicago crowd of two thousand had attended the opening game. Each of the games in St. Louis had attracted slightly above-average crowds of three thousand.[34] Four exciting games had been played, and momentum had been built to draw even larger crowds in Chicago and St. Louis. Ideally, the teams would have immediately traveled back to Chicago, where fans might well have flocked to the ballpark to see the White Stockings try to overcome the Browns' edge in games won. Then, if the White Stockings had succeeded in tightening up the series, the deciding games could have been played in front of huge gatherings in St. Louis. Instead, the 1885 World Series, once it was interrupted and continued elsewhere, never seemed to get back on track.

Prior to the start of the World Series, Von der Ahe had expressed support for the concept of using multiple playing sites "because the baseball enthusiasts of all those towns are wild to see the two clubs come together." He soon reconsidered. Arriving in the wintry weather of Pittsburgh and sensing the utter disinterest of local fans, he hastily wired Spalding. His telegram suggested that the World Series should be discontinued, due to "the cold and unfavorable weather," after completing the seventh game in Cincinnati.[35] The White Stockings' owner agreed to the proposal.

A mere five hundred spectators braved the cold in Pittsburgh for Game Five. This sparse audience watched a lopsided 9–2 Chicago victory. Newspaper accounts complained that the game had been played "listlessly," a far cry from the passionate intensity of the teams in Games Two and Four. Enthusiasm only marginally improved after reaching Cincinnati, where a crowd of fifteen hundred showed up for Game Six. Furthermore, Chicago again drubbed the Browns, 9–2, and this one-sided outcome hardly gave Cincinnati citizens extra incentive to return the next day for Game Seven. Only twelve hundred spectators assembled at

American Park in Cincinnati on Saturday, October 24, for the last game of the 1885 World Series.[36]

On the day of this seventh game, the *St. Louis Post-Dispatch* criticized the premature end of the World Series and printed a prophesy: "It is to be regretted that Von der Ahe and Spalding came to this conclusion, as the games between these clubs that have been played so far have been closely contested ones, and whether the Chicagos or Browns win today's game, it will still leave the question as to which club is superior entirely in the dark."[37] Of the six previous games, the first had been a tie, the second had been indecisive (although Chicago had been awarded the game by forfeit, St. Louis partisans believed it should not count in determining the result of the World Series), and each team had won two of the next four.

A brief announcement made prior to the seventh game was an apparent acquiescence to the St. Louis viewpoint. Umpire "Honest John" Kelly, acting upon a request from Anson and Comiskey, promised the Cincinnati crowd that they were about to view the seventh and deciding game of the 1885 World Series. Kelly explained that Chicago no longer claimed a victory in the disputed second game; thus each club had won twice, and, therefore, the upcoming game "would decide the series and the question of the championship."[38]

Anson and Comiskey probably hoped to stimulate excitement among spectators and players. Comiskey had nothing to lose. Anson had approved an important concession. He may have consented to portray Game Seven as the deciding contest out of a sense of overconfidence. After Game Three, Anson's remarks had clearly revealed that he viewed the White Stockings as a vastly superior team that would eventually wear down the plucky but overmatched Browns. The White Stockings' decisive back-to-back 9–2 wins likely convinced Anson that this process had indeed taken place.

Also, before Game Seven, Anson changed his pitching plans. He intended to use John Clarkson, until the pitcher arrived at the park five minutes late; Anson, ever the strict disciplinarian, benched him.[39] By punishing Clarkson, though, the White Stockings' manager forced McCormick to pitch for a second straight day. The Browns had a better-rested pitcher. Dave Foutz, after losing the fifth game to Clarkson, would now work with a day's rest.

The White Stockings opened the scoring with two runs in the first inning. But the Browns struck back with four runs in the third and six more in the fourth off of an obviously tired McCormick. McCormick, after limiting the Browns to only two hits the previous day, allowed a dozen base hits in Game Seven and received little support from the "miserable" White Stockings' defense. Staked to a commanding 10–2 lead, Foutz and the Browns coasted to a 13–4 triumph.[40]

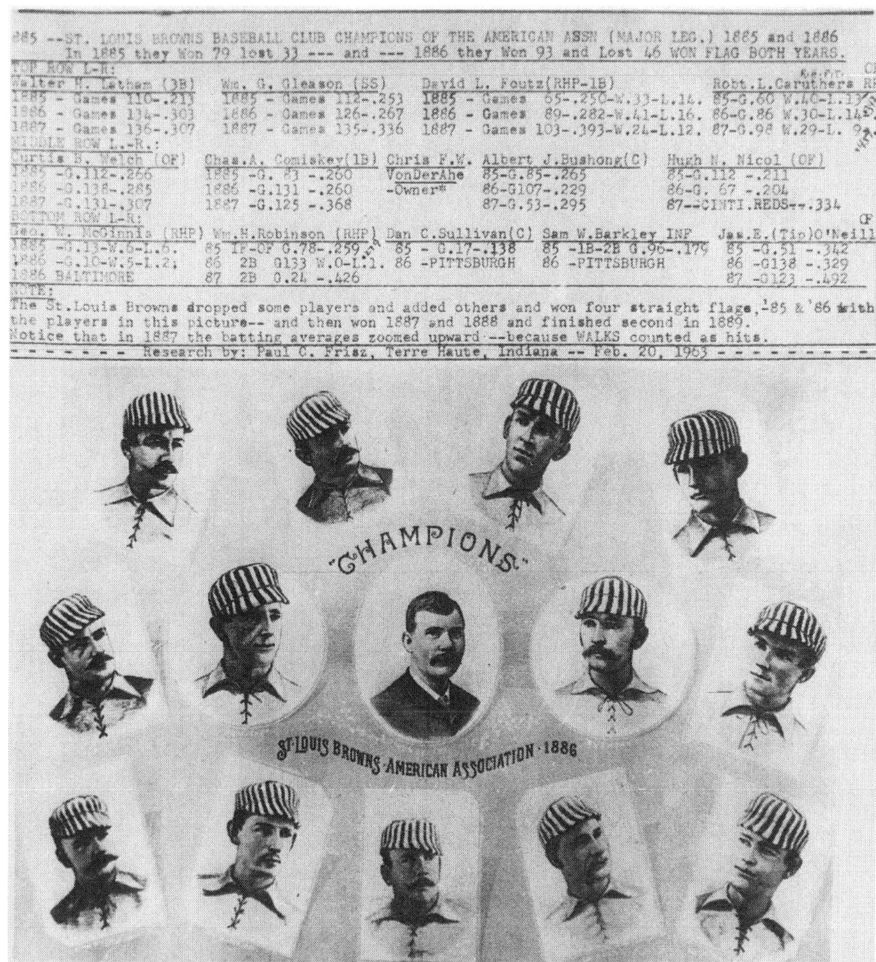

After defeating the Chicago White Stockings in the seventh game of the World Series, the St. Louis Browns claimed the title of world champions. Missouri Historical Society, St. Louis.

Following the seventh game, the Browns were immediately hailed as the World Series champions by newspapers in St. Louis, Chicago, and elsewhere. However, A. G. Spalding quickly challenged this interpretation. The White Stockings' owner protested that he had never renounced the forfeited game and Anson had lacked "any authority to take such a step." Spalding insisted that the series had ended in a tie. Furthermore, he downplayed the significance of the 1885 World

Series, dismissing as "nonsense" the idea that the games had been played "to decide the championship of the world." Finally, Spalding offered an excuse for his team's failure to beat the Browns: "Unquestionably, our boys have played very poor ball during the entire series, but their interest in play was gone, and, as a test of the playing strength of the two nines, the series has been a failure."[41]

Spalding prevailed upon *The Mirror of American Sports,* which was considered in St. Louis "an organ for Spalding," to split evenly the one thousand dollars in prize money that the two owners had put up. *Spalding's Official Baseball Guide* then cited the equal division of the prize money as proof that the 1885 World Series had truly been a tie. On the other hand, *Reach's Official American Association Baseball Guide* declared the Browns champions and, as documentation, referred to the public announcement made by Umpire Kelly before the seventh game. Contemporary opinion remained bitterly divided over the outcome, although most modern accounts depict the 1885 World Series as a tie.[42] The disputed result heightened interest tremendously when the same teams met again in the World Series of 1886.

7

"The $15,000 Slide"

> A Very Good Baseball Movie Could Be Made About: Baseball in St. Louis, 1883–86. It's got everything—great teams, unbelievable characters . . . pennant races, World Series. Best material for a baseball movie ever.
>
> —Bill James, *Historical Baseball Abstract,* 1988

Before the 1886 season started, a momentous baseball event occurred in St. Louis. On March 17 the first issue of the *Sporting News* rolled off the presses. Al Spink served as the founder, publisher, and editor of the new journal. Within the first year of operation, Charles C. Spink joined his brother in St. Louis. Charles Spink, who later succeeded his older brother as editor and publisher, originally functioned as a business manager while Al handled the creative end of the operation. Together, the two brothers established a weekly magazine that quickly boasted "the largest circulation of any sporting paper published west of Philadelphia."[1]

The Spinks carefully worded this claim to exclude the Philadelphia-based *Sporting Life.* In its first edition, the *Sporting News* respectfully acknowledged its eastern competitor: "From Philadelphia, [Francis] Richter, the editor of the liveliest sports journal in the land, sends friendly greetings and hopes the *News* may live forever a friendly rival of the *Life.*" In just four months, however, this civility was replaced by a fierce newspaper war. Yet conflicts between the two competing baseball journals enlivened the game until Richter's publication folded in 1910. As the survivor of the rivalry, the *Sporting News* proudly claimed the title, "The Bible of Baseball."[2]

Throughout its initial year of life, the *Sporting News* devoted a large amount of its baseball coverage to the defending pennant-winners. The March 17, 1886, premiere edition, for example, featured front-page articles on the St. Louis Browns and Chicago White Stockings. Readers learned that St. Louis ace pitcher Robert Lee Caruthers had agreed to terms with the Browns after a winter holdout spent in Paris. Another story reported that the White Stockings planned to assemble on March 15 at the popular health resort in Hot Springs, Arkansas, to get in shape for the upcoming season. Their owner, A. G. Spalding, explained the trip in his typical moralistic manner: "I have written a professor down there, and he is making arrangements to build a vat in which he can boil the whole nine at once. . . . I boil out all the alcoholic microbes, which may have impregnated the systems of these men, during the winter while they have been away from me."[3]

In 1886 both the Browns and White Stockings repeated as pennant-winners in their respective leagues. As in 1885, the Browns moved almost immediately to the top of the American Association standings and stayed there the remainder of the year. Fortunately for Chris Von der Ahe's gate receipts, the Browns did not sustain another long winning streak like the one that had given the 1885 team an illusion of invincibility. All through the first half of the 1886 season, other teams closely pursued them. An exciting pennant race enticed larger crowds to Sportsman's Park, and for the third time in five American Association seasons the Browns boasted the best home attendance in the major leagues. Still, the team steadily pulled away from the other contenders, finishing with a record of 93–46 and convincingly capturing the Association pennant by twelve games over the Pittsburgh Alleghenys.[4]

Meanwhile, in the National League, the White Stockings again survived a very tough struggle. After trailing the Detroit Wolverines for most of the season, the White Stockings finally overtook Detroit in August and held them off in the end by the narrow margin of two and a half games. As in 1885, the closer National League race pushed the White Stockings to a better winning percentage than the Browns compiled in the less competitive American Association.[5]

The second half of the 1886 regular season featured a slow buildup to a World Series rematch. When the White Stockings visited St. Louis for a mid-July series with the Maroons, Cap Anson provided a last spark that ignited the hottest baseball rivalry to that point in the game's history. A *St. Louis Post-Dispatch* reporter asked the White Stockings' manager how he thought the Browns might fare in the National League. Anson bluntly claimed that the Browns could expect to finish no higher than "somewhere around fifth or sixth." The newspaper promptly relayed this prediction to Charles Comiskey, who "recalled the Series with the Chicagos last fall" and then dismissed Anson's contention as "preposterous."[6]

The next day, Von der Ahe staged a banquet for the Browns and local newspapermen at Sportsman's Park. The *Sporting News* reported, "Tables were spread . . . in right field and were loaded down with good things. Wine flowed like water." At the climax of the festivities, the Browns toasted their boss, and Von der Ahe praised them as the finest baseball team in the world. Then he added, "I want you always to remain an honor to St. Louis and the Association."[7]

The top pitchers on the Browns, Dave Foutz and Bob Caruthers, decided to go looking for Anson in order to defend the slighted honor of St. Louis and the

Association. Confronting Anson at the Lindell Hotel, Caruthers, brandishing a fist full of money, loudly challenged the White Stockings' manager: "I'll bet you a thousand dollars that the Browns can beat your nine, and I'll put this money up as a forfeit." Foutz maintained that he wanted some of the same action while Anson "simply smiled and said nothing." The *Sporting News* concluded Anson had been "trying to get in a big bluff," but the Browns effectively "called on it."[8]

For the rest of the season, the Browns and White Stockings continued to raise the ante. First, a week after Foutz and Caruthers dared Anson to put his money where his mouth was, White Stocking shortstop Ned Williamson responded to the offer of the Browns' aces: "Anson and the rest of us will stand ready to cover all bets which Foutz and others of the Brown Stockings wish to make." The St. Louis Merchants Exchange got into the act by claiming that it would wager ten thousand dollars on the Browns in a series with the White Stockings. Then the Chicago Board of Trade engaged in a bit of one-upmanship by offering to bet up to one million dollars on the White Stockings. While dismissing most of these maneuverings as "a big game of bluff," the *Sporting News* editorialized, "If the Chicago folks think that their team can beat ours, they have simply to put up their stuff. Ours has been up. . . . Anson and others were asked to cover it, but they politely declined. Money is the only thing that talks nowadays so our Chicago friends will do well to either put up or shut up."[9]

Despite this strident challenge, the *Sporting News* cautioned in early August that all of the speculation remained virtually meaningless until the Browns and White Stockings wrapped up their respective pennants. But at the same time, the publication affirmed the local fervor for a St. Louis–Chicago rematch. Near the end of the regular season Al Spink often focused upon the St. Louis version of the 1885 World Series. For instance, on September 20, he noted in the *Sporting News* that Von der Ahe soon planned to erect a flagpole at Sportsman's Park in order to fly the Browns' 1886 American Association championship pennant. Then, Spink bravely foretold future developments: "After the Browns knock the eye out of the champions of the League, for a second time, there will be still another staff grow up like a bean stalk at Sportsman's Park, and on it will be inscribed 'Twice Champions of the World'. . . . The Chicagos can go on flying their one-horse banner."[10]

Within a week, Von der Ahe issued a formal challenge in a September 26 letter to Spalding. Von der Ahe's letter insisted on two conditions: the games between the Browns and White Stockings would "be known as the World's Championship Series," and would be played exclusively in St. Louis and Chicago. The Browns' owner included these terms in an attempt to avoid the problems of the year before. Before agreeing to participate, Spalding laid down certain ground rules of his own. He advocated an intriguing "winner take all" formula to settle the division of gate receipts. His other major concern involved the selection of umpires. Spalding urged each team to cooperate in choosing two umpires from each league, creating a four-man Board of Umpires that would serve as a "final" source of appeal in case of any dispute between the two teams. Also, under this plan, game umpires could be rotated on a daily basis. Once any contest started, the umpire of the day would be empowered as the "sole judge" whose "decision shall be final and not subject to appeal."[11]

Von der Ahe amicably accepted all of the ideas offered by Spalding: "Why, the terms suit me. I am willing to play him the series right on his own preposition, the winning club to take all the gate receipts." The Browns blamed conflicts with umpires for the shroud of controversy surrounding the outcome of the 1885 World Series. Therefore, their owner eagerly endorsed the proposed umpiring format, believing the Board of Umpires could ensure that there would be "no possible quibble after the result has been obtained."[12]

In the first week of October, the two owners hammered out the final details. They clashed over the length of the series. Spalding wanted to play nine games, while Von der Ahe, mindful of reserving some October playing dates for a City Series against the Maroons, preferred a five-game World Series. The owners then settled on a compromise solution of seven games. Next, they arranged a playing schedule, which called for six games in six days from Monday, October 18, through Saturday, October 23. After opening with three contests in Chicago, the Series would shift to St. Louis for the next three games. If the Series still remained undecided at that point, a climactic seventh game would be played on Tuesday, October 26, at a neutral site. Von der Ahe, through a coin flip with Spalding, won the right to select the scene of the seventh game. He chose Cincinnati, where the Browns had defeated the White Stockings in Game Seven of the 1885 World Series.[13]

On October 18, Chicago hosted the first game of the 1886 World Series. The pitching matchup featured the top winners on each staff. John Clarkson, victorious in thirty-six games for the White Stockings, opposed the Browns' Dave Foutz, who had led American Association hurlers in winning percentage and tied for the most games won with forty-one. Clarkson emerged triumphant, shutting out the Browns on just five hits. St. Louis newspapers, seeking solace in various excuses, blamed the Browns' 6–0 loss on the cold Chicago weather and the White Stockings' monopoly of hitting luck. Meanwhile, in its analysis of the game, the *Chicago News* revived Anson's midsummer claim of National League superiority: "The St. Louis club, while it is undoubtedly competent to contest with the clubs of such towns as Louisville or Pittsburgh, is entirely outclassed. . . . There are four clubs in the National League that play better ball than the champions of the American Association."[14]

A day later, the Browns punctured this myth of National League supremacy, shellacking Chicago 12–0 and handing the White Stockings the worst loss in the history of their organization. Bob Caruthers, the Browns' thirty-game winner, clearly outpitched Jim McCormick, the White Stockings' thirty-one game winner. Caruthers yielded only one hit, a lead-off single by the White Stockings' first batter, George Gore. In contrast, the Browns walloped McCormick's pitches "sky-west-and-crooked."[15]

James "Tip" O'Neill ignited the Browns' barrage with three hits and a pair of home runs, both of which landed among a number of carriages parked in the most distant regions of left field. Caruthers chipped in with three hits of his own. Out of the Browns' total of fourteen hits, six went for extra bases. Defensively, St. Louis committed only two errors as opposed to nine miscues made by Chicago.[16] In a nutshell, the Browns decisively defeated the White Stockings at virtually every facet of the game—pitching, hitting, and fielding.

Game Three, which wrapped up the Chicago phase of the World Series, took place the next afternoon. An overly enthusiastic Caruthers persuaded Von der Ahe to let him pitch for a second consecutive day. This decision, made over the objections of Comiskey and the other Browns, demonstrated once again the negative impact that Von der Ahe sometimes exerted. It immediately backfired. In the first inning, the overworked pitcher walked four of the first five Chicago batters that he faced. His wildness allowed two White Stockings to score without benefit of a base hit. When Caruthers finally located the strike zone, he failed to fool many of the White Stockings' hitters. Chicago pounded out eleven runs, a dozen hits, and a pair of home runs among their five extra-base hits. Clarkson coasted to an easy 11–4 win.[17]

Throughout the three games in Chicago, grudges had festered among some of the rival players and further fueled the feud between the ball clubs. Additionally, St. Louis and Chicago journalists had sharply escalated their war of words. The 1886 World Series had developed into an intense conflict, savagely fought in the columns of the newspapers, within the lines of the playing field, and even with fists in the bleachers. Prior to the opening game, the *Chicago Tribune* had established a shrill and partisan tone. The newspaper even recommended that the White Stockings should intentionally seek to injure Browns' third baseman Arlie Latham. The *St. Louis Post-Dispatch* promptly denounced the *Tribune* for printing "a piece of the vilest scurrility" that left the Browns and Von der Ahe "in a state of the wildest indignation."[18]

National League newspapers and players continued to view the champions of the American Association with condescension. Anson, for example, had informed reporters that the first game of the World Series merely constituted a "good practice" for the White Stockings. In the seventh inning of Game Two, as the Browns' Curt Welch crossed home with the eighth run against McCormick, the Chicago pitcher "struck him on the head, knocking his cap off without any provocation whatsoever."[19]

The Browns, already a highly aggressive base-running team, seemed increasingly determined to use the base paths to earn the respect of the White Stockings. In a play at home plate during Game Three, the Browns' William "Yank" Robinson had barreled into the Chicago catcher, Mike "King" Kelly. Kelly had been flipped over by the impact of Robinson's shoulder driving into his face, but he nevertheless managed to hold onto the ball and register an out. At the time, Anson had feigned a desire to hit Robinson with a bat.[20]

Arriving in St. Louis before the fourth game of the 1886 World Series, Anson granted an interview to the *Post-Dispatch,* in which he apparently criticized Robinson for being more interested in colliding with Kelly than in scoring a run. Then, in the same interview, Anson conveyed a veiled threat that the Browns' fielders should expect the same treatment from the White Stockings. By the time the series ended, the *Missouri Republican* pointed to the ferocious base-running of the two teams as perhaps the most prominent feature of play: "The championship series was not prolific of pretty plays. When no baseman can play anywhere near his base without the risk of having a leg broken, the conditions are not conducive to developing the beauties of the game. In truth, the play at times was somewhat too viciously honest."[21]

Early in Game Four, another Browns' runner slammed into Kelly at home plate. The Browns had quickly fallen behind, 3–0. In the second inning, with one out, they had Bill Gleason on third base and Curt Welch on first. The Browns, just as they had successfully done during the second game, attempted to perpetrate a double steal. But this time Kelly anticipated the play and unleashed a strong throw that resulted in Welch being tagged out by second baseman Fred Pfeffer. Pfeffer also had sufficient time to return the ball back to Kelly at almost the same moment that Gleason reached home plate. Gleason managed to score, though, by running directly into the hands of Kelly and denying him any opportunity to catch the ball. Kelly suffered a spike wound to his foot, and the game was halted for fifteen minutes while he was treated. During the delay, a belligerent Browns' booster bellowed words of encouragement to the home team: "That's right, kill some more of 'em." Kelly eventually recovered, confronted Gleason, and delivered some angry words to the Browns' shortstop.[22]

While the innings rolled along, the Browns benefited from a major pitching advantage. Clarkson had been forced to pitch back-to-back games because of the health problems of the other primary Chicago hurlers, McCormick and John "Jocko" Flynn. Although Clarkson struggled gallantly, the Browns scored in four of the last five innings in which they faced the weary Chicago hurler. Meanwhile, the better-rested Foutz actually improved his pitching for St. Louis as the game wore on. The White Stockings tallied three times in the opening inning, but Foutz shut them out five of the next six times that he matched wits with them.[23]

St. Louis edged closer in the third inning. With Caruthers on first base, O'Neill lined a long drive into the right-field beer garden. The peculiar ground rules of Sportsman's Park required the defensive team to return any balls hit into the beer garden to their pitcher before making a play on an opposing runner. White Stockings' right fielder Jimmy Ryan scrambled into the crowded beer garden, managed to locate the ball, and relayed it back toward the infield. Caruthers scored easily, and O'Neill rounded third to head home. Clarkson received the ball just in time to zip it to Kelly at the same instant that O'Neill arrived. National League umpire Joe Quest, a former Brown who had once been released by Von der Ahe, called O'Neill out on a controversial ruling.[24]

Neither side scored again until the fifth inning. In the top half of the fifth, Foutz blanked the White Stockings for the fourth straight inning. Then, with one out in the bottom of the fifth, Browns' catcher Albert "Doc" Bushong drew a walk. Arlie Latham, the Browns' lead-off hitter, pounded the ball past Chicago third baseman Tommy Burns for a single. With runners on first and second, Caruthers sent a deep fly ball to right field. After Ryan backtracked to make the catch, the Browns' runners tagged up and advanced a base apiece. Tip O'Neill, the slugging star of the series, advanced to the plate amidst "thunderous applause."[25]

The Chicago battery of Clarkson and Kelly quickly conferred. They decided to employ a strategy familiar to modern-day fans: with the game on the line, the opposition's best hitter at the plate, and first base open, O'Neill received an intentional walk. In 1886, however, this was unheard of, and the *St. Louis Globe-Democrat* even denounced the maneuver as "contemptible." The quick-thinking Kelly apparently devised the strategy, since Anson seemed befuddled.[26]

By walking O'Neill, Clarkson faced Gleason with the bases loaded. A huge crowd, estimated at anywhere between eight and thirteen thousand people, hushed as the local hero entered the batter's box. Gleason took the first two pitches from Clarkson, and Quest called both of them strikes. The second strike seemed questionable to St. Louis partisans, and they broke the silence by howling disapproval at the call. On the third pitch, Gleason lined the ball into center field for a two-run single.[27]

The jubilant crowd rejoiced as Bushong and Latham crossed home to give St. Louis a 4–3 lead. Indeed, this sudden good fortune provoked an unprecedented response. The *Globe-Democrat* claimed the celebration constituted "a scene at the park that has never been equaled on similar occasions in the past . . . Yelling, hand-clapping and cheering, which made a deafening roar of applause, lasted for fully five minutes. Hats, canes, and umbrellas were thrown in the air, men shook hands and embraced each other and the ladies showed their excitement by waving their handkerchiefs." The *Post-Dispatch* insisted that "the whole performance was a fine contrast to the cold showing in a Chicago audience, where enthusiasm is slow in comparison."[28]

However, a small minority of St. Louis supporters gave a darker side to the "five minutes of general insanity." In the left-field bleachers an argument broke out between devotees of the two teams. During the early stages of the game, an advocate of the White Stockings had continually enraged the hometown crowd by directing disparaging remarks at Latham. When Gleason's base hit put the Browns ahead, the Chicago partisan criticized the extended demonstration indulged in by St. Louis fans. Several backers of the Browns then bodily evicted the Chicago loyalist from the bleachers. He landed on the playing field and was pounced on by a furious follower of the Browns. The *Missouri Republican* reported that the two combatants "were rolling about the grass pummeling each other in a vigorous and apparently business-like manner." Meanwhile, approximately two hundred men and boys poured out of the bleachers to gather around the fight. Several other scuffles ensued within this group. Policemen promptly hurried to the melee; they forced the spectators back into the bleachers and evicted the two foremost trouble-makers from Sportsman's Park, but not before the vocal proponent of the White Stockings had been "terribly punished, getting both eyes blacked, a bruised face, and some hard kicks about the body."[29]

When the game finally started again, Comiskey singled into center, driving home O'Neill and putting St. Louis ahead by a score of 5–3. In the sixth inning, though, the White Stockings immediately rallied to tie the score. Chicago sympathizers, outnumbered and intimidated, made "scarcely a ripple of applause" as White Stockings' left fielder Abner Dalrymple tripled into the beer garden with one on and one out.[30] They remained virtually silent when Clarkson singled to right and tied the ball game.

In the bottom of the sixth, after one out, Robinson connected solidly with a Clarkson pitch. The game's longest drive soared into the left-field stands, but it curved slightly foul. Working more cautiously, Clarkson walked Robinson. Bushong, a crowd favorite for his endurance of the physical strains of catching, approached the plate next. He singled on a hard-hit grounder into left field, and the local fans reacted with "tremendous cheers." Then, taking advantage of the nineteenth-century rule that foul balls did not count as strikes, Latham fouled off so many pitches that Clarkson ultimately wound up walking him.[31]

With the bases loaded, Clarkson induced Caruthers to loft a high pop-up on the infield. Second baseman Pfeffer, stationed beneath the ball, could have recorded a simple put-out. However, in 1886, the absence of an infield fly rule allowed Pfeffer leeway to improvise. All three runners anticipated the ball would be caught. Therefore, they wisely stayed near their respective bases. But Pfeffer permitted the pop-up to drop, and all three runners were suddenly forced to advance a base. Hoping to start an inning-ending double play, Pfeffer pounced on the ball and tossed it to shortstop Williamson, covering at second base, for a force-out on Latham. Caruthers alertly ran down the line to first base, so Williamson threw the ball to third base instead. The ball beat Bushong to the bag, but third baseman Burns dropped the throw. Bushong slid in safely, and, meanwhile, Robinson scored the run that put the Browns back ahead, 6–5. With runners at first and third, Clarkson pitched very tentatively to O'Neill and again walked the Browns' slugger.[32] Regardless of whether Clarkson intended to walk O'Neill or not, he now faced Gleason in yet another bases-loaded situation. Gleason responded in precisely the same manner as in the preceding inning, lining another two-run single up the middle of the diamond and into center field. The crowd erupted once more into a frenzy of excitement.

Once the shouting subsided, Comiskey smashed a liner that Burns snared to retire the side. As darkness covered Sportsman's Park, the White Stockings sent up the heart of their batting order in what would obviously be Chicago's last opportunity to erase an 8–5 deficit. Foutz quickly finished them off. First, Anson sent a fly ball sailing into right field that was caught by Caruthers. Pfeffer popped the ball up, and Foutz made the catch. Ned Williamson, the last hope for Chicago, drove a pitch into center field where Welch made the play for the final putout in what the *Republican* portrayed as "one of the greatest games, if not the greatest, known to baseball history."[33]

The *Republican* based its high opinion of Game Four upon the fact that the contest was the first tight struggle of the 1886 World Series and possessed many "qualities which combined to make the game so important." It identified these "qualities" as "the amount of money indirectly involved, the distinguished honor for which the clubs were contending, the strong rivalry between the teams and the two great cities which they represented, the large crowd which witnessed the game and the national interest attending the result."[34]

Game Five contained the same potential as the preceding contest, but fell short of achieving the same epic proportions. Although enlivened by a pregame dispute between Von der Ahe and Spalding, it represented a return to the one-sided games played in Chicago. Von der Ahe, always a showman, arranged for a Mexican band to entertain the crowd prior to the game. The turnout either rivaled or exceeded the vast throng drawn the day before. At this game, the *Republican* observed a larger presence of Browns' fans from the hinterlands of neighboring towns in Missouri and Illinois. It also reported an increase in the number of female spectators, crediting the women for a "softening and refining effect" that resulted in a "more civil and respectful" audience.[35]

The game had been slated to begin at 3 P.M., but the dispute between Von der Ahe and Spalding delayed the start by twenty minutes. Spalding tried to slip Mark Baldwin into the White Stockings' lineup as their starting pitcher. Baldwin had pitched Duluth to the Northwestern League pennant in 1886, and two days after the start of the World Series he had signed an 1887 contract with Chicago.[36]

Von der Ahe objected to the idea of the White Stockings using a player not on their 1886 roster.[37] On the other hand, Spalding insisted that Baldwin truly belonged to the White Stockings since he had signed an 1887 contract with them. The two quarrelsome owners, as agreed in their prior arrangements, took their debate to the Board of Umpires. One of the umpires, "Gracie" Pierce, could not be found. This left the question of Baldwin's eligibility in the hands of John Kelly, Joe Quest, and John McQuade. Quest, perhaps still embittered over Von der Ahe releasing him from the Browns, sided with Spalding. McQuade, an Association umpire whose work was lauded in St. Louis newspapers and criticized by Chicago publications, supported Von der Ahe. Kelly refused to cast the tie-breaking vote. Instead, he instructed Quest and McQuade to resolve the matter with a coin flip. In winning the coin toss, McQuade earned the right to decide the question. He ruled that Baldwin would not be allowed to participate.[38]

This decision left the White Stockings with few pitching options for the fifth game. McCormick, hampered by rheumatism in his leg, had stayed in Chicago to recuperate. Flynn suffered such agonizing pain in his throwing arm that he could not even raise it, much less use it to pitch a baseball. The 1886 White Stockings' pitching staff, featuring a twenty-game winner and two thirty-game winners, had depleted its usefulness. Clarkson alone remained to shoulder the pitching burden. The White Stockings understood the necessity of giving him a day off, since he had pitched twice in a row and three games in four days.[39] In desperation, Anson turned to his shortstop, Ned Williamson.

Anson considered Williamson to be "the greatest all-around ballplayer the country ever saw."[40] Over the preceding six seasons, Williamson had compiled respectable statistics in a limited number of pitching appearances. In eleven games, he had worked a total of thirty-three innings, posted a record of 1–1, and registered an earned-run average of 3.00. Also, Williamson had pitched the final inning of the third game of the 1886 World Series, allowing the Browns only one unearned run. Still, the Browns held an obvious advantage. They simply called upon the usual third man in their rotation, Nat Hudson, who had notched a 16–10 record in his first major-league season.[41]

The Browns quickly capitalized on their superior pitching. After Hudson retired Chicago successfully, St. Louis scored twice against Williamson. In facing five Browns' batters, Williamson allowed three hits and a walk. He only escaped further damage because the Browns' aggressiveness backfired on them. Caruthers and Gleason, striving to stretch their hits into doubles, were both thrown out at second base.[42] A reshuffled defensive alignment compounded the White Stockings' problems. Kelly had been forced to take over Williamson's normal shortstop position, and Frank "Silver" Flint had substituted for him behind the plate. In the second inning, Anson pursued a new strategy. He sent Williamson back to the shortstop spot, moved Kelly to third base, shifted third baseman Burns to right field, and brought in right fielder Jimmy Ryan to pitch. As a rookie, Ryan had made five pitching appearances in 1886, hurling twenty-three innings while posting a rather high 4.63 earned-run average. Since Ryan registered no pitching decisions, Anson apparently used him in one-sided games when the White Stockings were either comfortably ahead or hopelessly behind.[43] Now, with Williamson so ineffective and none of his regular-season pitchers available, Anson turned to the youngster out of sheer desperation.

The Browns broke open a 3–2 contest with four runs in the third inning and three more in the sixth. These runs were partly facilitated by the fielding miscues of Burns in right, Kelly at third, and Flint behind the plate. Ryan's pitching efforts, however, were not solely undermined by shoddy defense. The Browns' batters contributed, too. Ryan pitched five innings, and in that time the Browns tallied eight runs on eight hits (half of them for extra bases). Caruthers spearheaded the Browns' offense with three hits in three at-bats.[44]

Meanwhile, Hudson restricted the entire Chicago team to only three hits, and St. Louis won in a 10–3 rout. Following the game, both Kelly and Pfeffer bestowed lavish praise upon Hudson, the rookie pitcher signed out of the Colorado State League. White Stockings' owner A. G. Spalding refused to accept defeat as graciously. Instead, he raged about Baldwin being declared ineligible. Spalding stubbornly claimed that the White Stockings possessed "a perfect right" to use Baldwin, accused an "unsportsmanlike" Von der Ahe of sticking his nose in where he "had no business to interfere," and concluded his tirade by expressing revulsion at the intense competitiveness of the 1886 World Series. In his typically overstated manner, Spalding portrayed his own actions as the salvation of the sport: "You may thank me that there was not a riot in your baseball park today; and to avoid such a disaster, which might have been ruinous to baseball for all time, I refrained from pitching Baldwin."[45]

Ironically, even though Spalding dwelled incessantly on the dispute over Baldwin, several Chicago newspapers paid little or even no attention to the controversy. They preferred an alternative of claiming a "hippodrome," or fix, was in effect to prolong the World Series and increase the gate receipts. The *Chicago News,* which had previously proclaimed that the White Stockings could defeat the Browns whenever they desired, served as the leading proponent of this conspiracy theory. "The baseball series in Chicago was cleverly worked," it insisted,

1886 Old Judge Cigarette baseball card of Nat Hudson. In the third game of the 1886 World Series, rookie pitcher Hudson was bypassed for the starting assignment. However, given the opportunity to pitch the pivotal fifth game, he turned in a masterful performance to lead the St. Louis Browns to a 10–3 triumph. Missouri Historical Society, St. Louis.

"the public felt that it was being humbugged, but the hippodrome was so artistically played that there really was no inclination to cry out against it. In St. Louis, however, the pins have been set up awkwardly and the wires have been worked bunglingly." Two other Chicago papers, the *Inter-Ocean* and *Times,* joined in the "hippodrome" chorus.[46]

The *News,* however, went much further than any other Chicago paper in flinging accusations at the White Stockings. While the *Inter-Ocean* and *Times* settled for raising suspicions of a fix, the *News* rashly asserted that one existed. In support of such a serious charge, the *News* offered only the flimsiest of purported evidence. For example, in fitting Game Five into its conspiracy theory, the *News* ignored all of the pitching problems faced by the White Stockings—Clarkson's inability to pitch three days in a row, McCormick's rheumatism that left him three hundred miles away in Chicago, Flynn's career-ending arm injury, and Baldwin's ineligibility. Instead of bothering with such facts, the *News* attributed the pitching choice of Williamson to the alleged fix: "The champion League club, having in its membership such pitchers as Clarkson, McCormick, Flynn and Baldwin disdained the services of all these gentlemen and put in the box the very estimable shortstop of the nine!" Similarly, the *News* disregarded the simple logic that Williamson was removed as the Chicago pitcher because of his ineffectiveness. Williamson had faced five St. Louis batters, and four of them had reached base. Rather than admitting the obvious, the *News* preferred to explain that Williamson had pitched very effectively, endangered the fix, and forced Anson to replace him with an inferior hurler. The *News,* after basing their whole case on these two inaccurate pieces of evidence, then deduced that the White Stockings were guilty of "brazenly giving away" Game Five.[47]

Quite understandably, the *Missouri Republican* dismissed such rantings as "sour grapes." The rumored "hippodrome" added, though, to a sense of urgency among St. Louisans. Under the scenario painted by the *Chicago News,* the White Stockings would seek to win the sixth and seventh games. Since the *News* believed the White Stockings could defeat the Browns anytime they wanted, it issued a bold prediction that Chicago would win Game Six to force a deciding seventh contest. The Browns, by winning the World Series in only six games, could forever silence any insinuations that the two teams had prolonged the series into a seven-game affair for the gate receipts. Oliver Wiseman, owner of a St. Louis gambling establishment frequently promoted by the *Sporting News,* appreciated the significance of the sixth game to public opinion: "There has been so much talk of this series being a hippodrome, that if the Browns should happen to lose, although honestly, no one will believe anything but that the Chicagos threw yesterday's game."[48]

Wiseman's Baseball Exchange eagerly covered all of the bets offered on Game Six by a large number of suddenly confident Chicagoans. The *Republican* reported: "Chicago money was brought in by the carload almost, and the cry of 'hippodrome' was raised." After reading their local papers, so many Chicagoans poured into St. Louis seeking to place bets on the White Stockings that they completely reversed the odds on the sixth game. When the baseball exchanges closed at 9 P.M. on Friday night, the Browns rated as slight favorites to win Game Six. But by the next morning, the White Stockings had become a solid 10–8 choice to take the sixth game.[49] The Browns, owing to their 3–2 advantage in games won, remained heavily favored to win the World Series. However, snatching up odds at either 100–70 or 100–80, the newly arrived Chicagoans placed a considerable number of bets upon the eventual outcome.

Anson and Spalding viewed reports of a "hippodrome" with disbelief. Yet both shared the Chicago boosters' faith that the White Stockings would prevail. In response to the talk of a fix, Anson sneered, "These games are for blood." Spalding also disparaged the rumors of the Chicago newspapers as being based upon "ignorance of human nature."[50]

Anson and Spalding derived their trust in a White Stockings' triumph from a more tangible factor. Clarkson, the White Stockings' ace pitcher, had received an off-day before Game Six and could have two more days to rest prior to a potential seventh game. Spalding, convinced that Clarkson was "in good condition," issued a prediction for the remainder of the World Series: "I am sure we will win it. . . . I am confident of winning both games." Immediately before Game Six started, Anson told a St. Louis sportswriter: "I am as satisfied that we will win this game as I am that I am alive."[51]

Throughout most of the afternoon, Clarkson seemed to move relentlessly toward justifying the assurances of Anson and Spalding. In the first four innings of Game Six, Clarkson struck out six Browns' batters and did not surrender any hits or runs. During this portion of the game, only one of the Browns even reached base—O'Neill, who drew a two-out walk in the first inning.[52]

While Clarkson overpowered the Browns, Pfeffer provided almost all of the White Stockings' offense. Leading off the second inning, Pfeffer singled into right field, then stole second and advanced to third on a passed ball. Caruthers nearly escaped the jam. He struck out both Williamson and Burns, but Ryan lined a single into left field to drive Pfeffer home with the game's first run. In the fourth inning, leading off again, Pfeffer knocked the ball deep into right field and circled the bases for a home run.[53]

The Browns, flustered by their inability to hit Clarkson, tried to get the game called in the top of the fifth inning. When a slight drizzle started falling, Comiskey insisted that Umpire "Gracie" Pierce should stop play. Pierce flatly refused, but while Comiskey pursued the argument, thousands of fans swarmed onto the field. A brief delay ensued. At this point, since the contest still fell short of going the five innings required to make it an official game, the Browns stood to gain a huge advantage from a rainout. The White Stockings would have squeezed four stellar innings out of their only able-bodied pitcher with nothing to show for it. Nature frowned, however, upon the attempted manipulations of Comiskey and the St. Louis spectators. The rain halted, a phalanx of twenty policemen forced the crowd back, and play resumed.[54]

Clarkson and Pfeffer picked up exactly where they had left off. After Clarkson again retired the Browns in order, Pfeffer continued his virtual one-man offensive crusade. In the top of the sixth inning, leading off once again, he smashed "a hot grounder" that went through the legs of second baseman Robinson "like greased lightning."[55] The ball also skipped past the grasp of right fielder Foutz, and Pfeffer raced all the way to third base. Welch caught a fly ball that Williamson had driven into deep center field, and Pfeffer tagged up and trotted home to score his third run of the day.

The sixth and seventh innings added further to the discomfort of the Browns and their frenzied followers. An estimated total of eight to twelve thousand people, most of them fiercely loyal to St. Louis, had flocked to Sportsman's Park for the game. They filled every seat, climbed atop the roof, and stood beside the right-field foul line. For a brief moment, in the sixth inning, these pro–St. Louis spectators thought that Bushong might collect their team's first hit against Clarkson. The Browns' catcher sent one of Clarkson's pitches "whizzing to right with great speed." But Pfeffer, again the Browns' nemesis, ranged far from his second-base position to catch up to the ball and throw Bushong out.[56]

Finally, in the seventh inning, the Browns' boosters received something to cheer about as O'Neill powered a pitch to deep right-center and reached third base ahead of Chicago's relay throw from the outfield. Such joy quickly subsided, though, after O'Neill overran the bag and was tagged out by third baseman Burns. Even the first St. Louis base hit resulted in an out.[57]

Caruthers had limited the White Stockings to only five hits, and he continued his fine work in the top of the eighth inning, in which neither of the National League's top two batters, Kelly or Anson, were able to hit the ball out of the infield. First, Caruthers disposed of Kelly on a pop-up that settled in the hands of third baseman Latham. Next, Anson rapped a grounder. Shortstop Gleason scooped it up and threw to first ahead of the Chicago player-manager. Then, Caruthers faced Pfeffer, his persistent plague. Pfeffer, a right-handed hitter, drove a pitch to the opposite field for the fourth straight time. On this occasion, though, right fielder Foutz loped under the fly ball and made the catch.[58]

Leading off the bottom of the eighth, Comiskey inspired his troops with a line-drive single into right field. The next batter, Welch, caught Chicago by surprise by bunting the ball down the third-base line. Welch, a very fast runner, sprinted to first base well in advance of the throw from third baseman Burns. Burns should have conceded the base hit and merely held onto the ball; instead, he tried in vain to throw Welch out at first. The hurried throw landed "in front of Anson . . . bounded, struck his left arm, and glanced off." While the bulky Anson lumbered after the baseball, the speedier Comiskey rushed all the way home with the Browns' first run of the game. Meanwhile, Welch reversed directions and advanced to second. The hometown crowd reacted so fervently that the proceedings were stopped for a few minutes.[59]

When the game commenced again, Clarkson temporarily recovered. He retired the following two hitters, although Welch sped to third when a pitch was momentarily fumbled by catcher Kelly. In order to close the 3–1 deficit, the Browns now required either a two-out hit or a Chicago mistake. They got both. First, Clarkson blundered by losing location of the strike zone and walking Bushong, whose .223 average marked him as the poorest-hitting player in St. Louis's starting lineup.[60] This brief lapse in control created a confrontation between Clarkson and the Browns' lead-off batter, Latham, with the potential tying runs on base.

Latham had been a target of controversy throughout the series. His constant chatter won him the nickname of "The Freshest Man on Earth," but earned the enmity of Chicago journalists as well.[61] Three different Chicago papers had portrayed Latham as, among many other insulting comments, "an antiquated idiot," "a hoodlum," and "the worst nuisance ever." A fourth, the *Chicago News,* complained that Latham's "tiresome exhibitions of alley wit" served to "degrade the national game in the estimation of reputable folk" by interjecting "the coarse, cheap buffoonery of the beer saloon and the stables." St. Louis newspapers had defended Latham; the *Globe-Democrat* wrote, "Latham's merry and entertaining way was decidedly refreshing . . . after gazing at the silent, statue-like Chicagos." The *Sporting News* conceded that Latham "reminds one of a calliope as he shoots off his mouth in one hundred different tones at the same time," but still gave him credit for infusing "life and spirit to the game."[62]

In Game Six, attempting to give Latham a taste of his own medicine, Anson and Kelly harassed him ceaselessly. Except for brief batting stints, Anson stood in the third-base coaching box whenever the White Stockings went to bat. From there, he ridiculed Latham by beseeching each Chicago batter: "Knock it right down here! This is the weak spot. Here's our puddin'!"[63]

Latham maintained an unusual quietness, bided his time, and then flamboyantly delivered the first "called shot" in World Series history. He broke his silence while Clarkson pitched to Bushong. When Bushong neared the total of six balls needed to draw a walk, Latham implored the teammate he had fought only a few months earlier: "Get your base now, Bush, and I'll bring you both in!"[64]

After Bushong walked, the Browns possessed runners at first and third—a situation where they frequently made use of the double steal. Moving to the plate, Latham paused and counseled Bushong against trying to steal second: "Stay there, Bush, and I'll bring you both in!" On a three-ball, two-strike count, Latham golfed a low pitch from Clarkson. The ball left the bat on a rising trajectory that fooled the Chicago left fielder, Abner Dalrymple. Dalrymple miscalculated the apex of the hit and dashed forward for what he mistook to be a sinking line drive. The baseball soared over his head, landed on the outfield grass, and rolled all the way to the left-field fence.[65] Before the White Stockings

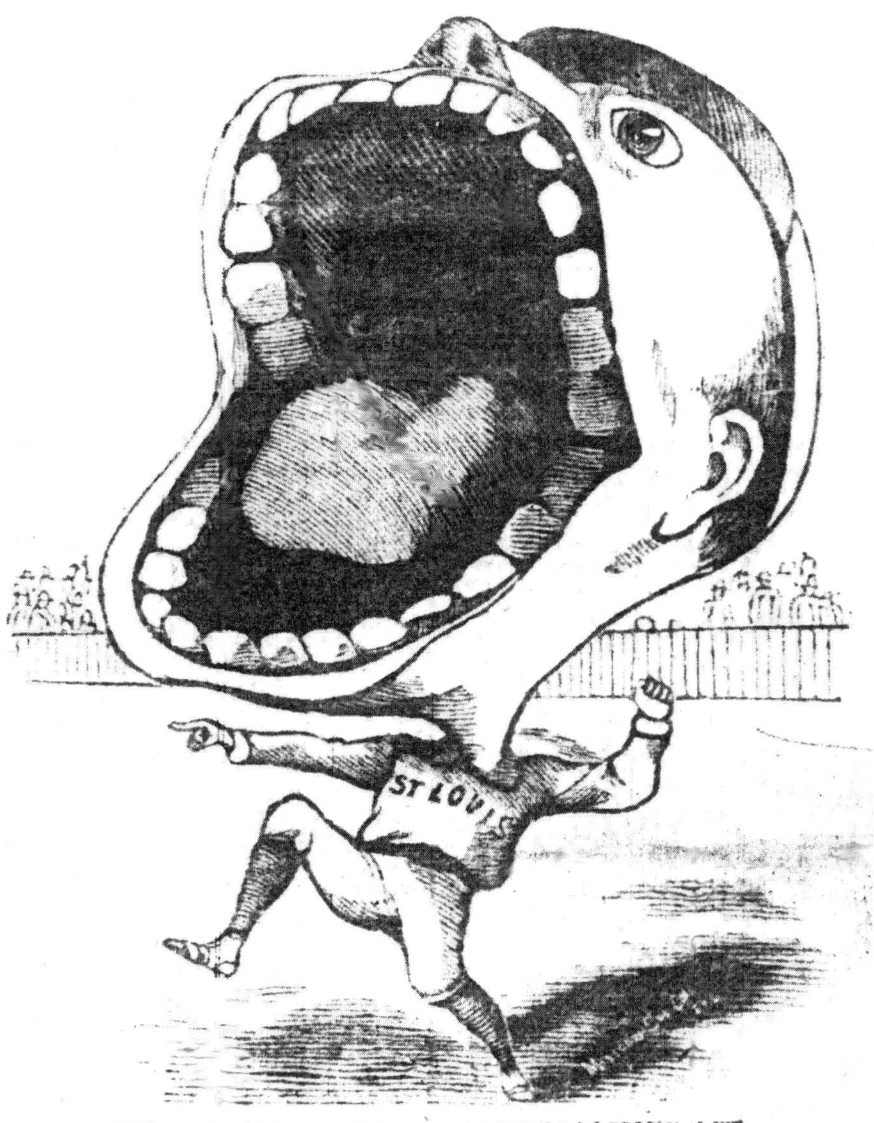
ARLIE LATHAM IN HIS GREAT COACHING ACT.

An 1887 *Sporting News* cartoon of Arlie Latham. State Historical Society of Missouri, Columbia.

could return the ball to the infield, both Welch and Bushong scored to tie the game at 3–3.

Latham hustled into third with a triple, and the pent-up emotions of the Sportsman's Park faithful finally erupted. The *Globe-Democrat* described "a scene that will never be forgotten by those who were present," an early form of participatory theater in which fans "yelled and cheered until they grew hoarse . . . shook hands and embraced each other, turned somersaults on the grandstand and [on] the field, and . . . actually wept tears of joy." Adhering to the nineteenth-century ritual of demonstrating enthusiasm, the crowd filled the sky with any article readily at hand—hats, handkerchiefs, and umbrellas. This general uproar lasted for five minutes before the game resumed. When it did, Caruthers missed an opportunity to give himself the lead. Instead, he bounced a grounder to third baseman Burns, who threw the St. Louis pitcher out at first.[66]

Caruthers took his spot in the pitcher's box to start the ninth inning. He struck out Williamson, but Burns doubled to right-center, becoming the first Chicago runner since Robinson's error on Pfeffer's sharply hit ball in the sixth. Caruthers, who had last surrendered a base hit back in the fourth inning, almost allowed another one to the very next batter. Ryan lashed a vicious grounder, but shortstop Gleason fielded it and threw to first for the out. With a runner at third, Caruthers struck out Dalrymple on three pitches.[67]

The Browns came to bat in the bottom of the ninth, needing only one run to claim the World Series title. O'Neill, their leading slugger, clouted a pitch to the deepest part of right-center. It looked like the ball might clear the fence for a game-winning homer, but at the last possible moment right fielder Ryan leaped high and "made one of the most remarkable catches ever seen." Clarkson then retired both Gleason and Comiskey, forcing the first extra-inning game in World Series play.[68]

Caruthers struck out Clarkson to start the tenth inning. He had registered only two strikeouts in the first eight innings, but had now victimized three of the last five batters. Left fielder O'Neill made consecutive putouts on fly balls from George Gore and Kelly to bring the top of the tenth to a close. Caruthers, who had retired nineteen of the last twenty-one Chicago hitters, sauntered off the diamond. The frail-looking Browns' pitcher, rumored to have a serious heart ailment, had effectively silenced the persistent gossip that poor health would prevent him from playing in the World Series. Instead, Caruthers had converted the series into a showcase of his versatile playing skills.[69]

The Browns came to bat again, still needing just one run to win the World Series. Their crafty center fielder, Welch, led off. In his last at-bat, he had reached base on a bunt single down the third-base line. This time, he ducked his shoulder into a Clarkson pitch. Umpire Pierce, enforcing an American Association rule, awarded first base to Welch. Anson vehemently objected that Welch should not be given first base, since he had failed to make any effort at avoiding the pitch. After listening to this contention, Pierce changed his mind and rescinded the original call. Welch stormed angrily back into the batter's box. On the next pitch from Clarkson, Welch slashed a single into center field.[70]

Then, Foutz, swinging down at the ball with a chopping motion, sent a high bounder over the head of the pitcher. Williamson, the Chicago shortstop, charged toward the ball as it descended midway between Clarkson and second base. He bobbled the ball and lost any possible chance to turn a difficult play. The Browns now had runners on second and first with nobody out.[71]

Amidst encouragement to "hit her out," Robinson moved to the plate. Comiskey, however, chose to pursue a different managerial strategy: Robinson bunted the ball down the third-base line. Even though Burns fielded the ball cleanly and threw Robinson out at first, Welch moved over to third. With a runner at third and only one out, Robinson's sacrifice bunt created a multitude of possible ways to score the winning run.[72]

The sacrifice bunt also set the stage for the most famous play in the history of nineteenth-century baseball. In a relatively recent publication, Lowell Reidenbaugh of the *Sporting News* described the winning play of the 1886 World Series: "The deciding run was scored in the tenth inning of the final game by Curt Welch. Newspaper accounts of the day reported that Welch scored on a wild pitch. [Modern] history has recorded the play as a steal of home."[73]

The uncertainty surrounding the winning run apparently stems from an account given by Charles Comiskey. In a 1919 biography, Gustav Axelson included Comiskey's recollection of the decisive run. Comiskey stated that Welch was running on the pitch, drew a pitchout, and crossed home safely on a "$15,000 Slide" that gave St. Louis the entire gate receipts of the winner-take-all World Series. Later, Arlie Latham related a similar version of Welch's "steal" to author Robert Smith, who included it in his landmark 1947 work *Baseball* and other books he wrote on the history of the sport. Together, Axelson and Smith ensured that the former Browns' narrative of the "$15,000 Slide" passed into baseball folklore.[74]

One contemporary newspaper report seems to corroborate part of the description offered by Comiskey and Latham. According to the *Chicago News,* as soon as third baseman Burns "gave Kelly a signal to catch Welch at third," the Chicago catcher responded by calling a pitchout. A mishap transpired, though, between the Chicago batterymates: "Kelly played away from the plate . . . but Clarkson put a ball over the plate which Kelly just touched with his fingers and bounded away to the grandstand, while Welch came in with the winning run."[75]

Other nineteenth-century newspapers said nothing about a steal, but instead debated whether Welch scored on a wild pitch or a passed ball. While the

Curt Welch. State Historical Society of Missouri, Columbia.

Chicago Tribune considered the play a passed ball on the part of Kelly, three St. Louis publications—the *Republican, Globe-Democrat,* and *Sporting News*—claimed Clarkson had been guilty of a wild pitch. The *Post-Dispatch* tried to settle the question by simply asking Kelly. The Chicago catcher seemed willing to accept responsibility ("I would say it was a passed ball"), yet he also emphasized how difficult it was to catch this particular pitch: "I signaled Clarkson for a low ball on one side, and when it came it was high up on the other. It struck my hand as I tried to get it. . . . Clarkson told me that it slipped from his hands."[76]

One might suspect that Comiskey and Latham embellished their tales of the play when they later recalled it, some thirty-three and sixty-one years after Welch scored. But it would be a very smug act on the part of present-day historians to state definitively that they understood an event better than two eyewitnesses.

Without photographic evidence of any sort, we must rely on the various first-hand accounts to recreate what may have happened on the "$15,000 Slide." Except for the reminiscences of Comiskey and Latham, no primary sources indicate that Welch was running with the pitch or ever slid across the plate. Still, Comiskey's detailed analysis of the play cannot be altogether dismissed as mere baseball mythology. In fact, the Comiskey/Latham explanation meshes well in some aspects with some of the contemporary newspaper reports. For example, the two old Browns agreed with the *Chicago News'* assertion that Kelly called for a pitchout. On Clarkson's first pitch to Bushong, Welch danced down the third-base line, straying so far from the bag that Kelly "could have nailed him easily" with a throw.[77] Seeing this, Burns and Kelly cooked up a scheme to trap the reckless Browns' runner in the snare of a pitchout. Meanwhile, Comiskey, stationed at the third-base coaching box, encouraged Welch to take another long lead. This strategy distressed Clarkson, and it would have enabled Welch to get a great start for home on any grounder hit by Bushong.

As the scene actually unfolded, the first of these advantages came into play. Clarkson, aware of Welch's capability to steal home, certainly seemed to ponder the prospect. While Welch scampered down the third-base line, the *Globe-Democrat* observed the disturbing effect this exerted upon the Chicago pitcher: "Clarkson, who is usually so cool, was visibly nervous. He rolled and twisted the ball around in his hands several times before he got in position to pitch it." A distracted pitcher, under such circumstances, might balk in a run, uncork a wild pitch, or even miss his catcher's signal for a pitchout. It appears plausible that Clarkson simply missed the pitchout signal and later, rather than admitting his mental mistake to Kelly, presented instead the physical alibi of a pitch that "slipped from his hands."[78] So at the same moment Kelly moved away from the plate in expectation of a low outside pitchout that would allow him to make a quick throw to third, Clarkson let go a high inside fastball designed to jam Bushong and force a futile infield pop-up. Kelly barely managed to reach back and get his fingers on the ball, but he could not prevent it from rolling all the way to the grandstand as Welch scored the winning run.

The only question left to resolve is precisely what Welch did once the pitch was released. It is possible to surmise that Welch instantly recognized the miscommunication between the Chicago batterymates, and as soon as the ball left Clarkson's hand, galloped ahead thinking he could reach home before Kelly ever got to the errant pitch. However, Ed Sheridan, reporting in both the *Republican* and the *Sporting News,* strongly suggested otherwise with his brief notation: "Welch trotted home."[79] This same comment also indicates that, in all probability, Welch did not slide home.

The primary significance of the "$15,000 Slide" was that it represented a dramatic "culminating point of a two-years' agitation." In recognition of this long struggle against the Chicago White Stockings, thousands of St. Louisans reacted euphorically. The *Republican* described an immediate "electrical" crowd response to the play. It noted that as soon as Welch crossed home with the winning run, "One fearful shout arose and then a portion of the crowd sprang out on the field." From a gathering estimated at ten thousand, the *Globe-Democrat* figured "more than half of them made a grand rush for the players, yelling and making all manner of noises and demonstrations." Reciprocating the enthusiasm of their fans, the Browns "joined in the shouting; tossed their caps in the air; performed somersaults and other difficult feats and acted in a manner that would impress a foreigner . . . with the idea that he was trespassing upon the ground set apart for the exclusive use of the violently insane." Eventually, rambunctious spectators hoisted the entire starting nine upon their shoulders and carried the victorious players off the field. Deposited at their dressing room, the Browns barricaded the door to ensure privacy. Some five thousand frenzied fans waited outside, "cheering and shouting for the Browns without a halt for fully half an hour." As the echoes of these vigorous yells reverberated again and again, the *Tribune* noticed that the grandstand of Sportsman's Park "shook and trembled like a leaf."[80]

The crowd remained until each of the Browns emerged in their street clothes to prolonged cheers and spirited handshakes. Many of these spectators viewed the players as heroes because the ball club had enabled them to win sizeable wagers. The *Republican* estimated that "fully $100,000 changed hands on the result of the game" in St. Louis alone.[81]

St. Louis newspapers responded to the Browns' victory with equal spirit. In the *Sporting News,* Al Spink reveled most in "the death blow it dealt to that class who are ever ready to shout hippodrome." The *Chicago News,* the primary agent for spreading this rumor, finally capitulated: "Humiliating as the confession is, we are obliged to admit that the champion baseball players of the world reside in St. Louis. . . . The fact is, the St. Louis Brown Stockings are, as a team, better players than the Chicago men." Besides reprinting such admissions of defeat, St. Louis newspapers delighted in ridiculing the city of Chicago, their baseball team, its manager, and the league in which it played. The *Globe-Democrat* could not resist offering a few wise words of advice to Chicago: "Let us hope that the lesson of defeat will not be entirely lost upon Chicago, but that she will soon learn that while wind and mortgages will go a certain length in building up a city, brains, capital and muscle will go a great deal further in the same direction." Anson served as a particular target for insults on the sports page, the editorial page, and even in an advertisement. One remark recalled his boastful comments following the White Stockings' opening-game victory: "Baby Anson can now tell his

KNOCKED OUT

THEY LAUGH THAT WIN.

Hurrah for Old St. Louis

After an exciting contest the St. Louis Browns, now dubbed the Champions of the World, knock out Anson's Babies from the windy city.

The Browns the Champions of the World.

Reader, we've gained our object---we've caught your eye. Read what we have to say about

The Apparel of Mankind!

Cartoon advertisement for a men's clothing store. State Historical Society of Missouri, Columbia.

Chicago admirers how his team practiced with the Browns." The editorial page of the *Republican* parodied the earlier assertions of National League superiority made by Anson and the *Chicago News:* "The Chicago baseball club plays a very good game for a League team. . . . If the windy city has any more stuffed clubs, St. Louis is prepared to reduce the swelling on very reasonable terms."[82]

Beneath a headline of "They Never Lie: Figures in the Case of the League Vs. the Association," the *Post-Dispatch* provided documentation of American Association superiority to the National League. The Association's best team, the Browns, defeated the League's top club, the White Stockings, in the 1886 World Series. In other postseason tests of comparative strength, the second-place Association team (the Pittsburgh Alleghenys) beat the second-place League club (the Detroit Wolverines); the third-place Association team (the Brooklyn Trolley-Dodgers) won against the third-place League team (the New York Giants); and the last-place team in the Association (the Baltimore Orioles) emerged victorious over the League's last-place finisher (the Washington Statesmen). Out of thirty postseason games between Association and League teams, the *Post-Dispatch* showed that American Association clubs won nineteen of these contests, lost nine times, and played two ties.[83]

Chris Von der Ahe seemingly derived his greatest pleasure from conquering A. G. Spalding, his rival who had insisted that the 1885 World Series was a tie. Reminiscing about the decisive sixth game of the 1886 Series, the Browns' owner mentioned that he spent the entire afternoon on the players' bench, sitting beside Spalding. This certainly constituted a bizarre scene—one of baseball's most strait-laced moralists, Spalding, and probably the game's most uninhibited promoter, Von der Ahe, side by side watching their two teams struggle for the title. Von der Ahe recalled that while the White Stockings were controlling the early portion of the contest, Spalding constantly pestered him to telegraph O. P. Caylor in Cincinnati and make arrangements for the deciding seventh game. Then, chuckling merrily, Von der Ahe pictured Spalding's reaction to the Browns' comeback: "When we began to count, you ought to see how his face dropped." After the reality of the "$15,000 Slide" had soaked in, Von der Ahe hastily wired Spalding, who had returned to Chicago, promising to make arrangements for the teams to play again at Cincinnati, *if* the White Stockings would enjoy participating in "an exhibition game." Spalding promptly wired back: "Friend Von der Ahe: We must decline with our compliments. We know when we have had enough. Yours truly, A. G. Spalding P.S. Anson joins me in the above message." Von der Ahe proudly displayed this telegram to St. Louis journalists, who then published it in their newspapers.[84]

Actually, the 1886 World Series represented a double triumph for Von der Ahe over Spalding: the Browns had defeated the White Stockings not only on the di-

1886 Old Judge Cigarette baseball card of Chris Von der Ahe. Von der Ahe, the Browns, and the American Association stood on top of the baseball world of 1886. The Old Judge Cigarette Company, clearly perceiving Von der Ahe's prominence, included the Browns' owner in their 1886 series of baseball cards. Missouri Historical Society, St. Louis.

amond but also at the box office. The three contests in Chicago yielded receipts of $6,554.25, while the three St. Louis games netted $7,365.85. These figures vindicated the business principles of Von der Ahe and the American Association; by drawing the masses to the ballpark with half-price tickets and then profiting from ensuing liquor sales, Von der Ahe had brought in more revenue than Spalding.

From the winner-take-all World Series, the Browns' owner pocketed $13,920.10. Von der Ahe split the proceeds evenly between himself and his players, meaning that the dozen members of the Browns each received a World Series share of $580, a reward better appreciated when compared to the average annual income for a manufacturing worker, which ranged from $345 in 1880 to $427 in 1890.[85]

On November 3, Von der Ahe held a banquet for the Browns at the Elks' Club. The Mermod-Jaccard Jewelry Company presented golden scarf-pins studded with diamonds to each member of the Browns. Congressman John J. O'Neill delivered a memorable speech. Scoffing about those "people at Washington [who] accused him of neglecting his official duties to look after baseball matters," O'Neill proclaimed a personal conviction "that when he was engaged in any service that would promote the national game, he was doing the public just as much good as he would be in talking tariff and labor in Congress."[86] Von der Ahe, within two decades of arriving in America as a German immigrant, owned a baseball team acclaimed as the best in the profession—one whose daily affairs concerned his local congressman equally as much as the leading political issues of the era.

The 1886 World Series marked the zenith for Von der Ahe, the Browns, and the American Association. Von der Ahe had enjoyed the best attendance in the major leagues for three of his five American Association seasons. His Browns unquestionably had beaten the White Stockings and settled beyond doubt their right to lay claim to the world's championship. For the second consecutive year, American Association teams had won a majority of their games against National League opponents. Furthermore, the Association, in all five years of its existence, had attracted more fans per game than the National League.[87]

The next five years would not be nearly as successful. Yet even over these five tumultuous seasons, the Association and its most visible franchise, Von der Ahe's St. Louis Browns, continued to exert a profound influence, and they would leave a lasting legacy to the sport of baseball.

Part III

The Survival of Major League Baseball in St. Louis, 1887–1891

8

Farewell to Five "Old War Horses"

> Baseball is a mighty uncertain business and for that reason it is hard to tell just what will happen. I have been offered a place in the [National] League time and again and so have other clubs in the American [Association], but as far as I am concerned, I am satisfied to remain just where I am.
>
> —Chris Von der Ahe, quoted in the *Sporting News,* September 27, 1886

> Each decade brings some great team to the front, some team that outclasses all the others and that shows the way until the break comes and then it must step aside and give way to a younger and better organization, for youth must be served.
>
> —Charles Comiskey, speaking to Al Spink, about the ebb and flow of baseball dynasties, 1910

In early November 1886, A. G. Spalding returned from a hunting retreat in the wilds of the Dakotas with renewed determination to overcome the superiority of the American Association. He barely stopped in Chicago before traveling to Pittsburgh. Less than a week after coming back from his hunting trip, the Chicago White Stockings' owner persuaded the Pittsburgh Alleghenys to defect from the American Association to the National League.[1]

Spalding had not introduced a new plan. Earlier, after the 1885 season, both the Alleghenys and the Brooklyn Trolley-Dodgers had rejected offers to join the National League. Likewise, on the eve of the 1886 World Series, Chris Von der Ahe, owner of the American Association champion St. Louis Browns, had proclaimed his intentions to resist National League overtures and keep the Browns in the Association.[2] Within a month of the Browns' triumph over the White Stockings in the World Series, Spalding achieved the League's first breakthrough at luring away an Association team. The National League owed this newfound success to Spalding's ability to capitalize upon the internal disputes of the Association.

The *Pittsburgh Referee* cited two major factors behind the Alleghenys' decision to switch leagues. "One of the principal reasons why the Allegheny directors entered the League," the paper explained, "was on account of their aversion to Sunday games. It has long been an open secret that they were opposed to having their players participate in games on Sunday." In fact, Pennsylvania blue laws did prevent the Alleghenys from playing Sunday games at home; therefore, the team's board of directors could not derive any financial benefits from Sunday games.[3] Since they could not profit from Sunday games at home, the Alleghenys certainly raised no objections to the National League's restriction against playing on the Sabbath. However, a year earlier, this professed "aversion to Sunday games" had not stopped the Alleghenys from choosing to stay in the American Association.

The Pittsburgh newspaper, with its second interpretation, provided a clearer analysis of the Alleghenys' change of heart. Praising the move to the National League as "a change for the better," the *Referee* explained: "Everybody knows the vast differences between the League and Association's manner of doing business, the one is straight-forward and on thorough business principles, while the other is considerably on the circus order." In their last American Association season, though, the Alleghenys had attained new heights of success. On the field they put together their best record and highest finish, trailing only the Browns in the standings. At the box office the team attracted more fans than ever before and outdrew every major-league team with the exception of the Browns.[4] Yet the Sam Barkley case had persuaded the Alleghenys that the Association operated its business affairs "considerably on the circus order."

Barkley, the starting second baseman on the Browns' first pennant-winner in 1885, had sought an opportunity to play somewhere else. Von der Ahe, trying to accommodate the disgruntled ballplayer, had shopped Barkley to both the Baltimore Orioles and the Alleghenys at a suggested purchase price of $1,000. Eventually, both clubs sent Von der Ahe his asking price, and both clubs signed Barkley to an 1886 contract. A quarrel commenced over which team legitimately owned Barkley's services. The Association's board of directors awarded Barkley to Pittsburgh as long as the player paid a hundred-dollar fine and served a year-long suspension for his "duplicity" and "dishonorable conduct" in signing multiple contracts.[5]

This decision had provoked controversy. It had increased displeasure within ownership circles over the performance of Denny McKnight, the American Association president and also an investor in the Pittsburgh team, who was perceived as giving his own club preferential treatment in the Barkley case. Consequently, in March 1886 the Association had ousted McKnight from power. Also, the year-long suspension had infuriated Barkley. At Pittsburgh he had filed suit in the Common Pleas Court, demanding to be reinstated immediately. The American

Association had settled out of court, raising Barkley's fine to five hundred dollars in exchange for dropping the suspension. Behind the scenes, though, it had apparently forced the Alleghenys to pay Barkley's fine and to provide compensation to Baltimore in the form of first baseman Milt Scott. William A. Nimick, the president of the Alleghenys' board of directors, had been outraged at the Association's actions of firing McKnight, fining Barkley, and compensating Baltimore.[6] When Spalding succeeded in convincing Nimick and the Alleghenys that such a "circus" would never have occurred in the National League, the Pittsburgh Alleghenys departed the Association and entered the League.

The loss of Pittsburgh marked the start of the decline of the American Association. The Alleghenys were a valuable franchise, both as a gate attraction in Pittsburgh and as a competitive team that enhanced attendance elsewhere. In 1886, for the fifth straight year, the Association had drawn larger crowds to their games than had the National League. Also, for the first time since their 1883 expansion, the Association had fielded eight teams that all turned a profit. The National League used the Alleghenys to replace the Kansas City Cowboys, the team with the worst attendance in the major leagues in 1886. As a poor substitute for Pittsburgh, the American Association turned to the Cleveland Blues, who would have the worst attendance in the major leagues in 1887. In 1887, for the first time the average attendance at League games exceeded the average attendance of Association games.[7]

Even more damaging, the National League's raid of Pittsburgh encouraged National League operators to persist in their efforts to entice away other American Association clubs. The remaining members of the American Association, a league composed of "cliques within cliques," presented inviting targets.[8] Following the transfer of Pittsburgh, each of the next three Association seasons unfolded under the shadow of rumored defections.

Throughout most of 1887, considerable speculation surrounded the defending world champion St. Louis Browns. At various points of the season, reports indicated that Von der Ahe seemed on the verge of: (1) selling the Browns for $100,000 to newspaper publisher Joseph Pulitzer, who planned to move them to New York and possibly into the National League as well; (2) buying an interest in the Philadelphia Athletics, dividing the current Browns' roster between Philadelphia and St. Louis, and then enlisting both the Athletics and the Browns in a consolidated partnership of the strongest Association and League clubs; (3) accepting a $25,000 offer to transfer the Browns into the National League; and (4) moving the Browns to New York and staying put in the American Association.[9]

Rumors about the Browns began circulating during an early season road trip; on June 4 the *Sporting News* featured a pair of front-page articles on the future prospects of the team. One account, filed by a New York correspondent, claimed "there is something more than smoke to the rumor that New York parties offered to purchase the St. Louis Browns." Pulitzer, who left the *St. Louis Post-Dispatch* to take over the *New York World* in 1883, allegedly proposed paying Von der Ahe $100,000 to buy the world champions. This report insisted that Von der Ahe accompanied the Browns on their eastern road trip just so he could meet Pulitzer "with a view to closing the deal." It implied that the sale would not be completed until November when Pulitzer could transfer the Browns to not only New York but also the National League. However, it also held out the possibility that Pulitzer might purchase the Browns, move them to New York, and keep the franchise in the American Association.[10]

The other report, written by the Browns' team secretary, George Munson, cautioned, "Believe no fairy tales emanating from New York concerning the sale of the St. Louis Browns to New York parties." In dismissing this New York "fairy tale," Munson included Von der Ahe's firm denial of the rumored sale: "The St. Louis Browns will stay in St. Louis until baseball ceases to be the national game. I have never for a moment thought of selling them to New York parties, nor would I sell them for twice a hundred thousand dollars."[11]

Pulitzer's involvement remains an open question. But over the next six months so many varying stories emerged that it now appears that Von der Ahe was thinking about transferring the Browns to either New York or Philadelphia, or possibly into the National League, or perhaps both. Continuing their road trip, the Browns traveled from New York to Philadelphia, where a new batch of rumors surfaced. This time, reports suggested that Von der Ahe wanted to acquire either a half or two-thirds interest in the Philadelphia Athletics. The *St. Louis Post-Dispatch* speculated that Von der Ahe's projected purchase of the Athletics "is part of the big scheme which has been maturing for some time past, looking to the consolidation of the best clubs in the American [Association] and National [League]." It claimed Von der Ahe was "known to be in co-operation" with other owners who favored consolidation, although "for prudential reasons he is unwilling to talk freely."[12]

The Athletics were jointly owned by three men: Lew Simmons, Charlie Mason, and Billy Sharsig. In his dispatch to the *Sporting News,* George Munson acknowledged that Von der Ahe had offered Simmons and Mason $35,000 for their interests. This offer, however, had been rebuffed; Simmons and Mason demanded $100,000. At that point, Von der Ahe cut off the negotiations, but he confided to the *Post-Dispatch* that he had planned some major personnel changes for the Philadelphia Athletics: "If I had got hold of the club, not a half interest, but a controlling interest, I would have transferred the Browns to this city, or at least enough of them to have formed a championship team."[13]

Perhaps Von der Ahe stopped pursuing the Philadelphia deal because he felt that Simmons and Mason would not accept a compromise settlement. Or, more likely, he lost interest after prominent National League figures expressed opposition to consolidation. During the same week that Von der Ahe was attempting to purchase the Athletics, the *Post-Dispatch* observed an apparent change in the attitude of Spalding, the most influential National League owner, toward the proposed merger: "The consolidation scheme is receiving favorable comment from every baseball manager in the country except from Spalding, the one man in the business who was its strongest advocate. This seems significant."[14]

Shortly afterwards, National League President Nick Young explained that the issue of Sunday games loomed as the major stumbling block in the path of the consolidation plan. Spalding held such adamant views on this particular issue that he reportedly intended "to wash his hands of the game" if the National League ever accepted Sunday play. Young felt that the League would "never have Sunday games" as long as "those now prominent in the councils continue to exert any influence." In contrast, he believed the Association would refuse any "terms of consolidation which did not embrace the Sunday contests."[15]

Despite Von der Ahe's conflict with the National League over Sunday games, another rumor quickly developed. It hinted that Von der Ahe intended to accept a $25,000 offer to transfer the Browns into the National League. Such gossip seemed plausible since Sunday baseball in St. Louis was undergoing its most severe test. Sabbatarians, in control of the Missouri legislature, threatened the future of Sunday games. In 1883 the state legislature passed the Downing Sunday law, "which prohibited amusements of all kinds." St. Louis brewery interests, however, managed to keep beer flowing every Sunday in local saloons by turning to "the law of 1857." In that year the Missouri state legislature had adopted an act allowing the citizens of each city within St. Louis County to decide the fate of Sunday beer and wine sales with a municipal election. A year later more than 70 percent of St. Louisans voted in favor of Sunday beer and wine sales. Thus due to this overwhelming expression of local support, such sales continued each Sunday in St. Louis, even after the passage of the Downing Sunday law. In March 1887, though, the Sabbatarians struck again, passing an act that repealed "the law of 1857." Sunday closing laws against a wide array of popular amusements—including baseball games and beer or wine sales—were to be strictly enforced in St. Louis, effective June 19, 1887.[16]

Von der Ahe, admitting that the Sunday law was "a subject which is now worrying me more than anything else," protested: "Whether baseball in St. Louis will pay without Sunday games is, I consider, a doubtful question. . . . I think it very strange that as harmless a sport as baseball should be interrupted in this way." Initially, Von der Ahe intended to circumvent the law. He rented a ball field in East St. Louis and planned to play Sunday games on the Illinois side of the Mississippi River. But the Illinois state legislature enacted their own prohibition against Sunday games and stymied Von der Ahe's efforts. Utterly disgusted with the sanctimonious Sabbatarians, the *Sporting News* complained, "The lot of the non-churchgoing people of this town from this time forward promises to be anything but a happy one."[17]

In exchange for police permission to stage Sunday games at Sportsman's Park, Von der Ahe offered to forgo beer sales for the day. The police board refused his request. Ultimately, however, Von der Ahe was not forced to give up either Sunday ball games or beer sales. Instead, Judge Edward A. Noonan, of the Court of Criminal Correction, saved Sunday baseball in St. Louis. The thirty-seven-year-old Noonan, a rising star in the state Democratic Party, had received a rare political endorsement the year before from the *Sporting News* for previous rulings that had maintained both Sunday baseball and boxing matches in the city. In the summer of 1887 Judge Noonan heard two important cases testing the legality of Sunday closing laws. On June 26, 1887—the second Sunday that the closing laws were enforced in St. Louis—a saloon owner named Joseph Schnaider deliberately defied the new restriction. Schnaider had been selected by the Brewers' Association to challenge the Sunday laws. As expected, the local police soon arrived at Schnaider's saloon, where they arrested him for selling Sunday beers to his thirsty customers. On July 8 the Court of Criminal Correction rendered a decision in the case: Noonan dismissed the charges against Schnaider, thus upholding the legal right of St. Louis saloons to sell beer and wine on Sundays.[18]

Noonan then tackled the question of Sunday baseball games. Originally, Von der Ahe had planned to test the Sunday law at the first opportunity that presented itself—Sunday, June 26. However, Joseph G. Lodge, who served as the primary defense attorney for both Schnaider and Von der Ahe, persuaded the Browns' owner to wait until after a decision had been reached in Schnaider's test case. Von der Ahe, encouraged by Noonan's verdict in favor of Schnaider, briefly hoped to avoid a confrontation with the police altogether. But the police board insisted upon a showdown. After the board convened for an hour on the night following Noonan's decision in the Schnaider case, Police Chief Anton Huebler announced that his department would henceforth focus upon enforcing the Sunday closing laws against "any saloon-keeper caught selling distilled liquors" or "any baseball or theatre manager who violates the law." Again, on the eve of the Browns' game scheduled for Sunday, July 10, Huebler proclaimed that there would be "no game tomorrow if the police in the city can prevent it." Von der Ahe refused to submit meekly to entrenched authority: "I will try to play tomorrow's game. If the men are arrested, I will have bond on hand and will make a test case of it. I do not

Edward A. Noonan. State Historical Society of Missouri, Columbia.

oppose the law merely because it deprives me of money, but because I do not believe the law is just."[19]

By game time on Sunday afternoon, approximately eight thousand spectators had gathered at Sportsman's Park. It was a substantial turnout, but the *Missouri Republican* thought that the matchup of the first-place Browns against the second-place Baltimore Orioles might have drawn "twelve thousand to fifteen thousand" if not for the anticipated interruption from the police. About three weeks earlier in Baltimore a game between the two teams had ended prematurely due to a near riot, and, under normal circumstances, the incident would have added to the size of the Sunday crowd at Sportsman's Park. However, many prospective spectators shied away from Sportsman's Park when they saw it was surrounded by twenty-five mounted policemen. The police presence probably would have hurt attendance even more if Von der Ahe, in a wily public relations move, had not carried out a promise made earlier that week to issue rain checks to all fans attending the Sunday game. Therefore, each spectator could redeem the rain check to see a future Browns' game.[20]

While the Browns and Orioles completed a scoreless first inning, the police searched futilely for Von der Ahe. The Browns' owner feared that the police might attempt to confiscate the day's proceeds. Therefore, he safely stored the money and arrived at his box seat near the end of the first inning. He was promptly arrested by Police Sergeant Phillipp Florreich. After turning Von der Ahe over to the custody of two other policemen, Florreich descended onto the field and instructed umpire Robert Ferguson to stop the game. As the police scattered across the diamond, St. Louis fans derisively chanted "Put 'em out!"

St. Louis newspaper editorials harshly criticized the local police. The *Republican* accused the police board of committing "petty tyranny" in applying the Sunday closing law to baseball. It considered all Sunday closing laws to be "unconstitutional," arguing that such blue laws were used "to discriminate in favor of this business or amusement and against that." The *Republican* opined, "The people of this town have exactly the same right to well-conducted Sunday baseball that they have to well-conducted Sunday newspapers or well-conducted Sunday churches." The *Sporting News* warned of the potential consequences of the police action: "The Browns will play Sunday games or St. Louis will lose them. Von der Ahe nor no one else will help keep up a losing venture and the Browns without Sunday games will certainly be ranked in that category." Finally, the *Post-Dispatch* criticized the Missouri legislature for passing "slipshod legislation" that had transformed "innocent amusements" into "the ranks of crime." But the *Post-Dispatch* focused most of its ire on the police, attacking their decision to shut down the game ("All that was needed was to make a test case and that could have been done without stopping the game").[21]

The Von der Ahe case reached Judge Noonan's courtroom on July 15. Prosecuting Attorney J. R. Claiborne tried a different approach from the strategy that had failed in the Schnaider trial. Rather than accusing Von der Ahe of violating the Downing Sunday law, Claiborne prosecuted the case as an infraction of a blue law that the state had adopted in 1839. This obscure, albeit broadly defined, 1839 statute denied an individual the legal right to "either labor himself or compel or permit his apprentice or servant or any other person under his charge or control to labor or perform any work" on a Sunday.[22]

In response, the defense called Congressman John J. O'Neill to the witness stand. O'Neill testified that the game of baseball should not be regarded as a business in which players labored, but instead as "the grandest recreation provided mankind for their edification and entertainment." Defense attorney Joseph Lodge then asked O'Neill to describe his views on the issue of Sunday ball games.

O'Neill provided an answer that the *Post-Dispatch* praised for its "moving eloquence" in cloaking baseball in a "semi-religious and poetic character which even its most ardent admirers had not previously discovered." First, O'Neill portrayed the effort to ban Sunday baseball as an assault upon personal liberties: "Ballplaying in every sense of the word is a recreation, and especially on Sundays should its pleasure be enjoyed in the free air, untrammeled by law or man." Next, O'Neill argued that Sunday baseball served as a safety valve for the working class. A Sunday ball game offered a preferable alternative to "the dives and low places to be found in every large city." Thus, O'Neill concluded that a Sunday game benefited society: "To the laboring man, who has to toil hard for his daily bread, the Sunday ballgame is considered a God send. . . . I have been repeatedly told by the Catholic clergy of St. Louis that Sunday baseball was literally the salvation of many a young man, who might, otherwise have gone to ruin."[23]

As an ambitious young politician, an Irishman, and a Democrat, Judge Noonan could not resist the allure of the words of O'Neill—a fellow Irishman, a fellow Democrat, and a congressman in his third term in office. Nor could Noonan ignore the fact that Von der Ahe, as the chairman of the Democratic Party's Eighth Congressional District, had been instrumental in O'Neill's successful reelection campaigns. Furthermore, Noonan had always opposed the political objectives of the Sabbatarians. His ruling in the Von der Ahe case relied more on these political realities than on legal technicalities. But in justifying his decision to permit Sunday baseball, Noonan reiterated O'Neill's premise that the game should be regarded as recreation or entertainment rather than as a business that compelled ballplayers to labor on Sundays.[24]

Local newspapers rejoiced over the decisions of Judge Noonan. The *Republican* exulted, "We now have both beer and baseball on Sunday," and the *Post-Dispatch* believed Noonan's two rulings would help St. Louisans survive the long months of summer: "With wine, beer and baseball on Sunday, there is every prospect that St. Louis will tide over the hot spell." Demonstrating political foresight, the *Sporting News* predicted that Judge Noonan would "forever carry with him the well wishes of every disciple and of every admirer of America's National game." One year later, as St. Louisans expressed their gratitude and elected Noonan mayor, Von der Ahe exulted over his personal impact upon the polls.[25]

Sunday baseball returned to St. Louis on July 17, 1887, just two days after Noonan authorized the Browns to play ball on the Sabbath. At least five thousand fans "braved the blistering sun, challenged death from sunstroke and were not even singed" while watching the Browns defeat the Philadelphia Athletics 10–8.[26] Judge Noonan, by rescuing Sunday baseball, simultaneously encouraged

Congressman John J. O'Neill. Missouri Historical Society, St. Louis. Photo by John A. Scholten.

Von der Ahe to maintain his affiliation with the American Association and to keep the Browns in St. Louis. Von der Ahe ultimately chose to follow both of these courses of action, but only after months of discussing other options.

Given the significance St. Louisans attached to Sunday baseball, most local residents believed Noonan had ensured that the Browns would remain in the American Association. After all, on the day before Von der Ahe appeared in Noonan's courtroom, Spalding had vowed to prevent the Browns from entering the National League unless they abided by "the same rules that govern us all and no others."[27] While Sunday baseball was under attack, the probability increased that Von der Ahe might accept the twenty-five-thousand-dollar offer to transfer the Browns from the Association to the League; but once Noonan allowed Sunday ball games in St. Louis, the possibility seemed more remote. It appeared doubtful that Von der Ahe would value a onetime payment enough to give up his most profitable payday. And besides prohibiting Sunday games, the National League also would impose its ban upon beer sales at the ballpark and thereby deny Von der Ahe another lucrative source of revenue.

Nevertheless, during a special American Association meeting held on July 27 in New York, Von der Ahe revived his threat to join the National League. This special meeting had been instigated by Von der Ahe, who had two objectives in mind: to fire American Association President Wheeler Wikoff and replace him with a St. Louisan, Joseph Pritchard, and to change the Association's method of distributing gate receipts to visiting ball clubs. To those ends, Von der Ahe accused Wikoff of being "totally incompetent and partial to certain clubs." Specifically, he attacked Wikoff's relationship with Charles H. Byrne, president of the Brooklyn Trolley-Dodgers. According to Von der Ahe, Wikoff had been nothing but "a catspaw in the hands of Byrne" since taking over the reins of the American Association. In response, Byrne lambasted Von der Ahe's complaints as "a case of abnormal enlargement of the cranium in a mentally small man."[28]

Von der Ahe's second proposal recommended that the American Association abandon its practice of paying a flat guarantee to visiting teams and instead reward visitors with a percentage of the gate receipts. The Association had relied upon the guarantee system, which allowed the home team to keep nearly all of the gate receipts, ever since its inaugural season of 1882. For five years, while the Browns were generally attracting the largest crowds in the major leagues to Sportsman's Park, Von der Ahe had raised no objections to the guarantee system. But as the 1887 season elapsed, he swiftly changed his mind and became a fervent advocate of the percentage plan.[29]

The *Sporting News* explained that Von der Ahe's conversion had been prompted by dwindling attendance at Sportsman's Park: "The St. Louis Browns have taken such a lead in the race for the pennant that all interest in it has gone. Therefore, the Browns have ceased to be a drawing attraction at home, where they are looked upon as easy winners, and where the club looks for revenue." This strange dilemma had surfaced initially in 1885 when the Browns reeled off their twenty-seven-game home winning streak. It had temporarily abated during the 1886 season, when the Browns had slowly pulled away from the other American Association pennant contenders. In 1887, however, an early season winning streak created the same problems that the team had experienced two years earlier. After losing three of their five opening games, the Browns won twenty-nine of the next thirty contests and quickly ended any suspense involving the Association pennant race.[30]

Von der Ahe, plagued by the "sparse numbers" at Sportsman's Park, turned to the percentage plan as a remedy for his declining profit margin. The percentage plan offered him an opportunity to capitalize on the Browns' status as "a big drawing card away from home." Von der Ahe insisted, however, that he was not acting solely in his own interest. He argued that the percentage plan would prove beneficial to the entire American Association: "To make money under the percentage plan, every member of the Association would have to put a good team in the field. . . . The percentage system in fact would be an incentive to every nine to build up. . . . It is under it that I look for the Association to take on new life and prosperity." Byrne, whose Brooklyn Trolley-Dodgers had replaced the Browns as the best home-drawing Association club, led the opposition to Von der Ahe's proposal. Byrne grumbled that the percentage plan would reward small-market teams "with a good fat pocketbook" whenever they visited Brooklyn, while the Trolley-Dodgers could only expect "small change" in return.[31]

In response to Von der Ahe's pair of proposals, the American Association split evenly into two warring factions. One group, headed by Von der Ahe and the Browns, included the Louisville Colonels, Cleveland Blues, and the New York Metropolitans. Intent upon firing Wikoff and gaining the percentage plan, they gathered eagerly at the meeting in New York. The other group, headed by Byrne and the Trolley-Dodgers, included the Cincinnati Red Stockings, Baltimore Orioles, and Philadelphia Athletics. To prevent Wikoff's dismissal and maintain the guarantee system, they boycotted the special Association meeting. Von der Ahe, denied the majority needed to pass his proposals, then threatened, "I will jump into the League." Prior to adjourning, though, Von der Ahe's faction wired Wikoff a message that implored him to convene an Association meeting in New York on September 3. The American Association later unanimously agreed to schedule this event and delay it until September 5. The editorial page of the *Sporting News,* while hopeful Von der Ahe's faction could secure a fifth and deciding vote, warned that if the deadlock persisted, "The Association will be a house divided evenly against itself, and then the Lord only knows what will happen."[32]

Slightly more than a month passed before the two factions could get together to try and resolve their differences. Then in New York City, during the noon hour on Monday, August 29, Byrne and Von der Ahe encountered each other at Westerman's Saloon. Both men appeared anxious to arrive at an amicable solution. Byrne, in a friendly gesture, clapped Von der Ahe on the back and asked: "How are you, Chris?" Responding in kind, Von der Ahe shook Byrne's hand and offered to buy him a drink. The two men then haggled over who would pick up the bar tab for their table. Von der Ahe won the argument when he exclaimed: "Brooklyn money is no good here. Nominate your medicine and I'll do the banker's act." Soon the other Association club owners joined them. A long and festive evening ensued.[33]

This harmonious party at Westerman's Saloon, described as "a regular love feast" by the *Sporting News,* informally laid the groundwork for a compromise settlement. On September 5, meeting formally at the Fifth Avenue Hotel, the American Association adopted a modified version of the percentage plan. Visiting teams would receive 30 percent of the total gate receipts, but were guaranteed a minimum payment of $130. Balancing Byrne's concession in granting visitors a percentage of the gate receipts, Von der Ahe did not push for Wikoff's dismissal as league president.[34]

Peace was restored to the American Association. Von der Ahe had triumphed in his battles to preserve Sunday baseball in St. Louis and to receive a percentage of the gate receipts on the road. With the Browns' future seemingly secure in St. Louis and the American Association, the spate of rumors surrounding the team subsided. Focus shifted instead to the upcoming World Series between the Browns and the National League champions, the Detroit Wolverines.

The arrangements for the contest proved controversial. Von der Ahe and Wolverines' president Fred Stearns decided to turn the 1887 World Series into a traveling carnival. After playing the first two games in St. Louis and Game Three in Detroit, the teams would journey east to stage the next nine contests at seven sites—Pittsburgh, Brooklyn, New York, Philadelphia, Boston, Washington, and Baltimore. Then, the World Series would wind up in the West with three final games to be played in Detroit, Chicago, and St. Louis.[35]

The *Sporting News* criticized these plans on both economic and competitive grounds. Economically, it argued that a home-and-home series in St. Louis and Detroit would be more profitable: "Anyone who has lived in a League or Association city is aware of the fact that, as soon as the championship season ends, interest in baseball ceases unless the local club may have captured first place." The *Sporting News* pointed to the example of the "miserable gatherings" the Browns and Chicago White Stockings had drawn when they played the last three games of the 1885 World Series in Pittsburgh and Cincinnati. In contrast, during the 1886 World Series, the same two teams played in front of robust crowds at Chicago and St. Louis.[36]

The *Sporting News* advised its hometown favorite Browns that from a competitive standpoint, "Such an arrangement will give the Detroit club all the best of it." At all of the eastern playing sites, the vast majority of spectators would support Detroit. National League fans bore no grudges against the Detroit team. The Wolverines had claimed their first pennant by dethroning the White Stockings, National League champions for five of the past seven seasons, a club loathed by League members outside of Chicago. Therefore, at National League sites, fans would root for the underdog Wolverines to deny the Browns' quest to claim a third consecutive world championship. However, the Browns could not count on similar support at American Association sites. Fans in Association cities, consistently frustrated by the failure of their hometown teams to defeat the Browns, would also tend to cheer for the underdog Wolverines.[37]

The outcome of the World Series validated these concerns. While attendance in the eastern cities proved better than the *Sporting News* had feared, the crowds generally were not as large as those drawn in St. Louis and Detroit. Without question, the quality of the Browns' performance declined once the teams headed east. The first three games in St. Louis and Detroit had shown great promise for a closely contested World Series. After splitting the two games in St. Louis, the Wolverines seized a narrow edge in the Series with a 2–1 thirteen-inning triumph in Detroit. In the East, though, Detroit defeated St. Louis in five of the next six contests and took a commanding advantage. Trailing seven games to two, the Browns needed to win six straight times to defend their title as world champions. In the morning game of a doubleheader on October 21, the Browns snapped a four-game losing streak and posted an 11–4 victory in Washington, D.C. But in Baltimore that afternoon the Wolverines clinched the World Series with a 13–3 win. Each team took two of the last four meaningless contests, which were played in front of diminishing audiences, to give Detroit ten wins in fifteen games.[38]

Two months later, St. Louisans discovered that the Browns' loss in the 1887 World Series had been beneficial to their city. If the Browns had captured a third consecutive world championship, Von der Ahe would have transferred the team to New York in search of larger profits. This report first surfaced through remarks made by Gus Abel, Byrne's business partner in the Brooklyn Trolley-Dodgers and other ventures. Abel told a *Cincinnati Commercial-Gazette* reporter, "It was Mr. Von der Ahe's intention, had he won the world's championship games with Detroit in the fall, to have transferred his team to New York City, and in a season he would have made a fortune. His losing the series spoiled the scheme." These comments were published in the *St. Louis Post-Dispatch* as well, and then the *Sporting News* queried Von der Ahe about the reliability of the rumor. Von der Ahe issued no denial. Instead, he explained, "There is more truth than poetry in the statement. The matter was not only seriously considered but a move of the kind had almost been determined on. As we did not beat the Detroits, however, the plan missed fire."[39]

The situation stemmed from the American Association's troublesome franchise in New York, the Metropolitans. The Metropolitans' original owner, John Day, also owned the New York Gothams in the National League. Day had always given preferential treatment to the Gothams. In case of scheduling conflicts, the Gothams received a better playing field than the Metropolitans; when the Association demanded that the teams share the same field, Day arranged the Gothams' games at more opportune playing times. Even worse, after the Metropolitans won the 1884 Association pennant, Day transferred two of the team's best players to his National League team, now rechristened the "Giants." In December 1885, under pressure from the American Association, Day sold the Metropolitans to Erastus Wiman. Wiman transferred the team from Manhattan to Staten Island, operated at an apparent financial loss for the next two years, and then sold the Metropolitans after the 1887 season to the Brooklyn Trolley-Dodgers.[40] Intrigue surrounded the Trolley-Dodgers' intentions for the future of the struggling Metropolitans franchise.

Abel had assured Von der Ahe that a world champion club in New York City could overcome the local popularity of the League's Giants and reap "a fortune." Von der Ahe strongly believed that the American Association should maintain a presence in New York, and, after listening to Abel, he defended the near move of the Browns with a discussion of potential profit margins: "We had talked the matter over and had come to the conclusion that the Browns as Champions of the World if located in New York could clear at least $100,000 a season . . . That is about twenty times what they could clear here even under the most favorable circumstances." Once the Browns had lost the 1887 World Series, however, Abel evidently shifted his pursuit to the victorious Detroit Wolverines. The Wolverines, after engaging in a brief flirtation with the American Association, decided to stay put in Detroit and the National League. Brooklyn claimed the best players off the Metropolitans' roster and then surrendered the franchise. The American Association replaced the Metropolitans with a franchise in Kansas City and depended on Brooklyn to maintain a presence in the metropolis of New York.[41]

Von der Ahe's Browns remained in St. Louis. However, by even considering a transfer of his team, he had demonstrated a profound change of business philosophy since the organization of the original Brown Stockings prior to the 1875 season. Unlike C. Orrick Bishop and the other directors of the original Brown Stockings, whose only incentive to invest in the team had been "civic pride," Von der Ahe expected monetary profits. The directors of the original Brown Stockings had been wealthy and socially prominent men before their involvement with baseball, but Von der Ahe relied upon baseball to advance upward in economic and social circles. Bishop and his partners would have been ecstatic if they had combined the prestige of winning a pennant with turning a modest profit. Von der Ahe, though, craved both the glory associated with winning and the financial windfall that he had come to expect from baseball. During his heyday in the 1880s, Von der Ahe earned approximately half a million dollars from the Browns. He used this baseball income to speculate wildly in real estate, building whole blocks in the area around Sportsman's Park and placing neighborhood bars on every corner.[42] Von der Ahe's attitude showed that despite Congressman O'Neill's sentiments and Judge Noonan's legal opinion, baseball was unquestionably a business.

Von der Ahe had likely exaggerated the downturn in the Browns' economic situation. Earlier in the 1887 season, after all, the *Post-Dispatch* estimated that the 1886 Browns had made forty-two thousand dollars "excluding the profits accruing from the sale of beer and refreshments, which, as everyone knows, is by no means insignificant." In fact, although the Browns had averaged more fans per game in both 1883 and 1884, the expanded Association schedule allowed the Browns to establish a team record for attendance in 1887. Two factors, however, had definitely reduced the ball club's profits. First, as mentioned earlier, the ease with which the Browns had won the Association pennant caused attendance to decline during the latter part of the season. Second, player salaries increased. After winning the 1886 World Series, Von der Ahe announced, "The season just closed has been a very successful one. The receipts at Sportsman's Park have been larger than for any season in its history, but we will not clear as much money this year as we did in 1883. Then you must remember our salary list was not as large by half as it was this year."[43]

Initially, in 1884, player salaries had increased due to the threat of raids from the newly formed Union Association. When the Union Association dissolved after only one year of play, club owners hoped that the cost of player salaries could be reduced. But this did not happen, even though both the American Association and National League accepted the reserve clause and thereby eliminated marketplace competition for players.

Ballplayers had acquired a sense of their economic power. Top players, aware that they were highly skilled laborers who possessed talents in short supply, resorted to contract holdouts until desperate owners capitulated to their demands. By October 1885 concern over rising salaries reached the point that club owners adopted a Limit Agreement which restricted the earnings of any individual player to two thousand dollars per season. For the remainder of the decade, major-league club owners paid a lot of lip service to their supposed strict compliance with the Limit Agreement while surreptitiously figuring out a variety of ways to evade its restrictions. For example, between the 1884 and 1887 seasons, even with the reserve clause and Limit Agreement both in effect, Von der Ahe's payroll increased an astronomical 49.7 percent. Von der Ahe had joined other club owners in blithely ignoring the provisions of the Limit Agreement. In 1887, when the Browns' owner claimed his team's payroll would "easily reach $35,000," the *Sporting News* observed that this salary structure meant the average income for a Browns' player would be "about $2450" (well above the maximum allowed under the Limit Agreement).[44]

Von der Ahe had intended to counteract the problems of declining attendance and rising player salaries by transferring a world championship ball club to the nation's largest market. When the 1887 World Series deprived Von der Ahe of this dream, he sought instead to restore interest among St. Louisans. He traveled to the East and traded away the rights to five valuable players from his championship team. For a total of $18,750, he sold to the Brooklyn Trolley-Dodgers the services of catcher Albert "Doc" Bushong and the two men who had served as a pitcher–right fielder tandem for the Browns, Dave Foutz and Bob Caruthers. In Philadelphia, Von der Ahe arranged another transaction, sending shortstop Bill Gleason and center fielder Curt Welch to the Athletics for catcher John "Jocko" Milligan, shortstop James "Chippy" McGarr, center fielder Fred Mann, and an additional eight thousand dollars.[45]

These deals compensated Von der Ahe for his decline in profits in 1887, but they also addressed the two underlying causes of the Browns' economic downturn. First, Von der Ahe replaced five highly paid veterans with less-heralded players in order to slash his rising payroll. Second, by promoting parity among Association teams, the transactions aimed to bolster attendance in St. Louis and the league's other cities. Von der Ahe admitted to the *Post-Dispatch,* "No interest whatever was taken in the games here last season for the simple reason that we were too strong for our opponents. Nobody comes to see a club play ball when it is eighteen games in the lead of the club next door to it."[46] Nor does it appear to be a coincidence that Von der Ahe's players went to the nation's two largest markets, less than two months after the Browns' owner had been assured he would receive 30 percent of the take for every game the Browns played on the road.

At the time of the trades, though, Von der Ahe often presented a different defense of the transactions. In criticizing his former players he was probably more interested in promoting a rivalry between the current and former Browns than in honestly assessing his motives for the trades. Von der Ahe's promotional instinct is clearly indicated by the fact that he immediately hired John B. Sage and Co., a Buffalo business, "to supply him with a lot of monster posters" of the former Browns. The *Sporting News* gleaned a purpose behind this "great scheme." It insisted that Von der Ahe was emulating the example set a year earlier when Spalding sold Mike "King" Kelly from the White Stockings to the Boston Beaneaters for ten thousand dollars following the White Stockings' loss of the 1886 World Series: "The coming of these . . . men is to be advertised in St. Louis next year, just as the coming of Ten Thousand Dollar Kelly was advertised in Chicago last year. If there is anything in precedent, the coming of these men will put money in Von der Ahe's pocket next year just as the coming of Kelly to Chicago."[47]

Von der Ahe's derogatory comments were probably intended to provoke a feud with his former players for the sake of publicity. Indeed, he succeeded in creating a war of words with the former Browns who were sold to Brooklyn. Von der Ahe claimed Bushong had been dealt because of a lack of team spirit: "Ever since . . . he had that quarrel with Latham [in June 1886], there was a coolness between the two, and Bushong has acted as though he cared little for the success of the team." Von der Ahe also complained that the veteran Bushong "appeared jealous" of twenty-one-year-old catcher Jack Boyle, who had joined the Browns in 1887 and assumed a share of the team's catching duties: "On one occasion when I asked

[Bushong] to go and catch, he said, 'What's the matter with the kid?' His work after that was lukewarm." Furthermore, Von der Ahe curtly dismissed Foutz, who had pitched the Browns to ninety-nine victories over the preceding three seasons and hit for a .303 average, as an over-the-hill liability: "It was the general opinion that his arm was gone." Von der Ahe did compliment Caruthers, who had likewise pitched the Browns to ninety-nine victories over the past three seasons and hit for a .317 average, as "the best pitcher in America and one of the best batsmen." Yet even while admitting that Caruthers was "the only man I regret losing," the Browns' owner still objected to his "very stubborn" nature, his tendency to hold out every spring for more money, and "his card playing proclivities."[48]

In addition, Von der Ahe made disparaging remarks about the two Browns sent to Philadelphia. He denounced Gleason's play in the 1887 World Series and deduced that the only shortstop in the six-year history of the Browns' Association franchise "had seen his better days." Von der Ahe accused Welch of creating "a breach in the team" due to his heavy drinking ("His conduct was of the Fred Lewis order"). Welch's own brilliant play, in the eyes of the Browns' owner, no longer compensated for the negative influence that he now exerted upon his teammates: "In his misdoings, he led away and demoralized all of the best of the remaining members of my nine. For this reason alone, I determined . . . to get rid of him." Gleason and Welch, however, were less inclined than the Brooklyn trio to allow Von der Ahe to goad them into a public exchange of taunts.[49]

When Von der Ahe officially announced his deals with Brooklyn and Philadelphia, most of the Browns were on a train en route to the West Coast. The team, with Foutz acting as business manager, had embarked upon a barnstorming tour opposing their old foes, the Chicago White Stockings, as soon as the World Series ended. "The Big Trip," as the *Sporting News* referred to the cross-country jaunt, started with an October 30 game in St. Louis, then continued across the South for the next three weeks. After making appearances in Memphis, Nashville, Atlanta, Charleston, and New Orleans, the Browns and White Stockings headed for San Francisco. Consequently, Foutz, Bushong, and Welch had a chance to complete their careers with the Browns in one last blaze of glory. For Welch, the games seemed so important that he disregarded an urgent message to return home to his wife, who had just given birth to twin boys, and instead stayed in San Francisco through the Christmas holidays.[50]

The Browns' "old war horses," trailing five games to four in the southern leg of the tour, served notice of their determination to win the "Winter Championship Series" when it opened at San Francisco's Central Park on November 27. With a virtuoso display of "numerous hits and a great many daring steals," the Browns defeated the White Stockings, 16–9, to even the series. The performance of "the Mound City lads" earned special praise from the *Sporting News*'s West Coast correspondent: "They played a circus game, every one moving from the moment game is called until the twenty-seventh man is retired. They take every chance, cover their uniform with dust in a glorious attempt to steal a bag, and scamper home on the slightest provocation."[51]

Despite this impressive beginning to the San Francisco trip, Chicago claimed two of the next three contests and held the series lead, seven games to six, as the teams took the field on Christmas Eve to start a concluding string of three ball games in three days. In front of two thousand fans, the Browns evened the series again. Foutz scored four runs, while Welch homered and tallied three times as St. Louis triumphed, 18–5. On Christmas Day four thousand baseball enthusiasts turned out to see the Browns stake themselves to the series lead with a hard-earned 6–5 victory. Foutz not only pitched the Browns to the win but also slugged a home run to support his own cause. Another "immense crowd" showed up a day later for the final game. The Browns easily clinched the series title, nine games to seven, as they crushed Chicago, 17–3. Foutz, with two triples and another home run, triggered the Browns' high-scoring attack. Bushong added an additional three hits. The three departing Browns combined to hit safely seven times in thirteen at-bats, score seven runs, and collectively record twenty-one of the twenty-seven putouts.[52]

After defeating Chicago, Bushong and Foutz turned their attention to the opportunity to compete against the Browns, the team they had played on together for three consecutive championship seasons. While still in San Francisco, Bushong simply stated, "Brooklyn will win the pennant next season." Later, upon his return from California, Foutz further inflamed the St. Louis–Brooklyn feud. Directly addressing Von der Ahe's allegation about his lack of arm strength, Foutz flexed the muscles of his pitching arm and complained, "Ain't she a daisy? Some people say it was dead. I pitched several games on the coast and I think my arm is all right. In fact, there never was anything the matter with my arm that I know of. The only thing that ever troubled me was my broken thumb. It is all right now." Foutz then went on to forecast that Brooklyn would win the Association pennant, while the Browns would "come out third or fourth." Within another month, Caruthers joined Bushong and Foutz in predicting a championship season for Brooklyn. Questioned at his wedding about the upcoming 1888 season, Caruthers boldly declared that Brooklyn had "without doubt secured the Association winners."[53]

In St. Louis, though, the Browns were in no mood to hand over the Association pennant to their former teammates. Third baseman Arlie Latham, who had scuffled with Bushong in 1886 on the Browns' bench in Baltimore, soon offered his opinion of the forthcoming American Association race: "The Browns are just going to fool them all the coming season." The *Sporting News* quoted Browns' manager Charles Comiskey as saying, "If I get hold of a good pitcher or two, the Browns will make them all hustle." Elsewhere in the same issue, the editorial page paraphrased Comiskey as predicting the Browns would repeat as Association champions. A supremely confident Von der Ahe gave notice to a *St. Louis Globe-Democrat* reporter that the Browns "will again win the pennant," interjecting, "I do not say this for a boast, but I mean every word of it."[54]

Von der Ahe's trades unleashed a fierce rivalry between the Browns and the Brooklyn team. The intense on-field rivalry reignited the personal animosity between Von der Ahe and Byrne, which had already divided the American Association once. Ultimately, Von der Ahe and Byrne would again divide the league into hostile factions. Their 1887 dispute had been settled with the adoption of the percentage plan. The Association would self-destruct the next time that it turned upon itself. But before internal discord could tear the league apart, St. Louis and Brooklyn would wage two memorable pennant races.

9

Browns versus Bridegrooms

> Baseball is the very symbol, the outward and visible expression of the drive and push and rush and struggle of the raging, tearing, booming nineteenth century.
>
> —Mark Twain, addressing a baseball banquet at Delmonico's restaurant in New York City, April 8, 1889

> I go on a field to win a game by any hook or crook. It is the game we are after, not reputations as society dudes.
>
> —Charles Comiskey, quoted in the *Sporting News,* April 27, 1889

The former members of the St. Louis Browns benefited the Brooklyn and Philadelphia ball clubs. The Philadelphia Athletics, a fifth-place team with a losing record in 1887, jumped to third place in each of the next two seasons and compiled records of 81–52 and 75–58. The Brooklyn Trolley-Dodgers improved even more. The 1887 Brooklyn team, with a record of 60–74, had finished a distant sixth in the American Association, thirty-four and a half games behind the champion Browns. Fortified by their new additions, Brooklyn battled St. Louis for the Association championship in both 1888 and 1889.[1]

In 1888, as the season headed into June, Brooklyn passed the Cincinnati Red Stockings and rose to the top of the Association standings. The Browns lurked in third place, two and a half games behind Brooklyn. On June 2 the *Sporting News,* in an editorial which predicted "The Browns Will Get There," warned the other Association teams that they had already missed their chance to dethrone the defending titleholders: "If the Browns were to be beaten this year, it was to be in the opening quarter of the race and before the new men had been broken in. They were not beaten in the opening quarter and the inference to be drawn from this fact is as conclusive as it is obvious—the Browns will win the . . . pennant again."[2]

Over the next few months, the St. Louis–Brooklyn duel took on a decidedly more personal flavor. In the last two weeks of June the Browns' manager–first baseman, Charles Comiskey, and the owner of the Brooklyn ball club, Charles Byrne, exchanged their own assessments of the pennant race. First, Comiskey, while acknowledging that the American Association would experience "one of the most interesting and exciting" pennant races in its history, described the fourth-place Philadelphia Athletics as "the strongest" eastern team. Questioned about front-running Brooklyn, Comiskey replied, "I believe the Brooklyns can't hold their high position. They are good hard sluggers, but are rather poor baserunners, and not as strong in batteries as most people suppose. Caruthers is not pitching the ball as he was last season. He is not near as speedy." Byrne quickly countered, saying that although the Association possessed many "good teams," he remained convinced "the Brooklyn club has a mortgage on first place." At the close of June, the Browns inched percentage points ahead of Brooklyn. In response, the *Sporting News* issued another editorial, "Comiskey and His Guard," which declared, "Like Napoleon with the Old Guard, Comiskey and his men are a power just now too swift and sure for the opposing legions of the American Association. These latter may some other season win the coveted pennant from the St. Louis Browns but not this season."[3]

A week later the Brooklyn ball club, increasingly known as the "Bridegrooms" because of the presence of seven newlyweds on their team, arrived in St. Louis for a four-game series against the Browns. From the outset, the Bridegrooms infuriated the Browns. A. J. Bushong, the former Brown turned Trolley-Dodger, sent a letter to St. Louis's star left fielder, Tip O'Neill. Bushong suggested that if O'Neill should slack off and play for his release, Brooklyn stood ready to sign him to a lucrative contract as soon as he gained his freedom. O'Neill remained with the Browns and went on to win his second consecutive American Association batting championship. Von der Ahe, though, claimed that Bushong had acted upon Byrne's advice. In August, following "a thorough investigation," the American Association reprimanded "the Brooklyn Club" for having been "indiscreet in instructing one of their players to communicate with Mr. O'Neill, in reference to his release from the St. Louis Club, and without having previously had information from Mr. Von der Ahe of the intention to release said player."[4] This tampering incident further kindled the flames of the St. Louis–Brooklyn rivalry.

The outcome of the four-game series added some extra sparks to the blaze. Brooklyn swept all four games, winning three of the contests by a single run. Enraged by the umpiring of Robert Ferguson, a Brooklyn native, Comiskey fumed, "Of the last four games with Brooklyn, we would have won three had it not been for the work of Ferguson. As it was, we did not capture a game. I do not think I can say more than that." If Comiskey had nothing more to say, the *Sporting News* certainly did. The journal insisted, "No sane man living west of the Alleghenies . . . will believe that Ferguson gave St. Louis a fair deal."[5]

Newspaper reports quoted Von der Ahe as alleging there had been "collusion" between Byrne and Ferguson. Later, at an American Association meeting in August, Von der Ahe maintained that he had been misquoted. The Association then passed a resolution proclaiming that it had "full confidence in the honesty and integrity of Mr. Byrne and Umpire Ferguson."[6]

St. Louis and Brooklyn remained stalemated atop the American Association standings for much of the rest of July. As the season entered August, the Browns clung to a slender half-game lead over Brooklyn. Cincinnati and Philadelphia remained in close pursuit, only three and three and a half games off the pace respectively.[7] The Browns, after completing an eastern road trip in Brooklyn and Philadelphia, would return to Sportsman's Park for a twelve-game home stand. At the same time, the Bridegrooms would head west to play a dozen games on the road. The upcoming scheduling advantage made the Browns' five remaining road games against the eastern contenders even more vital.

On August 3 in the opener of the Brooklyn series, the two teams competed with possession of first place on the line. Each club used its best pitcher. Bob Caruthers, the former Brown who had already defeated his former mates four times in 1888, handled the pitching chores for Brooklyn. The Browns handed the ball to "Silver" King. King, a hurler of German ancestry born in south St. Louis, had been a brick layer before launching his professional baseball career in 1886 with St. Joseph (Missouri) of the Western League. Late in the 1886 season King had reached the majors with the National League's Kansas City Cowboys. After the collapse of the Cowboys, King joined the Browns in 1887 and promptly topped St. Louis's pitching staff with thirty-two wins.[8]

Caruthers took a 6–3 lead into the fifth inning. Then, with two runners on base and two out, he faced Comiskey, the man who had publicly proclaimed that his pitching skills were eroding. Comiskey slammed one "into the center-field carriages" for a three-run homer, tying the game at six-all. Neither team scored in the next four innings. The Browns took the lead in the top of the tenth. With one out, second baseman Yank Robinson tripled to left, then tagged up and came home with the go-ahead run on O'Neill's fly-out to right field. King retired Brooklyn in order in the bottom of the inning to nail down the victory.[9]

The following day, in another taut extra-inning struggle, St. Louis and Brooklyn battled to a 4–4 eleven-inning tie before darkness forced the game to be called. King returned a day later and pitched a four-hitter to lead the Browns to a 3–1 triumph in the finale of the series. After an off-day to travel to Philadelphia, King pitched yet again. O'Neill contributed four hits in four at-bats and scored twice, while Comiskey clubbed a game-winning home run. The Browns defeated the Athletics, 5–4, as King earned his twenty-eighth victory of the season and third win in the Browns' last four games.[10]

1888 Old Judge Cigarette baseball card of Silver King. After the trades of Bob Caruthers and Dave Foutz, King's pitching heroics kept the 1888–1889 St. Louis Browns in pennant contention. Missouri Historical Society, St. Louis.

Despite losing their last game in Philadelphia, the Browns returned home with a two-game lead over Brooklyn for first place, a three-game advantage over Philadelphia, and a three-and-a-half-game edge over Cincinnati. St. Louis soon solidified its hold on first, winning fourteen of the next sixteen games. Meanwhile, Brooklyn struggled on its western trip, winning only five of their next sixteen games and falling all the way to fourth place, eleven games behind the Browns. As the first of September arrived, the Browns enjoyed a fairly comfortable six-and-a-half-game lead over second-place Philadelphia.[11]

Brooklyn recovered to post the best record in the American Association for September. Their late surge pushed them past Philadelphia and Cincinnati once again and into second place, but they still finished six and a half games behind the Browns. St. Louis clinched its fourth consecutive American Association pennant on September 20, and Von der Ahe raised another championship banner at Sportsman's Park—this one hailing his team as the "Four Time Winners."[12]

By capturing the 1888 pennant, the Browns had won the first round of their new feud with the Bridegrooms. Furthermore, during the course of the season Von der Ahe emerged victorious in his ongoing off-field fight with Byrne over a pair of American Association policy questions. Prior to the start of the 1888 season, Byrne, who was concerned with regaining the "outlay of capital" that he had expended in purchasing the three former Browns, persuaded Von der Ahe and other Association club owners to increase the price of admission for their games from a quarter to fifty cents. By early July, Von der Ahe, alarmed at the negative reaction to the new rate in St. Louis, argued that the fifty-cent fee had been given "a fair trial" and had failed. At a league meeting that month he pressed for a return to the twenty-five-cent ticket price. The Baltimore Orioles, Louisville Colonels, and Philadelphia Athletics sided with Von der Ahe. They outnumbered those clubs supporting the fifty-cent rate—Brooklyn, Cincinnati, and Cleveland—but fell short of the two-thirds majority needed to change the Association's constitution. In July, Byrne's forces conceded only that the Philadelphia Athletics could be given the local option to charge a quarter in order to compete with the National League's Philadelphia Quakers, who had won special approval from their league to drop ticket prices from fifty to twenty-five cents and had virtually quadrupled their attendance in the process.[13]

Undeterred, Von der Ahe in August demanded once again that the American Association return to its old twenty-five cent rate. As in July, the Kansas City Cowboys (recently revived by the Association) refused to take a stand one way or another. The Athletics sensibly advocated that each team should be given the same local option now possessed by Philadelphia. The other six Association members continued to be hopelessly split in their preference for charging either twenty-five or fifty cents. Finally, Byrne proposed a satisfactory compromise. In exchange for reverting back to twenty-five-cent ticket prices, Von der Ahe agreed to surrender the percentage system of distributing gate receipts to visiting teams. Rather than being required to pay Von der Ahe 30 percent of the total receipts, which totaled as much as $1,500 for one early season Sunday game, Byrne now needed to pay the Browns' owner only a $130 guarantee. Later, in November 1888, Von der Ahe successfully convinced the Association to abandon again the guarantee system and once more to grant visiting teams a percentage of the gate receipts.[14]

Von der Ahe thus had won not only the 1888 American Association pennant but also the policy disputes over ticket prices and the division of gate receipts. He did not fare as well when the Browns met the National League champions in the World Series. Again in 1888, the outcome of the World Series would put a tarnish on what had been a glorious season for the Browns.

In making World Series preparations with John Day, owner of the National League champion New York Giants, Von der Ahe once again foolishly conceded that a majority of the games would be played in the East. The schedule called for the first three games to be held at the home of the Giants, the Polo Grounds. After traveling to Brooklyn for the fourth game, the teams would return to the Polo Grounds for Game Five. Rather than holding the second half of the series at western sites, Von der Ahe permitted Game Six to be played in Philadelphia. Not until the final four contests would the World Series come to Sportsman's Park; St. Louis, one of the two participating cities, would not host any of the competition until the seventh game.[15]

For St. Louis, the most vivid image of the 1888 World Series would not be a resplendent moment of athletic triumph at Sportsman's Park, like Curt Welch's "$15,000 Slide" to win the 1886 World Series, but rather the gaudy spectacle of Von der Ahe's $20,000 special train. The Browns had finished the regular season in Cincinnati. From there, Von der Ahe had mailed a letter to Al Spink, the editor of the *Sporting News,* back in St. Louis. He requested that Spink, who had formerly served as the Browns' secretary, contact W. D. Wetherell of the Vandalia Railroad to arrange for a special train to transport the Browns and their supporters. As his personal guests, the Browns' owner wanted Spink to invite a representative from each St. Louis newspaper as well as "all our friends." Von der Ahe envisioned a long line of coaches draped with banners. He also ordered that Wetherell should make sure the train contained "plenty to eat and drink." "The Browns' Special" would depart St. Louis on the morning of October 6, stop in Ohio that night to pick up Von der Ahe and the Browns, continue on to New York, carry the team and its backers to the other eastern sites, and ultimately return them to St. Louis.[16]

When Spink relayed these plans to Wetherell, the railroad man incredulously proclaimed, "Why, Al, it's nonsense talking about a special train. One like Chris wants will cost nearly $20,000 for the round trip. You write and tell him he'd better travel on the regular trains." Spink conveyed these thoughts in a letter to Von der Ahe. He received a prompt response in the form of a telegram which read, "Tell Wetherell to mind his own business and fix up that special as I want it." In addition to the money that he spent on "The Browns' Special," Von der Ahe also picked up the tab for his guests' accommodations at the Grand Central Hotel.[17]

The World Series, like it had the preceding season, started with great promise for the Browns. But once again it ended listlessly in St. Louis in a meaningless game in front of a minuscule crowd. The opening two games of the series had provided hope for something far better. The first game featured a pitching duel between the Giants' Tim Keefe, who had led the National League in wins with thirty-five, and King, whose forty-five victories had led the American Association. Keefe narrowly outdueled King, 2–1. In Game Two, outstanding pitching again dominated the contest. The Browns took a 1–0 lead in the second inning when, with runners on first and third, right fielder Tommy McCarthy, the best of the players the 1888 Browns recruited to replace their former stars, stole home on the back end of a double steal.[18]

Through eight innings, McCarthy's theft still stood as the game's lone run. Finally, in the ninth, Giants' pitcher Mickey Welch surrendered two additional runs to the Browns. Elton "Icebox" Chamberlain, a late-season acquisition from the Louisville Colonels, completed a six-hit shutout to give the Browns a 3–0 triumph.[19] In hindsight, however, Al Spink viewed the victory as a mixed blessing: "The Browns played with all their best speed and vigor. But perhaps it would have been as well for them to have lost the game, for the players of the St. Louis team never quite recovered from the effect of the treatment they received on their return that evening to the Grand Central." Von der Ahe and virtually his entire "Browns' Special" entourage greeted the ball club warmly: "[They] took the boys into the great bar room and there in goblets of champagne drank to their health and their royal victory. The players responded, and so nobly that they failed to win another game of the series in New York and the East."[20]

After losing the next four contests, the Browns trailed five games to one in the World Series. They belatedly returned to St. Louis and staved off elimination in Game Seven with a 7–5 victory. A day later, though, the Giants scored six runs in the ninth inning to salt away an 11–3 win. The two games drew an average of more than 4,700 people, much larger than the crowds in the neutral sites of Brooklyn or Philadelphia. But once the outcome of the series was settled, few fans bothered to come watch the Browns in the last two meaningless games. An average of 562 spectators attended these contests. The Browns won both games, cutting the Giants' victory margin down to six games to four. Dismissing the last two outings as "mere farces," Giants' manager Jim Mutrie admitted, "Our boys did not care whether they won them or not."[21] The *Sporting News*, soon after this empty ending to an exciting season, observed a profound sadness among St. Louis baseball enthusiasts:

> The baseball world is very quiet. Whenever one speaks of the Browns, they are immediately sat down upon, so sore are the occupants of the Mound City over the defeats by the New Yorks of the Browns. But they'll get over it, and next year, these same individuals . . . will be found on the bleaching boards at Sportsman's Park cheering lustily for the same men they are now so loudly abusing.[22]

Indeed, in 1889 the Browns and the Brooklyn Bridegrooms waged another acrimonious pennant race, which revived the interest of those St. Louis fans who had watched the preceding season's competition. However, St. Louis attendance figures for Von der Ahe's Browns would never again reach their 1887 peak.[23] Von der Ahe's trades with Brooklyn and Philadelphia, although successful at increasing American Association parity, had not stimulated attendance in St. Louis. Many Browns' fans could not reconcile themselves to the loss of local favorites Caruthers, Bushong, Foutz, Welch, and Gleason.

The team's slipping attendance may have prompted Von der Ahe to curry local support with his lavish spending on "The Browns' Special." In 1888, attendance at the Browns' home games had tumbled by an astonishing 32 percent. Still, even though the Browns' decrease in attendance had been especially drastic, it partly mirrored a general trend in baseball. After reaching an all-time high in 1887, overall major-league attendance had declined by 17.4 percent in 1888. The drop-off had been particularly apparent in the American Association, whose experiment with selling fifty-cent tickets had been unsuccessful. National League attendance also had suffered, though.[24] Baseball rulemakers, in searching for a proper balance between hitting and pitching, had caused dramatic swings in styles of play. Fans apparently preferred the wide-open, high-scoring offensive battles of 1887 to the low-scoring pitching duels of 1888.

In 1889, after additional tinkering with the playing rules, batting averages and attendance figures both increased substantially, although neither quite regained the heights of 1887. Yet even with restored offensive firepower and the return of quarter tickets, attendance at Sportsman's Park improved only by 5.4 percent, an indication that St. Louis fans continued to resent Von der Ahe's trades of some of the Browns' most popular players.[25]

Three of the former Browns now with the Brooklyn Bridegrooms carried on their intense competition with St. Louis in the 1889 American Association pennant race. The battle between former teammates, along with the ongoing grudge between Von der Ahe and Byrne, continued to fuel the St. Louis–Brooklyn rivalry. One aspect of the Von der Ahe–Byrne feud again focused on the Browns' constant complaint that Byrne controlled the Association umpires. On September 7, during a hotly contested game played in front of more than fifteen thousand fans in Brooklyn, the hostility reached a fever pitch.

In a complete reversal of form from the previous year, the Browns had held the top spot in the Association for most of the season before losing it on a disastrous eastern road trip. As they entered Brooklyn's Washington Park on September 7, the Browns trailed the first-place Bridegrooms by two and a half games. After falling behind 2–0 in the first inning, the Browns scored once in the fifth and twice in the sixth to take a 3–2 lead. Immediately, Comiskey attempted to persuade umpire Fred Goldsmith to call the game on account of darkness. Goldsmith refused, and play continued. The Browns added another run in the seventh and led 4–2 as the eighth inning began.[26]

Despite an absence of any scoring, the eighth proved to be quite lively. While Brooklyn batted in the top half of the inning (having won the pregame coin toss and chosen to bat first), the Browns incessantly grumbled to Umpire Goldsmith that he should call the game. After retiring the Bridegrooms, the Browns persisted in this argument as they left the field. Once they arrived at the bench, someone—perhaps Von der Ahe—distributed candles. The Browns, as a comic reminder to Goldsmith that it was too dark to continue playing, lit the candles and positioned them in front of the bench. In response, a considerable number of Brooklyn fans threw their beer mugs at the Browns' candles. They succeeded in knocking down several of the candles, almost with tragic consequences. When the candles were toppled, they set off a chain reaction by igniting some stray paper, which in turn created a small fire that briefly threatened to set the wooden grandstand ablaze. Fortunately, the flames were extinguished before any real damage was done.[27]

The incident, however, further hardened Umpire Goldsmith's resolve to finish the ball game in its entirety. In the *St. Louis Globe-Democrat,* sports editor Joe Murphy noted that Goldsmith also might have been guided by his own desire for self-preservation: "No one blames Goldsmith much for not calling the game as he surely would have been killed by the Brooklyn and New York toughs." The ninth inning started at 6:25 P.M. All of the other games on the East Coast had been called because of darkness twenty minutes earlier, including a New York Giants' game played just across the Harlem River.[28] When Comiskey started agitating to have the game called following the sixth inning, Goldsmith may well have been correct to deny the Browns' request. But, without doubt, the game should have been called long before the ninth inning started. Apparently, the players could not even see the ball any more. Bob Clark, leading off the ninth inning for Brooklyn, struck out. He reached first base safely, though, when strike three sailed past Browns' catcher Jocko Milligan. With Caruthers at bat, Clark advanced to second when another one of Icebox Chamberlain's pitches eluded Milligan. At this point, Comiskey had seen enough. He ordered the Browns to leave the field.

Goldsmith informed the Browns that they had five minutes to take the field or risk a forfeit. When the five minutes elapsed, the Browns turned away from the diamond and instead headed toward the clubhouse. Goldsmith announced that the game had been forfeited to Brooklyn. Before the Browns could reach the clubhouse, many Brooklyn fans rioted. Hurling stones and bottles at the Browns, the Brooklynites connected with Comiskey, Robinson, and McCarthy, whose jaw was so swollen that he could not eat for the next couple of days. Comiskey nearly met an even worse fate as "he was caught in the crowd, and, just as several men were about to strike him, a bystander jumped in and sailed into the crowd," allowing the Browns' manager "a narrow escape."[29]

One day later the Browns and Bridegrooms were scheduled to meet again in a Sunday contest. New York state law actually banned all forms of popular amusements on the Sabbath, but the Bridegrooms had been getting around this restriction by playing their Sunday games at Ridgewood, where the Queens County sheriff elected not to enforce the law forbidding Sunday baseball. Since the sheriff was voluntarily ignoring a violation of the law, however, no police protection could be assigned to the games at Ridgewood. With tensions still running high over Saturday's contest, Von der Ahe expressed concern for the safety of his ball club and refused to play the Sunday game at Ridgewood: "If, with their police arrangements at Washington Park on Saturday they could not protect us, how would they do it at Ridgewood without police? I was stoned at Ridgewood last year, and I don't want any more of it. My players said that they would not go to Ridgewood. . . . They are afraid of their lives."[30] As a result of the Browns' failure to appear, Brooklyn obtained another forfeited victory.

Von der Ahe vowed that he would get the forfeits reversed at a special meeting of the American Association. He placed the blame for "this terrible state of affairs" upon Byrne: "At his door, the responsibility lies for inciting his mob of people to riotous demonstrations." From a starkly different perspective, Byrne demanded that the Association expel the Browns for refusing to play a scheduled game.[31] On September 23 the American Association convened to resolve the controversy.

The league's board of directors—which included representatives of the Cincinnati Red Stockings, Louisville Colonels, Columbus Buckeyes, and Philadelphia

Athletics—arrived at a compromise settlement. On the one hand, the board emphatically supported the Browns regarding the game played on Saturday, September 7, at Brooklyn's Washington Park. It overturned the forfeit and ruled that the Browns had won the game by a score of 4–2. Naturally, the board also canceled the automatic fifteen-hundred-dollar fine that had been imposed upon the Browns for forfeiting the game. Finally, Goldsmith, the umpire who had declared a forfeit, received an official reprimand and an abrupt dismissal from the Association's staff of umpires. On the other hand, the board refused to revoke the forfeit and fine for the Sunday game at Ridgewood.[32]

Initially, this decision seemed more popular in St. Louis than in Brooklyn. While the Browns joined the majority of the Association in a 6–2 vote favoring acceptance of the board's judgment, the Bridegrooms and the Baltimore Orioles dissented. The *Sporting News* considered the outcome "a famous victory for Von der Ahe" since the Browns' owner succeeded "in not only having the 4–2 game awarded them, but in having one of Byrne's props, Goldsmith, knocked out from under him."[33]

Ironically, though, the forfeit of the Sunday game ultimately cost the Browns an opportunity to gain their fifth consecutive Association pennant. When the regular season ended, Brooklyn's record stood at 93–44—two games better than the 90–45 mark of the Browns. If instead of forfeiting the Browns had played and won the Sunday game at Ridgewood, the margin would have been erased: St. Louis (with a record of 91–44) would have surpassed Brooklyn (92–45) in winning percentage by a margin of .674 to .672. Consequently, the *Sporting News* branded Brooklyn as the "Bogus Champions" of the American Association, and Von der Ahe protested, "We have lost, but it was scheming and not ballplaying which beat us."[34]

A month after the end of the regular season the American Association held its annual meeting at the Fifth Avenue Hotel in New York City. The major order of business involved electing a new president to replace the departing Wheeler Wikoff. The election would be shaped by the newfound realization that a single executive decision could determine the outcome of the pennant race. Both St. Louis and Brooklyn fought to get their own candidate elected to the position. Byrne backed L. C. Krauthoff of the Kansas City Cowboys, while Byrne's opponents, spearheaded by Von der Ahe, adamantly opposed Krauthoff.[35]

Earlier in the season, the *Sporting News* had harshly criticized the influence that Brooklyn exerted over the Kansas City ball club: "[Brooklyn] has a mortgage on the Kansas City franchise and threats to foreclose always brings the latter to time." Von der Ahe certainly did not want to replace Wikoff, whom he had denounced two years earlier as "a catspaw in the hands of Byrne," with a man apparently as pliable as Krauthoff. As an alternative, Von der Ahe nominated the Louisville Colonels' Zach Phelps. A deadlock developed between the nominees supported by Byrne and Von der Ahe.[36] For sixteen straight ballots, Von der Ahe, supported by the Philadelphia Athletics, Louisville Colonels, and Columbus Buckeyes, voted for Phelps. Byrne, backed by the Baltimore Orioles, Kansas City Cowboys, and Cincinnati Red Stockings, held out for Krauthoff. Following the sixteenth ballot, Byrne's faction proposed a recess for the day. The vote to recess divided evenly along the same lines as the balloting for president. When the St. Louis faction voted to stay in session, the Brooklyn faction walked out in disgust. Early the next morning, the Brooklyn faction returned, and another marathon session commenced. Yet the same deadlock persisted. That afternoon, Brooklyn and Cincinnati dramatically withdrew from the American Association and joined the National League.[37]

Although a sensational development, the transfer did not come entirely as a surprise. Throughout the previous two seasons, rumors had been circulating that the Bridegrooms and Red Stockings intended to abandon the American Association in favor of the National League.[38] Byrne preferred the League's fifty-cent ticket price; his Brooklyn team had drawn so well in the previous three seasons that he did not depend upon Sunday games for a big payday; and, most important, he did not want to stay in the American Association once Von der Ahe neutralized his control over it.

Aaron Stern, president of the Red Stockings, also had professed enthusiasm for the fifty-cent ticket price and publicly expressed his belief that "a winning club in the League at Cincinnati would prove a bonanza." Apparently, he only resisted transferring in 1888 because of the National League's prohibitions against beer sales and Sunday games. Then, two factors helped to push Cincinnati into the League. First, Stern bought out the interests of John Hauck, the remaining Red Stockings' investor most closely affiliated with brewery interests, thereby reducing the importance of beer sales to the Cincinnati organization. Second, local Sabbatarians temporarily managed to block Sunday games from being played in Cincinnati. As early as September 1889 Stern had announced, "Now that we are not allowed the privilege of playing Sunday games at Cincinnati, we belong in the League. I have for some time been a candidate for League honors, and, if the place is offered, I will most certainly accept."[39]

But even if the defections of Brooklyn and Cincinnati were not utterly unexpected, they undoubtedly sounded a death knell for the American Association. Shortly afterward, both the Baltimore Orioles and Kansas City Cowboys—the other two teams aligned with Byrne at the 1889 convention—resigned from the American Association. Kansas City joined the Western Association, and Baltimore entered the Atlantic Association.[40] By departing for minor leagues, the two clubs spoke volumes about the rapidly declining status of the American Association.

As late as 1886 the American Association could still bask in the glory of being the major league with the largest market size, the best attendance, and the most success in head-to-head competition. By the end of the decade, though, it clearly had been passed by the National League. The League had outdrawn the Association in attendance for three successive seasons and also had won the last three World Series. In the battle for New York, the biggest market, the rise of the League's New York Giants—the 1888–1889 World Series champions—had crowded the New York Metropolitans completely off the Association map. The National League, bolstered by its successful raids of the Association's Pittsburgh and Cleveland franchises, already enjoyed a large advantage in market size during the 1889 season. This advantage became even larger once the Cincinnati and Brooklyn clubs had been snatched away. Brooklyn had been major-league baseball's home attendance leader for the preceding year.[41]

Reeling from the loss of half its 1889 membership, the American Association could only respond by placing an inferior club in Brooklyn and trying to cultivate new teams in three small markets—Toledo, Syracuse, and Rochester. During the 1890 season the National League would enjoy a population base twice the size of the American Association. The *Sporting News* issued an ominous warning to the Association: "A circuit composed of clubs, a majority of whom represent second and third rate cities, is not calculated to draw out the masses of people who have been educated to think that the best and strongest clubs come only from the larger cities."[42]

The blows could not have occurred at a worse time for the American Association, which was forced to wage this uneven struggle after losing many of its biggest stars and best gate attractions to raids from an upstart, the Players' League. In 1890 the American Association would compete in a greatly weakened state against a pair of leagues with population bases twice its own size.

10

War and Peace

> The people that support the game here are those who have to work for their bread and butter. . . . The best supporters are those who work in the manufactories in South and North St. Louis and who find no time to devote to their favorite sport except on Sunday afternoons.
>
> —*Sporting News,* July 21, 1888

> I will tell you just what . . . the outcome of the Brotherhood business will be. They may try it for a while, but it won't work, and then we will have one big league of twelve or fifteen teams. It's coming to it, and all the organizations are bound to be merged into it. The trouble now is that we have to skirmish around each year, in each ball organization to find cities. Some of these don't amount to much—Indianapolis and Washington, for instance, but you have to take them in.
>
> —Chris Von der Ahe, speculating about the future prospects of the Players' League and major league baseball, quoted in the *Sporting News,* October 26, 1889

> That pure (?) and saintly body, the [National] League, with ostentatious godliness, has shouted itself hoarse over Sunday games and beer.
>
> —*Sporting News,* November 23, 1889

The Players' League had been formed as the by-product of a labor dispute between the National League and its players. In October 1885, nine players on the New York Giants formed the first local chapter of the Brotherhood of Professional Baseball Players. They selected the team's star shortstop, John Montgomery Ward, as the Brotherhood's president. Ward, an honor graduate of Columbia University Law School, organized chapters on every National League team. Originally, the Brotherhood merely sought to modify certain objectionable aspects of player contracts. For example, the Brotherhood wanted the owners to repeal officially the virtually ignored Limit Agreement on salaries. Also, while the Brotherhood was willing to accept the reserve clause, it asked the owners to refrain from reserving players at reduced salaries. The National League seemed receptive to discussing labor issues with the Brotherhood. The League even appeared prepared to grant concessions, although it eventually failed to abide by these promises. Since the Limit Agreement on salaries went unenforced, the Brotherhood remained willing to tolerate the status quo for baseball's labor relations.[1]

In November 1888 the attitudes of both the National League and the Brotherhood hardened when League officials adopted the Salary Classification Plan. This scheme called for salaries to be "limited, regulated and determined by the classification and grade to which such players may be assigned by the secretary of the League, after the termination of the championship season." Salaries were to range from $1,500 for a Class E player to a maximum of $2,500 for a Class A player, with a $250 incremental increase all the way up the scale for Class D, C, and B players. In arriving at this public grade for the value of each National League player, the Salary Classification Plan called upon the secretary to take into account both ball-playing ability and off-field personal conduct.[2]

In general, the Brotherhood deplored the idea of a limit on the potential annual earnings of a player. The top players of the era received salaries twice as much as the maximum $2,500 permitted under the Salary Classification Plan.[3] Furthermore, the Brotherhood specifically resented the notion of players being publicly graded on their personal and professional lives.

When the National League refused to engage in a simple discussion of the matter with Ward, the Brotherhood proceeded with its own secret plan to form a Players' League, locating entrepreneurs able to provide financial backing in every National League city except Cincinnati. Buffalo filled out the organization. The structure of the Players' League permitted the ballplayers to be active participants in both administrative and economic spheres. A sixteen-man Senate functioned as its government. Each team sent two representatives to the Senate—one capitalist and one player. As for finances, after paying expenses and salaries, each investor would be allowed to keep the first $10,000 of his anticipated profits. The next $10,000 in profits would be divided among all of the Brotherhood players. If any club earned more than $20,000 in a single season, the additional profits would be evenly distributed among all the teams in the Players' League. Unlike the National League and American Association, where only a few privileged player-managers such as Charles Comiskey or Cap Anson actually owned stock in their team, all Brotherhood ballplayers were encouraged to purchase shares in their clubs. In its player contracts, the Players' League discarded the salary levels of the Classification Plan and the restrictive reserve clause. The Players' League, however, did require that each player sign a three-year commitment at the same salary that he had received prior to the Classification Plan.[4]

The American Association at first hoped to stay out of this war between the National League and its ballplayers. In March 1889, trying to avoid the crossfire, the Association voted to reject the Salary Classification Plan. Eight months later, when Ward formally announced the organization of the Players' League, no Association player officially belonged to a Brotherhood chapter. The *Sporting News* conjectured, "In no way will the move of the Brotherhood affect the standing of the American Association. The new [Players' League] will say to the officers of the American Association, 'Keep out of the fight, and we will let your players alone.' "[5]

As the Players' League took shape, though, it turned out that the Association had been engaging in wishful thinking. Many Association players sympathized with the Brotherhood, and the Players' League did sign players off of American Association rosters. Altogether, out of the 124 players who saw action in ten or more games in the Players' League, 81 were former National League players, 28 were former American Association players, and 15 had come from the ranks of the minor leagues.[6]

The St. Louis Browns absorbed the most casualties of any Association ball club, losing seven players, including Comiskey. Three factors made the Browns particularly vulnerable to raids from the Players' League. First, their roster included some of the finest and most renowned players in the country. The Players' League, therefore, regarded numerous Browns as attractive additions to the Brotherhood. Second, in the 1889 season, relations between Von der Ahe and his players had grown increasingly strained. Third, Comiskey, so often effective in mediating disputes between Von der Ahe and the Browns players, complained that his influence on the team's owner had waned during the 1889 season. The second and third factors were obviously interrelated. Tensions mounted between Von der Ahe and his players because Comiskey could no longer act as a constraint on him. In 1889 Von der Ahe repeatedly fined players, accused them of throwing games, suspended four team members (third baseman Arlie Latham and a trio of pitchers—Nat Hudson, Silver King, and Icebox Chamberlain), and ultimately traded Hudson to Louisville. Comiskey blamed all of this turmoil on the presence of Von der Ahe's son, Eddie, as a newly established team official ("I was satisfied he was the mischief maker, as previous to his advent, I had always gotten along well with his father").[7]

In January 1890, after spending months denying that he intended to leave the Browns to become the player-manager on the Chicago Brotherhood team, Comiskey finally confirmed the truth of this persistent rumor. In a threefold explanation, he cited his deteriorating relationship with Von der Ahe, support for the Brotherhood cause, and a desire to play in his hometown of Chicago. Von der Ahe denounced Comiskey as "the most ungrateful of all men," claiming that he "was of a very ugly disposition and could never gain the good will of his men." It is apparent, given the later restoration of a close friendship between Von der Ahe and Comiskey, that Von der Ahe spoke out of his bitterness of the moment and his sense of anger, disappointment, and betrayal. Von der Ahe, after all, had made Comiskey one of only four major-league players to receive the game's largest annual salary of five thousand dollars. However, the Browns' owner certainly erred in claiming that Comiskey could not get along with his players. Of the six other Browns who signed contracts with the Players' League, four departed St. Louis to play for Comiskey in Chicago.[8]

All three major leagues suffered severe financial setbacks in 1890. For the first time since 1882, none of the major leagues surpassed the one million mark in total attendance. The Players' League not only maintained the National League's more expensive fifty-cent ticket price but also adhered to National League policies against liquor sales and Sunday games. These positions cost it support from its natural constituency of sympathetic working-class laborers. Nevertheless, the Players' League possessed the major advantage of having cornered the game's best talent, and the baseball public rewarded it with the best total attendance among the three leagues (980,877). Yet the new league still lost a reported $125,000. The total deficit of the Players' League, counting the construction costs of new ballparks, reached $340,000. Of all the Players' League teams, only the pennant-winning Boston Reds turned a profit.[9]

The American Association had been weakened by both the Players' League raids on its ballplayers *and* the National League raids on Association franchises. These dual raids so depleted the Association talent supply that the Louisville Colonels rose from last place in the 1889 Association standings to first place in 1890. However, although half of the Association was now composed of undesirable small markets (Syracuse, Toledo, Rochester, and Columbus), most of its franchises did benefit from avoiding direct competition with the other two leagues. Recent research has revealed that, contrary to previous historical accounts, the Association did not finish a distant third in 1890 attendance figures. In fact, the American Association, with a total attendance of 803,200 spectators, drew larger gatherings than the National League. But of its teams, only the Louisville champions could claim a profit.[10]

The National League finished last among the three leagues in attendance with a paltry total of 776,042. Estimates of National League losses ranged from $231,000 to $500,000. No National League team could turn a profit. The League did, however, cling to one important advantage. A. G. Spalding, the owner of the Chicago White Stockings and leader of the National League's War Committee, devised an imaginative strategy to dupe the capitalists of the Players' League. After the 1890 season, Spalding out-bluffed the owners of the Players' League teams, convincing them that the National League was absolutely resolved and perfectly willing to war through another season. The Brotherhood's uneasy capitalist sponsors, who had anticipated profits but instead acquired deficits, failed to grasp the desperate condition of the two older leagues. Acting independently of the Brotherhood, they negotiated a peace settlement with their fellow capitalists from the National League and American Association.[11] Most of the principal investors in the Players' League, even after selling out the Brotherhood, continued to hold shares in major-league ball clubs.

Three Players' League franchises—New York, Brooklyn, and Pittsburgh—merged with their National League counterparts. Al Johnson, owner of the Players' League franchise in Cleveland, could not work out a merger with his National League counterpart. However, in a tangled legal situation, he and other Players' League investors still held stock in the National League's Cincinnati club. John Addison, owner of the Chicago Pirates of the Players' League, received stock in the National League's New York Giants in exchange for permitting Spalding to buy out the Pirates.[12]

Two other Players' League teams, Philadelphia and Boston, joined the American Association. The American Association's franchise in Philadelphia, the Athletics, went bankrupt near the end of the 1890 season. Therefore, George and J. Earle Wagner, the brothers who owned the Philadelphia ball club in the Players' League, were accepted into the Association and allowed to take over the traditional nickname of "Athletics." Also, Charles Prince brought the pennant-winners of the Players' League, the Boston Reds, into the American Association. The owners of the National League's Boston franchise, as a price for surrendering their territorial rights of the National Agreement, forced Prince to return all of his former National League players. In the end, out of all the principal investors in the Players' League, only the owners of the Buffalo Bisons were denied a slice of the major-league pie. Buffalo lacked a National League counterpart to join forces with, and the Association shunned the city as an unpromising market.[13]

After only one tumultuous season, the Players' League ceased to exist. Yet peace did not immediately come to baseball circles. Trouble soon rose again when the National League and the American Association clashed over the rights to a pair of players, Harry Stovey and Louis Bierbauer. Following the 1890 season, some confusion persisted over the rights to the players who had belonged to the Brotherhood. In most cases, a Brotherhood player simply returned to the team that had reserved him back in 1889. However, some of the former Players' League investors wanted to keep their best performers. Consequently, special stipulations were occasionally involved in assigning the rights to Brotherhood players. Stovey had played in 1889 with the Association's Philadelphia Athletics, then had joined the Players' League champion Boston Reds in 1890, and was scheduled to move intact with the Reds into the Association for the 1891 season. On the other hand, Bierbauer had been slated simply to return to his 1889 team, the Philadelphia Athletics of the American Association.

Early in 1891, however, National League teams signed both Stovey and Bierbauer. The American Association, already angered at the National League's raids of its franchises, now decided that the League no longer recognized its player rights. If the League did not acknowledge the Association's right to its own franchises and players, then the National Agreement could not be considered as being worth the paper it was written on. In protest, the American Association withdrew from the National Agreement, which had maintained a tenuous peace between the two rival organizations since 1883, and plunged the baseball world into a second straight season of warfare.[14]

The American Association waged one last spirited battle against its old adversary. In August 1890 the Baltimore Orioles had rejoined the American Association to replace the Brooklyn Gladiators, a last-place team unable to find favor in a city that boasted pennant contenders in both of the other two leagues. Following the 1890 season, the Association bought out the three small-market franchises it had added that year—Toledo, Rochester, and Syracuse—for a combined total of twenty-four thousand dollars. To replace them, the Association picked up Boston from the Players' League and also organized new teams in Washington, D.C., and Cincinnati. Although the National League still held a considerable advantage in population base over the American Association, 5.713 million to 3.158 million, League markets no longer doubled the size of Association cities. Furthermore, while the National League regained its edge in attendance during 1891, both the Association and League recovered strongly at the box office from their dismal showing of the preceding season. In 1891, National League attendance rebounded by more than 74 percent, from 776,042 in 1890 to 1,352,487. American Association attendance also enjoyed a resurgence, increasing by 46 percent from 803,200 in 1890 to 1,173,000 a year later.[15]

In St. Louis especially, baseball enjoyed renewed excitement. The 1890 season had seen a local "dearth in patronage." The *Sporting News* believed that under the circumstances, the apathy of the St. Louis baseball public was inevitable:

> Not only did we lose the bone and sinew of a ballteam that has always held its own in the baseball world, but we were forced to travel in company of the one-

> horse order. . . . The Mound City was not only treated to a very mediocre team, but her men were put in competition with those of second and third rate cities so that even had it been victorious there would not have been much to crow about.[16]

However, in depicting the 1890 Browns as "a very mediocre team," the *Sporting News* revealed the high expectations that Comiskey's Browns had created for the ball club. The 1890 team had finished third in the American Association with a respectable record of 78–58. Nevertheless, attendance in St. Louis plunged to 105,000, the lowest total in any of the Browns' American Association years.[17]

With the demise of the Players' League, though, Comiskey returned to St. Louis to lead the 1891 Browns. Two former Browns who had followed Comiskey to Chicago, left fielder Tip O'Neill and catcher Jack Boyle, accompanied him on his homecoming. They reunited with three former teammates who had remained in St. Louis for the 1890 season—right fielder Tommy McCarthy, shortstop William "Shorty" Fuller, and pitcher Jack Stivetts. In a burst of nostalgia, St. Louisans flocked to Sportsman's Park to get a glimpse of Comiskey's Browns. On April 12, the first Sunday of the season, some fifteen thousand fans assembled there to see the Browns thrash Cincinnati, 10–2. The *Sporting News* proudly proclaimed, "St. Louis is again the baseball city of the West." Almost two months later, with the Browns and Boston Reds in a neck-and-neck race for the top spot in the Association standings, a Sportsman's Park record crowd of 17,439 turned out for a Sunday contest between the two pennant contenders.[18] Boston won the game, 8–6, but the two teams remained virtually deadlocked in the American Association standings until August.

In August, three developments distressed Chris Von der Ahe. First, the Browns dropped out of pennant contention. The Boston Reds pulled away to a comfortable lead, and they eventually claimed the American Association title by eight and a half games over the second-place Browns. Second, after continually losing money by bankrolling the Association's Cincinnati Porkers, Von der Ahe finally surrendered and sold the franchise to the Milwaukee Brewers of the Western Association. The American Association transferred the Porkers' famous player-manager, Mike "King" Kelly, back to Boston, where he was still revered for his past playing exploits. The Brewers took their pick of the other Porkers and joined the American Association, then further embarrassed Von der Ahe by easily surpassing the performance of his Cincinnati club, both on the playing field and at the box office.[19] To top the month off, Von der Ahe suffered yet another setback while pursuing a peace agreement with the National League.

In late August, following his strategic retreat from Cincinnati, Von der Ahe traveled to Washington, D.C., as part of a three-man Association peace delega-

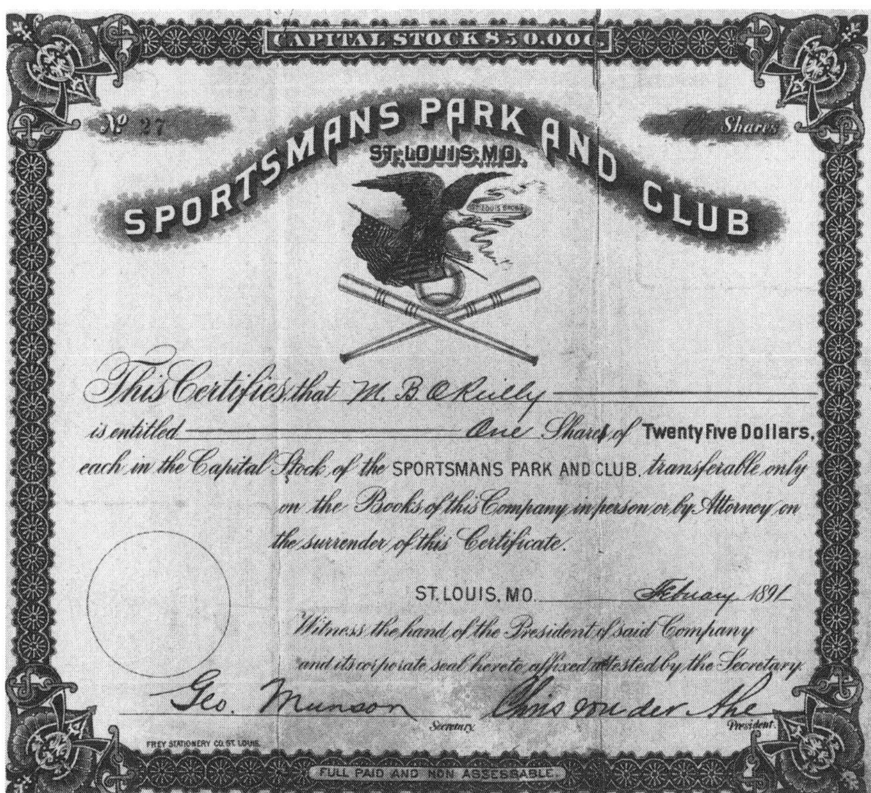
CAPITAL STOCK $50,000
No 27
SPORTSMANS PARK AND CLUB
ST. LOUIS, MO.
This Certifies that M. B. O'Reilly
is entitled One Share of Twenty Five Dollars,
each in the Capital Stock of the SPORTSMANS PARK AND CLUB, transferable only
on the Books of this Company in person or by Attorney on
the surrender of this Certificate.
ST. LOUIS, MO. February 1891
Witness the hand of the President of said Company
and its corporate seal hereto affixed attested by the Secretary.
Geo. Munson, Secretary
Chris Von der Ahe, President.
FREY STATIONERY CO. ST. LOUIS.
FULL PAID AND NON ASSESSABLE.

Stock certificate of the Sportsman's Park Club. In February 1891, amidst the local euphoria over the return of Charles Comiskey and other old Browns to St. Louis, M. B. O'Reilly purchased this share from President Von der Ahe. Missouri Historical Society, St. Louis.

tion. The National League sent a similar three-man committee. But shortly after the start of the Washington conference, a fateful telegram arrived from Boston. It informed the American Association peace committee that the National League's Boston Beaneaters had just raided the popular Kelly off the roster of the Boston Reds.[20] In the eyes of Von der Ahe and the Louisville Colonels' Zach Phelps, this action constituted a treacherous act of war conducted under the guise of a cease-fire. The news utterly disrupted the Washington conference.

Von der Ahe and Phelps threatened that unless the National League's peace committee promptly returned Kelly to the Reds, the American Association would terminate the negotiations. When the National League representatives protested that such a step exceeded their authority and could only be authorized by a majority vote of the entire League, the Association delegation departed.[21]

By signing Kelly, the Beaneaters provoked a flurry of player raids. Over the next few months twenty-eight ballplayers agreed to switch from one major league to the other for the 1892 season. Most of these players were lured from their teams by "exorbitant salaries." As raids and counter-raids escalated at a dizzying pace, the Association plucked thirteen players from National League rosters while the League snatched fifteen others from American Association squads. The Browns suffered the most damage, losing seven members of the team to the clutches of the National League: Comiskey, O'Neill, McCarthy, Stivetts, Boyle, Fuller, and third baseman Denny Lyons. Von der Ahe retaliated by raiding four National Leaguers. Among League teams, the New York Giants sustained the most losses with six players taken, followed closely by the Chicago White Stockings, who lost five.[22]

By mid-November, when National League owners gathered in New York City for their annual convention, this wild spending spree had finally started to subside. In its place, as the owners suddenly came to their senses, spiraling salaries again emerged as a chief concern. To combat this problem, the League formed another three-man peace committee and authorized it to seek a consolidation with some of the American Association clubs. The committee traveled to St. Louis in early December and met Von der Ahe at the Southern Hotel.[23]

The League's peace committee still regarded Von der Ahe, despite his recent reversals, as a power to be reckoned with. After all, in 1891 Von der Ahe's Browns had once more led the major leagues in total attendance. As far back as 1887, Von der Ahe had expressed interest in consolidating the strongest Association and League teams. At that time, the consolidation plan had been blocked by the National League's opposition to the American Association's business practices, especially Sunday games. But now the League's representatives conceded to Von der Ahe that the long-standing opposition to the Association's practices of twenty-five-cent ticket prices, beer sales, and Sunday games would be dropped. Instead, each team would be given the right to decide these questions for themselves.[24]

Von der Ahe, now assured of conducting his business as usual in St. Louis, could see no reason to continue the costly baseball war. The National League's peace committee had called for the same terms of consolidation, at long last, that Von der Ahe had been requesting for the preceding four years.[25] At the end of the Southern Hotel conference, Von der Ahe and the League's representatives signed a preliminary agreement. They arranged to present this document for approval from both leagues at a joint conference to be held at Indianapolis on December 15.

Prior to the Indianapolis conference, the *Sporting News* worried restlessly over whether the National League might reject the consolidation "on any terms which may lead to Sunday games." It particularly feared the influence of Arthur Soden, one of the owners of the Boston Beaneaters, and A. G. Spalding, who now held a controlling interest in both the Chicago White Stockings and the New York Giants.[26] In fact, the Philadelphia Quakers did raise an objection to Sunday games at the Indianapolis conference. If Soden and Spalding had sided with Philadelphia, the League would have deadlocked between the four teams that had originated in the National League (Chicago, Boston, New York, and Philadelphia) and the four franchises that originated in the Association and were then raided (Pittsburgh, Cleveland, Brooklyn, and Cincinnati).

Neither Soden nor Spalding voiced any support for the Philadelphia position, though, and the objection quickly died. Spalding later rationalized that although he was still personally opposed to Sunday games, the presence of so many former Association teams in the League had forced him to reconsider his attitude: "[When] the League circuit was composed exclusively of cities not desiring Sunday baseball, there was no reason to do otherwise than refrain from it, as all the clubs were a unit. Now, however, a number of new clubs have been admitted, and they desire to play on Sundays. Their wishes deserve consideration."[27] Yet Spalding had never articulated this belief in local option during 1885–1886 when he denied Henry Lucas and the St. Louis Maroons the right to play Sunday games.

Spalding actually wanted to avoid a convention divided like the 1889 American Association fiasco. He had no desire to see Charles Byrne of the Brooklyn Bridegrooms stage another walk-out, this time perhaps taking half of the National League franchises back into the American Association. Besides, Spalding and Soden each possessed an ulterior motive to stand behind the consolidation proposal. For Spalding, the planned Association franchise in Chicago would be bought out before it ever took the field. Likewise, Soden would benefit from having his local Association competitor bought out.[28]

The most difficult task at the Indianapolis conference, as it turned out, involved setting a price for the lame ducks of the American Association. But after a great deal of debate and dickering, the National League shelled out a grand total of $131,500 to persuade Philadelphia, Milwaukee, Chicago, and Boston to resign from the Association. In addition, Charles Prince, the owner of the Association's Boston Reds, received a quarter interest in Soden's National League Boston Beaneaters. J. Earle Wagner, owner of the Philadelphia Athletics of the American Association, also stayed in the baseball business by buying a controlling interest in one of the Association clubs to be consolidated, the Washington Senators. This left behind the four clubs slated to consolidate with the National League—the

St. Louis Browns, Louisville Colonels, Baltimore Orioles, and Washington. On December 17, 1891, these four franchises dissolved the American Association and then officially joined the National League.[29]

Ironically, because of one aspect of the consolidation agreement that the National League reneged on, most modern historians have failed to grasp that the December 1891 consolidation was a merger of business interests. The original plan had been to give the new "big league" a name that would have befitted the merger of the old rivals—the American League. However, at the last moment, National League owners rejected this name because it gave first billing to the word "American" rather than "National." Instead, in 1892 the "big league" took the field under the long-winded banner of the "National League and American Association." Sportswriters soon shortened the title back to the simpler "National League." This had unfortunate consequences for historical truth. Since the name of the "National League" survived and the name of the "American Association" vanished, most modern historians assume that the National League unequivocally "won" the baseball war.[30]

Such an interpretation is far too simplistic. From one perspective, the consolidation did mark a poignant end to the colorful career of the American Association. But looked at from a different angle, the American Association's cause triumphed. The twelve teams of the newly consolidated "big league" were composed of three evenly divided groups: the four newly admitted Association franchises, the four franchises that originated in the Association and had then been raided by the League, and the four franchises that had originated in the National League. Therefore, eight of the twelve members of the consolidated National League traced their origins to the American Association. Even after 1900, when the National League eliminated the franchises of four of the teams with Association roots, it still retained a distinct Association flavor. In the remarkably stable era of 1900–1952, the eight teams of the National League were equally composed of four franchises that had originated in the Association (St. Louis, Pittsburgh, Cincinnati, and Brooklyn) and four franchises that had originated in the League (Chicago, Boston, New York, and Philadelphia). Furthermore, while Chicago stands alone as the sole surviving charter member of the 1876 National League still playing baseball in the same city in which they started, three charter Association franchises (the St. Louis Cardinals, Cincinnati Reds, and Pittsburgh Pirates) continue in major-league baseball today as part of an unbroken chain beginning with the November 1881 formation of the American Association.[31]

The spirit of the American Association still persists. The National League of today bears a greater resemblance to the Association than to the pre-1892 League. All teams play Sunday games and serve beer in the ballpark, practices which might not have survived if the Association had not forced concessions on these questions in December 1891.

Von der Ahe took the St. Louis Browns into the National League on his own terms. The League conceded to him the right to play Sunday games, serve beer in the ballpark, and charge only twenty-five cents as the price of admission. Those concessions, though, represented Von der Ahe's last significant victory in baseball. The National League of the 1890s would be as frustrating for him as the American Association of the 1880s had been glorious.

Epilogue

Farewell to Chris Von der Ahe, 1892–1899

> Fans and players of the younger generation will only laugh, perhaps, at the German dialect stories that are told on the late Chris Von der Ahe as part of his obituary, and their main impression of the once famous owner of the old St. Louis Browns will be that he was a clown, given to much drink and squandering of money.
>
> But the veterans of the long ago, remembering what Chris really was and did, felt a choking in the throat and a scalding in the eyes when they read that he was no more. Mr. Von der Ahe had what convention terms faults, but they were only those of a plain and simple foreigner, suddenly elevated into a whirl of wealth and popularity. . . . As for Von der Ahe's virtues, they were those of a good-hearted, generous loyal character. . . . It is significant that those who knew him best held him in greatest regard.
>
> —the *Sporting News* obituary for Chris Von der Ahe, June 12, 1913

Throughout the 1880s, Chris Von der Ahe received appropriate public acclaim for saving major-league baseball in St. Louis from extinction. In June 1883 he had enhanced his favorable civic image even further, organizing a charity baseball game between his Browns and a team put together by the St. Louis Merchants Exchange that benefited local flood victims. Later, as the Browns claimed American Association championships from 1885–1888, Von der Ahe had been hailed for his role in building the "Four Time Winners." Along the route of the city's parade to celebrate the Browns' first Association pennant, the *St. Louis Globe-Democrat* observed that "cheer after cheer rent the air" as soon as Von der Ahe arrived. Von der Ahe lost some public support over his 1887 trades of five of the most popular Browns. However, despite his increasingly controversial reputation within national baseball circles, Von der Ahe remained generally popular in St. Louis as long as the Browns kept winning.[1]

After the Browns entered the National League, the public's perception of Von der Ahe became less positive. In the National League the Browns, stripped of

LEST WE FORGET!

By 1908, Chris Von der Ahe had fallen upon hard times, and a benefit baseball game was arranged on his behalf. This *St. Louis Globe-Democrat* cartoon tried to raise money to assist him by pointing out his vital role in St. Louis baseball history. State Historical Society of Missouri, Columbia.

practically their whole lineup, never gave Von der Ahe another winning record. Without the assistance of first baseman–manager Charles Comiskey, Von der Ahe lacked the skill and patience to rebuild the team. Over the next seven years he employed eighteen managers, even trying the job himself. Von der Ahe faced trouble off the field as well. Real estate values collapsed in the late 1880s, leaving him overextended and heavily indebted to the Northwestern Savings Bank of St. Louis. To pay his debts, Von der Ahe resorted to selling the services of many

Chris Von der Ahe's statue at Bellefontaine Cemetery in St. Louis. Photograph by author.

talented players. In the last two years of his ownership, the Browns finished last in the National League.[2]

As the nation slipped deeper into the economic depression of 1893–1897, Von der Ahe continued to squander his wealth in efforts to satisfy his passions for women and alcohol. In 1895 his affairs with two St. Louis women, Della Wells and Kittie Myers, provoked his wife, Emma, to sue him for divorce after twenty-five years of marriage. Emma received a generous alimony settlement, and Von der Ahe wed Wells. Edward Von der Ahe, the son of Chris and Emma, never spoke to his father again. Meanwhile, Chris Von der Ahe delighted in buying rounds of drink, especially champagne, for "a numerous army of flatterers and hangers-on." While establishing himself in St. Louis, Von der Ahe had been known as a thrifty businessman. But after baseball brought him fame and fortune, he frequently "handled $1000 bills as if they were peanuts to feed to monkeys."[3]

The new Sportsman's Park, built in 1893 at the corner of Vandeventer Avenue and Natural Bridge Road, was one of Von der Ahe's many risky real-estate ventures. On April 16, 1898, a disastrous fire virtually destroyed the ballpark. Von der Ahe sank his dwindling cash reserve into rebuilding it, but the fire hounded him. Some spectators, trampled in the rush to flee the burning ballpark, filed personal injury lawsuits against him. Confronted by too many creditors, Von der Ahe declared bankruptcy. He could not pay off the bonds used to finance the original construction of the new Sportsman's Park, and in March 1899 the Browns were sold at a public auction.[4]

Von der Ahe faded into the obscurity of the St. Louis saloon business. He did not prosper, and in the spring of 1908 a benefit baseball game was staged for him at the old Sportsman's Park on Grand Avenue. Amidst the other troubles of 1898, Von der Ahe had been divorced by his second wife, Della. He later married a third time, and this wife, the former Anna Kaiser, survived him. Von der Ahe died on June 5, 1913, of cirrhosis of the liver. Hundreds attended his funeral. Comiskey, then owner of the Chicago White Sox, eulogized his former boss as "the grandest figure baseball has ever known."[5] Von der Ahe is buried at Bellefontaine Cemetery in St. Louis beneath a life-sized marble statue of himself. His major-league baseball franchise lives on, now known as the Cardinals.

Appendix

"Only Doing What Is Right"

The Race Issue in Professional Baseball's Frontier Era

Philadelphia, September 10, 1887
-Chris Von der Ahe, Esq.:
DEAR SIR-

We, the undersigned members of the St. Louis Baseball Club, do not agree to play against negroes tomorrow. We will cheerfully play against white people at any time, and think by refusing to play we are only doing what is right, taking everything into consideration and the shape the team is in at present.

Signed-
W. A. Latham
John Boyle
J. E. O'Neill
R. L. Caruthers
W. Gleason
W. H. Robinson
Chas. King
and Curt Welch

—*A letter given by eight players of the St. Louis Browns to club owner Chris Von der Ahe before a scheduled exhibition game against the Cuban Giants,* St. Louis Globe-Democrat, *September 12, 1887*

On October 13, 1875, in the same ballpark where the Chicago White Stockings played their home games, two African-American baseball teams waged a heated contest. One club, the Blue Stockings, hailed from St. Louis; the other, the Uniques, were a local Chicago squad. Two days earlier, the visiting Blue Stockings had defeated the Uniques, 12–8, and now the home team sought with grim determination to earn a split in the rain-shortened series.[1] This game, with its premature ending and violent undertones, illustrated that African-American ball clubs were just as caught up in the regional rivalry between St. Louis and Chicago as their white counterparts in the major leagues.

The Blue Stockings trailed, 17–14, as they came to bat in the bottom half of the ninth inning. After the first two Blue Stockings batters reached base safely, the Uniques attempted to stall until the umpire called the game on account of darkness. However, when the Uniques' first baseman hid the game ball, umpire J. F. Thacker simply tossed another baseball to the pitcher and ordered the Uniques to "play ball." The Uniques refused to heed this admonition; as a consequence, the game abruptly ended. As the Blue Stockings tried to leave the ballfield, a stone-throwing mob approached them and inflicted severe injuries to two of their players, William Mitchell and William Pitts.[2]

A dispute ensued over the outcome of the game. According to the *Chicago Tribune,* umpire Thacker waved off the unfinished ninth inning and proclaimed the Uniques 15–14 winners in a darkness-shortened eight-inning contest. In a letter written to the *Tribune,* though, Thacker declared that the ball game had been forfeited to the Blue Stockings: "My decision . . . is that, upon the refusal of the Uniques to proceed with the game and their concealing the ball when called upon to produce it, under the circumstances, the game belongs to the Blue Stockings by 9 to 0."[3]

In 1875, the Blue Stockings and Uniques eerily foreshadowed a pair of disputed games played later by Chris Von der Ahe's St. Louis Browns—the controversial second game of the 1885 World Series against the Chicago White Stockings, and the riotous contest of September 7, 1889, with the Brooklyn Bridegrooms. The Blue Stockings–Uniques rivalry demonstrates that nineteenth-century African-American ball clubs, although usually segregated from white baseball, fought battles as intense as those waged by white major-leaguers.

Racial barriers in baseball extended back to its amateur days. In December 1867, at its annual convention, the National Association of Baseball Players adopted a resolution to deny admission to any teams "which might be composed of one or more colored persons."[4] Shunning an explicit written statement, the National League operated under a "gentleman's agreement" that banned African-American ballplayers from the time of the League's founding in 1876 until the arrival of Jackie Robinson in 1947.

Robinson, however, was not the first major-league ballplayer of African-American descent. That honor belongs to Moses Fleetwood Walker of the 1884 Toledo Blue Stockings of the American Association. Early that season, when Toledo visited Sportsman's Park to play the Browns, the *St. Louis Globe-Democrat* noted, "Among the spectators there were quite a number of colored individuals, attracted by the announcement that Walker, the colored catcher, would appear behind the bat for the visitors. They were enthusiastic over Walker, and manifested decided partiality for his club." Walker rewarded their support by singling twice in three at-bats and playing errorless ball. One of the better-hitting catchers in the game, Walker posted the fifth-highest batting average among twenty-four Association catchers. Late in the 1884 season his brother, Welday, played five games in the outfield for Toledo.[5] But when the Toledo ball club folded following the 1884 season, the Walker brothers disappeared from the major leagues. So did their entire race for the next sixty-three years.

The Walkers and other African-American players still continued to compete professionally in the minor leagues. A record total of twenty African-American ballplayers started the 1887 season on minor-league rosters, but a series of setbacks soon followed. Together, they set in motion a process that culminated in the exclusion of African-Americans from all of the organized minor leagues by 1892.[6]

In baseball mythology, Chicago White Stockings' player-manager Cap Anson has emerged as the villain supposedly responsible for singlehandedly imposing racial segregation on the sport. Robert Peterson, the first writer to examine thoroughly the history of racial segregation in the game, effectively argued that assigning Anson the sole blame for drawing baseball's color line "is to credit him with more influence than he had." Anson did threaten not to participate in a July 19, 1887, exhibition game against the Newark International League team if Newark used their top pitcher—George Stovey, an African-American, who won thirty-three games that year. Newark's capitulation allegedly ushered in a new era of racial segregation within the sport.[7]

Anson's action, however, did not occur within a social vacuum. It should be understood within the framework of the exclusionary racial standards that then prevailed both in baseball and the United States as a whole. Without doubt, Anson harbored racist thoughts. But his refusal to play against Newark and Stovey came five days *after* the International League had taken an even bigger step to segregate baseball. Home in 1887 to four other African-American stars besides Stovey, the International League voted to refrain from signing any additional African Americans. In defense of the vote, the International League explained, "Many of the best players in the League were anxious to leave on account of the colored element."[8] By refusing to bat against Stovey five days later, Anson could hardly have forced the International League to take a step that it had already taken.

Also, given the intense rivalry between Anson's White Stockings and the St. Louis Browns, it seems difficult to believe that the Browns would do anything simply to appease Anson. Yet a couple of months after Anson refused to take the field against Stovey, the world champion St. Louis Browns declined to play an exhibition game against the all-black Cuban Giants at West Farms, New York, with eight Browns signing the note to Chris Von der Ahe that voiced their objections.[9]

In the America of the late nineteenth century, many segregationists believed that they were "only doing what is right." Von der Ahe, aware of the social climate of the time, initially accepted his players' petition as a "matter of principle" and canceled the exhibition game. However, after investigating the matter further, he concluded that "this scheme" had been devised by "two or three" players to keep the Browns in Philadelphia, where they had made plans to attend the theater. The *Globe-Democrat* reported that "the leaders" behind the letter had been Arlie Latham, Jack Boyle, and Tip O'Neill—whose signatures, not so coincidentally, happened to be the first three appearing on the document. The newspaper also claimed that the three ringleaders "had considerable trouble in securing the signatures of some." Curt Welch, whose signature was the last added, had been a teammate of Moses Fleetwood Walker on the 1884 Toledo Blue Stockings. Obviously, he had signed with great reluctance. Ed Knouff, the newest member of the Browns, had refused to sign at all.[10]

Von der Ahe, after uncovering the circumstances behind the petition, protested, "The refusal of my men to play the Cuban Giants cost me at least $1000. . . . If it was a question of principle with any of my players, I would not say a word, but it is not." He likely fined Latham $100 and most assuredly rearranged the team's departure for Baltimore to deny Latham and the others their theater date in Philadelphia.[11]

If not for three factors, the whole rebellion might have been avoided. First, manager Charles Comiskey would probably have suppressed the revolt, but he had fractured his thumb earlier in the day and returned to St. Louis for treatment. Comiskey, contacted in St. Louis by the *Globe-Democrat,* immediately pointed out that the Browns had played previous exhibition games against the Cuban Giants and other African-American clubs "without a murmur." He instantly recognized the real motive behind the petition: "I think some of the boys wanted a day to themselves." Second, as the petition indicated, the Browns were truly a crippled ball club. Besides Comiskey, Dave Foutz and Doc Bushong were also in St. Louis recuperating from broken fingers. The Browns, down to nine players, were forced to continue starting Welch, Robinson, and Caruthers every day, despite their physical ailments.[12] Third, by the late nineteenth century, racism had become so ingrained in American society that weary and gimpy ballplayers turned to it as a convenient excuse for getting the day off.

It should be remembered that segregation in baseball is only a small part of a bigger story. In the late nineteenth century, the U.S. Supreme Court upheld Jim Crow–style racial segregation in a series of decisions, including its 1883 ruling on seven *Civil Rights Cases* that involved discrimination in places of public accommodation as well as the landmark 1896 *Plessy vs. Ferguson* decision.[13]

Notes

Prologue: Fall Festival

1. *Missouri Republican,* October 8, 1885; *St. Louis Globe-Democrat,* October 8, 1885; *St. Louis Post-Dispatch,* October 7–8, 1885; Robert Smith, *Baseball,* 137–38.

2. Lee Allen, *The World Series,* 18–19. Bill Gleason was born in St. Louis, Missouri, on November 12, 1858. His major-league playing career was in the American Association with the St. Louis Browns (1882–1887), Philadelphia Athletics (1888), and Louisville Colonels (1889). In six seasons with St. Louis, Gleason played on three consecutive pennant winners, averaged 92 runs scored per year, and hit for a .275 average. Rick Wolff, ed., *The Baseball Encyclopedia,* 8th ed., 90–92, 94–96, 99–100, 947–48; John Thorn, Pete Palmer, Michael Gershman, and David Pietrusza, eds., *Total Baseball,* 6th ed., 894, 1944–45, 1948–49, 1952–53.

Introduction: Take Me Out to the Nineteenth-Century Ball Game

1. *St. Louis Democrat,* May 7, 9, 1875; *St. Louis Globe-Democrat,* May 5, 1876. Thorn and Palmer, eds., *Total Baseball,* 3d ed., 2244–45, 2275, 2277–81; Harold Seymour, *Baseball: The Early Years,* 178; *Chicago Tribune,* May 6, 1876; *St. Louis Post-Dispatch,* July 4, 1885; Robert L. Tiemann, *Cardinal Classics: Outstanding Games from Each of the St. Louis Baseball Club's 100 Seasons, 1882–1981,* 14.

2. Bill James, *Historical Baseball Abstract,* 22; William Curran, *Mitts: A Celebration of the Art of Fielding,* 73–76; Benjamin G. Rader, *Baseball: A History of America's Game,* 64.

3. Seymour, *Baseball: The Early Years,* 176; John Thorn and John Holway, *The Pitcher,* 5, 7–8, 298–302; Thorn and Palmer, eds., *Total Baseball,* 3d ed., 2274, 2281–83, 2304. Tiemann, *Cardinal Classics,* 22; Rader, *Baseball,* 63–64; David Q. Voigt, *American Baseball,* vol. 1, 205; David Nemec, *The Beer and Whisky League: The Illustrated History of the American Association—Baseball's Renegade Major League,* 241.

4. Thorn and Holway, *The Pitcher,* 5–8, 300–301; Thorn and Palmer, eds., *Total Baseball,* 3d ed., 2279–80, 2283, 2304; Voigt, *American Baseball,* vol. 1, 205–6, 247–48; Rader, *Baseball,* 64. Seymour, *Baseball: The Early Years,* 60, 82, 177, 275. The National League, successor to the National Association, repeatedly enlarged the playing schedule. After its original season of 1876, the National League expanded its playing schedule in 1879, 1883, 1884, 1886, 1888, and 1891. In 1876, each National League team was expected to play seventy games. By 1891, the

number had doubled to 140 games. Similarly, in the American Association's debut season of 1882, each team in the league played eighty games; by 1886, four expansions later, Association teams were playing a 140-game schedule. Prior to the overhand delivery, the expanded playing schedule, and the increased pitching distance, David Nemec has noted in his historical text to *The Ultimate Baseball Book:* "Most pitchers routinely posted season win totals between 20 and 50, depending on the quality of the teams behind them." In the twenty-one years preceding the lengthening of the pitching distance to sixty feet and six inches, there were 119 occasions when a pitcher won thirty or more games in a single league during the course of a season. In more than one hundred years since the modern pitching distance was established, there have been only 35 thirty-game winners (and twelve of those achieved the feat from 1893–1896, the first four years at the new pitching distance). Thorn et al., eds., *Total Baseball,* 6th ed., 1908–2385; Daniel Okrent and Harris Lewine, eds., *The Ultimate Baseball Book,* 15–16; Rick Wolff, ed., *The Baseball Encyclopedia,* 8th ed., 63–539.

5. In 1880 the National League decreased the number of balls needed to draw a walk from nine to eight. The following year the number was reduced to seven. In 1884 the league dropped the necessary number of balls to walk to six, but briefly returned to the seven-ball requirement in 1886. The American Association maintained the seven-ball requirement for walks until 1886, when it dropped the number needed to six. At the joint League-Association rules conference of 1887, the two leagues agreed to pare the number of balls needed down to five. By 1889, both leagues had arrived at the current requirement of four balls for a walk. Seymour, *Baseball: The Early Years,* 176–77. In 1884, the American Association started awarding first base to a batter who had been hit by a pitch. The National League did not adopt this rule until 1887. Until the mid-1860s, fielders could record an out by merely catching a batted ball on the first bounce. Then, in either 1864 or 1865, the first-bound rule was eliminated for fair balls, but remained in effect for foul balls. In 1883 the National League dispensed altogether with the first-bound rule, but the American Association continued to count a foul ball snared on the first bounce as an out until June 7, 1885. Thorn and Holway, *The Pitcher,* 5, 299–300; Thorn and Palmer, eds., *Total Baseball,* 3d ed., 2272, 2278–82, 2303.

6. Thorn et al., eds., *Total Baseball,* 6th ed., 684; Okrent and Lewine, eds., *The Ultimate Baseball Book,* 13.

7. Thorn et al., eds., *Total Baseball,* 6th ed., 1176, 1906–19, 1989–2109; David Nemec, *The Great Encyclopedia of 19th Century Major League Baseball,* 17, 30, 45, 103; Thorn and Holway, *The Pitcher,* 6–11, 167; Harold Seymour, *Baseball: The Golden Age,* 423–25.

8. Thorn et al., eds., *Total Baseball,* 6th ed., 1907–2385. *St. Louis Dispatch,* May

5–7, 1875. Even the rival *Chicago Tribune* marveled at the power of Pike "to hoist a ball out among the freight-cars on the lake shore." *Chicago Tribune*, January 19, 1879.

9. Seymour, *Baseball: The Early Years*, 176–77, 275–76; Voigt, *American Baseball*, vol. 1, 207–8; Thorn and Holway, *The Pitcher*, 5–9, 299–302; James, *Historical Baseball Abstract*, 22, 58; Thorn and Palmer, eds., *Total Baseball*, 3d ed., 2279, 2282, 2285; Rader, *Baseball*, 64, 87.

10. Seymour, *Baseball: The Early Years*, 177; Voigt, *American Baseball*, vol. 1, 207; Thorn and Holway, *The Pitcher*, 8; Thorn and Palmer, eds., *Total Baseball*, 3d ed., 2281–82, 2306; Nemec, *Beer and Whisky League*, 130. Thorn et al., eds., *Total Baseball*, 6th ed., 1925–53. Three modern baseball encyclopedias have recalculated the 1887 batting averages of the major leagues to conform more closely with the standards of other seasons. They do not count walks as either a base hit or as an official at-bat. (Of course, even modern statisticians cannot take away the additional strike enjoyed by 1887 hitters.) In order to demonstrate the chaos wrought by the 1887 rule changes, I have adjusted the figures back to their original 1887 form. Or, in other words, I have taken the 6,053 walks drawn in the two major leagues during the 1887 season and added them to both the hits and at-bats categories. This increases the major-league batting average for 1887 from .271 to .325. A contemporary newspaper clipping, reprinted in Jordan A. Deutsch, Richard M. Cohen, Roland T. Johnson, and David S. Neft, eds., *The Scrapbook History of Baseball* (p. 24) reveals that eleven Association players were credited in 1887 with a batting average of .400 or higher. Modern baseball encyclopedias refuse to accept the 1887 rule that credited batters with a hit whenever they drew a walk, thus reducing the number of .400 hitters for the 1887 season to two in the American Association and none in the National League. Thorn et al., eds., *Total Baseball*, 6th ed., 1951–53; Wolff, ed., *Baseball Encyclopedia*, 8th ed., 98, 100; Nemec, *Encyclopedia of 19th Century Major League Baseball*, 320, 331.

11. Seymour, *Baseball: The Early Years*, 178; Voigt, *American Baseball*, vol. 1, 207–8; Thorn and Holway, *The Pitcher*, 8; Thorn and Palmer, eds., *Total Baseball*, 3d ed., 2279, 2281–83, 2304, 2306; Thorn et al., eds., *Total Baseball*, 6th ed., 1907–87; Rader, *Baseball*, 63–64.

12. Seymour, *Baseball: The Early Years*, 178, 275–76; Voigt, *American Baseball*, vol. 1, 207–8, 288; Seymour, *Baseball: The Golden Age*, 123, 423–25; Thorn and Holway, *The Pitcher*, 9–11, 13–14, 302; Thorn and Palmer, eds., *Total Baseball*, 3d ed., 1882–2109, 2300–2301; James, *Historical Baseball Abstract*, 58; Rader, *Baseball*, 64, 87.

13. Baseball, as depicted by Tristram Potter Coffin, has served since the nineteenth century as "a popular means of working out village-to-village rivalries." Thus, the game has functioned in the role of a "semi-civilized" substitute for

"village-to-village wars." Being only "semi-civilized," many fiercely contested ballgames "ended up in brawls." Coffin, *The Old Ball Game: Baseball in Folklore and Fiction,* 7.

Chapter 1: St. Louis versus Chicago

1. Wyatt Winton Belcher, *The Economic Rivalry between St. Louis and Chicago, 1850–1880;*

James Neal Primm, *Lion of the Valley: St. Louis, Missouri,* 234, 238; Jonathan Schnell, "Chicago Versus St. Louis: A Reassessment of the Great Rivalry," 247, 265.

2. Primm, *Lion of the Valley,* 285, 287.

3. Belcher, *Economic Rivalry,* 175–76, 206.

4. Another new arena of competition arrived when St. Louis hosted the 1904 World's Fair and sought to transcend the 1893 Columbian Exposition staged in Chicago. When the seven-month event closed in December 1904, former St. Louis mayor and Missouri governor David R. Francis, the fair's president, proudly noted that it had drawn larger numbers of out-of-state and foreign tourists than Chicago's Columbian Exposition. Sports were included in this as St. Louis used the attraction of the World's Fair to win selection over Chicago as the first U.S. city to host the Olympic Games. Primm, *Lion of the Valley,* 395–415; Harry M. Hagen, *This Is Our St. Louis,* 377–89; Mark Dyreson, "The Playing Fields of Progress: American Athletic Nationalism and the 1904 Olympics," 4–23. On early professional baseball teams, see Seymour, *Baseball: The Early Years,* 56–59; Voigt, *American Baseball,* vol. 1, 23–24, 33; Voigt, *Baseball: An Illustrated History,* 23–28; Charles C. Alexander, *Our Game: An American Baseball History,* 19–21; Rader, *Baseball,* 26–27; David Nemec and Saul Wisnia, *Baseball: More Than 150 Years,* 24–28; *Chicago Tribune,* April 30, 1870; May 2, 1870; E. H. Tobias, "Paid Players," *Sporting News,* December 14, 1895; "Down in Dixie," *Sporting News,* December 28, 1895; Alfred H. Spink, *The National Game,* 39.

5. Bill Borst, *Baseball through a Knothole: A St. Louis History,* 5; *Chicago Tribune,* April 30, May 2, 1870, May 6–10, 1874; *St. Louis Daily Globe,* May 1, 1874, also quoted in Gregg Lee Carter, "Baseball in St. Louis, 1867–1875: An Historical Case Study in Civic Pride," 261; Tobias, "Paid Players," *Sporting News,* January 18, 1896; Tobias, "Down in Dixie"; Tobias, "A Bad Beating," *Sporting News,* February 1, 1896; "First Browns," *Sporting News,* February 8, 1896; Spink, *National Game,* 38–39. In fairness to the St. Louis amateur teams, it should be pointed out that from 1867 through 1872 the Empires posted an excellent win-loss record of 19–9 against their out-of-state competitors, who were legitimate amateurs themselves and never joined the National Association.

6. Borst, *Baseball through a Knothole,* 5, 10; Tobias, "A Bad Beating"; "First Browns"; Anthony B. Lampe, "The Background of Professional Baseball in St. Louis," 31; *St. Louis Dispatch,* May 6, 1875.

7. Julian S. Rammelkamp claims that J. B. C. Lucas II was the wealthiest man in St. Louis. James Neal Primm simply places the Lucases and a few others "at the peak of the power structure" within the city. Julian S. Rammelkamp, *Pulitzer's Post-Dispatch, 1878–1883,* 51; Primm, *Lion of the Valley,* 191. See also Dumas Malone, ed., *Dictionary of American Biography,* vol. 11, 484–86; Primm, *Lion of the Valley,* 82, 86, 107–8, 190, 360; Harold Seymour, "St. Louis and the Union Baseball War," 257–69. J. B. C. Lucas II served as president of the original St. Louis Brown Stockings for all three years of their existence; in 1884 his younger brother, Henry V. Lucas, served as the president of a new league, the Union Association, which lasted only one season. It dissolved when Lucas accepted an offer to move his own St. Louis Maroons, the runaway pennant winners, into the more established National League. Lucas operated the Maroons in the National League for the next two seasons before selling the team to local interests in August of 1886. The Maroons completed the 1886 season in St. Louis, but were subsequently sold to John Brush, the owner of an Indianapolis department store. After Brush moved the team to Indianapolis for the 1887 season, he renamed it the "Hoosiers." Henry V. Lucas Vertical File, Missouri Historical Society Library, St. Louis; *Sporting News,* August 23, 1886; Borst, *Baseball through a Knothole,* 15. The sources for team nicknames are Wolff, ed., *Baseball Encyclopedia,* 8th ed., 60–61; and Nemec, *Encyclopedia of 19th Century Major League Baseball.*

8. Tobias, "First Browns"; Spink, *National Game,* 44; Primm, *Lion of the Valley,* 83, 360, 363, 449–50; Charles H. Turner Vertical File, Missouri Historical Society Library, St. Louis; Charles Van Ravenswaay, *St. Louis: An Informal History of the City and Its People, 1764–1865,* 131; William E. Foley, "William C. Carr," in Lawrence O. Christensen, William E. Foley, Gary R. Kremer, and Kenneth H. Winn, eds., *Dictionary of Missouri Biography,* 152–53. J. B. C. Lucas and William C. Carr, through discrediting large Spanish land grants held by the area's older French families, sought to open up the region for newcomers eager to purchase land—including themselves. Walter B. Stevens, *History of St. Louis: The Fourth City, 1764–1909,* vol. 2, 970–73; Borst, *Baseball through a Knothole,* 3, 9–11; Lampe, "Background of Professional Baseball in St. Louis," 14, 16.

9. Borst, *Baseball through a Knothole,* 7; Nemec, *Encyclopedia of 19th Century Major League Baseball,* 17, 30, 45, 74–75; Thorn et al., eds., *Total Baseball,* 6th ed., 764, 815, 1164, 1176, 1907, 1909, 1911, 1914; Wolff, ed., *Baseball Encyclopedia,* 8th ed., 2553–54, 2564, 2571. Robert Slater has unequivocally stated that Pike became the first professional baseball player in 1866, but other accounts

demonstrate that the practice of paying players predated 1866. Slater, *Great Jews in Sports,* 167; Seymour, *Baseball: The Early Years,* 47–48; Voigt, *American Baseball,* vol. 1, 15, 17, 19; Rader, *Baseball,* 21; Nemec and Wisnia, *Baseball,* 14, 16. Bob Carroll contributed an article to a 1987 book edited by John Thorn, *The National Pastime,* which credited Dickey Pearce with being "the first to play what we would consider the shortstop position." Carroll explained that, prior to Pearce pioneering the modern-day conception of a shortstop, the position had functioned closer to the role of a current softball rover: "Until Pearce came along in 1856, the 'shortstop' was a fourth outfielder whose job was to catch flares (or whatever they called them in those days) and to take short throws from the deep outfielders and relay them to the infield. (The early ball was so light that no one could throw it more than 200 feet or so.)" Later, Thorn wrote an article, in the 1993 third edition of the *Total Baseball* encyclopedia that he co-edited, which credited Daniel "Doc" Adams of the New York Knickerbockers with creating the position of shortstop in 1849 or 1850. Thorn added, however, that the position played by Adams differed from the function of a modern-day shortstop: "When Adams first went out to short, it was not to bolster the infield but to assist in relays from the outfield. The early Knickerbocker ball was so light that it could not be thrown even 200 feet; thus the need for a short fielder to send the ball in to the pitcher's point." Hence, when one carefully compares the Carroll article in a Thorn-edited book with Thorn's own article in another Thorn-edited book, the two articles appear to be more complementary than contradictory. Taken together, these articles indicate that "Doc" Adams invented a prototype of the shortstop position, which Dickey Pearce subsequently converted into the role of a modern-day shortstop. Bob Carroll, "For the Hall of Fame: Twelve Good Men," in Thorn, ed., *National Pastime,* 74–75; Thorn, "The True Father of Baseball," in Thorn and Palmer, eds., *Total Baseball,* 3d ed., 5–6; Seymour R. Church, *Baseball: The History, Statistics, and Romance of the American National Game,* 28–31.

10. *St. Louis Dispatch,* May 6, 1875; Lampe, "Background of Professional Baseball in St. Louis," 30; William J. Ryczek, *Blackguards and Red Stockings: A History of Baseball's National Association, 1871–1875,* 147, 187; Thorn et al., eds., *Total Baseball,* 6th ed., 689, 917, 1104; Wolff, ed., *Baseball Encyclopedia,* 8th ed., 2557, 2563; Nemec, *Encyclopedia of 19th Century Major League Baseball,* 49, 60.

11. *Sporting News,* October 11, November 20, 1886, February 11, 1905; Ed Fitzgerald, ed., *The National League,* 7; Robert Smith, *Baseball in the Afternoon: Tales from a Bygone Era,* 57; Thorn et al., eds., *Total Baseball,* 6th ed., 802, 913, 1906–7, 1910–11; Nemec, *Encyclopedia of 19th Century Major League Baseball,* 16–18, 31, 33, 46–47, 62; *Missouri Republican,* October 30, 1885; *St. Louis Globe-Democrat,* April 15, 1951, October 5, 1952, contained in the *Sports Scrapbook,* vol. 1, 15, 39–40, Missouri Historical Society Library, St. Louis; Jim Rygelski, "Base-

ball's 'Boss President': Chris Von der Ahe and the Nineteenth-Century St. Louis Browns," 44.

12. *St. Louis Dispatch,* May 6, 1875.

13. Ibid.; Thorn et al., eds., *Total Baseball,* 6th ed., 1683, 1910; Wolff, ed., *Baseball Encyclopedia,* 8th ed., 2563, 2571; Nemec, *Encyclopedia of 19th Century Major League Baseball,* 60–61.

14. Tobias, "First Browns."

15. *St. Louis Democrat,* February 16, 1875; also quoted in Carter, "Baseball in St. Louis," 262.

16. Tobias, "First Browns." McNeary, co-owner of a combination grocery store and saloon, was in an uncomfortable position. Lacking the financial reserves of J. B. C. Lucas II, McNeary fronted the Red Stockings almost singlehandedly. Meanwhile, Lucas's Brown Stockings received more support from small-scale investors, whose backing McNeary urgently needed. Robert L. Tiemann, ed., *St. Louis's Favorite Sport: Convention Brochure of the 22nd National SABR Convention,* 10–11; Carter, "Baseball in St. Louis," 262–63; Thorn et al., eds., *Total Baseball,* 6th ed., 105, 150, 274, 277, 1544; Borst, *Baseball through a Knothole,* 6. Ironically, after being included on the original Brown Stockings as a political necessity to offset resentment about the team's New York and Pennsylvania composition, Galvin later performed his greatest pitching exploits for Buffalo and Pittsburgh. While the Brown Stockings drew an average of more than 2,300 people per game in 1875, the Red Stockings' average crowd was around 465. Thorn and Palmer, eds., *Total Baseball,* 2d ed., 2522, provides the number of home games played.

17. Tobias, "First Browns"; *St. Louis Dispatch,* May 5, 1875.

18. Gregg Lee Carter claims that the Brown Stockings' game against Chicago on May 6 marked the team's debut. In fact, opening day occurred two days earlier. However, the Red Stockings were newcomers to the National Association, included largely to protest the Brown Stockings' exclusion of homegrown talent. Therefore, contemporary opinion viewed the Chicago game as the first major threat to the Brown Stockings. The *St. Louis Democrat,* for example, saw the contest with Chicago as "the first big game of the season" or "the first great game." Carter, "Baseball in St. Louis," 255, 262; *St. Louis Democrat,* May 6–7, 1875.

19. *St. Louis Democrat,* May 7, 1875, also quoted in Carter, "Baseball in St. Louis," 256; *St. Louis Dispatch,* May 6, 1875; *Chicago Tribune,* May 6, 1875.

20. *St. Louis Dispatch,* May 7, 1875. This is a very early portrayal of baseball as a psychological release from the troubles in a fan's daily life. The notion that baseball acted as a safety valve for urban laborers closely paralleled older theories which proclaimed that the agricultural frontier performed the same function for

this socioeconomic group. *St. Louis Democrat,* May 7, 1875; Tobias, "Marks An Era," *Sporting News,* November 23, 1895. Grand Avenue Park would later be renamed Sportsman's Park in 1881, and it became one of the most famous and revered ballparks in the country. After hosting its last major-league game on May 8, 1966, the site was divided into two baseball diamonds, where members of the Herbert Hoover Boys and Girls Club still play the game today. *Sporting News,* August 20, 1990.

21. *St. Louis Democrat,* May 7, 1875; *St. Louis Dispatch,* May 7, 1875. The Mississippi Valley Agricultural and Mechanical Fair was held annually in St. Louis each October from 1855 through 1903. "Big Thursday" had been a school holiday in St. Louis since the 1860s. Donald B. Oster, *Community Image in the History of St. Louis and Kansas City,* 220.

22. *St. Louis Dispatch,* May 6, 1875. Higham is now remembered in baseball history chiefly because of a brief umpiring career after his playing days. In 1882, after a series of dishonest decisions made by Higham were proved to have been made in collusion with gambling interests, he became the first and only major-league umpire to be permanently barred from the game. Lee Allen, *100 Years of Baseball,* 60–61; Seymour, *Baseball: The Early Years,* 343; James, *Historical Baseball Abstract,* 28; John Bowman and Joel Zoss, *Diamonds in the Rough: The Untold History of Baseball,* 302; Dan Gutman, *Baseball Babylon,* 352–53. Thorn et al., eds., *Total Baseball,* 6th ed., 948; Nemec, *Encyclopedia of 19th Century Major League Baseball,* 726; *St. Louis Democrat,* May 7, 1875; *St. Louis Dispatch,* May 7, 1875; *Chicago Tribune,* May 7, 1875.

23. *St. Louis Democrat,* May 7, 1875; *St. Louis Dispatch,* May 7, 1875; *Chicago Tribune,* May 7, 1875.

24. *St. Louis Democrat,* May 7, 9, 1875; *St. Louis Dispatch,* May 7, 1875; Thorn et al., eds., *Total Baseball,* 6th ed., 764; *Chicago Tribune,* May 7, 1875.

25. *St. Louis Dispatch,* May 7, 1875; *St. Louis Democrat,* May 7, 9, 1875.

26. In July 1870 the New York Mutuals shut out the Chicago White Stockings, 9–0. Baseball insiders derisively started using the term "Chicagoed" to designate a team that had gone a whole game without scoring. Church, *Baseball,* 24.

27. *St. Louis Democrat,* May 7, 1875; *St. Louis Dispatch,* May 7, 1875; *Chicago Tribune,* May 7, 1875.

28. *St. Louis Dispatch,* May 7, 1875.

29. *St. Louis Democrat,* May 7, 1875; also quoted in Carter, "Baseball in St. Louis," 256.

30. *St. Louis Republican,* May 7, 1875; also partially quoted in Carter, "Baseball in St. Louis," 256.

31. *St. Louis Democrat,* "Short Stops," May 7, 1875.

32. *St. Louis Republican,* May 7, 1875; also quoted in Carter, "Baseball in St. Louis," 256.

33. *St. Louis Dispatch,* May 7–8, 1875; *St. Louis Democrat,* May 9, 1875; *Chicago Tribune,* August 5, 1868, also quoted in Belcher, *Economic Rivalry,* 138; Carter, "Baseball in St. Louis," 257–58.

34. *St. Louis Democrat,* May 9, 1875.

35. Ibid.

36. Ibid.

37. Ibid. *Chicago Tribune* quoted in *St. Louis Democrat,* May 10, 1875. *Chicago Times,* May 8, 1875; also quoted in Carter, "Baseball in St. Louis," 257.

38. *St. Louis Democrat,* May 15, 1875; also quoted in Carter, "Baseball in St. Louis," 253–54.

Chapter 2: "Champions of the West"

1. *Chicago Tribune* quoted in *St. Louis Democrat,* May 10, 1875. Thorn et al., eds., *Total Baseball,* 6th ed., 1915; Wolff, ed., *Baseball Encyclopedia,* 8th ed., 2571; Nemec, *Great Encyclopedia of 19th Century Major League Baseball,* 71.

2. Daniel T. Rodgers, *The Work Ethic in Industrial America: 1850–1920,* 106; Daniel Nelson, *Managers and Workers: Origins of the New Factory System in the United States, 1880–1920,* 126–27, 210*n20;* Thorn et al., eds., *Total Baseball,* 6th ed., 105; Thorn and Palmer, eds., *Total Baseball,* 2d ed., 2522, provides the number of home games played.

3. Allen, *100 Years of Baseball,* 31; Seymour, *Baseball: The Early Years,* 79; Voigt, *American Baseball,* vol. 1, 62.

4. *Sporting News* interview with C. Orrick Bishop, July 16, 1887; Ryczek, *Blackguards and Red Stockings,* 187.

5. Ryczek, *Blackguards and Red Stockings,* 187–89; Thorn et al., eds., *Total Baseball,* 6th ed., 866.

6. *Sporting News* interview with Bishop, July 16, 1887.

7. Ibid.

8. *St. Louis Globe-Democrat,* February 4–5, 1876.

9. Voigt, *American Baseball,* vol. 1, 62; Rader, *Baseball,* 41.

10. Seymour, *Baseball: The Early Years,* 60; Ryczek, *Blackguards and Red Stockings,* 181, 204–8; *St. Louis Republican,* May 7, 1875; *Chicago Tribune,* October 10, 1875, October 8, 1876; *St. Louis Dispatch,* "Life in St. Louis," October 10, 1876.

11. Seymour, *Baseball: The Early Years,* 53–54, 75; Voigt, *American Baseball,* vol. 1, 20, 50, 53, 61; Ryczek, *Blackguards and Red Stockings,* 64–67, 211–13,

215; Rader, *Baseball,* 20, 40; Nemec and Wisnia, *Baseball,* 18, 22, 27, 29–30, 40; A. G. Spalding, *America's National Game,* 189–90.

12. *Sporting News* interview with Bishop, July 16, 1887; Seymour, *Baseball: The Early Years,* 79; Voigt, *American Baseball,* vol. 1, 62–63.

13. *St. Louis Globe-Democrat,* February 4–5, 1876; *Sporting News* interview with Bishop, July 16, 1887; Seymour, *Baseball: The Early Years,* 79–80; Voigt, *American Baseball,* vol. 1, 63–64.

14. *Sporting News* interview with Bishop, July 16, 1887; *Spalding's Official Baseball Guide: 1876,* 17; Seymour, *Baseball: The Early Years,* 21.

15. *Spalding's Official Baseball Guide: 1876,* 17–18, 21.

16. The 1870 census revealed that only fourteen U.S. cities had populations greater than 100,000. Of the eight charter members of the National League, seven represented cities with 100,000 or more inhabitants. The only exception was Hartford, with a population of just 37,180. C. Orrick Bishop, the St. Louisan who wrote the National League constitution, recalled that Hartford was included "because it had a very strong club which we were anxious to get." In contrast, the 1871–1875 National Association had included (at various times) such small-market sites as Elizabeth, Fort Wayne, Keokuk, Middletown, New Haven, Rockford, and Troy. *Compendium of the Ninth Census, 1870,* 444; *Sporting News* interview with Bishop, July 16, 1887; *Spalding's Official Baseball Guide: 1876,* 7, 11, 12, 19; *St. Louis Globe-Democrat,* February 5, 1876; Wolff, ed., *Baseball Encyclopedia,* 8th ed., 60; Thorn et al., eds., *Total Baseball,* 6th ed., 2538; Nemec, *Encyclopedia of 19th Century Major League Baseball,* 16, 30, 45, 71; Seymour, *Baseball: The Early Years,* 81–82; Rader, *Baseball,* 30–31, 37, 41–42.

17. *Chicago Tribune,* May 5, 1876.

18. Gunther Barth, *City People: The Rise of Modern City Culture in Nineteenth Century America,* 156. In his insightful study of the nineteenth-century city, Barth has noted that "gambling on sports was widespread." He offered this explanation of the phenomenon: "Betting provided a way of responding to a world of change and chance. Poor men became rich overnight, and rich men poor; and between these extremes of good and bad lay a wide range of chances that cried out to be exploited by betting." The motivation to gamble, according to Barth, varied from individual to individual: "Gambling appealed to some city people as a mark of gentility, or struck others as an exciting diversion from everyday problems." Hagen, *This Is Our St. Louis,* 255–56. *Spalding's Official Baseball Guide: 1877,* 57; *St. Louis Globe-Democrat,* May 4, 1876; *Chicago Tribune,* May 5, 1876.

19. The *Globe-Democrat*'s idea was similar in spirit to the rain-check system eventually adopted throughout major-league baseball. Although never implemented by the original Brown Stockings, in 1884 St. Louis apparently became

the first city to put such a plan into effect. Paul Dickson, *The Baseball Dictionary,* 318; *St. Louis Globe-Democrat,* May 5–6, 1876.

20. The *St. Louis Globe-Democrat* described Pike's game-winning hit as a "fine bounder to right field." The *Chicago Tribune,* on the other hand, believed that substitute first baseman John Glenn "muffed" Pike's grounder, which "should have been an out." This view remained consistent with the *Tribune*'s assertion that the defeat of the White Stockings could be attributed to the absence of regular first baseman Cal McVey, who had missed the game to be with his sick child. Aside from McVey's absence, the Chicago newspaper also placed part of the blame on the wretched playing conditions: "Home plate, pitcher's position, and first base were putty beds. . . . Before the third inning was closed, the ball became dumpty, and instead of responding with a click when hit, it simply gave a dull thud like a chunk of mud." This excuse failed to explain why Bradley himself managed to register as many hits (two) as he allowed the entire White Stockings' lineup. *St. Louis Globe-Democrat,* May 6, 1876; *Chicago Tribune,* May 6, 1876.

21. *Chicago Tribune,* April 30, May 6, 1876.

22. *St. Louis Globe-Democrat,* September 26, 1876.

23. *Chicago Tribune,* October 10, 1875; October 1, 6, 8, 1876.

24. *St. Louis Globe-Democrat,* October 6, 8, 1876; *Chicago Tribune,* October 6, 8, 1876; Thorn et al., eds., *Total Baseball,* 6th ed., 1917, 2440; Nemec, *Encyclopedia of 19th Century Major League Baseball,* 86, 91–92. Bradley's 1876 total of sixteen shutouts remains a major-league record for one season. It has since been tied only by twentieth-century Hall-of-Famer Grover Cleveland Alexander.

25. *Chicago Tribune,* October 10, 1876; *St. Louis Globe-Democrat,* October 10, 1876. St. Louis took a 1–0 lead in the first inning. Herman "Dutch" Dehlman singled, stole second, and advanced to third when White threw errantly in an effort to prevent the steal. Dehlman then scored on Lipman Pike's sacrifice fly. Anson's overthrow of first base allowed Dehlman to reach safely and move to second in leading off a two-run sixth inning. Again, Pike immediately drove Dehlman home, this time with a run-scoring single. Pike then scored on John Clapp's double and another Chicago miscue.

26. *Chicago Tribune,* October 10, 1876; *St. Louis Globe-Democrat,* October 10, 1876.

27. *Chicago Tribune,* October 11, 1876.

28. Ibid.; *St. Louis Globe-Democrat,* October 11, 1876. Although not as hard-hitting a pitcher as A. G. Spalding, Bradley was a respectable hitter. In two seasons with St. Louis (1875–1876) he averaged .247, and his lifetime average over eleven seasons was .229. Bradley had not hit a home run in either the 1875 or 1876 regular seasons, so the homer he clouted off Spalding in Game Four was his first since joining the major leagues. Before his career ended, Bradley hit three

more home runs during regular season play. Thorn et al., eds., *Total Baseball,* 6th ed., 721; Nemec, *Encyclopedia of 19th Century Major League Baseball,* 74, 93, 162, 207, 758.

29. *Chicago Tribune,* October 12, 1876. It is simply shocking that the Brown Stockings defeated the White Stockings in both of these high-scoring games. The St. Louis club was known for its strong defense and Bradley's superb pitching. However, Chicago possessed far more imposing hitting credentials. In 1876, eight of the nine White Stocking starters hit better than .300, and their team average of .337 surpassed all other National League teams. As a team, the 1876 Brown Stockings averaged .259, fifth among the eight league teams. Thorn et al., eds., *Total Baseball,* 6th ed., 1917; Wolff, ed., *Baseball Encyclopedia,* 8th ed., 63–64; Nemec, *Encyclopedia of 19th Century Major League Baseball,* 92.

30. *St. Louis Republican,* May 4, 1876, quoted in *Chicago Tribune,* May 6, 1876. Spending $21,500 on salaries during the 1876 season, Chicago paid their players more money than any other National League club. St. Louis, with a payroll estimated at somewhere between $16,800 and $18,300, rated anywhere from second to fifth among league teams in salary expenditures. *St. Louis Globe-Democrat,* July 13, October 10, 1876; *St. Louis Dispatch,* "Life in St. Louis," October 10, 1876.

31. Seymour, *Baseball: The Early Years,* 86, 88, 135–36; Rader, *Baseball,* 42, 44; Thorn et al., eds., *Total Baseball,* 6th ed., 105; Nemec, *Encyclopedia of 19th Century Major League Baseball,* 84; *Spalding's Official Baseball Guide: 1876,* 12; *Spalding's Official Baseball Guide: 1877,* 41–45; Voigt, *American Baseball,* vol. 1, 69; James, *Historical Baseball Abstract,* 10; Nemec and Wisnia, *Baseball,* 36, 42.

Chapter 3: The Collapse of the Original Brown Stockings

1. *Chicago Tribune,* October 22, 1876; Nemec, *Encyclopedia of 19th Century Major League Baseball,* 74–75, 90, 93, 103, 107; Thorn et al., eds., *Total Baseball,* 6th ed., 1432, 1917–19; Wolff, ed., *Baseball Encyclopedia,* 8th ed., 64–66. On August 4, 1873, Pike had received the hundred-dollar first prize for winning the Maryland state hundred-yard dash championship. Matched up later that month against "Clarence," a champion trotting horse, Pike again triumphed to claim a $250 prize. In both races, Pike completed the hundred-yard distance in exactly ten seconds. Slater, *Great Jews in Sports,* 167; James, *Historical Baseball Abstract,* 13.

2. J. E. Findling, "The Louisville Grays' Scandal of 1877," 182–83; *St. Louis Globe-Democrat,* October 24–25, 1877.

3. During the 1877 season the Cincinnati Red Stockings folded and then reorganized under new ownership. Newspapers published three different versions of the National League standings that year. One counted all of the Cincin-

nati games, another counted none of the Cincinnati games, and a third counted only the games played by the original Cincinnati organization. The National League ultimately decided at its winter meeting to count none of the Red Stockings' games in the final 1877 standings. However, modern baseball encyclopedias now include all of the Cincinnati games. Findling, "Louisville Grays' Scandal," 178, 183; *Louisville Courier-Journal,* reprinted in both the *Chicago Tribune* and *St. Louis Globe-Democrat,* November 4, 1877; Voigt, *American Baseball,* vol. 1, 72; James, *Historical Baseball Abstract,* 16.

4. The *Louisville Courier-Journal* offered a damning assessment of Hague's performance: "Bad muffs on easy chances did much to mar his playing and spoil his club's chances for several victories, noticeably one or two at Boston where the Grays had things all their own way up to the very last of the game, at which point Hague stepped in and switched the cars to a side track." *Louisville Courier-Journal,* October 12, 1877; also quoted in Findling, "Louisville Grays' Scandal," 181, 183–84. *Louisville Courier-Journal,* quoted in *St. Louis Globe-Democrat,* October 31, November 4, 1877; *Chicago Tribune,* November 4, 1877.

5. Spink, *National Game,* 345–46; *Sporting News,* April 30, 1914.

6. *St. Louis Globe-Democrat,* November 1, 1877.

7. Ibid.; *Chicago Tribune,* November 3, 1877; Thorn et al., eds., *Total Baseball,* 6th ed., 2489–94.

8. *St. Louis Globe-Democrat,* November 1, 1877.

9. Ibid.

10. Ibid., August 25–26, 1877.

11. Ibid., November 1, 1877; Findling, "Louisville Grays' Scandal," 184.

12. *Chicago Tribune,* November 4, 1877.

13. Ibid., November 3–4, 18, December 2, 1877. The *Chicago Tribune* claimed, "There has been as much crookedness in St. Louis as Louisville. The attempt to cut off the investigation by hanging Joe Blong and Joe Battin is like stopping a fountain with a handful of salt." *Chicago Tribune,* November 4, 1877.

14. *St. Louis Globe-Democrat,* August 25, October 24–25, 31, 1877.

15. In August of 1875, McGeary accused two teammates on the Philadelphia White Stockings, pitcher George "The Charmer" Zettlein and outfielder Fred Treacey, with fixing a game against Hartford. They countercharged that McGeary himself had been guilty of attempting to fix several games. The National Association held a hearing and acquitted all three players, blaming the accusations on "personal animosities." A year later, at the end of the first season that McGeary spent with St. Louis, the *Chicago Tribune* sarcastically complained: "The League at its annual meeting ought to provide a special tribunal to try Mike regularly. It is very annoying to the club officers to have to go through the form of exonerating him every season. It has got to be a regular thing nowadays, and

the matter ought to be set apart and a special trial calendar made." Ryczek, *Blackguards and Red Stockings,* 211–12; *Chicago Tribune,* October 29, 1876.

16. *Brooklyn Eagle* and *New York Clipper,* both quoted in the *Chicago Tribune,* November 18, 1877. Henry Chadwick, born in England, arrived in Brooklyn as an adolescent with his father, Sir James Chadwick. He spent the rest of his life there, serving overlapping thirty-year stints as sports editor of both the *Clipper* (1857–1888) and the *Eagle* (1864–1894). He also edited the first annual baseball guides, selling more than fifty thousand copies a year of *Beadle's Dime Baseball Player* (1860–1881) and later *DeWitt's Baseball Guide* (1869–1880). In 1881, the official National League guide, *Spalding's Guide,* named Chadwick as its editor, a position he maintained until his death in 1908. Church, *Baseball,* 24; Martin Appel and Burt Goldblatt, *Baseball's Best: The Hall of Fame Gallery,* 66; Lowell Reidenbaugh, ed., *Baseball's Hall of Fame: Cooperstown, Where the Legends Live Forever,* 52.

17. *St. Louis Globe-Democrat,* November 18, 1877.

18. *Missouri Republican,* November 4, 1877; *St. Louis Globe-Democrat,* November 1, 11, 1877; *Chicago Tribune,* December 2, 1877.

19. *Chicago Tribune,* reprinted in the *St. Louis Globe-Democrat,* July 4, 21, 1876; *St. Louis Globe-Democrat,* July 4, 12, 14, 16, 1876; *New York Clipper,* quoted in *St. Louis Globe-Democrat,* July 21, 1876.

20. *Chicago Tribune,* October 28, 1877. The *Tribune* also claimed that the Brown Stockings had lost a combined total of twenty thousand dollars in their two preceding seasons. This assertion is extremely doubtful. It hardly seems plausible that the Brown Stockings' financial setbacks averaged more in 1875 and 1876, when their attendance was higher, than in 1877, when their attendance dropped to its lowest ebb. *Chicago Tribune,* December 16, 1877; Thorn et al., eds., *Total Baseball,* 6th ed., 105. *St. Louis Globe-Democrat,* October 31, November 1, 1877; *Missouri Republican,* November 1, 1877.

21. *St. Louis Globe-Democrat,* October 31, November 1, 18, December 9, 1877; *Missouri Republican,* November 1, 4, 11, 1877; *Boston Daily Globe,* November 11, 1877. The *Republican,* in its account of the stockholders' meeting, cited a figure of $2,791 as the amount of the debt. Another report, dispatched to the *Daily Globe,* claimed the debt totaled $2,700. Later, even after some fund-raising had been conducted, the *Globe-Democrat* insisted that $2,900 was still needed to pay the debt, while the *Republican* called for an additional $2,700. Three different reports provided three different figures for the amount of money raised. One account, dispatched to the *Daily Globe,* estimated that "$300 or $400" had been collected. The *Globe-Democrat* set the total at $400, while the *Republican* believed $525 had been contributed.

22. *St. Louis Globe-Democrat,* November 1, 1877.

23. *Chicago Tribune,* November 4, 1877.

24. *Missouri Republican,* November 4, 1877.

25. *St. Louis Globe-Democrat,* November 1, 18, 1877.

26. Ibid., November 18, December 9, 1877; *Missouri Republican,* November 4, 11, 1877.

27. *St. Louis Globe-Democrat,* December 2, 9, 1877; *Missouri Republican,* December 9, 1877; *Spalding's Official Baseball Guide: 1878,* 47–48; *New York Clipper,* quoted in *Chicago Tribune,* December 30, 1877. It later became a subject of debate whether the Brown Stockings ever paid their players the money still owed on the overdue final paychecks for the 1877 season. A year after the Brown Stockings resigned from the league, the *Globe-Democrat* quoted "a gentleman who takes great interest in baseball matters," who claimed the team had never paid its debts and that "the old St. Louis organization is heavily in arrears." The *St. Louis Post-Dispatch* quickly denied the charge that the Brown Stockings had "left their players in the lurch," protesting, "If our contemporary will brush up its memory, it may remember that . . . the St. Louis club paid its players." More than forty years later, in an interview with the *Globe-Democrat,* one of the most influential of the original Brown Stockings' directors, C. Orrick Bishop, simply recalled, "After three seasons, we . . . paid our debts and quit." *St. Louis Globe-Democrat,* December 15, 1878, and interview with Bishop, quoted in Borst, *Baseball through a Knothole,* 10–11; *St. Louis Post-Dispatch,* December 21, 1878.

28. *St. Louis Globe-Democrat,* May 22, 1878; *Spalding's Official Baseball Guide: 1878,* 38; Thorn et al., eds., *Total Baseball,* 6th ed., 689, 710, 866, 1083, 1424; Wolff, ed., *Baseball Encyclopedia,* 8th ed., 67–69, 662, 689–90, 908, 1210, 1685; Seymour, *Baseball: The Early Years,* 94; *Chicago Tribune,* November 10, 1878; Nemec, *Encyclopedia of 19th Century Major League Baseball,* 127, 129.

29. Seymour, *Baseball: The Early Years,* 86; Rader, *Baseball,* 42; Thorn et al., eds., *Total Baseball,* 6th ed., 105, 1918; *Chicago Tribune,* October 28, 1877; *St. Louis Globe-Democrat,* August 25–26, October 24–25, 31, November 1, 13, 18, 1877; *Missouri Republican,* November 1, 4, 11, 1877; Wolff, ed., *Baseball Encyclopedia,* 8th ed., 63–65. The Louisville Grays left the league for reasons similar to St. Louis's problems. When the Grays resigned from the National League in March 1878, the *Louisville Commercial* explained that the Louisville gambling scandal had caused baseball to lose the financial backing of local citizens: "Our people were so thoroughly disgusted with the conduct of the players last season that a call upon them now to support a new set would meet with a cold response." The Hartford Dark Blues also had withdrawn due to a combination of financial reversals and negative feedback from the Louisville gambling scandal. During the first year of the National League, attendance at Hartford games had slipped 56 percent from the last season of the National Association. In response, the

Dark Blues, while still officially representing Hartford, had played their 1877 home games in Brooklyn. Brooklyn did not warmly embrace a team that still represented the capital of Connecticut. The Dark Blues' home attendance in 1877 was marginally better than it had been at Hartford the previous year, but still lagged 46 percent below its 1875 level. Yet the Hartford organization had continued to make plans for the 1878 season. However, as part of their 1878 team, Hartford had signed Bill Craver, who later became one of the four accused Louisville players. The Louisville gambling scandal apparently supplied the final nail in the coffin of the Hartford club, which withdrew from the National League on December 6, 1877, one day after St. Louis's resignation. Findling, "Louisville Grays' Scandal," 178–79, 181, 183–86; *Spalding's Official Baseball Guide: 1878,* 46–48.

30. Thorn et al., eds., *Total Baseball,* 6th ed., 1918–25; Wolff, ed., *Baseball Encyclopedia,* 8th ed., 61, 64–71; Seymour, *Baseball: The Early Years,* 86–87.

31. Rader, *Baseball,* 45; *Compendium of the Tenth Census, 1880,* 542.

32. *Chicago Tribune,* September 29–30, October 2, 1879; Allen, *100 Years of Baseball,* 71; Fitzgerald, ed., *The National League,* 76–77; Okrent and Lewine, eds., *The Ultimate Baseball Book,* 17.

33. *Chicago Tribune,* September 29–30, October 2, 1879, August 15, October 6, 1880.

34. Seymour, *Baseball: The Early Years,* 91–92; for further complaints about beer-selling, see the *Worcester Spy,* quoted in the *Chicago Tribune,* July 18, 1880. *Cincinnati Enquirer,* quoted in Seymour, *Baseball: The Early Years,* 92, and Robert Harris Walker, *Cincinnati and the Big Red Machine,* 14; *Chicago Tribune,* August 1, 15, 1880.

35. *Chicago Tribune,* October 6–7, 1880; *Spalding's Official Baseball Guide: 1881,* 85–87. Historian Harold Seymour, with considerable justification, has noted: "Cincinnati was expelled for past acts which the League intended to prohibit in the future. The Constitution of the United States might ban ex post facto laws, but the National League could and did use them with a vengeance." Seymour, *Baseball: The Early Years,* 92. *Cincinnati Enquirer,* quoted in *St. Louis Globe-Democrat,* October 31, 1880, and Rader, *Baseball,* 44.

36. *Chicago Tribune,* August 22, October 10, 1880.

37. *St. Louis Dispatch,* "Life in St. Louis," December 6, 1877; *Missouri Republican,* March 31, 1878; *St. Louis Globe-Democrat,* reprinted in the *Chicago Tribune,* November 3, 1878; *St. Louis Post-Dispatch,* May 8, 1880, also quoted in Julian S. Rammelkamp, *Pulitzer's Post-Dispatch, 1878–1883,* 180–81; *Philadelphia Evening Bulletin,* quoted in the *Chicago Tribune,* October 7, 1877; *New York Times,* reprinted in Ira L. and H. Allen Smith, *Low and Inside,* 136–40.

Chapter 4: Beer and Baseball

1. *Sporting News,* December 5, 1891. For Westfalia, "one of the most emigration-prone areas of Germany," Missouri was a preferred site of relocation. The desire of Westfalians to discover greater economic opportunities and to avoid Prussian military service represented the primary reasons for leaving. Walter Kamphoefner, *The Westfalians: From Germany to Missouri,* 8; Audrey L. Olson, *St. Louis Germans, 1850–1920,* 10; Rygelski, "Baseball's 'Boss President,'" 43.

2. *Sporting News,* December 5, 1891, June 12, 1913; *St. Louis Republic,* January 19, 1913, reprinted in Missouri Historical Society Library, St. Louis, *Necrologies,* vol. 6 (1913), 16–18; Rygelski, "Baseball's 'Boss President,'" 43–44; Spink, *National Game,* 298; J. Roy Stockton, "The St. Louis Cardinals," in Fitzgerald, ed., *The National League,* 167–68; William A. Borst, "Christian Frederick Wilhelm Von der Ahe," in David L. Porter, ed., *Biographical Dictionary of American Sports: Baseball,* 575; George Lipsitz, *The Sidewalks of St. Louis: Places, People, and Politics in an American City,* 58; Jon David Cash, "Christian Frederick Wilhelm Von der Ahe," in Christensen et al., eds., *Dictionary of Missouri Biography,* 775; J. Thomas Hetrick, *Chris Von der Ahe and the St. Louis Browns,* 3–4.

3. *St. Louis Globe-Democrat,* April 29, May 2, 5–7, 15, 21–23, 1878; *Missouri Republican,* April 29, May 2, 5–6, 1878; Tiemann, ed., *St. Louis's Favorite Sport,* 10–11. First, Joe Battin agreed to terms with the New Haven, Connecticut, club of the International Association. Next, the Springfield, Massachusetts, team signed three members of the Brown Stockings—Joe Blong, catcher George Baker, and first baseman Charles Houtz. In addition, the Milwaukee Cream Citys of the National League secured the services of center-fielder Bill Morgan.

4. *St. Louis Globe-Democrat,* April 29, May 2, 5–6, 1878; *Missouri Republican,* May 2, 1878.

5. *St. Louis Globe-Democrat,* April 14, 1879.

6. Thorn et al., eds., *Total Baseball,* 6th ed., 105; Thorn and Palmer, eds., *Total Baseball,* 2d ed., 2522, provides the number of home games played. *St. Louis Globe-Democrat,* April 20, 1879.

7. *St. Louis Globe-Democrat,* June 29, July 13, 1879.

8. Ibid., July 27, August 7, 10, 1879.

9. Ibid., April 14, 21, 28, May 5, 12, June 9, 16, 23, 30, July 7, 14, 21, 28, August 3–5, 7, 1879.

10. Ibid., June 29, August 18, 1879.

11. Ibid., August 31, September 1, 7–8, 15, 22, 29, October 13, 1879.

12. Ibid., October 19–20, 26–27, 1879.

13. Spink, *National Game,* 46.

14. Ibid.; *St. Louis Globe-Democrat,* August 22–23, September 6, 13, 27, 1880; *Missouri Republican,* September 6, October 11, 1880. The *Globe-Democrat* proclaimed that the season-ending series would decide the local championship: "Those evenly-matched local rivals, the Reds and the Browns, will be the contending forces, and rare sport will ensue. Honors are about even between the two clubs, and, for that reason, each will struggle valiantly for supremacy." The Brown Stockings ultimately defeated the Red Stockings, three games to two.

15. *Missouri Republican,* October 7, 1880; Hetrick, *Chris Von der Ahe and the St. Louis Browns,* 6; for the origins of the ballpark, see E. H. Tobias, "Marks An Era."

16. Robert L. Burnes, "Baseball Flourished Here before Von der Ahe," *St. Louis Globe-Democrat,* October 5, 1952, in Missouri Historical Society Scrapbook, St. Louis, *Sports I,* 39.

17. *St. Louis Globe-Democrat,* February 7, 1905; also quoted in Rygelski, "Baseball's 'Boss President,'" 44.

18. Robert L. Burnes, "'It Looks Like First Division!'" *St. Louis Globe-Democrat,* April 15, 1951, in Missouri Historical Society Scrapbook, St. Louis, *Sports I,* 15; Burnes, "Baseball Flourished Here before Von der Ahe," 39; Spink, *National Game,* 46; *Missouri Republican,* October 11, 1880; *St. Louis Globe-Democrat,* June 6, 1913; Stockton, "St. Louis Cardinals," 168; Stan N. Carlson, "St. Louis Cardinals: Baseball's Perennial Gas House Gang," in Peter C. Bjarkman, ed., *Encyclopedia of Major League Baseball Teams: National League,* 513–14.

19. *Missouri Republican,* December 9, 1877, May 8, 1881; Tiemann, ed., *St. Louis's Favorite Sport,* 26.

20. *Missouri Republican,* May 23, 1881; *St. Louis Globe-Democrat,* August 29, 1881; Tiemann, ed., *St. Louis's Favorite Sport,* 26–27; Robert E. Hannon, "A Century of Baseball," *St. Louis Commerce,* May 1966, 14; Philip J. Lowry, *Green Cathedrals: The Ultimate Celebration of All 271 Major League and Negro League Ballparks Past and Present,* 226–27.

21. Lowry, *Green Cathedrals,* 226–27.

22. Spink, *National Game,* 46–47; Hetrick, *Chris Von der Ahe and the St. Louis Browns,* 7; Allen, *100 Years of Baseball,* 64–65; Seymour, *Baseball: The Early Years,* 136. The Brown Stockings had actually played their first game at the renovated Sportsman's Park on the preceding Sunday, May 22. A crowd of "fully 2800 persons" watched the St. Louis Red Stockings upset the Brown Stockings, 2–1, for what turned out to be the first of only two victories that the Red Stockings posted in eight 1881 encounters with their local rivals. However, Al Spink billed the Cincinnati series as the "grand opening," for a couple of reasons. First, he had decided months earlier to have the Brown Stockings stage the "grand opening" of Sportsman's Park against Cincinnati. Second, he needed the additional week to

complete several of "the finishing touches" on the redesigned ballpark—painting the grandstand and constructing the beer garden, bowling alleys, and handball courts in right field. Thus, even on the eve of the May 22 game, Spink announced in the *Missouri Republican:* "By Saturday next [May 28], upon which day the Browns play the Cincinnati Reds, everything will be ship-shape out there, and the grand opening will be grand indeed." *Missouri Republican,* October 11, 1880, May 22–23, 28–29, 1881; *St. Louis Globe-Democrat,* November 20, 1881.

23. *Missouri Republican,* May 29–30, 1881; *St. Louis Globe-Democrat,* May 29–30, 1881; Rodgers, *Work Ethic in Industrial America,* 106; Nelson, *Managers and Workers,* 126–27, 210*n20.*

24. Spink, *National Game,* 47.

25. Ibid., 48; *St. Louis Globe-Democrat,* May 11, 1879.

26. Spink, *National Game,* 48.

27. Ibid.; *St. Louis Globe-Democrat,* August 29, September 5, October 4, 9–10, 16–17, November 20, 1881; Seymour, *Baseball: The Early Years,* 136; *St. Louis Republic,* January 19, 1913, reprinted in Missouri Historical Society Library, St. Louis, *Necrologies,* vol. 6 (1913), 16–18; *Sporting News,* June 12, 1913; Rygelski, "Baseball's 'Boss President,'" 44–45; Thorn et al., eds., *Total Baseball,* 6th ed., 1926; Cash, "Christian Frederick Wilhelm Von der Ahe," 775; Hetrick, *Chris Von der Ahe and the St. Louis Browns,* 8. The Brown Stockings won their season series against eleven rivals and split with two other teams, the Louisville Eclipse and the Akrons. The Brooklyn Atlantics, victorious in two of three games, were the only semi-professional team to own a winning record against the Brown Stockings. At the end of the season, the Brown Stockings suffered five of their fifteen losses when they were swept in a series against a traveling troupe of National League all-stars.

28. *St. Louis Globe-Democrat,* September 3, November 3–4, 1881; Allen, *100 Years of Baseball,* 66–67; Voigt, *American Baseball,* vol. 1, 122–23; Richard C. Wade, *The Urban Frontier: The Rise of Western Cities, 1790–1830,* 18, 29, 39, 42, 48, 53, 62–64, 66, 70–71, 178, 192–93; Seymour, *Baseball: The Early Years,* 136–39; Rygelski, "Baseball's 'Boss President,'" 45; Cash, "Christian Frederick Wilhelm Von der Ahe," 775–76; Hetrick, *Chris Von der Ahe and the St. Louis Browns,* 9–10; Steven A. Reiss, *Touching Base: Professional Baseball and American Culture in the Progressive Era,* 32; Bowman and Zoss, *Diamonds in the Rough,* 318; David Pietrusza, *Major Leagues: The Formation, Sometimes Absorption, and Mostly Inevitable Demise of Eighteen Professional Baseball Organizations, 1871 to Present,* 67; Alexander, *Our Game,* 35–36; Rader, *Baseball,* 47; Nemec, *Beer and Whisky League,* 21–22; Nemec, *Great Encyclopedia of 19th Century Major League Baseball,* 167.

29. *St. Louis Globe-Democrat,* November 4, 1881; Reiss, *Touching Base,* 32, 121, 125; Alexander, *Our Game,* 36; Nemec, *Beer and Whisky League,* 22; Allen, *100 Years of Baseball,* 66–67; Seymour, *Baseball: The Early Years,* 139; Rader, *Baseball,* 47; Nemec and Wisnia, *Baseball,* 36.

30. Richard Jensen, *The Winning of the Midwest: Social and Political Conflict, 1886–1896,* 58–88; *Sporting News,* December 5, 1891; Rader, *Baseball,* 40, 42–43, 47; Seymour, *Baseball: The Early Years,* 77; Reiss, *Touching Base,* 32, 121; Alexander, *Our Game,* 27, 35–36; Nemec, *Encyclopedia of 19th Century Major League Baseball,* 84; Nemec, *Beer and Whisky League,* 16; Allen, *100 Years of Baseball,* 67.

31. Allen, *100 Years of Baseball,* 66–67; Seymour, *Baseball: The Early Years,* 144; Voigt, *American Baseball,* vol. 1, 122–23; Pietrusza, *Major Leagues,* 67, 72; Rader, *Baseball,* 47; Nemec, *Encyclopedia of 19th Century Major League Baseball,* 167; Hetrick, *Chris Von der Ahe and the St. Louis Browns,* 10. *Chicago Tribune,* November 6, 1881.

32. In 1882 the National League slightly exceeded the American Association in total attendance, 404,388 to 400,000. However, the eight National League teams played a total of 338 games, while the six Association clubs participated in only 234 contests. Therefore, the American Association attracted an average crowd of 1,709 spectators, compared to the National League's average attendance of 1,196 per game. Thorn et al., eds., *Total Baseball,* 6th ed., 105, 1929, 1931. *Chicago Tribune,* October 28, 1877; *St. Louis Globe-Democrat,* October 10, 1880; Seymour, *Baseball: The Early Years,* 86–87; Voigt, *American Baseball,* vol. 1, 123; Nemec, *Encyclopedia of 19th Century Major League Baseball,* 167; Cash, "Christian Frederick Wilhelm Von der Ahe," 776; Hetrick, *Chris Von der Ahe and the St. Louis Browns,* 16.

33. *Compendium of the Tenth Census, 1880,* 542; Wolff, ed., *Baseball Encyclopedia,* 8th ed., 75–77; Nemec, *Encyclopedia of 19th Century Major League Baseball,* 176, 183; Thorn et al., *Total Baseball,* 6th ed., 1929, 1931.

34. Seymour, *Baseball: The Early Years,* 144–47; Voigt, *American Baseball,* vol. 1, 127–28.

35. Nemec, *Beer and Whisky League,* 55. The rivalry between the two leagues, which fostered profits for both, also inspired innovations to popularize the game even further. Portraying the 1880s as the decade when baseball blossomed into "a mass cultural movement, a large-scale, passionate American affair," Ronald Story credited the era's many pioneering trends—such as "gaudy promotionalism, kaleidoscopic franchise and league formation, spring training and transcontinental and international barnstorming treks, expanded seasons, city and world series, tobacco cards, product endorsements . . . booster clubs, flamboyant daredevil players and weekly baseball newspapers." Ronald Story, "The Country of

the Young: The Meaning of Baseball in Early American Culture," in Alvin L. Hall, ed., *Cooperstown Symposium on Baseball and the American Culture [1989],* 324.

36. Thorn et al., eds., *Total Baseball,* 6th ed., 105, 1933, 1935; *St. Louis Globe-Democrat,* January 27, 1884, also cited in Voigt, *American Baseball,* vol. 1, 130, and Hetrick, *Chris Von der Ahe and the St. Louis Browns,* 26; Seymour, *Baseball: The Early Years,* 119. According to the figures supplied by the *Globe-Democrat,* four American Association teams (Philadelphia, St. Louis, Cincinnati, and Baltimore) combined for $160,000 in profits. Two others, Louisville and Columbus, reportedly broke even. Pittsburgh endured a $3,000 deficit, and no figures were available for New York.

37. Two thousand people attended the Brown Stockings' 1882 season opener on a Tuesday, but a month later eight thousand spectators turned out for the first Sunday contest of the year. *St. Louis Globe-Democrat,* May 3, June 5, 1882, May 1–3, 1884, October 22, 1886; Thorn et al., eds., *Total Baseball,* 6th ed., 105; Thorn and Palmer, eds., *Total Baseball,* 2d ed., 2522, provides the number of home games played. Seymour, *Baseball: The Early Years,* 196; Borst, *Baseball through a Knothole,* 29; Lipsitz, *Sidewalks of St. Louis,* 59; *St. Louis Post-Dispatch,* May 2, 1884, April 9, 1908; Tiemann, *Cardinal Classics,* 8; *Missouri Republican,* October 22, 1886; Borst, "Christian Frederick Wilhelm Von der Ahe," 576; Hetrick, *Chris Von der Ahe and the St. Louis Browns,* 13; Mac Davis, *Lore and Legends of Baseball,* 78.

38. *Reach's Official American Association Baseball Guide: 1883,* 59–62; Wolff, ed., *Baseball Encyclopedia,* 8th ed., 75–77; Nemec, *Encyclopedia of 19th Century Major League Baseball,* 183; Thorn et al., eds., *Total Baseball,* 6th ed., 1931.

39. Nemec, *Encyclopedia of 19th Century Major League Baseball,* 185–90; Thorn et al., eds., *Total Baseball,* 6th ed., 656–1383, 1387–1902; Tiemann, *Cardinal Classics,* 8–9; Wolff, ed., *Baseball Encyclopedia,* 8th ed., 76; *St. Louis Globe-Democrat,* April 29, June 1, 1878, August 23, October 31, 1880, October 4, 10, 16, 1881, October 8, 1885; *Missouri Republican,* October 17, 1880, May 9, 1881; *Sporting News,* July 12, 1886, February 11, 1905, July 28, 1932; Spink, *National Game,* 46–47.

40. *St. Louis Globe-Democrat,* April 29, June 1, 1878, August 23, 1880, October 8, 1885; *Sporting News,* July 12, 1886, October 29, 1931, July 28, 1932; Wolff, ed., *Baseball Encyclopedia,* 8th ed., 76, 79, 83, 947–48; Nemec, *Encyclopedia of 19th Century Major League Baseball,* 188–89, 208, 236; Thorn et al., eds., *Total Baseball,* 6th ed., 894, 1689; *Missouri Republican,* May 9, 1881; *St. Louis Post-Dispatch,* August 3, 1883; Spink, *National Game,* 46–47.

41. Gustav W. Axelson, *"Commy": The Life Story of Charles A. Comiskey,* 10–11, 32–35, 37, 50; *Sporting News,* October 29, 1931.

42. Spink, *National Game,* 178; *Sporting News,* October 29, 1931; Steven A. Reiss, "Charles Albert Comiskey," in Porter, ed., *Biographical Dictionary of American Sports: Baseball,* 107.

43. Axelson, *"Commy,"* 42–44, 49–50; *Sporting News,* October 29, 1931; Robert Smith, *Baseball in America,* 49–51.

44. *Sporting News,* December 11, 1886, October 29, 1931; Spink, *National Game,* 176; Axelson, *"Commy,"* 50–52, 57–58.

45. *St. Louis Globe-Democrat,* May 3, 1882; *Missouri Republican,* May 3, 1882; Wolff, ed., *Baseball Encyclopedia,* 8th ed., 76. Historian Harold Seymour claims that, contrary to public perception, Comiskey had not been the originator of first basemen playing off the bag. Instead, Seymour insists that this style of play had been prevalent as far back as the 1860s. But a couple of Comiskey's contemporaries—sportswriter Al Spink and teammate Jumbo McGinnis—unhesitatingly paid homage to him as the game's foremost innovator for first basemen. Seymour, *Baseball: The Early Years,* 61–62; Spink, *National Game,* 176, 178, 394; *Sporting News,* "Al Spink, Writing in 1921, Gave Graphic Picture of Comiskey as Player and Manager," October 29, 1931.

46. Axelson, *"Commy,"* 64; Stockton, "St. Louis Cardinals," 170; Spink, *National Game,* 50; Wolff, ed., *Baseball Encyclopedia,* 8th ed., 835, 852, 1129, 1143, 1177, 1285, 1499, 2076; Thorn et al., eds., *Total Baseball,* 6th ed., 813, 826, 1025, 1035, 1060, 1136, 1289, 1716.

47. *Missouri Republican,* November 1, 1883; *St. Louis Post-Dispatch,* May 8, 1884; *St. Louis Globe-Democrat,* October 8, 1885; Spink, *National Game,* 214–16; Thorn et al., eds., *Total Baseball,* 6th ed., 639, 1025; *Sporting News,* December 10, 1952.

48. Clark Nardinelli, "Anthony John Mullane," in Porter, ed., *Biographical Dictionary of American Sports: Baseball,* 406–7; Wolff, ed., *Baseball Encyclopedia,* 8th ed., 76–77, 79–80, 2076; Nemec, *Encyclopedia of 19th Century Major League Baseball,* 187, 208, 239, 265, 309, 333; Thorn et al., *Total Baseball,* 6th ed., 1716–17; Mike Shatzkin, *The Ballplayers: Baseball's Ultimate Biographical Reference,* 769. Nardinelli offers this explanation of Mullane's ambidextrous playing style: "During the 1881 season, he . . . began pitching with his left arm following an injury to his right arm. The recovery of Mullane's right arm enabled him to pitch with either arm, but he rarely hurled left-handed. His ambidexterity allowed the barehanded pitcher to field and throw with either hand and gave him a devastating pickoff move."

49. Wolff, ed., *Baseball Encyclopedia,* 8th ed., 79, 2040, 2076; Nemec, *Encyclopedia of 19th Century Major League Baseball,* 208; Thorn et al., eds., *Total Baseball,* 6th ed., 1689, 1716–17; *St. Louis Post-Dispatch,* July 27, August 31, September 8, 1883.

50. *St. Louis Post-Dispatch,* July 27, 1883; Axelson, *"Commy,"* 59–62.

51. *St. Louis Post-Dispatch,* August 18, 1883.

52. Ibid.

53. *Missouri Republican,* August 26–29, 1883.

54. Ibid., August 24–30, September 9, 1883.

55. Ibid., August 30, September 2, 1883. In the 1883 season, the Philadelphia Athletics welcomed 305,000 customers to establish a new major-league peak for home attendance. This record was not surpassed until 1888. Thorn et al., eds., *Total Baseball,* 6th ed., 105, 109.

56. *St. Louis Post-Dispatch,* August 31, 1883; *Missouri Republican,* August 31, 1883, also cited in Rygelski, "Baseball's 'Boss President,'" 46.

57. *St. Louis Post-Dispatch,* August 31, 1883.

58. Ibid.; *St. Louis Globe-Democrat,* September 1–4, 1883.

59. *St. Louis Globe-Democrat,* September 5–7, 1883; *Missouri Republican,* September 5, 1883; *St. Louis Post-Dispatch,* September 5–7, 1883.

60. *St. Louis Globe-Democrat,* September 2–16, 1883; *Missouri Republican,* September 2, 17–19, 1883.

61. *St. Louis Globe-Democrat,* September 8–16, 1883; *Missouri Republican,* September 17–24, 1883; *St. Louis Post-Dispatch,* September 22, 24, 1883.

62. *Missouri Republican,* September 27–October 1, 1883; *St. Louis Post-Dispatch,* September 29, 1883.

63. Thorn et al., eds., *Total Baseball,* 6th ed., 105; Thorn and Palmer, eds., *Total Baseball,* 2d ed., 2522, provides the number of home games played. *St. Louis Globe-Democrat,* January 27, 1884, also cited in Voigt, *American Baseball,* vol. 1, 130; Nemec, *Beer and Whisky League,* 55.

64. Henry V. Lucas Vertical File, Missouri Historical Society Library, St. Louis; Spink, *National Game,* 26–27; Harold Seymour, "St. Louis and the Union Baseball War," 259; Seymour, *Baseball: The Early Years,* 149; *St. Louis Republic,* November 16, 1910, in Henry V. Lucas Vertical File; Borst, *Baseball through a Knothole,* 13.

65. *St. Louis Republic,* November 16, 1910, in Henry V. Lucas Vertical File, Missouri Historical Society Library, St. Louis; Seymour, "St. Louis and the Union Baseball War," 259–60; Seymour, *Baseball: The Early Years,* 147, 149.

66. Seymour, "St. Louis and the Union Baseball War," 260; Seymour, *Baseball: The Early Years,* 149; Pietrusza, *Major Leagues,* 82.

67. Seymour, "St. Louis and the Union Baseball War," 257, 259; Seymour, *Baseball: The Early Years,* 148–49.

68. *St. Louis Post-Dispatch,* October 23, November 6, 1883; Seymour, "St. Louis and the Union Baseball War," 262–64; Hetrick, *Chris Von der Ahe and the St. Louis Browns,* 18. According to a subsequent report, McGinnis actually

received $1,975 for the 1884 season. Three other players on the 1884 Browns also earned in excess of $1,900. Based on their 1884 spring roster, the projected yearly payroll for the thirteen members of the Browns—considered to be "the highest salaried club in the American Association"—totaled $23,275, an average of $1,798.08 per player. Deutsch et al., eds., *The Scrapbook History of Baseball,* 19.

Chapter 5: Von der Ahe versus Lucas

1. *St. Louis Globe-Democrat,* May 8, 1884; Seymour, "St. Louis and the Union Baseball War," 262–63; Seymour, *Baseball: The Early Years,* 152–55; Robert F. Burk, *Never Just a Game: Players, Owners, and American Baseball to 1920,* 75; Hetrick, *Chris Von der Ahe and the St. Louis Browns,* 28–29.

2. *St. Louis Globe-Democrat,* May 8, 1884; Seymour, "St. Louis and the Union Baseball War," 262–63; Seymour, *Baseball: The Early Years,* 152–55; Robert F. Burk, *Never Just a Game: Players, Owners, and American Baseball to 1920,* 75; Hetrick, *Chris Von der Ahe and the St. Louis Browns,* 28–29.

3. *St. Louis Globe-Democrat,* May 6, 11, 14, 1884; Seymour, "St. Louis and the Union Baseball War," 263–64; Seymour, *Baseball: The Early Years,* 155–56; *Sporting News,* March 15, 1887. Mullane circumvented the intent of the Missouri court when he appeared sometimes in St. Louis to pitch against the Browns "on Sundays only, as no legal action can be taken on that day." *Sporting News,* May 10, 1886.

4. Seymour, "St. Louis and the Union Baseball War," 261, 263; Seymour, *Baseball: The Early Years,* 152, 154.

5. Deutsch et al., eds., *Scrapbook History of Baseball,* 19; for the salary levels of the Browns in the preceding season of 1883, see the *St. Louis Post-Dispatch,* July 28, 1883.

6. Spink, *National Game,* 26–27; Seymour, "St. Louis and the Union Baseball War," 260; Seymour, *Baseball: The Early Years,* 149.

7. Seymour, *Baseball: The Early Years,* 117–18; *St. Louis Post-Dispatch,* July 28, 1883; Reiss, *Touching Base,* 32; Rodgers, *Work Ethic in Industrial America,* 106; Nelson, *Managers and Workers,* 126–27, 210*n20.*

8. Nemec, *Great Encyclopedia of 19th Century Major League Baseball,* 246–58; Thorn et al., eds., *Total Baseball,* 6th ed., 656–1383, 1387–1902.

9. *Missouri Republican,* November 25, 1883. For more on the expansion of the American Association, see the *Missouri Republican,* November 14, December 11–13, 16, 1883.

10. *Sporting Life* quoted in *Missouri Republican,* November 25, 1883; *Philadelphia Times* quoted in *Missouri Republican,* December 11, 1883; *Missouri Republican,* December 16, 1883.

11. Aside from Brooklyn, the three new American Association markets (Washington, Toledo, and Indianapolis) spent a combined twenty-seven seasons in the nineteenth-century major leagues and never produced a single ball club that rated in the upper half of average attendance per game. Thorn et al., eds., *Total Baseball,* 6th ed., 105–6, 109; Thorn and Palmer, eds., *Total Baseball,* 2d ed., 2522–27, provides the number of home games played by each team.

12. *Sporting News,* December 11, 1886; *St. Louis Post-Dispatch,* May 17, 24, 26, June 7, July 5, 1884.

13. *St. Louis Globe-Democrat,* May 4, 1884; Seymour, "St. Louis and the Union Baseball War," 265; Seymour, *Baseball: The Early Years,* 159; Thorn et al., eds., *Total Baseball,* 6th ed., 69, 105, 109, 1940–41; Nemec, *Encyclopedia of 19th Century Major League Baseball,* 244; Wolff, ed., *Baseball Encyclopedia,* 8th ed., 88. Altoona had attracted an average crowd of only 611 spectators, twenty-eighth among the thirty-two major-league franchises with available home attendance figures for 1884. However, even with a worse winning percentage than Altoona, Kansas City still rated eleventh among major league teams in average home attendance per game. Thorn and Palmer, eds., *Total Baseball,* 2d ed., 2522–23, 2525, provides the number of home games played by each team.

14. Seymour, "St. Louis and the Union Baseball War," 265; Seymour, *Baseball: The Early Years,* 159; Wolff, ed., *Baseball Encyclopedia,* 8th ed., 88; Nemec, *Encyclopedia of 19th Century Major League Baseball,* 244; Thorn et al., eds., *Total Baseball,* 6th ed., 1940–41.

15. Wolff, ed., *Baseball Encyclopedia,* 8th ed., 84, 88, 846, 866, 948, 1402, 1440, 1515–16, 2243. *St. Louis Globe-Democrat,* July 2, 10, 23–25, 28–30, August 2, 10–11, 13, 15, 1884; Frederick Ivor-Campbell, "1884: Old Hoss Radbourne and the Providence Grays," in Thorn, ed., *National Pastime,* 158, 162–63; Peter Wallan, "Old Hoss," in Wallan et al., eds., *The 01' Ball Game,* 1–2; Seymour, "St. Louis and the Union Baseball War," 264; Seymour, *Baseball: The Early Years,* 156; Allen, *100 Years of Baseball,* 67; Nemec, *Encyclopedia of 19th Century Major League Baseball,* 244; Thorn et al., eds., *Total Baseball,* 6th ed., 1941.

16. *St. Louis Globe-Democrat,* May 15, 1884; *St. Louis Post-Dispatch,* May 26, July 5, 7, 1884. The Browns drew a major-league-high 212,000 spectators to Sportsman's Park. The Maroons attracted a total attendance of 116,000 at the Union Grounds. Thorn et al., eds., *Total Baseball,* 6th ed., 105, 109.

17. *Missouri Republican,* November 25, 1883; also quoted in Seymour, "St. Louis and the Union Baseball War," 261, and Seymour, *Baseball: The Early Years,* 150; *St. Louis Post-Dispatch,* April 19, 21, 1884. The *Post-Dispatch* article of April 19, "The Lucas Nine," is also contained in the "St. Louis Unions" Vertical File, Missouri Historical Society Library, St. Louis. For more information on the op-

position of the *Post-Dispatch* to the reserve clause, see *St. Louis Post-Dispatch,* July 17, August 16, 1884. *St. Louis Globe-Democrat,* April 21, 1884. The *Post-Dispatch* adjusted the attendance figure down to six thousand. It later noted, "People look at the size of crowds in a very different light, and make their estimates accordingly." *St. Louis Post-Dispatch,* April 21, 26, 1884.

18. *St. Louis Globe-Democrat,* April 21, 25, 27–28, May 2–3, 5, 7–10, 1884; *St. Louis Post-Dispatch,* May 10, 1884.

19. *Missouri Republican,* May 9–11, 1884; *St. Louis Post-Dispatch,* May 10–12, 1884; *St. Louis Globe-Democrat,* May 12, 1884. While the *Post-Dispatch* concurred that twelve thousand spectators were present for the Browns' game, it substantially lowered the attendance figure for the Maroons' game, placing it at only two hundred.

20. Voigt, *American Baseball,* vol. 1, 134. Besides surpassing the Maroons in total attendance, the Browns claimed top billing in the sports columns that appeared in local newspapers. Both the *St. Louis Post-Dispatch* and the *St. Louis Globe-Democrat* devoted far more space to their accounts of the Browns' game. The *Post-Dispatch* devoted 107 lines of newsprint to the Browns' ballgame and only 13 lines to the Maroons' contest, while the *Globe-Democrat* ran 111 lines on the Browns and just 27 lines on the Maroons. *St. Louis Post-Dispatch,* May 12, 1884; *St. Louis Globe-Democrat,* May 12, 1884. Thorn et al., eds., *Total Baseball,* 6th ed., 105, 109; Thorn and Palmer, eds., *Total Baseball,* 2d ed., 2522–23, 2525, provides the number of home games played by each team.

21. *St. Louis Post-Dispatch,* December 1, 4–5, 1883; Seymour, *Baseball: The Early Years,* 165–66.

22. *St. Louis Post-Dispatch,* October 27, December 1, 4, 1883.

23. Ibid., May 3, 1884; *St. Louis Globe-Democrat,* October 8, 1885; Wolff, ed., *Baseball Encyclopedia,* 8th ed., 1305, 2100; Nemec, *Encyclopedia of 19th Century Major League Baseball,* 202–3, 733, 792; Thorn et al., eds., *Total Baseball,* 6th ed., 546, 1149, 1735; William Humber, *Cheering for the Home Team: The Story of Baseball in Canada,* 28–36, 45–46, 53, 54, 65, 87, 106, 119, 146.

24. *St. Louis Post-Dispatch,* April 28, May 2–3, 1884; *St. Louis Globe-Democrat,* May 2–17, July 22, August 25, 1884.

25. *St. Louis Post-Dispatch,* May 21, 1884.

26. *St. Louis Globe-Democrat,* May 14, 17, 1884.

27. Ibid., May 18–June 1, 1884.

28. *St. Louis Post-Dispatch,* May 21, June 2, 7, 28, 30, 1884.

29. Ibid., June 2–3, 19–20, 1884.

30. Ibid., June 20, September 16, 20, 1884.

31. Ibid., May 24, June 3–4, 6–7, 1884; *St. Louis Globe-Democrat,* May 18, 23, 26, 31, 1884.

32. *St. Louis Post-Dispatch,* June 18, 20, 1884.

33. Ibid., June 21, 23, 1884; *St. Louis Globe-Democrat,* June 27, 1884.

34. *St. Louis Post-Dispatch,* June 21, 23–25, 27–28, 30, 1884; *St. Louis Globe-Democrat,* June 22–30, July 2, 1884.

35. *St. Louis Post-Dispatch,* July 4, 1884.

36. *Missouri Republican,* July 3, 1884.

37. Ibid.; *St. Louis Globe-Democrat,* July 3, 10, 12, 1884.

38. *St. Louis Globe-Democrat,* June 10, 13, 23, 28, 30, July 3, 5, 1884; *St. Louis Post-Dispatch,* July 3, 5, 7, 1884; May 19, 1885.

39. *St. Louis Post-Dispatch,* July 19, 1884; Tiemann, *Cardinal Classics,* 12; Deutsch et al., eds., *Scrapbook History of Baseball,* 19; Duane A. Smith, "David Luther Foutz," in David L. Porter, ed., *Biographical Dictionary of American Sports: Baseball,* 194; Hetrick, *Chris Von der Ahe and the St. Louis Browns,* 35.

40. Smith, "David Luther Foutz," 194; Hetrick, *Chris Von der Ahe and the St. Louis Browns,* 35; Duane A. Smith, "Baseball Champions of Colorado: The Leadville Blues of 1882," 56, 59–61, 65, 68, 71; Nemec, *Beer and Whisky League,* 98–99; *St. Louis Post-Dispatch,* July 26, 1884; Tiemann, *Cardinal Classics,* 12. Foutz's tall tale about his pitching exploits for the Leadville Blues followed him to St. Louis. *St. Louis Globe-Democrat,* July 20, 1884.

41. *St. Louis Post-Dispatch,* July 30, August 1, 1884; *St. Louis Globe-Democrat,* July 30, 1884; Tiemann, *Cardinal Classics,* 12–13.

42. *St. Louis Globe-Democrat,* July 30, August 1, 18, 1884; Tiemann, *Cardinal Classics,* 12–13; *St. Louis Post-Dispatch,* July 26, 28, August 2, 1884.

43. *St. Louis Post-Dispatch,* August 16, 19, 20–21, 27, September 11, 1884; *St. Louis Globe-Democrat,* August 27, September 11, 1884; *Missouri Republican,* August 27, September 11, 1884.

44. *St. Louis Globe-Democrat,* August 20–22, 24, 30, September 1, 4, 1884; *St. Louis Post-Dispatch,* August 25, September 4, 1884; Hetrick, *Chris Von der Ahe and the St. Louis Browns,* 30–31.

45. *St. Louis Post-Dispatch,* September 5–6, 1884; *Sporting News,* November 27, 1886. In 1885, Von der Ahe gave Comiskey the opportunity to manage a full season, and the Browns started their fourth year in the American Association under the guidance of their fourth different manager. Wolff, ed., *Baseball Encyclopedia,* 8th ed., 76, 79, 83, 90; Nemec, *Encyclopedia of 19th Century Major League Baseball,* 188, 208, 235, 279.

46. *St. Louis Post-Dispatch,* September 5, 8, 1884; *Missouri Republican,* December 6, 1887; Frederick Ivor-Campbell, "Robert Lee Caruthers," in Porter, ed., *Biographical Dictionary of American Sports: Baseball,* 78; Craig Carter, ed., *Daguerreotypes: The Complete Major and Minor League Records of Baseball's Greats,* 8th ed., 45; Hetrick, *Chris Von der Ahe and the St. Louis Browns,* 35; Wolff, ed., *Baseball Encyclopedia,* 8th ed., 1731; Nemec, *Encyclopedia of 19th Century Major League Baseball,* 236; Thorn et al., eds., *Total Baseball,* 6th ed., 1459.

47. Tiemann, *Cardinal Classics,* 13; Wolff, ed., *Baseball Encyclopedia,* 8th ed., 83, 85, 1835; Nemec, *Encyclopedia of 19th Century Major League Baseball,* 231, 236; Thorn et al., eds., *Total Baseball,* 6th ed., 1536, 1939.

48. *St. Louis Post-Dispatch,* September 16, 1884; Nemec, *Encyclopedia of 19th Century Major League Baseball,* 236. The eighth edition of *The Baseball Encyclopedia,* then the official encyclopedia of Major League Baseball, credits Caruthers as the all-time leading pitcher in career winning percentage (.692) with Foutz a close second (.690). In the recent sixth edition of *Total Baseball,* now the official encyclopedia of Major League Baseball, the editors list Foutz as the all-time leading pitcher in career winning percentage (still at .690) and Caruthers in third place with a .688 winning percentage. Even in the *Total Baseball* version, the Foutz-Caruthers combination surpasses the next closest pair of teammates, the New York Yankees' Whitey Ford and Vic Raschi, who rate second and fifth respectively. The discrepancy in Caruthers' record stems from the fact that *Total Baseball* charges him with two additional losses in 1892. Wolff, ed., *Baseball Encyclopedia,* 8th ed., 45, 1731; Thorn et al., eds., *Total Baseball,* 6th ed., 640–41, 1459, 2406.

49. In his Triple Crown season of 1887, O'Neill slugged 14 home runs, drove in 123 runs, and batted .435. Thorn et al., eds., *Total Baseball,* 6th ed., 238–41, 1149.

50. *St. Louis Post-Dispatch,* September 20, October 6, 16, December 17, 1884; *St. Louis Globe-Democrat,* September 21, October 13, 1884; Wolff, ed., *Baseball Encyclopedia,* 8th ed., 79, 83, 1143; Nemec, *Encyclopedia of 19th Century Major League Baseball,* 207, 235, 246; Hetrick, *Chris Von der Ahe and the St. Louis Browns,* 34; Nemec, *Beer and Whisky League,* 98.

51. *St. Louis Post-Dispatch,* September 16, 1884.

52. Von der Ahe quoted in *St. Louis Post-Dispatch,* October 27, 1884; for a discussion of this transaction between the Browns and the Toledo Blue Stockings, see Seymour, *Baseball: The Early Years,* 168.

53. *St. Louis Post-Dispatch,* October 27–28, 31, 1884; Nemec, *Beer and Whisky League,* 98.

54. Wolff, ed., *Baseball Encyclopedia,* 8th ed., 1581; Thorn et al., eds., *Total Baseball,* 6th ed., 1349; Nemec, *Beer and Whisky League,* 98; *St. Louis Post-Dispatch,* October 27, 1884.

55. Wolff, ed., *Baseball Encyclopedia,* 8th ed., 90, 94, 99, 1581; Nemec, *Encyclopedia of 19th Century Major League Baseball,* 277, 279, 303, 305, 330, 332; Thorn et al., eds., *Total Baseball,* 6th ed., 1349, 1945, 1949, 1953; Spink, *National Game,* 268; Gustav W. Axelson, *"Commy,"* 100.

56. Quest hit only .206, and his fielding average was .894. Wolff, ed., *Baseball Encyclopedia,* 8th ed., 83, 90. Allen, *100 Years of Baseball,* 111; Seymour, *Baseball: The Early Years,* 217–18, 220.

57. *St. Louis Post-Dispatch,* October 27, 31, November 8, 1884; Deutsch et al., eds., *Scrapbook History of Baseball,* 20; Seymour, *Baseball: The Early Years,* 68.

58. *St. Louis Post-Dispatch,* November 8, 1884; Seymour, *Baseball: The Early Years,* 168–69; Hetrick, *Chris Von der Ahe and the St. Louis Browns,* 32.

59. *St. Louis Post-Dispatch,* August 16, 1885; Thorn et al., eds., *Total Baseball,* 6th ed., 274–86, 1716–17, 2406; Nemec, *Encyclopedia of 19th Century Major League Baseball,* 265; Reidenbaugh, ed., *Baseball's Hall of Fame,* 5, 47, 59, 117, 133, 164, 170, 215, 239–40, 249, 251–52, 274, 281, 292, 301, 323, 337, 342.

60. Seymour, *Baseball: The Early Years,* 168–69.

61. In 1885, after winning more than twenty games for three consecutive seasons, McGinnis won six games and lost six. Wolff, ed., *Baseball Encyclopedia,* 8th ed., 2040; Thorn et al., eds., *Total Baseball,* 6th ed., 1689.

62. Wolff, ed., *Baseball Encyclopedia,* 8th ed., 86, 1390, 2161; Nemec, *Encyclopedia of 19th Century Major League Baseball,* 246, 249–50; Thorn et al., eds., *Total Baseball,* 6th ed., 1212; *St. Louis Post-Dispatch,* July 25, 1884.

63. Wolff, ed., *Baseball Encyclopedia,* 8th ed., 88; *St. Louis Post-Dispatch,* October 22, December 17–18, 1884; Seymour, "St. Louis and the Union Baseball War," 265; Seymour, *Baseball: The Early Years,* 159.

64. *St. Louis Post-Dispatch,* January 17, 19, 1885; Daniel M. Pearson, *Baseball in 1889: Players vs. Owners,* 212. Most of the Cleveland players, a total of six, had already been snatched up by the Brooklyn Trolley-Dodgers of the American Association.

65. *St. Louis Post-Dispatch,* January 19, June 20, July 2, September 4, 1885; Wolff, ed., *Baseball Encyclopedia,* 8th ed., 90, 92, 94, 96, 99–100, 103–4, 107, 738, 1390; Axelson, *"Commy,"* 101; Nemec, *Beer and Whisky League,* 99; Nemec, *Encyclopedia of 19th Century Major League Baseball,* 277, 279, 303, 305, 330, 332, 360, 362–63, 391; Thorn et al., eds., *Total Baseball,* 6th ed., 1212, 1945, 1949, 1953, 1957.

66. *St. Louis Post-Dispatch,* December 18, 1884; *St. Louis Republic,* November 16, 1910, in Henry V. Lucas Vertical File, Missouri Historical Society Library, St. Louis; *Sporting News,* August 23, 1886; Seymour, "St. Louis and the Union Baseball War," 266; Seymour, *Baseball: The Early Years,* 160. Henry Lucas admitted only to losing seventeen thousand dollars. In all likelihood, he lost more money than he acknowledged. Lucas, through business reversals in baseball and other financial investments, eventually lost all of the one million dollars that he had inherited from his father. Al Spink, secretary of the Maroons' board of directors, estimated the overall losses of the Union Association at $250,000. Given these facts, it seems likely that Lucas had intentionally downplayed his losses on the Union Association. Spink, *National Game,* 26.

67. *St. Louis Globe-Democrat,* May 8, 1884; *St. Louis Post-Dispatch,* August 4, 16, 1884; *Missouri Republican,* October 10, 1885; *Sporting News,* June 18, 1887.

68. Seymour, *Baseball: The Early Years,* 162.

69. Ibid.; Hagen, *This Is Our St. Louis,* 200; *Sporting News,* December 5, 1891; Seymour, *Baseball: The Early Years,* 162.

70. Seymour, *Baseball: The Early Years,* 160; Seymour, "St. Louis and the Union Baseball War," 266. *St. Louis Post-Dispatch,* January 22, 1885.

71. *St. Louis Post-Dispatch,* January 22, 1885; Seymour, *Baseball: The Early Years,* 163.

72. Seymour, "St. Louis and the Union Baseball War," 267. For details on the life and political career of John J. O'Neill, refer to the following: United States Biographical and Publishing Company, *The United States Biographical Dictionary and Portrait Gallery of Eminent and Self-Made Men, Missouri Volume,* 811; William Hyde and Howard L. Conrad, eds., *Encyclopedia of the History of St. Louis,* vol. 3, 1673; American Biographical Publishing Company, *The Bench and Bar of St. Louis, Kansas City, Jefferson City, and Other Missouri Cities,* 286–87; *St. Louis Republic,* February 20, 1898, reprinted in Missouri Historical Society Library, St. Louis, *Necrology Scrapbook,* vol. 2c, 127; Dan Morris and Inez Morris, *Who Was Who in American Politics,* 449. *Sporting News,* December 5, 1891. Dickson Terry, "Browns—Rich in Tradition," *St. Louis Post-Dispatch,* March 22, 1953, in Missouri Historical Society Scrapbook, St. Louis, Mo., Sports I, 40; *St. Louis Republic,* January 19, 1913, reprinted in Missouri Historical Society Library, St. Louis, *Necrologies,* vol. 6 (1913), 16–18; *Reach's Official American Association Baseball Guide: 1883,* 47.

73. Seymour, "St. Louis and the Union Baseball War," 267*n53;* Seymour, *Baseball: The Early Years,* 163; Nemec, *Beer and Whisky League,* 85; Hetrick, *Chris Von der Ahe and the St. Louis Browns,* 33.

74. *St. Louis Republic,* November 16, 1910, in Henry V. Lucas Vertical File, Missouri Historical Society Library, St. Louis; *St. Louis Post-Dispatch,* July 2, 10, August 2, 1884, September 7, 1885; *Sporting News,* March 29, 1886. By comparing the 1884 and 1885 records of some of the Maroons' prominent holdover players, one can easily comprehend the superiority of the National League to the Union Association. In 1884 the Maroons' second baseman, Fred Dunlap, led all Union Association players in runs, hits, home runs, total bases, and batting average (.412). The next year, in the National League, Dunlap's batting average dipped to a solid but unspectacular .270. Right fielder George "Orator" Shaffer had led the Union Association in doubles, while trailing only Dunlap in runs, hits, total bases, and batting average (.360). But in 1885, Shaffer hit an anemic .195 in the National League. Similarly, the earned run averages of two of the Maroons' pitchers, Henry Boyle and Charles Sweeney, shot dramatically upward once these pitchers were in the National League. Boyle's earned run average increased from 1.74 in 1884 to 2.75 in 1885, and Sweeney's earned run average leaped from 1.83

to 3.93. Wolff, ed., *Baseball Encyclopedia,* 8th ed., 88, 90, 866, 1440, 1695, 2240; Nemec, *Encyclopedia of 19th Century Major League Baseball,* 266; Thorn et al., eds., *Total Baseball,* 6th ed., 1943.

75. Thorn et al., eds., *Total Baseball,* 6th ed., 105, 109; Thorn and Palmer, eds., *Total Baseball,* 2d ed., 2522–23, 2525, provides the number of home games played.

76. Sullivan quoted in Pearson, *Baseball in 1889,* 13, 90, and Hetrick, *Chris Von der Ahe and the St. Louis Browns,* 36; *St. Louis Globe-Democrat,* October 8, 1885; *St. Louis Post-Dispatch,* April 10, 1885.

77. *St. Louis Globe-Democrat,* April 9, 12, 14, 17, 18, 1885.

78. Ibid., April 17, 1885; *St. Louis Post-Dispatch,* April 20, 22, 24–25, 27, 1885. Bob Caruthers narrowly edged "Cannonball" Morris for the most wins among 1885 American Association pitchers, 40 to 39. Wolff, ed., *Baseball Encyclopedia,* 8th ed., 92; Nemec, *Encyclopedia of 19th Century Major League Baseball,* 278; Thorn et al., eds., *Total Baseball,* 6th ed., 1945.

79. *St. Louis Post-Dispatch,* April 27–July 20, 1885; Tiemann, *Cardinal Classics,* 14–15; Thorn et al., eds., *Total Baseball,* 6th ed., 1944.

80. *St. Louis Post-Dispatch,* May 21–23, 1885.

81. Ibid., May 30, June 1–30, July 1–4, 6, 8, 10–11, 13, 1885.

82. Ibid., July 15–16, 1885; Tiemann, *Cardinal Classics,* 14.

83. Harry Stovey had started his major-league career with Worcester of the National League; in his rookie season of 1880, he led the league in home runs and triples. After the 1882 season the small-market Worcester club was forced out of the National League, and Stovey joined the Philadelphia Athletics in the American Association. Over the course of the next seven seasons he would top the American Association in runs scored (four times), home runs (three times), triples (twice), doubles, stolen bases, and runs batted in. When he retired in 1893, Stovey held the major-league career records for runs scored (1,492) and home runs (122). Nemec, *Beer and Whisky League,* 44–45; Thorn et al., eds., *Total Baseball,* 6th ed., 638–39, 1287–88.

84. *St. Louis Post-Dispatch,* July 17, 1885; Tiemann, *Cardinal Classics,* 14–15.

85. *St. Louis Post-Dispatch,* April 25, 27, 30, July 18, 20, 25, August 1, 8, 15, 22, 26, 29, September 5, 11–12, 1885; Tiemann, *Cardinal Classics,* 14–15; Thorn et al., eds., *Total Baseball,* 6th ed., 1944.

86. Wolff, ed., *Baseball Encyclopedia,* 8th ed., 92; Nemec, *Encyclopedia of 19th Century Major League Baseball,* 277; Thorn et al., eds., *Total Baseball,* 6th ed., 1945; *Missouri Republican,* October 8, 1885; *St. Louis Globe-Democrat,* October 8, 1885.

87. *Missouri Republican,* October 19, 26, 28, November 2, 1885; Jerry Lanasche, *The Forgotten Championships: Postseason Baseball, 1882–1981,* 81; Het-

rick, *Chris Von der Ahe and the St. Louis Browns,* 49; Henry V. Lucas Vertical File, Missouri Historical Society Library, St. Louis; *Sporting News,* August 23, 1886; Borst, *Baseball through a Knothole,* 15; Thorn et al., eds., *Total Baseball,* 6th ed., 1950.

88. Allen, *The World Series,* 19; Glenn Dickey, *The History of the World Series,* 16. Following the end of the 1882 season, in the prototype of the modern World Series, the American Association pennant-winners, the Cincinnati Red Stockings, split a pair of games against the National League champions for three years running, the Chicago White Stockings. Two years later, in the first postseason matchup between champions of rival leagues to be played to completion, the National League's Providence Grays swept three straight games from the American Association's New York Metropolitans. Al Kermisch, " 'The First World Series,' " in Thorn, ed., *National Pastime,* 53–54; Thorn et al., eds., *Total Baseball,* 6th ed., 308.

Chapter 6: "Champions of the World"

1. *St. Louis Globe-Democrat,* September 27, 30, October 1–2, 4, 7, 1885.

2. *Chicago Tribune,* October 15, 1885. For Spalding's political affiliation, see Peter Levine, *A. G. Spalding and the Rise of Baseball,* 134–42, and Arthur Bartlett, *Baseball and Mr. Spalding: The History and Romance of Baseball,* 290–93; for the best discussion of Spalding's ethnic background, see the autobiography of another Albert Spalding, a renowned violinist and the nephew of A. G. Spalding; Albert Spalding, *Rise to Follow: An Autobiography,* 16, 20.

3. In an excellent study of the art of fielding, David Falkner observes that these distinctive styles echo down to the modern-day game: "When the imagery of a first baseman comes to mind today, it is remarkable how the picture still seems to divide between Anson, the immobile, big target, able to stretch, to 'perfect the plays,' and Comiskey, the smaller man, patrolling, prowling, testing, challenging, calculating." David Falkner, *Nine Sides of the Diamond: Baseball's Great Glove Men on the Fine Art of Defense,* 35. The superiority of Anson at the plate and Comiskey at first base is clearly demonstrated through a year-by-year comparison of their offensive and defensive statistics from 1882–1885. A comparison of their stolen base records is not possible for any season prior to 1886. In that year, Comiskey showed his superiority on the basepaths, stealing 41 bases compared to the 29 stolen by Anson. Wolff, ed., *The Baseball Encyclopedia,* 8th ed., 73, 76–77, 79, 81, 83, 88, 90; Nemec, *Encyclopedia of 19th Century Major League Baseball,* 295, 305.

4. Voigt, *American Baseball,* vol. 1, 103–4. Spalding had instructed Anson, "I will accept no excuse for any infraction of any rule." Mike "King" Kelly, a frequent target of punishment from White Stockings' management, conceded that Anson

was "apt to be harsh," yet he felt that Anson commanded respect from his players because he had "no favorites" and treated "all men alike." Levine, *A. G. Spalding and the Rise of Baseball,* 43; Mike "King" Kelly, *"Play Ball": Stories of the Ball Field,* 34. Axelson, *"Commy,"* 59–62; *Sporting News,* June 14, 1886.

5. The Browns' Curt Welch and the White Stockings' King Kelly shared a proclivity to partake of alcoholic beverages in the midst of a ballgame. These two players merely represented the most conspicuous drinkers on each team. Anson considered Kelly, Jim McCormick, and George Gore to be alcohol abusers while they played for the White Stockings. On the Browns, Yank Robinson, Dave Foutz, and Bob Caruthers also consumed alcohol heavily. Voigt, *American Baseball,* vol. 1, 173; Nemec, *Beer and Whisky League,* 98; Seymour, *Baseball: The Early Years,* 331; *Missouri Republican,* October 22, 1886; Adrian C. Anson, *A Ballplayer's Career,* 115; Pearson, *Baseball in 1889,* 204, 211, 215. Wolff, ed., *Baseball Encyclopedia,* 8th ed., 88, 90, 617–2320; Paul Dickson, *Baseball's Greatest Quotations,* 219; Spink, *National Game,* 50; Thorn et al., eds., *Total Baseball,* 6th ed., 1943, 1945, 1947, 1949. The White Stockings argued with umpires so much that Kelly described his teammates as "chronic kickers." Francis Richter, in the Philadelphia-based weekly *Sporting Life,* labeled the Browns as "about the toughest and roughest gang that ever struck this city," a ball club which featured players "vile of speech, insolent in bearing . . . [who] set at defiance all rules, grossly insulting the umpires and exciting the wrath of the spectators." Kelly, *"Play Ball,"* 8; Richter quoted in Voigt, *American Baseball,* vol. I, 140, Alexander, *Our Game,* 41, and Hetrick, *Chris Von der Ahe and the St. Louis Browns,* 20.

6. Wolff, ed., *Baseball Encyclopedia,* 8th ed., 90, 92; Nemec, *Encyclopedia of 19th Century Major League Baseball,* 267, 278; Thorn et al., eds., *Total Baseball,* 6th ed., 1943, 1945; *Missouri Republican,* October 15, 1885; *St. Louis Globe-Democrat,* October 15, 1885; *Chicago Tribune,* October 15, 1885; Lanasche, *Forgotten Championships,* 9–10.

7. The attendance figure of three thousand comes from the *Chicago Tribune,* October 16, 1885. Frederick Ivor-Campbell adjusts the figure down to two thousand in Thorn et al., eds., *Total Baseball,* 6th ed., 309.

8. The *Missouri Republican* labeled the shoddy fielding exhibition of the National League champions as "simply disgusting." *Missouri Republican,* October 16, 1885.

9. *Missouri Republican,* October 16, 1885; *St. Louis Globe-Democrat,* October 16, 1885. The roots of the term "fans" reach back to St. Louis in the 1880s. Browns' owner Chris Von der Ahe referred to one of the team's enthusiasts, Charles E. Haas, as "the greatest fanatic in baseball." Sportswriters picked up the term, applied it to the growing masses of baseball aficionados, and short-

ened the word to "fans" in the process. Missouri Historical Society Vertical File: Baseball-Missouri.

10. *Chicago Tribune,* October 16, 1885. Sunday, a reserve outfielder for the White Stockings, started only because regular center fielder George Gore had been suspended after the opening tie in Chicago for "indifferent playing and indulging too freely in stimulants." In October 1885 Sunday still caroused with teammates such as Gore, but in June of the following year he underwent a religious conversion. Within five years, Sunday retired from baseball in order to devote his life to preaching. By the time of his death in 1935, Sunday had preached to more than a hundred million people and taken in more than a million dollars in love offerings. One of his staple sermons, "Get on the Water Wagon," which attacked saloons and the liquor industry, played a major role in securing the adoption and ratification of the Prohibition Amendment that banned the legal sale of alcohol in the United States between the years of 1920 and 1933. Lyle W. Dorsett, *Billy Sunday and the Redemption of Urban America,* 23–26, 43–113; Roger A. Bruns, *Preacher: Billy Sunday and Big-Time American Evangelism,* 43–44.

11. *Missouri Republican,* October 16, 1885; for details of the argument between Anson and O'Neill, see *St. Louis Globe-Democrat,* October 16, 1885.

12. *Chicago Tribune,* October 16, 1885.

13. *Missouri Republican,* October 16, 1885; *St. Louis Globe-Democrat,* October 16, 1885; *Chicago Tribune,* October 16, 1885.

14. *Missouri Republican,* October 16, 1885; *St. Louis Globe-Democrat,* October 16, 1885; *Chicago Tribune,* October 16, 1885. The applicable rule on this play, adopted after the 1876 season to eliminate the fair-foul hit, stated that the determination of fair or foul on any groundball was dependent on the position of the ball as it passed first or third base. If the ball hit the bag, it would be deemed a fair ball; therefore, Sullivan's original call had been accurate. Okrent and Lewine, eds., *The Ultimate Baseball Book,* 13.

15. *Chicago Tribune,* October 16, 1885; *Missouri Republican,* October 16, 1885; *St. Louis Globe-Democrat,* October 16, 1885.

16. *Chicago Tribune,* October 16, 1885. The *St. Louis Globe-Democrat* condemned Comiskey's alleged decision to leave the diamond as "a serious blunder" which cost the Browns an "irretrievable loss of a game that they had a chance to win." But the *St. Louis Post-Dispatch* strongly endorsed the behavior attributed to the Browns' manager: "Comiskey, seeing that Sullivan was determined to have Chicago win, wisely determined to withdraw his men from the field, as forfeiting the game was much more acceptable than playing for nine innings only to be robbed." A third local opinion, printed by the *Missouri Republican,* sought to strike a more moderate position: "Comiskey may have been a little injudicious in calling off his men, but he can hardly be blamed for it, as the way Sullivan had

been giving decisions against them, made it look as though he was determined to keep the Browns from winning." *St. Louis Globe-Democrat,* October 16, 1885; *St. Louis Post-Dispatch,* October 16, 1885; *Missouri Republican,* October 16, 1885.

17. James, *Historical Baseball Abstract,* 39.

18. David Voigt, *America through Baseball,* 167–68; Voigt, *American Baseball,* vol. 1, 186. Both Voigt and Bill James blame Chris Von der Ahe for turning St. Louis into a model of umpire-baiting that was emulated by other cities. In reality, rather than boldly shaping public opinion, Von der Ahe and Sportsman's Park partisans merely reflected the spirit of the times. Historian Harold Seymour insightfully suggested a sociopsychological perspective of the antipathy that fans expressed toward umpires: "The umpire is a symbol of authority, and many people dislike authority. . . . A contributing explanation of the umpire's position may lie in America's frontier tradition of violence and disrespect for law. For the baseball fan the umpire represents law." James, *Historical Baseball Abstract,* 23, 39; Seymour, *Baseball: The Early Years,* 337.

19. The White Stockings scored 834 runs during the 1885 regular season; their closest challengers for offensive production within the National League, the New York Giants, totaled 691 runs. Thorn et al., eds., *Total Baseball,* 6th ed., 1943.

20. *Missouri Republican,* October 17, 1885; *St. Louis Globe-Democrat,* October 17, 1885; *Chicago Tribune,* October 17, 1885.

21. *St. Louis Globe-Democrat,* October 17, 18, 1885; *Missouri Republican,* October 18, 1885; *Chicago Tribune,* October 17, 1885. The *Missouri Republican* reported a thirty-minute delay over choosing an umpire while the *Globe-Democrat* stated that the dispute caused the game to start forty minutes late.

22. Wolff, ed., *Baseball Encyclopedia,* 8th ed., 88, 92, 2035; Nemec, *Encyclopedia of 19th Century Major League Baseball,* 269, 278; Thorn et al., eds., *Total Baseball,* 6th ed., 1685, 1945.

23. *Missouri Republican,* October 18, 1885; *St. Louis Globe-Democrat,* October 18, 1885; *Chicago Tribune,* October 18, 1885.

24. Robinson started behind the plate because the Browns' regular catcher, Albert "Doc" Bushong, fell prey to the most prevalent occupational hazard for backstops of the era—a hand injury. Tiemann, *Cardinal Classics,* 16. *Missouri Republican,* October 18, 1885; Wolff, ed., *Baseball Encyclopedia,* 8th ed., 90; Nemec, *Encyclopedia of 19th Century Major League Baseball,* 267; Thorn et al., eds., *Total Baseball,* 6th ed., 1943.

25. *Missouri Republican,* October 18, 1885.

26. Ibid.; *St. Louis Globe-Democrat,* October 18, 1885.

27. *Chicago Tribune,* October 18, 1885. The *Globe-Democrat* noted that McCormick "tried to get back, but did not succeed." *St. Louis Globe-Democrat,* October 18, 1885; *Missouri Republican,* October 18, 1885.

28. *St. Louis Globe-Democrat,* October 18, 1885.

29. Ibid.; *Missouri Republican,* October 18, 1885; *Chicago Tribune,* October 18, 1885.

30. Gore had been suspended after the opening tie in Chicago for "indifferent playing and indulging too freely in stimulants." His place in center field was taken by reserve outfielder Billy Sunday. However, a hand injury to White Stockings' catcher Frank "Silver" Flint then caused Mike "King" Kelly to transfer from right field to the backstop position. Since Sunday was already substituting for the suspended Gore, Clarkson was pressed into service in right field. *Chicago Tribune,* October 16, 1885; Tiemann, *Cardinal Classics,* 16.

31. *St. Louis Globe-Democrat,* October 18, 1885; *Missouri Republican,* October 18, 1885; *Chicago Tribune,* October 18, 1885 Later, with Cincinnati from 1889–1898, Holliday compiled a career major-league batting average of .311. Thorn et al., eds., *Total Baseball,* 6th ed., 955.

32. *St. Louis Globe-Democrat,* October 18, 1885.

33. Thorn and Palmer, eds., *Total Baseball,* 3d ed., 2244, 2250–51; *Chicago Tribune,* October 15, 1885.

34. In 1885 the average home attendance for the Chicago White Stockings had been 2,062 spectators, so the two thousand attending the World Series opener was only slightly less than the normal Chicago turnout. Frederick Ivor-Campbell, writing in *Total Baseball,* provides a lower attendance figure of two thousand for Game Two in St. Louis than the three thousand reported by the *Chicago Tribune.* Given the nature of the rivalry between these cities, I doubt very much that the *Tribune* would have exaggerated the attendance count and, in the process, bestow St. Louis with the recognition of having drawn more fans to Game Two than Chicago drew in Game One. The crowds of three thousand at the World Series games in St. Louis surpassed the Browns' average home attendance for 1885 of 2,345 spectators. Thorn et al., eds., *Total Baseball,* 6th ed., 105, 309; *Chicago Tribune,* October 15–16, 1885; Thorn and Palmer, eds., *Total Baseball,* 2d ed., 2523, 2525, provides the number of home games played by the teams in 1885.

35. *Missouri Republican,* September 28, October 24, 1885.

36. Ibid., October 23–25, 1885; *St. Louis Globe-Democrat,* October 23–25, 1885; *Chicago Tribune,* October 23–25, 1885.

37. *St. Louis Post-Dispatch,* October 24, 1885.

38. *Missouri Republican,* October 25, 1885; *St. Louis Globe-Democrat,* October 25, 1885; *Chicago Tribune,* October 25, 1885; *Cincinnati Commercial-Gazette,* quoted in *Chicago Tribune,* October 26, 1885; *Reach's Official American Association Baseball Guide: 1886,* 12.

39. *Missouri Republican,* October 25, 1885; *St. Louis Globe-Democrat,* October 25, 1885; *Chicago Tribune,* October 25, 1885.

40. *Missouri Republican,* October 25, 1885; *St. Louis Globe-Democrat,* October 25, 1885; *Chicago Tribune,* October 25, 1885.

41. The similarity of game descriptions in the *Chicago Tribune, Missouri Republican,* and *St. Louis Globe-Democrat,* after the World Series left St. Louis, evidently stemmed from the three newspapers' reliance upon the same accounts wired to them by local correspondents, first in Pittsburgh and then in Cincinnati. This situation led to the baffling contradictions of the *Chicago Tribune* in its Sunday edition of October 25. The *Tribune* gave the same description of Game Seven appearing in the St. Louis newspapers, printed underneath the headline: "Chicago Badly Beaten by the St. Louis Browns—The Latter Now Champions of the World." Elsewhere on the very same page, the *Tribune* offered this assessment of the 1885 World Series: "The result of the series (a tie) certainly cannot be taken as a true test . . . of playing strength." These apparently paradoxical reports became a bit clearer the next day. The *Tribune,* on Monday, established the *Cincinnati Commercial-Gazette* as the probable source of the account of Game Seven appearing in the St. Louis newspapers and the *Tribune.* It did so by reprinting a commentary on the World Series from the Sunday edition of the *Commercial-Gazette* that emphasized the same points previously made in the *Tribune, Republican,* and *Globe-Democrat:* "The St. Louis team . . . has the right to lay claim to the championship of the world. They won three games on their merits, while Chicago won but two. It was agreed before the game yesterday to call off . . . the games in the East, and decide the series with the game about to be played." Spalding likely provided the Sunday *Tribune* with the assertion that the World Series ended in a tie that "certainly cannot be taken as a true test . . . of playing strength." This deduction is supported by the similarity between those remarks and Spalding's heated protest in Monday's *Tribune,* which also maintained, among its many other complaints, that the series between the Browns and White Stockings "as a test of strength of the two nines has been a failure." Meanwhile, in Philadelphia, *Sporting Life* also printed contradictory interpretations of the 1885 World Series. First it conceded that the Browns were the champions: "The Chicago club is much chagrined at the defeats inflicted by St. Louis, a club they underrated, and the loss of the 'world championship.'" Then, after Spalding raised his objections, *Sporting Life* changed its mind in late November: "The championship of the United States for 1885 remains in abeyance." *Chicago Tribune,* October 25–26, 1885; *Missouri Republican,* October 25, 1885; *St. Louis Globe-Democrat,* October 25, 1885; *Cincinnati Commercial-Gazette* quoted in *Chicago Tribune,* October 26, 1885; *Sporting Life* quoted in Nemec, *Beer and Whisky League,* 104.

42. For a St. Louis view of the connection between Spalding and *The Mirror of American Sports,* see the *St. Louis Globe-Democrat,* April 12, 1885. The sharp divisions over the outcome of the series can be seen through a small sampling of published opinions. Generally, modern accounts depict the 1885 World Series as a tie, although many writers present balanced perspectives by offering the

St. Louis interpretation as well. Occasionally, one still encounters an unvarnished modern version of the St. Louis interpretation. Contemporary views that the Browns legitimately earned the title of 1885 world champions: *Missouri Republican,* October 25, 1885; October 24, 1886; *St. Louis Globe-Democrat,* October 25, 1885; October 24, 1886; *Cincinnati Commercial-Gazette* quoted in *Chicago Tribune,* October 26, 1885; *Reach's Official American Association Baseball Guide: 1886,* 11–12. Contemporary views of the 1885 World Series as a tie: *Chicago Tribune,* October 26, 1885; *Sporting Life* quoted in Nemec, *Beer and Whisky League,* 104; *Spalding's Official Baseball Guide: 1886,* 66–67. Modern accounts offering a balanced perspective: Allen, *The World Series,* 21; Thorn et al., eds., *Total Baseball,* 6th ed., 309. Modern works where the St. Louis version of the 1885 World Series has survived unchallenged: Harry Grayson, *They Played the Game: The Story of Baseball Greats,* 52; Deutsch et al., eds., *Scrapbook History of Baseball,* 21; A. D. Suehsdorf, *The Great American Baseball Scrapbook,* 23; Rygelski, "Baseball's 'Boss President,'" 45–46.

Chapter 7: "The $15,000 Slide"

1. *Sporting News,* May 10, 1886.

2. Ibid., March 17, July 19, 1886. *Sporting Life* accused Spink of plagiarizing their material. Denouncing the charge as a "base insinuation," Al Spink fired back in an inflammatory editorial, "The *Philadelphia Sewer* has not had a live item in it since the *News* jumped into the world and scared Grandmother Richter out of her wits. . . . We would as soon think of going to a cemetery after news." Seymour, *Baseball: The Early Years,* 349–50; Voigt, *American Baseball,* vol. 1, 193–95, 322; Lowell Reidenbaugh, ed., *The Sporting News' First Hundred Years, 1886–1986,* 14, 16; Steve Gietschier, "Before 'The Bible of Baseball': The First Quarter Century of *The Sporting News,*" in Tiemann, ed., *St. Louis's Favorite Sport,* 31–34.

3. *Sporting News,* March 17, 1886.

4. *Spalding's Official Baseball Guide: 1886,* 52–57; *Spalding's Official Baseball Guide: 1887,* 63–67; Thorn et al., eds., *Total Baseball,* 6th ed., 105, 109, 1949. The Browns led the American Association race by a game and a half at the end of April, two-and-a-half games at the end of May, four-and-a-half at the end of June, eight at the end of July, ten-and-a-half at the end of August, eleven-and-a-half at the end of September, and twelve when the regular season ended on October 10. *St. Louis Globe-Democrat,* October 11, 1886; *Missouri Republican,* October 11, 1886; Wolff, ed., *Baseball Encyclopedia,* 8th ed., 96; Nemec, *Encyclopedia of 19th Century Major League Baseball,* 303.

5. *Spalding's Official Baseball Guide: 1887,* 15–19. In 1885 the Browns posted a 79–33 record to outdistance second-place Cincinnati by the substantial margin of

sixteen games. A year later they went 93–46 and claimed the Association pennant by twelve games over Pittsburgh. The White Stockings' 1885 mark of 87–25 gave them a two-game edge over the second-place New York Giants. Then, in 1886, the White Stockings finished two-and-a-half games ahead of second-place Detroit with a record of 90–34. Wolff, ed., *Baseball Encyclopedia,* 8th ed., 90, 92, 94, 96; Nemec, *Encyclopedia of 19th Century Major League Baseball,* 266, 277, 293, 303; Thorn et al., eds., *Total Baseball,* 6th ed., 1943, 1945, 1947, 1949.

6. *St. Louis Post-Dispatch,* July 12, 14, 1886. Later, Comiskey countered that he felt the White Stockings would probably finish fifth in the American Association race. *Sporting News,* August 2, 1886.

7. *Sporting News,* July 19, 1886.

8. Ibid.

9. Ibid., July 26, August 2, 1886.

10. Ibid., August 2, September 20, 1886. Two weeks later the *Sporting News* similarly proclaimed, "The St. Louis Browns are ready to defend their title of 'Champions of the World.' Mr. Spalding will please take notice." *Sporting News,* October 4, 1886.

11. *Missouri Republican,* September 26, October 1–2, 1886; *Sporting News,* September 27, October 4, 1886; *St. Louis Post-Dispatch,* October 23, 1886.

12. *Missouri Republican,* October 2, 1886; *St. Louis Globe-Democrat,* October 2, 1886; *Sporting News,* October 4, 1886.

13. *Missouri Republican,* October 2, 4–5, 8, 1886; *St. Louis Globe-Democrat,* October 2, 8, 1886; *Sporting News,* October 11, 1886; *St. Louis Post-Dispatch,* October 18, 1886.

14. Wolff, ed., *Baseball Encyclopedia,* 8th ed., 96; Nemec, *Encyclopedia of 19th Century Major League Baseball,* 295, 304; Thorn et al., eds., *Total Baseball,* 6th ed., 1469, 1949; *Missouri Republican,* October 19, 1886; *St. Louis Globe-Democrat,* October 19, 1886; *Chicago News* reprinted in *Missouri Republican,* October 20, 1886.

15. *St. Louis Globe-Democrat,* October 20, 1886. The *Missouri Republican* hailed the Browns' triumph as "the greatest baseball victory of the ages." *Missouri Republican,* October 20, 1886. Wolff, ed., *Baseball Encyclopedia,* 8th ed., 92, 94; Nemec, *Encyclopedia of 19th Century Major League Baseball,* 295, 305; *Sporting News,* October 25, 1886; *Chicago News* reprinted in *Missouri Republican,* October 21, 1886.

16. O'Neill's first homer, with a runner on base and one out in the opening inning, staked St. Louis to a 2–0 lead. He led off the fifth inning with a solo shot to build a 5–0 advantage. The *St. Louis Globe-Democrat* described O'Neill's pair of home runs as "the longest hits ever seen on the grounds." Apparently, the hometown *Chicago Tribune* concurred; it stated that the blows struck by O'Neill

were "the prettiest ever made on the grounds." *St. Louis Globe-Democrat,* October 20, 1886; *Chicago Tribune,* October 20, 1886; *Sporting News,* October 25, 1886.

17. *St. Louis Globe-Democrat,* October 21, 1886; *St. Louis Post-Dispatch,* October 21, 1886; *Sporting News,* October 25, 1886.

18. The *Tribune* reacted bitterly to a prediction Comiskey made. Before leaving St. Louis, the Browns' manager suggested that his team needed to win at least one game in Chicago so they could wrap up the series with a sweep of the three games scheduled for Sportsman's Park. In response, the *Tribune* announced that the Browns departed for Chicago "full of confidence and beer." *Chicago Tribune,* October 18, 1886; *St. Louis Post-Dispatch,* October 18, 1886.

19. The outcome of Game Three had restored the faith of the *Chicago News* in claims of National League superiority: "Yesterday's game is no surprise. . . . It was confidently expected that the home team would deal with the visitors just about as they pleased." The *Chicago Times* assumed a similar smug tone in issuing a vitrolic farewell to the Browns that stressed the moralistic pretensions of the National League: "Chicago is well rid of a gang of hoodlums who make a living by exhibiting themselves on Sundays at 25 cents a spectator, and bear the same relation to honest baseball as a nigger minstrel show to the legitimate drama." *Chicago News* and *Chicago Times* reprinted in *Missouri Republican,* October 22, 1886; *St. Louis Globe-Democrat,* October 20, 1886.

20. The *Chicago Tribune* condemned Robinson for his "hoodlum action" that left Kelly with a "badly" cut face. However, the *Missouri Republican* diagnosed Kelly as being only "slightly" shaken on the play. It insisted that "the accident was clearly Kelly's fault whether he intended to get in Robinson's way or not." *Chicago Tribune,* October 21, 1886; *Missouri Republican,* October 21, 1886.

21. *St. Louis Post-Dispatch,* October 21, 1886; *Missouri Republican,* October 24, 1886.

22. *Missouri Republican,* October 20, 22, 1886; *Chicago Tribune,* October 22, 1886; *Sporting News,* October 25, 1886.

23. *St. Louis Post-Dispatch,* October 21, 1886; *St. Louis Globe-Democrat,* October 29, 1886; *Sporting News,* October 25, 1886.

24. *St. Louis Globe-Democrat,* October 8–9, 22, 1886; *Missouri Republican,* October 8–9, 1886. The *Globe-Democrat* felt O'Neill reached the plate "certainly as quick as, if not before, the ball did." Since Kelly also had to apply a tag, the *Globe-Democrat* argued that "a poor decision on the part of umpire Quest" denied O'Neill his third home run of the World Series.

25. *Missouri Republican,* October 22, 1886; *Sporting News,* October 25, 1886.

26. *St. Louis Globe-Democrat,* October 22, 1886; *Missouri Republican,* October 22, 1886; *Sporting News,* October 25, 1886. Kelly's quick thinking is noted in several secondary sources, including James, *Historical Baseball Abstract,* 23–24.

27. The *St. Louis Post-Dispatch* gleefully noted that even the lowest estimates of the St. Louis turnout "exceeded by three thousand the number of the best audiences in Chicago." *St. Louis Post-Dispatch,* October 22, 1886; *Missouri Republican,* October 22, 1886.

28. *St. Louis Globe-Democrat,* October 22, 1886; *St. Louis Post-Dispatch,* October 22, 1886.

29. *Missouri Republican,* October 22, 1886; *St. Louis Globe-Democrat,* October 22, 1886.

30. *St. Louis Globe-Democrat,* October 22, 1886. In contrast to the accounts of the *Globe-Democrat* and *Chicago Tribune,* both the *Missouri Republican* and *Sporting News* claimed that Comiskey had singled "past third." Ed Sheridan, an outstanding baseball reporter for the *Republican* whose game accounts also ran in the *Sporting News,* had given a vivid description of the "side show" brawl between the supporters of the Browns and White Stockings. I believe that Sheridan's detailed coverage of this "side show" had delayed him in getting back to the resumption of the game. It seems likely that Sheridan then asked somebody else where Comiskey's hit had gone. That observer, perhaps similarly distracted by the chaotic proceedings, provided erroneous information. *Missouri Republican,* October 22, 1886; *Sporting News,* October 25, 1886; *Chicago Tribune,* October 22, 1886.

31. *Missouri Republican,* October 22, 1886; *Sporting News,* October 25, 1886. This approach at the plate had helped Latham to improve considerably as a hitter. In three previous years with the Browns, Latham walked fifty-five times (3.9 percent of his plate appearances) and posted a batting average of .240. However, during the 1886 season Latham equaled the number of walks he drew in the preceding three years combined. In 1886, by walking 55 times (8.7 percent of his plate appearances) and often getting so far ahead in the ball-strike count that he forced opposing hurlers to throw pitches over the fat part of the plate, Latham managed to record a batting average of .301 for the season. Wolff, ed., *Baseball Encyclopedia,* 8th ed., 1129.

32. Ed Sheridan, reporting in both the *Missouri Republican* and the *Sporting News,* blamed the walk upon the "terror" that Clarkson encountered every time O'Neill entered the batter's box. The *St. Louis Globe-Democrat* and Clarkson himself, however, stressed that the Chicago pitcher at least made an effort to retire O'Neill this time. *Missouri Republican,* October 22, 1886; *Sporting News,* October 25, 1886; *St. Louis Globe-Democrat,* October 22, 1886; *St. Louis Post-Dispatch,* October 22, 1886.

33. *Missouri Republican,* October 22, 1886.

34. Ibid.

35. Ibid., October 22–23, 1886. The *Chicago Tribune* claimed that Game Four

drew eight thousand fans and a larger crowd of ten thousand flocked to Sportsman's Park for Game Five. Frederick Ivor-Campbell, in the encyclopedic *Total Baseball,* cites the same figures. The *St. Louis Globe-Democrat,* however, maintained "at least 12,000 people" were present for the fourth game and noted that "attendance was about the same" at the fifth contest. *Chicago Tribune,* October 22–23, 1886; Thorn et al., eds., *Total Baseball,* 6th ed., 310; *St. Louis Globe-Democrat,* October 22–23, 1886.

36. *Chicago Tribune,* October 21, 23, 1886; *Missouri Republican,* October 22–23, 1886; *St. Louis Post-Dispatch,* October 23, 1886; *St. Louis Globe-Democrat,* October 23, 1886; *Sporting News,* October 25, 30, 1886.

37. Von der Ahe believed an earlier controversy provided an important precedent in favor of his argument. Immediately before the start of the World Series, various newspapers circulated rumors that Von der Ahe had engaged Louisville pitcher Tom Ramsey to pitch against the White Stockings. In Chicago, the *Tribune* had harshly attacked Von der Ahe for "resorting to trickery" and undermining the public perception that "the League pennant-winners were to be pitted against the Association champions." Von der Ahe vehemently denied the allegation that he had contacted Ramsey: "There is not a word of truth in it. . . . We will use only our own men, and, if we can't beat Chicago with them, we will not try to beat them in any other way." By seeking to bring in Baldwin, Von der Ahe felt that Chicago now violated the very principle for which the *Tribune* had condemned him. In his denial of the Ramsey rumor, Von der Ahe had promised, "As for myself if Chicago tried to ring in any new players, I should take my nine off the field [instantly]." *Louisville Commercial* cited in *Missouri Republican,* October 15, 1886; *Chicago Tribune,* October 15, 17, 1886; *Sporting News,* October 18, 1886.

38. *St. Louis Post-Dispatch,* October 23, 1886.

39. Ibid., October 21, 1886; *St. Louis Globe-Democrat,* October 29, 1886; Wolff, ed., *Baseball Encyclopedia,* 8th ed., 92; Nemec, *Encyclopedia of 19th Century Major League Baseball,* 295. Baldwin would post an 18–17 record with the White Stockings in 1887. Thorn et al., eds., *Total Baseball,* 6th ed., 1404.

40. Anson, *A Ballplayer's Career,* 113.

41. Wolff, ed., *Baseball Encyclopedia,* 8th ed., 94, 1924, 2299; Thorn et al., eds., *Total Baseball,* 6th ed., 310, 1604, 1886; *Missouri Republican,* October 23, 1886; *Sporting News,* October 25, 1886.

42. *Missouri Republican,* October 23, 1886; *St. Louis Globe-Democrat,* October 23, 1886; *Chicago Tribune,* October 23, 1886.

43. Wolff, ed., *Baseball Encyclopedia,* 8th ed., 2174; Thorn et al., eds., *Total Baseball,* 6th ed., 1792.

44. *Missouri Republican,* October 23, 1886; *St. Louis Globe-Democrat,* October 23, 1886.

45. *St. Louis Globe-Democrat,* October 23, 1886. Hudson arrived in St. Louis directly out of the Colorado State League, where he spent the 1885 season pitching for the Denver Browns. *Sporting News,* March 17, 1886. Spalding blamed his own winner-take-all format for the fierce combativeness of the 1886 World Series: "I will never consent again to play games of this description with anybody for the money that is in them. . . . They have become altogether too earnest and I think it very fortunate that the games have passed off thus far without any more serious trouble than that which has already occurred." *St. Louis Post-Dispatch,* October 23, 1886.

46. *Chicago News* reprinted in *Missouri Republican,* October 24, 1886. The *Chicago Inter-Ocean* suggested the 1886 World Series had been tainted by "a flavor of the hippodrome . . . that has been to the disadvantage rather than the advantage of the sport of baseball." The *Chicago Times* questioned if the World Series represented "a genuine contest of baseball or . . . a hippodrome run for the benefits of the gate receipts." *Chicago Inter-Ocean* and *Chicago Times* reprinted in *Missouri Republican,* October 24, 1886.

47. Also, in forcing Game Four into its "hippodrome" theory, the *Chicago News* conveniently ignored the fact that pitchers—especially one of Foutz's caliber—could often finish a game strongly even if they got off to a poor start. Instead, it reported sinisterly, "The Chicagos made three runs in the first inning, and then, all at once, discovered that they could not hit Mr. Foutz's delivery!" *Chicago News* reprinted in *Missouri Republican,* October 24, 1886.

48. *Missouri Republican,* October 24, 1886; *Chicago News* reprinted in *Missouri Republican,* October 24, 1886; *Sporting News,* October 30, 1886. For examples of the *Sporting News* advertising Wiseman's Baseball Exchange, see that publication's issues of June 7, 14, 21, July 5, 26, August 2, 1886.

49. *Missouri Republican,* October 23–24, 1886; *St. Louis Globe-Democrat,* October 23–24, 1886.

50. *Sporting News,* October 30, 1886.

51. *St. Louis Post-Dispatch,* October 23, 1886; *Sporting News,* October 30, 1886.

52. *Sporting News,* October 30, 1886; *Missouri Republican,* October 24, 1886.

53. *Missouri Republican,* October 24, 1886; *Chicago Tribune,* October 24, 1886; *Chicago News* reprinted in *St. Louis Globe-Democrat,* October 26, 1886; *Sporting News,* October 30, 1886.

54. *Missouri Republican,* October 24, 1886; *Chicago Tribune,* October 24, 1886; *Chicago News* reprinted in *St. Louis Globe-Democrat,* October 26, 1886; *Sporting News,* October 30, 1886.

55. *Chicago Tribune,* October 24, 1886.

56. *St. Louis Globe-Democrat,* October 24, 1886; *Missouri Republican,* October 24, 1886; *Sporting News,* October 30, 1886; Thorn et al., eds., *Total Baseball,*

6th ed., 310; *Chicago News* reprinted in *St. Louis Globe-Democrat,* October 26, 1886.

57. *Missouri Republican,* October 24, 1886; *Sporting News,* October 30, 1886.

58. Kelly won the National League batting championship with a .388 average. Anson's .371 average placed him only behind Kelly. Wolff, ed., *Baseball Encyclopedia,* 8th ed., 94; Nemec, *Encyclopedia of 19th Century Major League Baseball,* 293; Thorn et al., eds., *Total Baseball,* 6th ed., 1947. *Missouri Republican,* October 24, 1886; *Sporting News,* October 30, 1886.

59. *Chicago News* reprinted in *St. Louis Globe-Democrat,* October 26, 1886; *Missouri Republican,* October 24, 1886; *Sporting News,* October 30, 1886.

60. *Chicago Tribune,* October 24, 1886; *Sporting News,* October 30, 1886; Wolff, ed., *Baseball Encyclopedia,* 8th ed., 94; Nemec, *Encyclopedia of 19th Century Major League Baseball,* 305.

61. For Latham's nickname, see Smith, *Baseball in the Afternoon,* 86–87; Wolff, ed., *Baseball Encyclopedia,* 8th ed., 1129; Nemec, *Encyclopedia of 19th Century Major League Baseball,* 702; Thorn et al., eds., *Total Baseball,* 6th ed., 1025.

62. *Chicago Times* and *Chicago Inter-Ocean* reprinted in *Missouri Republican,* October 21, 1886; *Chicago Tribune,* October 19, 1886; *Chicago News* reprinted in *Missouri Republican,* October 22, 1886; *St. Louis Globe-Democrat,* October 19, 1886; *Sporting News,* June 21, October 25, 1886.

63. *Missouri Republican,* October 24, 1886; *Sporting News,* October 30, 1886.

64. *Missouri Republican,* October 24, 1886. For more on the Latham-Bushong tussle, see *Sporting News,* June 14, 21, 1886.

65. *Missouri Republican,* October 24, 1886; *Chicago Tribune,* October 24, 1886; *Sporting News,* October 30, 1886. Although the *Chicago News* claimed Latham's triple "dropped where [Dalrymple] had been standing," Ed Sheridan believed the Chicago left fielder received excessive criticism for his misjudgment: "Dalrymple made a very bad attempt to judge the ball, but it is doubtful if he could have reached it." *Chicago News* reprinted in *St. Louis Globe-Democrat,* October 26, 1886; *Sporting News,* October 30, 1886.

66. *St. Louis Globe-Democrat,* October 24, 1886; *Missouri Republican,* October 24, 1886; *Chicago Tribune,* October 24, 1886; *Sporting News,* October 30, 1886.

67. *Missouri Republican,* October 24, 1886; *Sporting News,* October 30, 1886.

68. *St. Louis Globe-Democrat,* October 24, 1886; Thorn et al., eds., *Total Baseball,* 6th ed., 308–10; Lanasche, *Forgotten Championships,* 1–18.

69. The health of Caruthers posed a major question on the eve of the World Series. He had been sidelined for more than a week during the late stages of the regular season. Sensational accounts attributed his illness to typhoid fever or heart palpitations. On October 3, allegedly pitching under the treatment of

morphine, Caruthers had returned to action and pitched the Browns to a 6–4 triumph over the New York Metropolitans. *Missouri Republican,* September 25–27, 29–30, October 3–4, 1886. Besides pitching superbly in Games Two and Six, Caruthers also tied for the series lead in triples (two) and runs batted in (five). His six runs scored trailed only the seven tallies totaled by both teammate Curt Welch and the White Stockings' Fred Pfeffer. Thorn et al., eds., *Total Baseball,* 6th ed., 310.

70. *Missouri Republican,* October 24, 1886; *St. Louis Globe-Democrat,* October 24, 1886; *Sporting News,* October 30, 1886. In 1884 the American Association adopted a rule stipulating, "If a batsman be solidly hit by a ball from the pitcher when he evidently cannot avoid the same, he shall be given his base by the umpire." The National League did not accept the rule until 1887. Thorn and Palmer, eds., *Total Baseball,* 3d ed., 2280–81.

71. *Missouri Republican,* October 24, 1886; *St. Louis Globe-Democrat,* October 24, 1886; *Chicago News* reprinted in *St. Louis Globe-Democrat,* October 26, 1886; *Sporting News,* October 30, 1886.

72. *Missouri Republican,* October 24, 1886; *Chicago Tribune,* October 24, 1886; *Sporting News,* October 30, 1886. Regarded as a controversial tactic, the sacrifice bunt underwent a period of critical acceptance in the late nineteenth century. Henry Chadwick, a veteran baseball reporter with the *New York Clipper* and *Brooklyn Eagle,* opposed the concept. He called it "veritable stupidity" for a batter to voluntarily enhance the chances of the opposition to put him out—even if the batter succeeded in advancing a vital base runner. In his description of Robinson's tenth-inning sacrifice, Ed Sheridan displayed a greater appreciation for the merits of the play: "The result showed that Robbie was level headed." The ascendancy of Sheridan's perspective over the viewpoint of Chadwick became officially recognized in 1894, the year that batters started receiving credit for sacrifices and were no longer charged with an at-bat whenever they sacrificed. Seymour, *Baseball: The Early Years,* 280; Thorn and Palmer, eds., *Total Baseball,* 3d ed., 2307.

73. Lowell Reidenbaugh, ed., *The Sporting News' Take Me Out to the Ballpark,* 232.

74. Axelson, *"Commy,"* 77, 89–91; Robert Smith, *Baseball,* 103; Robert Smith, *An Illustrated History of Baseball,* 64, 66; Smith, *Baseball in the Afternoon,* 87; Seymour, *Baseball: The Early Years,* 181, 186; Voigt, *American Baseball,* vol. 1, 143; James, *Historical Baseball Abstract,* 31; Frederick Lieb, *The Story of the World Series: An Informal History,* 12; Joseph Gies and Robert H. Shoemaker, *Stars of the Series: A Complete History of the World Series,* 3–4; John Thorn, *A Century of Baseball Lore,* 19; Thorn et al., eds., *Total Baseball,* 6th ed., 310.

75. *Chicago News* reprinted in *St. Louis Globe-Democrat,* October 26, 1886.

76. *Chicago Tribune,* October 24, 1886; *Missouri Republican,* October 24, 1886; *St. Louis Globe-Democrat,* October 24, 1886; *Sporting News,* October 30, 1886; *St. Louis Post-Dispatch,* October 25, 1886.

77. Axelson, *"Commy,"* 89–90.

78. In 1886 Welch placed third among American Association base stealers with fifty-nine, and he had stolen home in the past. Nemec, *Encyclopedia of 19th Century Major League Baseball,* 303; Thorn et al., eds., *Total Baseball,* 6th ed., 1949; *St. Louis Post-Dispatch,* July 4, 1885; *St. Louis Globe-Democrat,* October 24, 1886. Since 1858, baseball rules had contained a provision calling for runners to advance a base in the event of a balk committed by the opposition pitcher. In 1886 umpires defined a balk as occurring "whenever the pitcher, when about to deliver the ball to the bat while standing in his position, makes any one of a series of actions he habitually makes in delivery, and he fails to deliver the ball to the bat." Thorn and Palmer, eds., *Total Baseball,* 3d ed., 2271, 2281, 2302; *St. Louis Post-Dispatch,* October 25, 1886.

79. *Missouri Republican,* October 24, 1886; *Sporting News,* October 30, 1886.

80. *St. Louis Post-Dispatch,* October 30, 1886; *Missouri Republican,* October 24, 1886; *St. Louis Globe-Democrat,* October 24, 1886; *Sporting News,* October 30, 1886; *Chicago Tribune,* October 24, 1886.

81. *St. Louis Globe-Democrat,* October 24, 1886; *Sporting News,* October 30, 1886; *Missouri Republican,* October 24, 1886. This $100,000, which changed hands in St. Louis after Game Six of the World Series as a result of gambling, would convert to a modern-day equivalent somewhere between $1.2 million and $1.5 million. Alexander, *Our Game,* 27; James, *Historical Baseball Abstract,* 29.

82. *Sporting News,* October 30, 1886; *Chicago News* reprinted in *Missouri Republican,* October 26, 1886; *St. Louis Globe-Democrat,* October 24, 1886; *Missouri Republican,* October 24, 1886.

83. *St. Louis Post-Dispatch,* October 30, 1886.

84. *St. Louis Post-Dispatch,* October 25, 1886; *St. Louis Globe-Democrat,* October 24, 1886; *Missouri Republican,* October 24, 1886; *Sporting News,* October 30, 1886.

85. *St. Louis Globe-Democrat,* October 24, 1886; *Missouri Republican,* October 24, 1886; *Sporting News,* October 30, 1886; Reiss, *Touching Base,* 32. The gate receipts of the 1886 World Series would convert to a modern-day equivalent somewhere between $167,000 and $200,000. Each player's share would range somewhere between the modern-day equivalent of $6,960 to $8,337.50. Alexander, *Our Game,* 27; James, *Historical Baseball Abstract,* 29.

86. *St. Louis Globe-Democrat,* November 4, 1886.

87. Thorn et al., eds., *Total Baseball,* 6th ed., 105, 109, 310, 1929, 1931, 1933, 1935, 1937, 1939, 1943, 1945, 1947, 1949; *Reach's Official American Association*

Baseball Guide: 1887, 16–18; *Reach's Official American Association Baseball Guide: 1886,* 9–11; *Spalding's Official Baseball Guide: 1887,* 28–31; *Spalding's Official Baseball Guide: 1886,* 63–65.

Chapter 8: Farewell to Five "Old War Horses"

1. *Sporting News,* November 13, 20, 1886.
2. *Reach's Official American Association Baseball Guide: 1886,* 8; *Sporting News,* August 23, September 27, 1886.
3. *Pittsburgh Referee* quoted in *Sporting News,* December 4, 1886; Robert F. Martin, "Sports versus the Sabbath: Professional Baseball and Blue Laws," 38.
4. *Pittsburgh Referee* quoted in *Sporting News,* December 4, 1886; Thorn et al., eds., *Total Baseball,* 6th ed., 105, 1931, 1935, 1939, 1945, 1949.
5. *Reach's Official American Association Baseball Guide: 1886,* 35–38; Seymour, *Baseball: The Early Years,* 217–18.
6. *Sporting News,* March 29, December 4, 1886; Seymour, *Baseball: The Early Years,* 218.
7. Thorn et al., eds., *Total Baseball,* 6th ed., 105, 1929–49; *Reach's Official American Association Baseball Guide: 1887,* 5; Nemec, *Encyclopedia of 19th Century Major League Baseball,* 313; Nemec, *Beer and Whisky League,* 6.
8. *Sporting News,* June 11, 1887.
9. Ibid., June 4, 11, 25, July 30, August 6, 13, December 31, 1887; *St. Louis Post-Dispatch,* June 9–10, December 15, 1887.
10. *Sporting News,* June 4, 1887.
11. Ibid.
12. Ibid., June 11, 1887; *St. Louis Post-Dispatch,* June 9–10, 1887.
13. *Sporting News,* June 11, 1887; *St. Louis Post-Dispatch,* June 10, 1887.
14. *St. Louis Post-Dispatch,* June 11, 1887.
15. *Chicago Tribune,* November 15, 1885; *Sporting News,* June 18, 1887.
16. *Sporting News,* June 25, 1887; *St. Louis Post-Dispatch,* June 25, 1887; *Missouri Republican,* June 19, July 9, 1887. In 1857 the *Missouri Republican* noted that the beer drinking of German immigrants had been "well-nigh universally adopted by the English-speaking population, and the spacious beer halls and extensive gardens nightly show that." By 1880, twenty-three St. Louis breweries employed 1,335 workers who produced $4,535,630 worth of beer. During 1887 alone, St. Louis breweries turned out 1,383,361 barrels or 43,575,872 gallons of beer. *Missouri Republican,* June 21, 1857, also quoted in Primm, *Lion of the Valley,* 206; Olson, *St. Louis Germans,* 215–16.
17. *Missouri Republican,* June 28, 1887; *St. Louis Post-Dispatch,* June 25, 1887; *Sporting News,* June 11, 1887.

18. *Missouri Republican,* June 28, July 9, 1887; James Cox, *Old and New St. Louis,* 275; Albert Nelson Marquis, *Book of St. Louisans,* 448–49; *Sporting News,* October 30, 1886.

19. *Missouri Republican,* July 9–10, 1887.

20. Ibid., July 11, 1887; *Sporting News,* June 18, 1887.

21. *Missouri Republican,* July 10, 1887; *Sporting News,* June 25, 1887; *St. Louis Post-Dispatch,* July 11, 1887. This opposition to blue laws reflected the views of the Democratic Party on the issue. The *Missouri Republican,* despite its misleading name, staunchly supported the Democrats. The newspaper traced its origins back to 1808, and it had been named in support of Jeffersonian political ideals.

22. *Missouri Republican,* July 12, 16, 1887.

23. *Sporting News,* July 16, 1887; *St. Louis Post-Dispatch,* July 16, 1887.

24. United States Biographical and Publishing Company, *United States Biographical Dictionary and Portrait Gallery,* 811; Hyde and Conrad, eds., *Encyclopedia of the History of St. Louis,* vol. 3, 1673; *Bench and Bar of St. Louis . . . ,* 286–87; Morris and Morris, *Who Was Who in American Politics,* 449; *Sporting News,* December 5, 1891. Explaining that he considered baseball "a reasonable sport and use of nature's power," Judge Noonan ruled, "While the evidence showed that money was taken [from spectators] and money paid to the players, it in my mind is not within the meaning of this statute any more than would be the playing of any piano player or singer that might come into the home of a citizen on Sunday to contribute to his entertainment." *Missouri Republican,* July 16, 1887.

25. *Missouri Republican,* July 16, 1887; *St. Louis Post-Dispatch,* July 16, 1887; *Sporting News,* July 16, 1887; Cox, *Old and New St. Louis,* 275; Marquis, *Book of St. Louisans,* 448–49; Hetrick, *Chris Von der Ahe and the St. Louis Browns,* 257.

26. *Missouri Republican,* July 18, 1887. While the *Republican* estimated the attendance at five thousand, the July 23, 1887, edition of the *Sporting News* claimed that a crowd of eight thousand turned out.

27. *Missouri Republican,* July 14, 1887.

28. *Sporting News,* July 30, August 6, 13, 1887; Seymour, *Baseball: The Early Years,* 210.

29. Seymour, *Baseball: The Early Years,* 208–10.

30. *Sporting News,* August 6, 1887; *St. Louis Post-Dispatch,* May 23, 1885; *Spalding's Official Baseball Guide: 1887,* 63–67; Tiemann, *Cardinal Classics,* 14–15, 22–23. The 1887 Browns finished fourteen games ahead of second-place Cincinnati, the third successive season that they had claimed the Association pennant with a winning margin of at least a dozen games. Their winning percentage, .704, narrowly failed to match the American Association's record winning percentage (.705) established by the 1885 Browns. Nemec, *Encyclopedia of 19th Century Ma-*

jor League Baseball, 183, 205, 231, 277, 303, 330; Thorn et al., eds., *Total Baseball,* 6th ed., 1931, 1935, 1939, 1945, 1949, 1953.

31. *Sporting News,* August 6, 13, September 10, 1887; Seymour, *Baseball: The Early Years,* 210.

32. *Sporting News,* July 30, August 27, 1887.

33. Ibid., September 3, 1887.

34. Ibid., September 3, 10, 1887.

35. Nemec, *Encyclopedia of 19th Century Major League Baseball,* 329; Thorn et al., eds., *Total Baseball,* 6th ed., 311.

36. *Sporting News,* September 10, 1887. For a comparison of attendance figures between the 1885 and 1886 World Series, see Thorn et al., eds., *Total Baseball,* 6th ed., 309–10.

37. *Sporting News,* September 10, 1887.

38. Thorn et al., eds., *Total Baseball,* 6th ed., 311; Tiemann, *Cardinal Classics,* 24–25.

39. *Cincinnati Commercial-Gazette* quoted in *St. Louis Post-Dispatch,* December 15, 1887; *Sporting News,* December 31, 1887.

40. *Reach's Official American Association Baseball Guide: 1886,* 17–24; Seymour, *Baseball: The Early Years,* 165–66, 214–16; Nemec, *Beer and Whisky League,* 62–63, 91–92. Seymour notes that Wiman "reputedly lost $30,000" on the Metropolitans in two years of ownership. Yet he also comments that baseball increased the volume of traffic on a Wiman-operated ferry, the Staten Island Rapid Transit Railway, thus elevating the price that the Baltimore & Ohio Railroad paid Wiman to buy out the Staten Island Rapid Transit Railway. Furthermore, *Reach's Official American Association Baseball Guide: 1887* (p. 5) insisted that all eight American Association teams turned a profit in 1886, the first of the two years that Wiman owned the Metropolitans.

41. *Sporting News,* December 31, 1887; *St. Louis Globe-Democrat,* November 15, 18, 1887; *St. Louis Post-Dispatch,* December 15, 1887; Seymour, *Baseball: The Early Years,* 216; Nemec, *Beer and Whisky League,* 147–48.

42. Borst, *Baseball through a Knothole,* 10; *St. Louis Republic,* January 19, 1913, reprinted in Missouri Historical Society Library, St. Louis, *Necrologies,* vol. 6 (1913), 16–18; *Sporting News,* June 12, 1913; Lipsitz, *Sidewalks of St. Louis,* 58.

43. *St. Louis Post-Dispatch,* June 18, 1887; Thorn et al., eds., *Total Baseball,* 6th ed., 105; Thorn and Palmer, eds., *Total Baseball,* 2d ed., 2522–23, provides the yearly number of home games played by the Browns. *Sporting News,* November 13, 1886.

44. *Reach's Official American Association Baseball Guide: 1886,* 5–6; Seymour, *Baseball: The Early Years,* 119–21. Von der Ahe's projected 1884 payroll for "the highest salaried club in the American Association" totaled $23,375. Three years

later, Von der Ahe declared that his $35,000 payroll would make the Browns "the highest salaried team in America." Deutsch et al., eds., *Scrapbook History of Baseball,* 19; *Sporting News,* May 7, 1887.

45. *Sporting News,* November 26, December 17, 1887.

46. *St. Louis Post-Dispatch,* November 20, 1887.

47. *Sporting News,* December 17, 1887.

48. Ibid., November 26, 1887. For the records of Foutz and Caruthers with the Browns, see Nemec, *Encyclopedia of 19th Century Major League Baseball,* 279, 305, 332–33; Thorn et al., eds., *Total Baseball,* 6th ed., 757, 869, 1459, 1536.

49. *Sporting News,* November 26, 1887. Bill Gleason, while not providing many details, did clearly express to the *St. Louis Globe-Democrat* that he believed his contributions to the Browns had been underappreciated by Von der Ahe. He also expressed relief over playing for someone else. Welch, while reluctant to make a public statement, must have felt the same way. Later, during his last road trip with the team, the San Francisco correspondent to the *St. Louis Post-Dispatch* reported that Welch, Foutz, and Bushong were all "glad to escape from Von der Ahe." *St. Louis Globe-Democrat,* November 26, 1887; *St. Louis Post-Dispatch,* January 1, 1888.

50. *Sporting News,* November 19, 26, 1887; December 10, 1887–January 7, 1888.

51. Ibid., December 10, 1887; January 28, 1888.

52. Ibid., December 17, 31, 1887; January 7, 1888.

53. Ibid., December 31, 1887; February 18, March 19, 1888.

54. Ibid., February 4, 1888; *St. Louis Globe-Democrat,* December 4, 1887.

Chapter 9: Browns versus Bridegrooms

1. Wolff, ed., *Baseball Encyclopedia,* 8th ed., 100, 104, 108; Nemec, *Great Encyclopedia of 19th Century Major League Baseball,* 330, 360, 388; Thorn et al., eds., *Total Baseball,* 6th ed., 1953, 1957, 1961.

2. *Sporting News,* June 2, 1888.

3. Ibid., June 23, 30, 1888.

4. Ibid., June 30, July 14, 21, August 11, 1888; Pearson, *Baseball in 1889,* 20; Wolff, ed., *Baseball Encyclopedia,* 8th ed., 100, 104; Nemec, *Encyclopedia of 19th Century Major League Baseball,* 331, 361; Thorn et al., eds., *Total Baseball,* 6th ed., 1953, 1957; *Sporting News,* August 11, 1888. In an accompanying resolution the American Association declared, "It is the sense of the Association that no clubs be permitted to negotiate with any player under contract with another club."

5. *Sporting News,* July 21, 1888. For other editorials critical of Ferguson, see the same publication's editions for July 28, August 11, and September 1, 1888.

6. Ibid., August 11, 1888.

7. Ibid., July 21, August 4, 1888.

8. Tiemann, *Cardinal Classics,* 26; *Sporting News,* March 10, 1888; Nemec, *Beer and Whisky League,* 128, 158; Nemec, *Encyclopedia of 19th Century Major League Baseball,* 333; Wolff, ed., *Baseball Encyclopedia,* 8th ed., 1962; Thorn et al., eds., *Total Baseball,* 6th ed., 1632.

9. *Sporting News,* August 11, 1888; Tiemann, *Cardinal Classics,* 27.

10. *Sporting News,* August 11, 1888; Tiemann, *Cardinal Classics,* 27.

11. *Sporting News,* August 11, September 1, 1888.

12. Ibid., September 1, 8, 22, 29, 1888; Wolff, ed., *Baseball Encyclopedia,* 8th ed., 104; Nemec, *Encyclopedia of 19th Century Major League Baseball,* 360; Thorn et al., eds., *Total Baseball,* 6th ed., 1957.

13. *Sporting News,* December 17, 1887; July 7, 1888; Seymour, *Baseball: The Early Years,* 208.

14. *Sporting News,* September 10, 1887; June 9, August 11, November 17, 24, 1888. Also, in November, the Cleveland Blues, still angered over the Association's acceptance of the twenty-five-cent ticket price, transferred to the National League. Besides holding a firm conviction in favor of the fifty-cent price of admission, Cleveland Blues' president Frank Robison resented the tendency of Von der Ahe and Byrne "to run the Association for their own benefit."

15. *Sporting News,* September 22, 1888; Nemec, *Encyclopedia of 19th Century Major League Baseball,* 359; Thorn et al., eds., *Total Baseball,* 6th ed., 312.

16. Spink, *National Game,* 298, 300.

17. Ibid.

18. Wolff, ed., *Baseball Encyclopedia,* 8th ed., 102, 104, 1201; Nemec, *Encyclopedia of 19th Century Major League Baseball,* 350, 359, 361; Thorn et al., eds., *Total Baseball,* 6th ed., 312, 1076, 1955, 1957; Tiemann, *Cardinal Classics,* 26, 28–29; Lanasche, *Forgotten Championships,* 29–30.

19. Nemec, *Beer and Whisky League,* 159; Nemec, *Encyclopedia of 19th Century Major League Baseball,* 359; Thorn et al., eds., *Total Baseball,* 6th ed., 312, 1462; Lanasche, *Forgotten Championships,* 30.

20. Spink, *National Game,* 300.

21. Thorn et al., eds., *Total Baseball,* 6th ed., 312; Lanasche, *Forgotten Championships,* 33–34.

22. *Sporting News,* November 10, 1888.

23. Thorn et al., eds., *Total Baseball,* 6th ed., 105–6.

24. The *St. Louis Post-Dispatch* observed, "As a baseball magnate Von der Ahe was known from one end of the country to the other because of lavish expen-

ditures of money, not only in building up his team, but also in cultivating the good will of the so-called 'sporting element,' which at that time was thought to be the prime factor in making or breaking a ball club." *St. Louis Post-Dispatch,* June 6, 1913. American Association attendance plunged by 26.2 percent in 1888, but National League attendance fell 9.2 percent as well. Thorn et al., eds., *Total Baseball,* 6th ed., 105.

25. Thorn et al., eds., *Total Baseball,* 6th ed., 105, 1951, 1953, 1955, 1957, 1959, 1961.

26. *Reach's Official American Association Baseball Guide: 1890,* 5; *St. Louis Post-Dispatch,* September 8, 1889; *Sporting News,* September 14, 1889; Tiemann, *Cardinal Classics,* 30–31.

27. *St. Louis Post-Dispatch,* September 8, 1889; *Sporting News,* September 14, 1889; Tiemann, *Cardinal Classics,* 30–31; Seymour, *Baseball: The Early Years,* 219.

28. *Sporting News,* September 14, 1889; *St. Louis Globe-Democrat* quoted in *Sporting News,* September 14, 1889.

29. *Sporting News,* September 14, 1889; Tiemann, *Cardinal Classics,* 31; Seymour, *Baseball: The Early Years,* 219.

30. *Sporting News,* September 14, 1889.

31. Ibid. Pearson, *Baseball in 1889,* 133.

32. *Sporting News,* September 28, 1889.

33. Ibid.

34. Borst, *Baseball through a Knothole,* 27–28; *Sporting News,* October 19, 1889. Rain-outs put additional strategy and intrigue into the pennant race. In the American Association, whether to make up rain-outs was determined by a joint decision of the teams involved. Rain-outs could be made up at the end of the regular season between October 15 and October 17. The Browns made tentative arrangements to make up three games at Philadelphia against the Athletics with a doubleheader on October 16 and a single game on October 17. The Bridegrooms, though, elected not to reschedule their home game against St. Louis that had been rained out on September 10 (it could have been made up on the afternoon of October 17 after the Browns played a morning game in Philadelphia). Then, after losing to Cincinnati on October 15, the Browns canceled their make-up games in Philadelphia since even a sweep would have left St. Louis a half game behind Brooklyn. However, if the Association had ordered the Browns and Bridegrooms to play the disputed forfeit from Sunday, September 8, Brooklyn would have been more tempted to reschedule the rain-out of September 10. A two-game closing series could have been created on October 17–18 between the Browns and Bridegrooms with the pennant in the balance. Nemec, *Beer and Whisky League,* 177–78.

35. *Sporting News,* November 16, 1889; Spink, *National Game,* 22; Seymour, *Baseball: The Early Years,* 219–20.

36. *Sporting News,* August 13, 1887; September 14, November 16, 1889; Spink, *National Game,* 22; Seymour, *Baseball: The Early Years,* 220.

37. *Sporting News,* November 16, 1889; *Reach's Official American Association Baseball Guide: 1890,* 12.

38. *Sporting News,* July 28, September 8, October 20, November 17, 24, 1888; February 2, 9, September 21, 28, 1889.

39. Ibid., July 7, September 8, October 20, 1888; September 21, 1889; Voigt, *American Baseball,* vol. 1, 123; Nemec, *Beer and Whisky League,* 112, 122.

40. Spink, *National Game,* 22; *Reach's Official American Association Baseball Guide: 1890,* 12.

41. *Compendium of the Tenth Census, 1880,* 542; *Abstract of the Eleventh Census, 1890,* 34–35; Wolff, ed., *Baseball Encyclopedia,* 8th ed., 94, 96, 106, 108; Nemec, *Encyclopedia of 19th Century Major League Baseball,* 293, 302–3, 378, 388; Thorn et al., eds., *Total Baseball,* 6th ed., 105, 310–13, 1947, 1949, 1959–61; *Reach's Official American Association Baseball Guide: 1887,* 16–19; *Spalding's Official Baseball Guide: 1887,* 22, 28–31; *Spalding's Official Baseball Guide: 1892,* 117.

42. Nemec, *Beer and Whisky League,* 187–89; Nemec, *Encyclopedia of 19th Century Major League Baseball,* 400–401, 403, 407, 418; *Abstract of the Eleventh Census, 1890,* 34–35; *Spalding's Official Baseball Guide: 1892,* 117; Wolff, ed., *Baseball Encyclopedia,* 8th ed., 111, 113; Thorn et al., eds., *Total Baseball,* 6th ed., 1963, 1965; *Sporting News,* November 23, 1889.

Chapter 10: War and Peace

1. Seymour, *Baseball: The Early Years,* 221–24; Voigt, *American Baseball,* vol. 1, 155–59.

2. *Sporting News,* November 24, 1888; Seymour, *Baseball: The Early Years,* 129.

3. Pearson, *Baseball in 1889,* 223–24.

4. Seymour, *Baseball: The Early Years,* 224–29; Voigt, *American Baseball,* vol. 1, 159–60.

5. Nemec, *Beer and Whisky League,* 166, 185; *Sporting News,* September 28, 1889.

6. Nemec, *Beer and Whisky League,* 211; Alexander, *Our Game,* 55.

7. *Reach's Official American Association Baseball Guide: 1890,* 40–41, 43; Pearson, *Baseball in 1889,* 88–89, 96–98, 102, 117–18, 143, 160, 162–64, 167–69; *Sporting News,* February 1, 1890.

8. *Sporting News,* October 5, 19, November 2, 9, 23, December 21, 28, 1889; January 18, February 1, 1890; Pearson, *Baseball in 1889,* 223–24; *Reach's Official American Association Baseball Guide: 1890,* 40–41, 43; Wolff, ed., *Baseball Encyclopedia,* 8th ed., 107, 113; Nemec, *Encyclopedia of 19th Century Major League Baseball,* 391, 433.

9. Nemec, *Encyclopedia of 19th Century Major League Baseball,* 398; Rader, *Baseball,* 60; Thorn et al., eds., *Total Baseball,* 6th ed., 105, 109; Seymour, *Baseball: The Early Years,* 238; Voigt, *American Baseball,* vol. 1, 167–68.

10. Recent research on major-league attendance appears in Thorn et al., eds., *Total Baseball,* 6th ed., 105. For other accounts of the 1890 American Association season, see Seymour, *Baseball: The Early Years,* 235; Voigt, *American Baseball,* vol. 1, 149–50; Alexander, *Our Game,* 57; Nemec and Wisnia, *Baseball,* 57; Nemec, *Encyclopedia of 19th Century Major League Baseball,* 403.

11. Thorn et al., eds., *Total Baseball,* 6th ed., 105, 109; Seymour, *Baseball: The Early Years,* 237–38, 240–49; Voigt, *American Baseball,* vol. 1, 166–69; Rader, *Baseball,* 60; Nemec and Wisnia, *Baseball,* 57; Spalding, *America's National Game,* 288; Geoffrey C. Ward and Ken Burns, *Baseball: An Illustrated History,* 39–40.

12. Seymour, *Baseball: The Early Years,* 240–45, 247–48, 254–55.

13. Ibid., 245–47.

14. Ibid., 251–53; Voigt, *American Baseball,* vol. 1, 150.

15. Seymour, *Baseball: The Early Years,* 245, 247; Voigt, *American Baseball,* vol. 1, 149–51; Nemec, *Encyclopedia of 19th Century Major League Baseball,* 438, 444, 454; *Abstract of the Eleventh Census, 1890,* 34–35; *Spalding's Official Baseball Guide: 1892,* 117; Wolff, ed., *Baseball Encyclopedia,* 8th ed., 117, 119; Thorn et al., eds., *Total Baseball,* 6th ed., 105–6, 1969, 1971.

16. *Sporting News,* November 22, 1890.

17. Thorn et al., eds., *Total Baseball,* 6th ed., 105, 1965.

18. *Sporting News,* April 18, 1891; *St. Louis Post-Dispatch,* June 8, 1891; Tiemann, ed., *St. Louis's Favorite Sport,* 26–27.

19. *Reach's Official 1892 Baseball Guide,* 11; Wolff, ed., *Baseball Encyclopedia,* 8th ed., 119; Nemec, *Encyclopedia of 19th Century Major League Baseball,* 454; Thorn et al., eds., *Total Baseball,* 6th ed., 105, 1971; Seymour, *Baseball: The Early Years,* 255; Tiemann, *Cardinal Classics,* 35; Rygelski, "Baseball's 'Boss President,'" 49; Thorn and Palmer, eds., *Total Baseball,* 2d ed., 2523, 2525.

20. *Reach's Official 1892 Baseball Guide,* 15; Seymour, *Baseball: The Early Years,* 257–58.

21. *Reach's Official 1892 Baseball Guide,* 15; Seymour, *Baseball: The Early Years,* 257–58.

22. *Reach's Official 1892 Baseball Guide,* 15–17. Apparently, Comiskey received $7,000 to sign with the Cincinnati Reds, some $2,000 more than he had been earning with the Browns. Therefore, Comiskey's salary increased from the modern-day range of $60,000-$71,875 to the equivalent of the modern-day range of $84,000-$100,625. Deutsch et al., eds., *Scrapbook History of Baseball,* 32; Alexander, *Our Game,* 27; James, *Historical Baseball Abstract,* 29.

23. *Reach's Official 1892 Baseball Guide,* 17, 19; *Sporting News,* December 12,

19, 1891; *St. Louis Post-Dispatch,* December 12, 1891; *Spalding's Official Baseball Guide: 1892,* 9; Seymour, *Baseball: The Early Years,* 260.

24. Thorn et al., eds., *Total Baseball,* 6th ed., 105; *St. Louis Post-Dispatch,* June 9, 11, 1887; December 12, 20, 1891; *Sporting News,* June 18, 1887; December 12, 19, 26, 1891; Seymour, *Baseball: The Early Years,* 198, 260–61; Martin, "Sports versus the Sabbath," 36–37.

25. At the beginning of the Southern Hotel negotiations, Von der Ahe remained "bitterly opposed to the union of the Association and League interests." But as the discussions proceeded, Von der Ahe sensed his original objections melting away: "My opposition . . . was based upon my past experience in dealing with the League. But when I saw the nature of the presentations by Messrs. Robison, Brush, and Byrne . . . were the embodiment of sincerity and honesty of purpose, it did not take me long to make up my mind to join hands." *Sporting News,* December 26, 1891.

26. *Sporting News,* December 12, 1891.

27. *Reach's Official 1892 Baseball Guide,* 20–21; *St. Louis Globe-Democrat,* December 19, 1891.

28. *Reach's Official 1892 Baseball Guide,* 20; *Sporting News,* December 19, 1891; Seymour, *Baseball: The Early Years,* 261.

29. *Reach's Official 1892 Baseball Guide,* 20–21; Seymour, *Baseball: The Early Years,* 261.

30. Nemec, *Beer and Whisky League,* 235; Nemec, *Encyclopedia of 19th Century Major League Baseball,* 467–68. For interpretations emphasizing that the National League decisively defeated the American Association in the consolidation agreement, see Seymour, *Baseball: The Early Years,* 262; Nemec, *Beer and Whisky League,* 242–44; Ward and Burns, *Baseball,* 40; Nemec and Wisnia, *Baseball,* 58.

31. Nemec, *Beer and Whisky League,* 235; Nemec, *Encyclopedia of 19th Century Major League Baseball,* 467; Wolff, ed., *Baseball Encyclopedia,* 8th ed., 60; Thorn et al., eds., *Total Baseball,* 6th ed., 20–22, 25–27, 51–57, 2538.

Epilogue: Farewell to Chris Von der Ahe, 1892–1899

1. "The St. Louis Merchants Exchange Collection," 53–54. For a fine explanation of Von der Ahe's early popularity in St. Louis, see a laudatory letter that appeared in the *St. Louis Post-Dispatch,* August 23, 1884. *St. Louis Globe-Democrat,* October 8, 1885. One St. Louisan, Frank Hotchkiss, complained in a July 1889 letter to the Philadelphia-based weekly, *Sporting Life,* that Von der Ahe had traded away five of the most popular Browns following the 1887 season and then immediately supported raising ticket prices from a quarter to fifty cents. The Browns' attendance declined more drastically from 1887–1888 and recovered

more sluggishly from 1888–1889 than major-league norms. These attendance figures indicate that many St. Louis baseball fans shared Hotchkiss's lingering resentment over Von der Ahe's 1887 trades. *Sporting Life,* July 10, 1889, quoted in Pearson, *Baseball in 1889,* 88; Thorn et al., eds., *Total Baseball,* 6th ed., 105. For examples of vituperative late 1880s criticism of Von der Ahe outside of St. Louis, see Pearson, *Baseball in 1889,* 143. Yet in St. Louis as late as December 1891, the hometown *Sporting News* referred to Von der Ahe as "the popular president of the famous St. Louis Browns and one of the most popular men in the West." At the same time, the *Sporting News* also paid tribute to Von der Ahe as "one of the most generous, genial, and enterprising gentlemen" in the baseball business, a clubowner who combined an "energetic and bold" personality with a visionary "far seeing eye." *Sporting News,* December 5, 1891.

2. Rygelski, "Baseball's 'Boss President,'" 49–50; Reidenbaugh, ed., *The Sporting News' First Hundred Years,* 20–21; Wolff, ed., *Baseball Encyclopedia,* 8th ed., 121, 124, 126, 129, 132, 135–36, 138; Pearson, *Baseball in 1889,* 203; Seymour, *Baseball: The Early Years,* 300; Borst, *Baseball through a Knothole,* 30; Borst, "Christian Frederick Wilhelm Von der Ahe," in David Porter, ed., *Biographical Dictionary of American Sports: Baseball,* 576; Nemec, *Encyclopedia of 19th Century Major League Baseball,* 591, 614; Thorn et al., eds., *Total Baseball,* 6th ed., 1983, 1985.

3. Seymour, *Baseball: The Early Years,* 300; Borst, *Baseball through a Knothole,* 30; Rygelski, "Baseball's 'Boss President,'" 50; Hetrick, *Chris Von der Ahe and the St. Louis Browns,* 166–67; *St. Louis Post-Dispatch,* June 6, 1913; *St. Louis Republic,* January 19, 1913, reprinted in Missouri Historical Society Library, St. Louis, *Necrologies,* vol. 6 (1913), 16–18.

4. Borst, *Baseball through a Knothole,* 30; Tiemann, *Cardinal Classics,* 50–51; Borst, "Christian Frederick Wilhelm Von der Ahe," 576; Rygelski, "Baseball's 'Boss President,'" 50.

5. *St. Louis Globe-Democrat,* March 28, April 9–10, 1908; *St. Louis Post-Dispatch,* April 9–11, 13, 1908; Borst, "Christian Frederick Wilhelm Von der Ahe," 576; *Sporting News,* June 12, 1913.

Appendix: "Only Doing What Is Right": The Race Issue in Professional Baseball's Frontier Era

1. *St. Louis Globe-Democrat,* October 11, 15, 1875.
2. Ibid., October 15, 1875.
3. *Chicago Tribune,* October 14, 1875.

4. Seymour, *Baseball: The Early Years,* 42; Robert Peterson, *Only the Ball Was White,* 16–17.

5. *St. Louis Globe-Democrat,* May 7, 1884; Wolff, ed., *Baseball Encyclopedia,* 8th ed., 83–85, 1563, 1565; Thorn et al., eds., *Total Baseball,* 6th ed., 69, 1338; Seymour, *Baseball: The Early Years,* 334.

6. Jules Tygiel, *Baseball's Great Experiment: Jackie Robinson and His Legacy,* 13–15.

7. Peterson, *Only the Ball Was White,* 29–30; Tygiel, *Baseball's Great Experiment,* 14.

8. Tygiel, *Baseball's Great Experiment,* 11.

9. *St. Louis Globe-Democrat,* September 12, 1887; also quoted in Peterson, *Only the Ball Was White,* 30–31.

10. *St. Louis Globe-Democrat,* September 12–13, 1887.

11. Ibid., September 13, 1887.

12. Ibid., September 5, 11–14, 16, 1887.

13. For more on segregation in United States history, see C. Vann Woodward, *The Strange Career of Jim Crow.*

Bibliography

I. Newspapers

Boston Daily Globe
Brooklyn Eagle
Chicago Inter-Ocean
Chicago News
Chicago Times
Chicago Tribune
Cincinnati Commercial-Gazette
Cincinnati Enquirer
Louisville Commercial
Louisville Courier-Journal
New York Clipper
New York Times
Philadelphia Evening Bulletin
(Philadelphia) *Sporting Life*
Philadelphia Times
Pittsburgh Referee
St. Louis Daily Globe
St. Louis Democrat
St. Louis Dispatch
St. Louis Globe-Democrat
(St. Louis) *Missouri Republican*
St. Louis Post-Dispatch
St. Louis Republic
St. Louis Republican
(St. Louis) *Sporting News*
Worcester Spy

II. Baseball Guides

Reach's Official American Association Baseball Guide. 1883; reprt., St. Louis: Horton Publishing Company, 1991.

Reach's Official American Association Baseball Guide. 1886; reprt., St. Louis: Horton Publishing Company, 1989.

Reach's Official American Association Baseball Guide. 1887; reprt., St. Louis: Horton Publishing Company, 1989.
Reach's Official American Association Baseball Guide. 1890; reprt., St. Louis: Horton Publishing Company, 1989.
Reach's Official Baseball Guide. 1892; reprt., St. Louis: Horton Publishing Company, 1989.
Spalding's Official Baseball Guide. 1876; reprt., St. Louis: Horton Publishing Company, 1988.
Spalding's Official Baseball Guide. 1877; reprt., St. Louis: Horton Publishing Company, 1988.
Spalding's Official Baseball Guide. 1878; reprt., St. Louis: Horton Publishing Company, 1988.
Spalding's Official Baseball Guide. 1881; reprt., St. Louis: Horton Publishing Company, 1988.
Spalding's Official Baseball Guide. 1886; reprt., St. Louis: Horton Publishing Company, 1987.
Spalding's Official Baseball Guide. 1887; reprt., St. Louis: Horton Publishing Company, 1988.
Spalding's Official Baseball Guide. 1892; reprt., St. Louis: Horton Publishing Company, 1989.

III. Censuses

Compendium of the Ninth Census, 1870. New York: Arno Press, 1976.
Compendium of the Tenth Census, 1880. New York: Arno Press, 1976.
Abstract of the Eleventh Census, 1890. New York: Arno Press, 1976.

IV. Books

Alexander, Charles C. *Our Game: An American Baseball History.* New York: MJF Books, 1991.
Allen, Lee. *100 Years of Baseball.* New York: Bartholomew House, 1950.
———. *The World Series.* New York: G. P. Putnam's Sons, 1969.
Anson, Adrian C. *A Ballplayer's Career.* Chicago: Era Publishing Company, 1900.
Appel, Martin, and Burt Goldblatt. *Baseball's Best: The Hall of Fame Gallery.* New York: McGraw-Hill, 1980.
Axelson, Gustav W. *"Commy": The Life Story of Charles A. Comiskey.* Chicago: Reilly and Lee, 1919.
Barth, Gunther. *City People: The Rise of Modern City Culture in Nineteenth Century America.* New York: Oxford University Press, 1980.

Bartlett, Arthur. *Baseball and Mr. Spalding: The History and Romance of Baseball.* New York: Farrar, Straus, and Young, 1951.

Belcher, Wyatt Winton. *The Economic Rivalry between St. Louis and Chicago, 1850–1880.* New York: Columbia University Press, 1947.

Bench and Bar of St. Louis, Kansas City, Jefferson City, and Other Missouri Cities. St. Louis: American Biographical Publishing Company, 1884.

Bjarkman, Peter C., ed. *Encyclopedia of Major League Baseball Teams: National League.* Westport, Conn.: Meckler Publishing, 1991.

Borst, Bill. *Baseball through a Knothole: A St. Louis History.* St. Louis: Krank Press, 1980.

Bowman, John, and Joel Zoss. *Diamonds in the Rough: The Untold History of Baseball.* New York: Macmillan, 1989.

Broeg, Bob. *Redbirds: A Century of Cardinals Baseball.* St. Louis: River City Publishers, 1981.

Bruns, Roger A. *Preacher: Billy Sunday and Big-Time American Evangelism.* New York: W. W. Norton and Co., 1992.

Burk, Robert F. *Never Just a Game: Players, Owners, and American Baseball to 1920.* Chapel Hill: University of North Carolina Press, 1994.

Carter, Craig, ed. *Daguerreotypes: The Complete Major and Minor League Records of Baseball's Greats.* 8th ed. St. Louis: Sporting News Publishing, 1990.

Christensen, Lawrence O., William E. Foley, Gary R. Kremer, and Kenneth H. Winn, eds. *Dictionary of Missouri Biography.* Columbia: University of Missouri Press, 1999.

Church, Seymour R. *Baseball: The History, Statistics, and Romance of the American National Game.* 1902; reprt., Princeton, N.J.: Pyne Press, 1974.

Coffin, Tristram Potter. *The Old Ball Game: Baseball in Folklore and Fiction.* New York: Herder and Herder, 1971.

Cox, James. *Old and New St. Louis.* St. Louis: Central Biographical Publishing Company, 1894.

Cronon, William. *Nature's Metropolis: Chicago and the Great West.* New York: W. W. Norton and Co., 1991.

Curran, William. *Mitts: A Celebration of the Art of Fielding.* New York: William Morrow, 1985.

Davis, Mac. *Lore and Legends of Baseball.* New York: Lantern Press, Inc., 1953.

Deutsch, Jordan A., Richard M. Cohen, Roland T. Johnson, and David S. Neft, eds. *The Scrapbook History of Baseball.* Indianapolis: Bobbs-Merrill, 1975.

Dickey, Glenn. *The History of the World Series.* New York: Stein and Day, 1984.

Dickson, Paul. *The Baseball Dictionary.* New York: Facts on File, 1989.

———. *Baseball's Greatest Quotations.* New York: Harper Perennial, 1991.

Dorsett, Lyle W. *Billy Sunday and the Redemption of Urban America.* Grand Rapids, Mich.: William B. Eerdmans Publishing, 1991.

Falkner, David. *Nine Sides of the Diamond: Baseball's Great Glove Men on the Fine Art of Defense.* New York: Times Books, 1990.

Fitzgerald, Ed, ed. *The National League.* New York: Grosset and Dunlap, 1959.

Frazier, Thomas R., ed. *The Underside of American History: Other Readings.* Vol. 2, since 1865. New York: Harcourt Brace Jovanovich, 1971.

Gershman, Michael. *Diamonds: The Evolution of the Ballpark.* Boston: Houghton Mifflin, 1993.

Gies, Joseph, and Robert H. Shoemaker. *Stars of the Series: A Complete History of the World Series.* New York: Thomas Y. Crowell Company, 1965.

Goldstein, Warren. *Playing for Keeps: A History of Early Baseball.* Ithaca, N.Y.: Cornell University Press, 1989.

Grayson, Harry. *They Played the Game: The Story of Baseball Greats.* New York: A. S. Barnes and Co., 1944.

Gutman, Dan. *Baseball Babylon.* New York: Penguin Books, 1992.

Hagen, Harry M. *This Is Our St. Louis.* St. Louis: Knight Publishing, 1970.

Hall, Alvin L., ed. *Cooperstown Symposium on Baseball and the American Culture (1989).* Westport, Conn.: Meckler Publishing, 1991.

Hart, Jim Allee. *A History of the St. Louis Globe-Democrat.* Columbia: University of Missouri Press, 1961.

Hetrick, J. Thomas. *Chris Von der Ahe and the St. Louis Browns.* Lanham, Md.: Scarecrow Press, 1999.

Humber, William. *Cheering for the Home Team: The Story of Baseball in Canada.* Erin, Ontario: Boston Mills Press, 1983.

Hyde, William, and Howard L. Conrad, eds. *Encyclopedia of the History of St. Louis.* Vol. 3. New York: Southern History Company, 1899.

James, Bill. *Historical Baseball Abstract.* New York: Villard Books, 1988.

Jensen, Richard. *The Winning of the Midwest: Social and Political Conflict, 1886–1896.* Chicago: University of Chicago Press, 1971.

Kamphoefner, Walter. *The Westfalians: From Germany to Missouri.* Princeton, N.J.: Princeton University Press, 1987.

Kelly, Mike "King." *"Play Ball": Stories of the Ball Field.* Boston: Emery and Hughes, 1888.

Lanasche, Jerry. *The Forgotten Championships: Postseason Baseball, 1882–1981.* Jefferson, N.C.: McFarland and Company, 1989.

Leonard, John W. *The Book of St. Louisans: A Biographical Dictionary of Leading Living Men of the City of St. Louis.* St. Louis: St. Louis Republic, 1906.

Levine, Peter. *A. G. Spalding and the Rise of Baseball: The Promise of American Sport.* New York: Oxford University Press, 1985.

Lieb, Frederick G. *The Story of the World Series: An Informal History.* New York: G. P. Putnam's Sons, 1949.

Lipsitz, George. *The Sidewalks of St. Louis: Places, People, and Politics in an American City.* Columbia: University of Missouri Press, 1991.

Lowry, Philip J. *Green Cathedrals: The Ultimate Celebration of All 271 Major League and Negro League Ballparks Past and Present.* Reading, Mass.: Addison-Wesley, 1992.

Malone, Dumas, ed. *Dictionary of American Biography.* Vol. 11. New York: Charles Scribner's Sons, 1933.

Marquis, Albert Nelson. *Book of St. Louisans.* St. Louis: St. Louis Republic, 1912.

Morris, Dan, and Inez Morris. *Who Was Who in American Politics.* New York: Hawthorn Books, 1974.

Nelson, Daniel. *Managers and Workers: Origins of the New Factory System in the United States, 1880–1920.* Madison: University of Wisconsin Press, 1975.

Nemec, David. *The Beer and Whisky League: The Illustrated History of the American Association—Baseball's Renegade Major League.* New York: Lyons and Burford, 1994.

———. *The Great Encyclopedia of 19th Century Major League Baseball.* New York: Donald I. Fine Books, 1997.

Nemec, David, and Saul Wisnia. *Baseball: More than 150 Years.* Lincolnwood, Ill.: Publications International, 1997.

Okrent, Daniel, and Harris Lewine, eds. *The Ultimate Baseball Book.* Boston: Houghton Mifflin, 1984.

Olson, Audrey L. *St. Louis Germans, 1850–1920.* New York: Arno Press, 1980.

Oster, Donald B. *Community Image in the History of St. Louis and Kansas City.* Ann Arbor, Mich.: University Microfilms, 1978.

Pearson, Daniel. *Baseball in 1889: Players versus Owners.* Bowling Green, Ohio: Bowling Green State University Popular Press, 1993.

Peterson, Robert. *Only the Ball Was White.* Englewood Cliffs, N.J.: Prentice Hall, 1970.

Pietrusza, David. *Major Leagues: The Formation, Sometimes Absorption, and Mostly Inevitable Demise of Eighteen Professional Baseball Organizations, 1871 to Present.* Jefferson, N.C.: McFarland and Company, 1991.

Porter, David L., ed. *Biographical Dictionary of American Sports: Baseball.* New York: Greenwood Press, 1987.

Primm, James Neal. *Lion of the Valley: St. Louis, Missouri.* Boulder, Colo.: Pruett Publishing, 1981.

Quirk, Charles E., ed. *Sports and the Law: Major Legal Cases.* New York: Garland Publishing, 1996.

Rader, Benjamin G. *Baseball: A History of America's Game.* Urbana: University of Illinois Press, 1992.

Rammelkamp, Julian S. *Pulitzer's Post-Dispatch, 1878–1883.* Princeton, N.J.: Princeton University Press, 1967.

Reidenbaugh, Lowell. *Baseball's Hall of Fame: Cooperstown, Where the Legends Live Forever.* New York: Gramercy Books, 1999.

———, ed. *The Sporting News' First Hundred Years, 1886–1986.* St. Louis: Sporting News Publishing, 1985.

———. *The Sporting News' Take Me Out to the Ballpark.* St. Louis: Sporting News Publishing, 1987.

Reiss, Steven A. *Touching Base: Professional Baseball and American Culture in the Progressive Era.* Westport, Conn.: Greenwood Press, 1980.

Rodgers, Daniel T. *The Work Ethic in Industrial America: 1850–1920.* Chicago: University of Chicago Press, 1974.

Ryczek, William J. *Blackguards and Red Stockings: A History of Baseball's National Association, 1871–1875.* Jefferson, N.C.: McFarland and Company, 1992.

Seymour, Harold. *Baseball: The Early Years.* New York: Oxford University Press, 1960.

———. *Baseball: The Golden Age.* New York: Oxford University Press, 1971.

Shatzkin, Mike. *The Ballplayers: Baseball's Ultimate Biographical Reference.* New York: Arbor House/William Morrow, 1990.

Slater, Robert. *Great Jews in Sports.* Middle Village, N.Y.: Jonathan David, 1983.

Smith, Henry Nash. *Virgin Land: The American West as Symbol and Myth.* Cambridge, Mass.: Harvard University Press, 1950.

Smith, Ira L., and H. Allen. *Low and Inside: A Book of Baseball Anecdotes, Oddities, and Curiosities.* Garden City, N.Y.: Doubleday and Company, 1949.

Smith, Robert. *Baseball.* New York: Simon and Schuster, 1947.

———. *Baseball in America.* New York: Holt, Rhinehart, and Winston, 1961.

———. *Baseball in the Afternoon: Tales from a Bygone Era.* New York: Simon and Schuster, 1993.

———. *An Illustrated History of Baseball.* New York: Grosset and Dunlap, 1973.

Spalding, A. G. *America's National Game.* New York: American Sports Publishing Co., 1911.

Spalding, Albert. *Rise to Follow: An Autobiography.* New York: Henry Holt and Co., 1943.

Spink, Alfred H. *The National Game.* St. Louis: National Game Publishing Co., 1910.

Stevens, Walter B. *History of St. Louis: The Fourth City, 1764–1909.* Vol. 2. St. Louis: S. J. Clarke Publishing Company, 1909.

Suehsdorf, A. D. *The Great American Baseball Scrapbook.* New York: Rutledge Books, 1978.

Tiemann, Robert L. *Cardinal Classics: Outstanding Games from Each of the St. Louis Baseball Club's 100 Seasons, 1882–1981.* St. Louis: Baseball Histories, 1982.

———, ed. *St. Louis's Favorite Sport: Convention Brochure of the 22nd National SABR Convention.* St. Louis: Society for American Baseball Research, 1992.

Thorn, John. *A Century of Baseball Lore.* New York: Galahad Books, 1980.

———, ed. *The National Pastime.* New York: Warner Books, 1987.

Thorn, John, and John Holway. *The Pitcher.* New York: Prentice Hall, 1987.

Thorn, John, and Pete Palmer, eds. *Total Baseball.* 2d ed. New York: Warner Books, 1991.

———. *Total Baseball.* 3d ed. New York: Harper Perennial, 1993.

Thorn, John, Pete Palmer, Michael Gershman, and David Pietrusza, eds. *Total Baseball.* 6th ed. New York: Total Sports, 1999.

Turner, Frederick Jackson. *The Frontier in American History.* New York: Henry Holt and Company, 1920.

Tygiel, Jules. *Baseball's Great Experiment: Jackie Robinson and His Legacy.* New York: Vintage Books, 1983.

United States Biographical Publishing Company. *The United States Biographical Dictionary and Portrait Gallery of Eminent and Self-Made Men, Missouri Volume.* St. Louis: United States Biographical Publishing Company, 1878.

Van Ravenswaay, Charles. *St. Louis: An Informal History of the City and Its People, 1764–1865.* St. Louis: Missouri Historical Society Press, 1991.

Voigt, David Q. *American Baseball.* Vol. 1. Norman: University of Oklahoma Press, 1966.

———. *America through Baseball.* Chicago: Nelson-Hall, 1976.

———. *Baseball: An Illustrated History.* University Park, Pa.: Pennsylvania State University Press, 1987.

Wade, Richard C. *The Urban Frontier: The Rise of Western Cities, 1790–1830.* Cambridge, Mass.: Harvard University Press, 1959.

Walker, Robert Harris. *Cincinnati and the Big Red Machine.* Bloomington: Indiana University Press, 1988.

Wallan, Peter, et al., eds. *The Ol' Ball Game.* Harrisburg, Pa.: Stackpole Books, 1990.

Ward, Geoffrey C., and Ken Burns. *Baseball: An Illustrated History.* New York: Alfred A. Knopf, 1994.

Wolff, Rick, ed. *The Baseball Encyclopedia.* 8th ed. New York: Macmillan, 1990.

Woodward, C. Vann. *The Strange Career of Jim Crow.* 3d ed. New York: Oxford University Press, 1974.

V. Articles

Barclay, Thomas S. "James H. Lucas." In Dumas Malone, ed., *Dictionary of American Biography,* vol. 11. New York: Charles Scribner's Sons, 1933.

Borst, William A. "Christian Frederick Wilhelm Von der Ahe." In David L. Porter, ed., *Biographical Dictionary of American Sports: Baseball.* New York: Greenwood Press, 1987.

Burnes, Robert L. "It Looks Like First Division." *St. Louis Globe-Democrat,* April 15, 1951. In Missouri Historical Society Scrapbook, *Sports I.*

———. "Baseball Flourished Here before Von der Ahe." *St. Louis Globe-Democrat,* October 5, 1952. In Missouri Historical Society Scrapbook, *Sports I.*

Carlson, Stan N. "St. Louis Cardinals: Baseball's Perennial Gas House Gang." In Peter C. Bjarkman, ed., *Encyclopedia of Major League Baseball Teams: National League.* Westport, Conn.: Meckler Publishing, 1991.

Carroll, Bob. "For the Hall of Fame: Twelve Good Men." In John Thorn, ed., *The National Pastime.* New York: Warner Books, 1987.

Carter, Gregg Lee. "Baseball in St. Louis, 1867–1875: An Historical Case Study in Civic Pride." *Bulletin of the Missouri Historical Society* (July 1975).

Cash, J. D. "Origins—The Spirit of St. Louis in the History of Professional Baseball: May 4–8, 1875." *Gateway Heritage: Quarterly Magazine of the Missouri Historical Society* (spring 1995).

Cash, Jon David. "Christian Frederick Wilhelm Von der Ahe." In Lawrence O. Christensen, William E. Foley, Gary R. Kremer, and Kenneth H. Winn, eds., *Dictionary of Missouri Biography.* Columbia: University of Missouri Press, 1999.

Dyreson, Mark. "The Playing Fields of Progress: American Athletic Nationalism and the 1904 Olympics." *Gateway Heritage: Quarterly Magazine of the Missouri Historical Society* (fall 1993).

Findling, J. E. "The Louisville Grays' Scandal of 1877." *Journal of Sport History* (summer 1976).

Foley, William E. "William C. Carr." In Lawrence O. Christensen, William E. Foley, Gary R. Kremer, and Kenneth H. Winn, eds., *Dictionary of Missouri Biography.* Columbia: University of Missouri Press, 1999.

———. "John B. C. Lucas." In Lawrence O. Christensen, William E. Foley, Gary R. Kremer, and Kenneth H. Winn, eds., *Dictionary of Missouri Biography.* Columbia: University of Missouri Press, 1999.

Gietschier, Steve. "Before 'The Bible of Baseball': The First Quarter Century of the *Sporting News*." In Robert L. Tiemann, ed., *St. Louis's Favorite Sport: Convention Brochure of the 22nd National SABR Convention.* St. Louis: Society for American Baseball Research, 1992.

Hannon, Robert E. "A Century of Baseball." *St. Louis Commerce* (May 1966).

Ivor-Campbell, Frederick. "1884: Old Hoss Radbourne and the Providence Grays." In John Thorn, ed., *The National Pastime.* New York: Warner Books, 1987.

———. "Robert Lee Caruthers." In David L. Porter, ed., *Biographical Dictionary of American Sports: Baseball.* New York: Greenwood Press, 1987.

Kermisch, Al. "The First World Series." In John Thorn, ed., *The National Pastime.* New York: Warner Books, 1987.

Lampe, Anthony B. "The Background of Professional Baseball in St. Louis." *Bulletin of the Missouri Historical Society* (October 1950).

Martin, Robert F. "Sports versus the Sabbath: Professional Baseball and Blue Laws." In Charles E. Quirk, ed., *Sports and the Law: Major Legal Cases.* New York: Garland Publishing Company, 1996.

Nardinelli, Clark. "Anthony John Mullane." In David L. Porter, ed., *Biographical Dictionary of American Sports: Baseball.* New York: Greenwood Press, 1987.

Reiss, Steven A. "Charles Albert Comiskey." In David L. Porter, ed., *Biographical Dictionary of American Sports: Baseball.* New York: Greenwood Press, 1987.

Rosen, Richard Allen. "Rethinking the Row House: The Development of Lucas Place, 1850–1865." *Gateway Heritage: Quarterly Magazine of the Missouri Historical Society* (summer 1992).

Rygelski, Jim. "Baseball's 'Boss President': Chris Von der Ahe and the Nineteenth-Century St. Louis Browns." *Gateway Heritage: Quarterly Magazine of the Missouri Historical Society* (summer 1992).

Schnell, Jonathan. "Chicago versus St. Louis: A Reassessment of the Great Rivalry." *Missouri Historical Review* (April 1977).

Seymour, Harold. "St. Louis and the Union Baseball War." *Missouri Historical Review* (April 1957).

Smith, Duane A. "Baseball Champions of Colorado: The Leadville Blues of 1882." *Journal of Sports History* 4, no. 1 (spring 1977).

———. "David Luther Foutz." In David L. Porter, ed., *Biographical Dictionary of American Sports: Baseball.* New York: Greenwood Press, 1987.

Spink, Alfred H. "Al Spink, Writing in 1921, Gave Graphic Picture of Comiskey as Player and Manager." *Sporting News,* October 29, 1931.

Stockton, J. Roy. "The St. Louis Cardinals." In Ed Fitzgerald, ed., *The National League.* New York: Grosset and Dunlap, 1959.

Story, Ronald. "The Country of the Young: The Meaning of Baseball in Early American Culture." In Alvin L. Hall, ed., *Cooperstown Symposium on Baseball and the American Culture (1989).* Westport, Conn.: Meckler Publishing, 1991.

Terry, Dickson. "Browns—Rich in Tradition." *St. Louis Post-Dispatch,* March 22, 1953. In Missouri Historical Society Scrapbook, *Sports I.*

Thorn, John. "The True Father of Baseball." In John Thorn and Pete Palmer, eds., *Total Baseball.* 3d ed. New York: Harper Perennial, 1993.

Tobias, E. H. "Series on Early Baseball in St. Louis." *Sporting News,* October 26, 1895–February 15, 1896.

Wallan, Peter. "Old Hoss." In Wallan et al., eds., *The Ol' Ball Game.* Harrisburg, Pa.: Stackpole Books, 1990.

White, Melvin J. "John Baptiste Charles Lucas." In Dumas Malone, ed., *Dictionary of American Biography,* vol. 11. New York: Charles Scribner's Sons, 1933.

VI. Missouri Historical Society Holdings

Baseball—Missouri. Vertical File.

Lucas, Henry. Vertical File.

Missouri Historical Society Bulletin. Vol. 6 (1949–1950). "St. Louis Merchants Exchange Collection."

Missouri Historical Society Collections. Vol. 3 (1911).

Missouri Historical Society Scrapbooks. *Sports I* and *Sports II.*

Necrologies. Vol. 6 (1913).

Necrology Scrapbook. Vol. II c.

Turner, Charles H. Vertical File.

Index

About the Author

Jon David Cash is Adjunct Professor of History at the University of Arkansas–Monticello. He resides in Crossett, Arkansas.